D1532952

Foundations of Vocational Education

A publication in the Merrill Series in Career Programs

Robert E. Taylor, Editorial Director

Foundations of Vocational Education
Second Edition

Rupert N. Evans
University of Illinois at Urbana-Champaign

Edwin L. Herr
The Pennsylvania State University

Charles E. Merrill Publishing Company
A Bell & Howell Company
Columbus Toronto London Sydney

Published by
Charles E. Merrill Publishing Company
A Bell & Howell Company
Columbus, Ohio 43216

This book was set in Times Roman.
The production editor was Lynn Stephenson Walcoff.
The cover was prepared by Will Chenoweth.

Cover photo courtesy of the Salt Lake Valley Convention and Visitors Bureau.

Library of Congress Catalog Card Number: 77–89745

International Standard Book Number: 0–675–08442–3

6 7 8 9 10 — 83

Printed in the United States of America

Contents

Photo Credits

Chapter 2	Larry Hamill
Chapter 3	Eastland Joint Vocational School District
Chapter 4	William Stoll
Chapter 6	Larry Hamill
Chapter 7	Ohio Bureau of Employment Services
Chapter 8	General Electric, Lamp Business Group, Nela Park, Cleveland, Ohio
Chapter 9	Ohio Bureau of Employment Services
Chapter 11	Dan Krivicich
Chapter 12	Eastland Joint Vocational School District
Chapter 13	Bernstein Photos
Chapter 15	Eastland Joint Vocational School District
Chapter 16	Eastland Joint Vocational School District
Chapter 17	Junior Achievement of Central Ohio
Chapter 18	Neil A. Miller
Chapter 19	State of Ohio, Rehabilitation Services Commission
Chapter 20	Eastland Joint Vocational School District

Foreword

Throughout its history, vocational education has enjoyed a vigorous eclectic philosophy. This pragmatism has its roots in many disciplines and is influenced by humanistic, social, economic, and political forces. The authors explicate the empirical bases of these contributing disciplines and provide their rationale and some of their strengths and limitations. They have identified critical problems and issues and, more importantly, their interrelationships. The book is thought-provoking. It extends horizons and perspectives and, as its title implies, provides the kinds of insights and understanding essential for building foundations for vocational education.

The addition of Dr. Herr as a co-author and the new chapters on vocational development and guidance greatly enhance the value and "foundation quality" of this reference. Dr. Herr is widely known as a leader and scholar in this area.

Dr. Evans, the senior author, is eminently qualified to author such a text, having been intimately involved in vocational education through several decades in a variety of roles. His experience as a local vocational teacher, a university professor, a college of education dean, and as an eminent researcher, member of national boards, councils and advisory groups cumulatively provide him with a unique and rich background which he has brought to bear in this text.

Robert E. Taylor

Editorial Director

Preface

This edition, as was the earlier edition, is designed for potential and in-service vocational educators who are pursuing a program of personal development which will insure competency in that specialty. A complete knowledge of vocational education and its relationships with society is essential to effective performance. With this in mind, the book concentrates on basic principles affecting all of human resource development.

In the United States, vocational education has come to mean education for any occupation which normally requires less than a baccalaureate degree for the beginning worker. It is used in that sense in this book and covers all such education, whether public or private, in school or out of school, and regardless of the source of funds which pay for it. The distinction between vocational education and education for the professions is an arbitrary one, and a term is needed to refer to the full range of education for work. In this book, *occupational education* is used to cover all education programs which prepare people for work, regardless of the occupational level. *Career education* is an even broader term which includes programs and activities which aid awareness and exploration of the world of work and of the self in relation to work, and preparation for work. Thus career education includes occupational education and vocational education. But vocational education is a large and complex field in its own right and demands intensive study.

In addition to normal revision treatment as a result of comments from the many users of the first edition, this second edition has totally new chapters on vocational development and guidance to accommodate the increasing inclusion of these areas in this basic course.

The first section of this book is devoted to the goals of vocational education. It describes how these goals have shifted toward an emphasis on human resource development and away from a narrow concern for meeting the needs of local employers. The second section presents an overview of the contributions of four social sciences toward these goals and toward the means of achieving them. The third section deals with vocational development and guidance and career education. The fourth section is concerned with present programs of vocational education and trends which are likely to affect the ways in which we achieve our goals. It is organized, not in terms of subject-matter areas within vocational education, but rather in terms of social organizations which conduct programs of vocational education. This is followed by a section on methods of preparing personnel to conduct programs of vocational education. The final chapter looks at the future of vocational education and its part in the development of all occupational education, with particular attention to its role in the development of every individual's full human potential.

Any book of this type is written by many people other than the "authors." Particular acknowledgment is due, however, to Professors Willard Hill and Harry Belman of Purdue and to the senior author's father, Loren Evans, who inducted him into the mysteries of vocational education. The following individuals have offered many suggestions for improving this book:

Joseph Arnold, Robert Campbell, Ulrich Ernst, Donald Lux, William Nelson, Robert Taylor, and Robert Young of the Ohio State University; Harry Broudy, Joe Burnett, Bernard Karsh, Ernest Robinson, Hazel Spitze, Jacob Stern, and Robert Tomlinson of the University of Illinois; Howard Rosen of the Department of Labor; Jack Willers of George Peabody College; William Schill of the University of Washington; Sar Levitan of George Washington University; Leslie Cochran of Central Michigan University; Ronald Stadt of Southern Illinois University; Garth Mangum of the University of Utah; Dale Riepe of the State University of New York at Buffalo; and many of our graduate students. Final responsibility, of course, rests with the authors, and many of the suggestions which have been offered have not been included. The result is a personal document in many ways. Its success should be judged in terms of its effect in suggesting ways in which vocational education can better serve the needs of youth and adults. Vocational education has no other reason for existing.

R.N.E.
E.L.H.

Foundations of Vocational Education

part I

Objectives of Vocational Education

1

Introduction

In its broadest sense vocational education is that part of education which makes an individual more employable in one group of occupations than in another. It may be differentiated from general education, which is of almost equal value regardless of the occupation to be pursued.

According to the previous definition, foreign language study is vocational education for those students planning to be interpreters. Driver's education is vocational education for those pursuing an occupation which requires the ability to drive an automobile. And education in *any* specialized field is vocational education for those planning to teach in that field.

While students' intentions have a great deal to do with determining whether or not a particular subject is vocational education for them, it is possible, by choosing subject matter and methods of presenting that subject matter, to insure that a subject has little or no vocational value for any of the students enrolled. However, all general education subjects can and should be taught in a way which emphasizes their occupational value and relevance to society as a whole. This is one of the key concepts of career education.

Often the term *vocational education* is used, especially in federal legislation, to include only instruction designed to enable people to succeed in occupations requiring less than a baccalaureate degree. While this distinction may be useful in subsidizing educational programs which tend to be neglected by schools controlled by individuals who emphasize only the preparation of students for the professions, it has little utility outside this realm. Vocational education is a much broader concept and is intimately interwoven with general education.

Every general education course can have occupational value, and awareness of career goals can lead students to see the relevance of certain content which otherwise might appear highly irrelevant.

Basic Objectives

There are three basic objectives in any public school vocational education curriculum. Listed in chronological order of their acceptance as goals, they are; (1) meeting society's needs for workers, (2) increasing the options available to each student, and (3) serving as a motivating force to enhance all types of learning. A few vocational education programs sponsored by employers have these same three goals, but most do not. Very often they are designed only to meet the short-term needs of a single employer.

Not all public human resources development programs attempt to achieve all three objectives. For example, most Comprehensive Employment and Training Act (CETA) programs include no general education component except for the occasional teaching of reading to students who are functionally illiterate. When the adult CETA trainees see that reading is essential for success in many types of jobs, they acquire reading skills rapidly. The same type of facilitation could apply to other general education subjects, but these subjects are rarely taught concurrently with vocational skills in CETA programs.

The managers and stockholders of profit-making organizations rarely see justification for using their funds and facilities to train more people than they need. Nor do they wish to educate personnel in ways which will increase the probability that they will change employers. On the other hand, they are interested in providing education programs which will increase employees' options within their own company, increase the job satisfaction of their employees, and meet the company's current and anticipated needs for skilled employees.

Profit-making vocational schools are seldom interested in providing training to individuals who are unable to pay the cost of training (though this objection disappears if the federal government will pay these costs). They also prefer offering programs in occupations where the demand is greater than the supply, and they avoid programs where enrollments are apt to be small and placement of graduates difficult. Since their students are interested in securing employment as rapidly as possible, general education courses are not included in the curriculum unless they are masked by names which indicate to the students that they will help employability, e.g., technical report writing for engineering technicians. Because their teachers rarely have tenure and because the managers of private schools tend to measure efficiency in terms of repeat business, their instruction tends to be more up-to-date than in some public school programs. Private vocational schools seem (1) interested in increasing the options of some students but not indigent or disadvantaged ones, (2) interested in helping to meet some of the nation's employment needs, (3) not at all interested in designing instruction to increase the intelligibility of general education, and yet (4) relatively effective in achieving their limited goals.

Despite the many obstacles imposed by their institutional roles, teachers in public vocational schools and vocational departments in comprehensive public schools and community colleges usually have all three basic objectives in mind and work toward their achievement. It seems reasonable to assume that teachers who strive to achieve all three goals are more likely to reach all of them than teachers who strive for only one or two.

Specific Objectives of the Instructor

In addition to the three basic objectives which should apply to all of vocational education, each course usually has its own objectives. These specific objectives should be in accord with all three basic objectives.

Unfortunately, too often specific objectives are warped by the goals and structure of the sponsoring organization, by personal prejudices of the instructor, and by the availability of unneeded equipment and unavailability of needed equipment. More frequently, they are distorted by instructors who lack competence in certain needed phases of instruction and therefore substitute other nonessential instruction. The worst situation occurs when instruction is offered by individuals who have no specific goals or no means of achieving the goals they do have.

Specific Objectives of the Student

Surprisingly little is known about students' objectives in vocational education programs. It is believed that students frequently seek vocational goals in courses that teachers believe to be nonvocational in nature. For example, a student who wishes to be a writer may take elective English composition courses and may attempt to shape the character of the assignments in ways which will further his or her vocational aspirations. One may infer that this is frequently the case by examining data from *Formal Occupational Training of Adult Workers* (2, p. 11), which indicated that 37.7 percent of adults over age twenty-two with less than three years of college education said that they had had vocational courses in high school. Since courses in which instructors have vocational objectives are not offered to this proportion of students, it would appear that as adults, some of these people saw vocational value in nonvocational courses. Whether or not they saw these values when they were students is open to question.

Similarly, the instructor may have a vocational objective while the students do not. This probably occurs most frequently when students have strong avocational interests, such as in increasing the performance of automobiles, and enroll in vocational courses like automobile mechanics to further their avocational rather than their vocational interests. Since, however, such students are almost invariably excluded if their lack of vocational interest becomes apparent to the instructor, these discrepancies between instructor and student goals are very often concealed.

Taxonomies of Educational Objectives

As we study the objectives of instructors and students, it is helpful to have a means of listing and describing them. Bloom (1), Krathwohl (3), and Simpson (4) have developed taxonomies for classifying educational objectives in the cognitive, affective, and psychomotor domains. Each of these three taxonomies provides a classification scheme which enables one to develop a hierarchy of objectives. Thus, within the psychomotor domain, objectives dealing with perception come first in the taxonomy. Perception is followed by set, guided response, mechanism, complex response, adaptation, and origination. Perception is necessary before guided response can be accomplished, and complex response is necessary before adaptation or origination can occur.

By using a taxonomy, instructors can determine whether or not they inadvertently are setting objectives early in the course which should be preceded by the attainment of simpler objectives. Instructors can also use the checklist to determine whether or not they are concentrating too much of their instruction within the cognitive, affective, or psychomotor domains and to determine whether or not they will move the class toward sufficiently high goals within each domain.

Behavioral Objectives

There has been considerable controversy about the desirability of specifying objectives in behavioral terms. An objective specified in behavioral terms identifies precisely the types of behavior a student should be able to exhibit at the end of the instructional program. Proponents of behavioral objectives feel that more general objectives are of little value in guiding an instructor's actions from day to day and are of little value to students in determining whether or not an objective has been achieved. Opponents feel that the use of behavioral objectives tends to tie the hands of capable instructors by restricting them from taking advantage of chance opportunities (unusual events in the community, a series of questions which show that students are particularly interested in an unusual topic, and the like) which can facilitate learning markedly. Moreover, they feel that many worthwhile outcomes of education, especially in the field of values, are difficult if not impossible to state in behavioral terms. This controversy is far from being resolved.

Conflicts in Objectives

A vocational education program which is designed to help meet national needs for workers may actually decrease individual options and vice versa. For example, for many years orderlies, aides, and even practical and registered nurses have been markedly underpaid compared to other individuals performing work of a similar level of importance and requiring similar amounts of intelligence and education. Clearly society needs workers in service-oriented fields, so in order to help meet the nation's needs for workers, vocational education should establish programs to prepare workers for these positions.

At the same time, one of the obvious reasons for shortages of employees in these fields has been their relatively low pay and poor working conditions. If the shortages of skilled workers in these fields become severe enough, wages are almost certain to rise and working conditions to improve. The extent to which vocational education provides programs which meet the nation's shortages of workers determines the number of individual options its trainees will have. These options will be decreased if the students have been prepared for an occupational field which does not produce as much income as another. Moreover, the options of current workers are decreased if too many trainees are produced. On this basis, some economists have argued that federal funds should not be spent for vocational training for fields in which wages and working conditions are substandard.

On the other hand, failure to produce skilled workers to meet society's needs for workers may also decrease individual options. Obviously people denied any sort of vocational training suffer because they do not have salable skills. Equally important but less obvious is the fact that when a particular occupation lacks enough skilled workers, employers seek ways to substitute workers in other occupations to meet their needs. Thus, the shortage of terrazzo workers has virtually eliminated the use of terrazzo floors in many parts of the United States and has provided employment for cement finishers, tile setters, and carpet layers who were trained to produce or install alternative types of floor coverings. Thus, a shortage of skilled workers not only raises the price of that skilled labor in the short run, but it may in the long run succeed in pricing the entire occupation out of the market. Obviously this decreases the options of workers in that occupation.

A vocational program which concentrates too heavily on achieving one of the basic objectives is certain to neglect the other two. Thus, a program offered by an employer may contribute markedly to meeting the nation's needs for workers (though it set out to meet the needs of the employer), but completely neglect the goal of making general education more meaningful. More often, a program with a single goal achieves that goal and in the process accidentally achieves the other two in part. It seems clear, however, that a program which is designed deliberately to meet all three of the goals of vocational education is more likely to meet all these goals in substantial measure than a program which achieves one goal on purpose, and two by accident. Though there are instances in which there are conflicts among basic goals, in the great majority of cases, the three goals complement each other. The next section of this book looks at the three basic goals of vocational education in greater detail.

REFERENCES

1. Bloom, Benjamin S. et al. *Taxonomy of Educational Objectives: Cognitive Domain.* New York: Longmans, Green and Co., 1956.
2. *Formal Occupational Training of Adult Workers.* Manpower/Automation Research Monograph No. 2. Washington, D.C.: U.S. Department of Labor, 1964.
3. Krathwohl, David R. et al. *Taxonomy of Educational Objectives: Affective Domain.* New York: David McKay Co., Inc., 1964.
4. Simpson, Elizabeth J. "The Classification of Educational Objectives, Psychomotor Domain," *Illinois Teacher of Home Economics* 10, no. 4 (Winter 1966–67):110–44.

2

Meeting Society's Needs for Workers

The earliest and most widely accepted objective of vocational education was to provide a mechanism for meeting the needs of the local community for skilled workers. Today it should be recognized that the needs of the nation and of society as a whole are as important or more important. Industry, government, the schools, and indeed all institutions of society require trained people if they are to survive. While the needs of the family are almost invariably ignored in statements of needs for workers, society is gradually recognizing that consumer education and homemaking education of high quality are essential to the survival of the family as well. If specially educated personnel are needed for the survival of each of these institutions, some mechanism must be found to provide these people. The history of society is interwoven with attempts to meet these needs.

While the need for trained personnel has been recognized throughout history, the problem of providing such personnel has become increasingly difficult as the rate of change in needs for workers has accelerated. When people could expect to spend a lifetime in the same occupation and could expect to transmit to their children in essentially unchanged form the skills, knowledges, and attitudes which they had acquired, the need for institutionalizing vocational education was much less than it is now, when few people can expect to engage in exactly the same productive activities for even a year.

Methods of Providing Workers

The oldest method of meeting needs for workers was for the father to pass on to his sons and for the mother to pass on to her daughters the occupational information they had acquired from their parents, plus what they had learned by trial and error during a generation of productive work. But when a technological revolution such as the substitution of agriculture for hunting or the substitution of bronze for stone tools occurred, transmission of the family heritage was no longer a satisfactory method of educating workers in the newly generated occupations.

On-the-Job Training

While training by the parent was accomplished almost entirely at the place of work and was carried out simultaneously with productive activity, the next type of on-the-job training included a new element. The instructor was a worker who was not necessarily a member of the family. On-the-job training (OJT) by individuals other than parents occurred whenever members of more than one family were engaged in a productive activity. It had the advantage of providing for the orphan, and it allowed the new worker to learn from more than one instructor; it had the disadvantage that the trainer did not have a vested interest in seeing that the new worker was fully trained. OJT continues in occupations from the simplest to the most complex, but in most vocations, it emphasizes the teaching of those skills and knowledges which are unique to a particular employer and hence are not suitable for more institutionalized types of vocational education.

Apprenticeship

OJT has always been relatively haphazard. The new worker observes, practices, learns by trial and error, and occasionally receives direct instruction (if the experienced worker does not feel threatened by the potential competition). There is no guarantee that the new worker will learn everything about the occupation. Instead he or she probably will learn only a portion of what is practiced in a particular place of employment at a certain time.

Apprenticeship attempted to combine the best of family instruction and OJT by having an experienced worker agree to teach the full range of an occupation, acting in lieu of the parent. In return the trainer received the services of the apprentice for a certain time span—often ten or more years. The method of instruction was similar to that used by the family, and by on-the-job training, but was more complete because the trainer agreed not to withhold any of the mysteries of the craft as was (and is) so commonly the case in OJT. For this reason apprenticeship has always been a practical necessity for a cadre of workers in highly skilled occupations which could not be learned efficiently through on-the-job training.

Apprenticeship reached its peak in Europe just prior to the beginning of the Industrial Revolution in the seventeenth century. At that time, it was the primary means of instruction for most skilled and semiskilled occupations. It was highly formalized, and graduates of the apprenticeship system were the only people licensed to practice in many occupations. Apprenticeship continues today, though in this country it is largely restricted to the construction crafts, certain highly skilled metalworking occupations, and certain occupations in the printing industry. The principal changes have been that apprenticeship begins later in life, lasts for a shorter period (often three to six years), and instruction is guaranteed by a group of employers or employees, rather than by a single craftsman.

Schools

The newest method of society for providing occupational skills has been the school. Originally schools had a vocational purpose only and were instituted for the priesthood, which was regarded as being so highly skilled that apprenticeship would not suffice. The school required the presence of several novices who could be given nearly identical instruction in the theory and practice of an occupation. Schools for the priesthood began more than three thousand years ago.

As time went on other occupations acquired sufficient importance and content to warrant the development of special schools to meet societal needs. By the Middle Ages, instruction in bookkeeping and algebra was provided in formal schools, and by 1900 almost every professional occupation had one or more schools devoted to it. At present, almost every skilled, technical, and professional occupation inducts at least part of its workers through formal school programs offered in high schools, community colleges, universities, and private occupational schools. In addition to their occupational purposes, schools are now used as a means of imparting knowledge which is useful to all citizens, regardless of occupation. Unfortunately they also serve to provide instruction which once had occupational value for the upper class but which now is largely irrelevant for anyone.

Private and Public Schools

Usually new occupational education programs are introduced in the private schools first. Later, if a program thrives, it is introduced into the public schools.

Most private schools are more flexible than public schools in adapting to changed needs for workers. They depend on tuition for financial support, and if they cannot attract students, they must go out of business. Students are influenced to a certain extent by sales pitches and by the availability of training in glamorous occupations; however, a private vocational school which does not place its students in good jobs will die eventually. Public schools, on the other hand, too seldom are concerned with placing their students, or even with attempting to attract students who can profit from vocational education. One of the major factors which enables private schools to cope rapidly with changing needs for workers is the fact that their instructors are rarely on tenure. Thus if an instructor is no longer needed, he or she can be discharged with no difficulty, while many public schools prefer to continue an unnecessary vocational program until the death or retirement of an existing instructor. Moreover, public schools are afraid to enter new occupational training programs until the long-term necessity for such training is clearly established, for they do not like to be saddled with excess staff. Still another reason for the flexibility of the private school is that its owner is free to revise an old course or install a new one, while "public schools . . . must . . . secure approval of school boards and local and state educators and legislators" (3, p. 27).

The principal incentive for the establishment of a public school occupational education program in a particular field, when an existing private institution could expand to meet needs for workers, is the shifting of the cost of instruction from the student to society. The tuition charge in a private vocational school is approximately the same as the total educational costs per individual in public schools. Since a major part of this latter cost is paid by society, obviously tuition costs paid by the individual are much lower in the public school setting.

Local advisory committees can be of marked assistance to school programs in providing education which meets local needs for workers. A mechanism is needed for providing information from employer and employee groups, government, and lay citizens on improvement of vocational education on a state and national basis. The establishment of state and national advisory councils who will annually evaluate vocational education programs clearly seems to be a step in the right direction.

Placement of Graduates

There is no perfect method for determining whether or not a particular vocational education program is helping meet the needs of the nation for workers. Most job placements are local rather than national and are affected markedly by local labor market needs, which may be at considerable variance from national needs. In addition, both local and national worker needs may be affected sharply in the short run by current economic conditions, which have little significance in terms of the long-range work needs of the nation but which do have marked effects upon placement rates. Eninger (5) has shown clearly that schools which operate placement offices for their students have better vocational education programs than schools which do not offer such a service. The most likely reason for this finding is that the placement office serves as a feedback mechanism for adjustment in the content and methods of the vocational training program to meet local labor market needs.

Industry-Operated Schools

Not all schools, of course, are operated by public institutions or by private educational organizations. Many large industries operate schools of their own. Less publicized schools are operated by trade associations in fields such as baking, cleaning, and dyeing, restaurant management, manufacturing engineering, and water plant operation. This extremely important part of vocational education is covered in detail later.

Institutionalization Trends

With the exception of a few very recently developed occupations, instruction in almost every field has progressed through the various types of occupational education institutions in the same order in which society invented them. Thus the practice of medicine was first taught by physicians to their children, then was taught on-the-job, then through apprenticeship, and only in the late nineteenth century became an accepted part of formal instruction in the schools. Generally, the older and more highly skilled the occupation, the earlier it made the transition through these various institutions to become part of the school curriculum.

Shifts in the method of providing instruction occurred gradually. Thus, in the late nineteenth century one could find physicians being prepared in every institution of society devoted to occupational education. Only recently have all practitioners of medicine been required to go to school. At the present time, most occupations outside the professions are still in the process of transition, with gradually increasing proportions of workers being prepared in the school and gradually decreasing proportions being prepared through the family and on-the-job training. With few exceptions, the semiskilled vocations have not reached the point where they are included in school curricula.

None of society's means for providing occupational instruction has ever been discarded totally. Instead, the simplest means of instruction have tended to become devoted to the simplest occupations. However, even in the most complex fields, e.g., medicine, OJT continues as a means of teaching content which applies only to a particular place of employment. New jobs which have developed and technical occupations which have split off from existing vocations tend to start farther up the hierarchy of vocational education institutions. Thus, new workers in the field of engineering technology have seldom if ever been prepared through family instruction and were taught only briefly through on-the-job training or apprenticeship. Instead, the bulk of such occupational preparation has from the beginning been provided in schools. Indeed, the availability of schools has been the primary limiting factor in the development of these occupations. Without schools to develop trained workers, the occupations within engineering technology or other highly technical fields cannot flourish.

Why We Are Not Meeting Needs for Workers

During the nineteenth century, the United States met many of its work needs through the immigration of skilled workers from Europe. This delayed the establishment of significant public vocational education programs in this country until the start of World War I. Many developing countries have used a similar labor pool, but they nearly all face a demand that native workers be trained and employed so that they can take over the best positions from foreigners. Clearly we cannot depend on other nations to meet our needs. Indeed we have obligations to help underdeveloped nations train their own people to meet needs for workers abroad, but how can we do this when we are not meeting our own needs?

During the fifties, the population in the United States increased 19 percent, and the number of households increased 20 percent. During this same period the number of electricians and plumbers increased 10 percent, or half as much as the number of households, and the number of carpenters actually decreased. During the following decade, the resulting shortage in the construction trades led to very rapid wage rate increases as contractors in most parts of the country attempted to attract skilled workers. This, in turn, resulted in increased costs of conventional housing and was a major factor in the more than 20 percent annual growth rate of the mobile home industry (1, p. 4).

It has been argued that the failure to train enough construction workers is because these trades are tightly unionized. Certainly at times the unions (and employers) in the construction industry, like almost every other occupational association from the American Medical Association to associations of morticians, have acted to restrict the entry of new workers. What is overlooked in this criticism is the fact that during the fifties, the numbers of cars and trucks in the United States increased by 50 percent, while the number of automobile mechanics increased by only 3 percent (2, p. 68). Since this is a field which is not tightly unionized, and since this example in the repair fields can be duplicated in occupation after occupation, the argument that restrictive union practices have produced our shortage of skilled workers is not very sound. Indeed, one can argue that if the construction workers' unions had not been the nation's leaders in fostering apprenticeship programs, the shortage of construction workers would be far greater than it is today.

The problem is more basic and rests in the attitudes of the public toward certain occupations. John Gardner stated the problem well when he said,

> An excellent plumber is infinitely more admirable than an incompetent philosopher. The society which scorns excellence in plumbing, because plumbing is a humble activity and tolerates shoddiness in philosophy because it is an exalted activity will have neither good plumbing nor good philosophy. Neither its pipes nor its theories will hold water. (6, p. 86)

If we assume that these attitudes can be changed, we are still faced with the problem of learning what we as a society should do in vocational education to meet the needs of the nation for workers. Work needs are changing to the point that it has been said, "There is no place in the world of work for the uneducated person or the educated person who has not learned how to work" (9, p. 124). It might be more accurate to say that times have changed so that unless a person has learned to work, he or she is not educated.

Changes in Needs for Workers

Long-Term Trends

The proportion of the labor force which is made up of unskilled workers has decreased sharply and steadily for over one hundred years. Except for interruptions caused by war, pestilence, and governmental or religious suppression of innovation, this proportion probably has decreased since the beginning of recorded history. Mechanization is selective in its effects, and during the last century it has been easy to replace unskilled workers with power from sources such as coal, petroleum, falling water, and atomic energy. Certain types of skilled labor can also be replaced by machines, but when this is done, other skilled labor is needed to manufacture, install, adjust, and repair machines. Once unskilled labor is replaced, it is no longer needed.

A second long-term trend has been a continued decrease in the proportion of the labor force involved in producing goods. Agriculture has become one of our most mechanized and efficient industries. While decreasing proportions of the labor force are required to produce our food and fiber, the knowledge and skill required of those who do produce them has increased. Similar effects are taking place in the manufacturing industry. These effects became apparent earlier in agriculture, however, because the demand for agricultural products is relatively static, while the demand for manufactured goods can be increased considerably. Despite increases in demand, the proportion of the population employed in manufacturing has declined for at least the past fifty years, with only the production of war goods temporarily reversing the long-term trend. As in agriculture, the skills of the labor force required for manufacturing continue to increase. Along with the decrease in the need for unskilled workers and the decrease in the proportion of the labor force involved in the production of goods, there has been a corresponding increase in employment in service occupations and in clerical work. In the mid fifties, the United States became the first nation in history to have less than half its workers employed in producing goods and more than half in white-collar activities, especially in service and clerical work.

Many routine clerical activities have been replaced by electronic hardware, with the net effect being an increase in the skill level of the clerical occupations which remain. During the late fifties, computer corporations, which were rapidly expanding in certain manufacturing and clerical fields, predicted that they would soon be able to replace a large portion of the labor force through a revolution which would mean the end of work as we have known it. The result would be a large portion of the population doing no work at all, and the remainder working two or three days per week.

This prospect generated a great deal of unsophisticated writing and discussion. Among the predictions was that all of humanity would be reduced to the status of button pushers and gauge watchers. Since button pushing and gauge watching are among the activities which are most easily automated, these predictions hardly merited notice. But they were noticed, and vocational education was provided for smaller proportions of the adult population and the male school population, on the grounds that vocational education would soon be obsolete.

Youth Unemployment

During the thirties, youth unemployment was one and a half times as high as adult unemployment. By the sixties, the youth unemployment rate was more than three times as high as the adult unemployment rate. Among industrialized nations, only the United States and Canada have had a severe youth unemployment problem. Those who have attempted to explain this anomaly have cited

1. *effects of minimum wage laws.* The hypothesis is that since many employers are forced to pay youth a minimum wage which is higher than their productive capacity, these employers choose not to employ youth. Folk (4, p. 92, ff.) points out that youth unemployment has not increased more rapidly following the imposition of higher minimum wage standards.
2. *the increased supply of job seekers in the 1960s and 1970s.* Although the number of jobs increased it never caught up with the demand for jobs by youth and women. It is yet to be seen if the decreased number of births in the early 1970s will create a shortage of young workers in the late eighties.
3. *a belief that youth no longer want to work.* This explanation usually ignores the definition of unemployment, which includes among the unemployed only those people who wish to work but are unable to find work. A few more sophisticated individuals who know how unemployment is measured hold to this belief, claiming that some youth reject the types of jobs open to them. Increased affluence and rising job expectations probably play a part.
4. *effects of education.* Students are more likely than adults to seek part-time or summer work. Parnes (11, p. 65) found that both white and black students had unemployment rates more than three times as high as the rates for comparable nonstudents. This would suggest that the long-term increase in youth unemployment might be associated with the long-term increase in the proportion of late teenage youth enrolled in school. However, labor department figures quoted by Folk show student and nonstudent youth unemployment as being at about the same level.

   A factor which may be related to education and youth unemployment is the probable effect of education's causing youth to want to work only in occupations which have better working conditions than inexperienced youth can command. Since graduates of high school vocational programs have considerably lower unemployment rates than graduates of other curricula, bring more salable skills to the marketplace, and command higher annual pay, this explanation seems plausible. Moreover, emphasis in the college preparatory curriculum on professional occupations, which most high school graduates are not equipped to follow, may lead to unrealistic expectations on the part of graduates and dropouts from this curriculum who seek employment without collegiate training (7).

Cyclical Changes

About once each generation the United States suddenly recognizes that it faces a critical shortage of workers capable of performing well in semiskilled, clerical, sales, and technical occupations. These are the occupational fields with which vocational education is most concerned. Recognition of these shortages leads to sharply increased federal, state, and local expenditures for vocational education in the public schools. In the forties and sixties it also brought about the creation of nonpublic school institutional mechanisms for meeting these shortages. In the forties this took the form of the establishment of war production training programs which were operated largely by public schools. In the sixties the additional mechanisms included Manpower Development and Training Act and Job Corps programs operated by the United States Department of Labor.

During the periods of recognized shortage of workers, vocational education is hailed in the nation's press and in the educational literature as vital to the nation's welfare. Half a generation later, when the most acute of these worker shortages have been met and the remaining shortages have been forgotten, vocational education is either ignored (as in the late twenties and early thirties) or sharply attacked as a waste of the taxpayer's money (as in the mid fifties). There are two parts to this problem. One is related to the nation's worker needs themselves, and the other is related to our perception of the nation's needs for workers.

Although the long-term needs noted earlier in this chapter continue with little change, there are sharp short-term trends which are affected by expansion or contraction of the total job market. When employers and consumers are optimistic, the job market expands rapidly and demands many more workers than have been employed in the past. Until recently, these new workers could be employed on unskilled jobs, so the transition to full employment was relatively painless. People were removed from unemployment rolls, part-time workers took on full-time jobs, and people who had not been working for pay at all accepted full-time employment. But the long-term trends make it clear that fewer and fewer unskilled workers will be needed. This means that with every successive expansion in the total economy, the process of adjustment becomes increasingly difficult. People want to work, but do not have the necessary skills and knowledge to participate in a technologically oriented labor force. Training periods for skilled workers are far longer than for unskilled workers, so training costs to employers rise, and employers are more likely to demand public assistance in meeting their training needs. This means, among other things, that they will demand more vocational education programs supported by public funds.

However, vocational teachers cannot be created overnight. Some experienced workers who are naturally good teachers are recruited to become teachers of vocational education. Along with them are recruited many workers who are unqualified as teachers, and a few people who are unqualified both as teachers and as workers. The net result is a dilution in quality but an increase in the quantity of vocational education offered. In about the length of time that it takes to create a good vocational teacher, employer and consumer optimism ebbs, the total labor force needs begin to decline, and the well-trained new teachers have difficulty in securing suitable employment.

When the total labor market needs decrease, the age group which is hit hardest is the youth group, which has no employment experience. Four million of these youth are ready to enter the labor market every year. Seniority systems guarantee that present workers receive first consideration in employment. Once their needs are met, employers turn to experienced workers who are most likely to be immediately productive. Youth, who have neither work experience nor seniority, are most likely to suffer. Middle class youth often secure jobs through the influence of family and friends; lower class youth who have salable skills acquired through vocational education come next; lower class youth who do not have salable skills find employment almost impossible to secure. Ironically it is at this very time that vocational education begins to appear as a needless luxury to many lay people. They suggest that the solution is to keep youth off the labor market inexpensively by enrolling them in general courses with large classes and little or no instructional equipment. It seems reasonable to assume that youth who are conditioned by education (both general and vocational) to expect meaningful employment will not react passively to denial of the right to work. Moreover, in the future youth are less likely to come from families where the major wage earner is unskilled and accustomed to low wages, seasonal unemployment, and the lack of material goods. Rising youth expectations for employment could make the expected sharp decrease in the size of the labor force a national disaster.

Cyclical Changes and Vocational Education

Until the early sixties, vocational education had the meeting of the nation's needs for workers as its principal objective. So long as this was the case, vocational education should have had no alternative but to expand and contract in accordance with the perceived needs for workers. In practice, however, vocational education, as does any bureaucracy, fought reductions in support and managed instead to secure constant levels of appropriations during periods of labor surplus. And when the nation's needs for workers were perceived to be great, vocational education profited from sharply increased appropriations.

The principal casualty of cyclical changes in perceived employment needs was the development of teachers, administrators, researchers, and other leadership personnel in vocational education. Not only did these personnel development programs suffer from a double acceleration effect (see chapter 7), but by the time such programs were put into effect, the need for their graduates had largely disappeared. This meant that leadership personnel in vocational education came almost entirely from the ranks of those trained on-the-job as vocational teachers and administrators during periods of rapid expansion in vocational education.

Perceived Needs for Workers

Actual needs for workers are affected by expansions and contractions in total labor force needs and by shifts in demand from one occupation to another. The public perception of these needs, however, is often quite different from reality. Public perception responds to shortages and surpluses reported by the media. During the early fifties, the popular press was full of articles stating flatly that we no longer needed large numbers of engineers. By the time this began to affect youth enrolling in engineering colleges, we were faced with a critical need for engineers and low enrollments in the first year of engineering. There is such a lag between professional awareness of imbalances, publicity about imbalances, and public action in response to publicity that often the public acts in the opposite direction to the way it should.

Another factor which creates a disparity between real and perceived manpower needs is the tendency of employers to hoard highly skilled workers in anticipation of future expansions. Extremely capable skilled workers have always been very difficult to find. If employers expect to increase their need for such workers in the near future, they will probably retain all the highly skilled personnel they can and recruit additional skilled staff beyond the immediate needs. This tends to create an illusion of a greater shortage than actually exists. When employers no longer anticipate immediate expansion, they will release these excess workers, temporarily creating the impression of a widespread surplus of skilled workers. Since unskilled and semiskilled workers seldom are hoarded in any significant quantities, and since the long-term trends suggest that they will be a continually decreasing proportion of the labor force, it appears that hoarding will become an increasingly important factor in creating a discrepancy between perceived and real shortages.

Forecasting the Need for Workers

For vocational education to serve the work needs of society effectively, a system of long-term forecasting of the needs for workers would be highly desirable. The forecasting which exists now is highly inaccurate even in the short-term. Indeed, many labor economists are of the opinion that given the present state of knowledge, long-term forecasting with any degree of accuracy is impossible.

Attempts have been made to ask employers what their anticipated employment needs will be. The results have been highly inaccurate partly because employers have not practiced forecasting their own needs for workers except to judge the quantity of managers and supervisors they will need. However, the problem involves more than the lack of practice in forecasting by employers. A major problem has been sudden shifts in government policy which affect jobs. Several attempts have been made to learn employers' current job vacancies. This would appear to be less complicated than trying to predict future vacancies. Nevertheless these studies have proved to be inaccurate because employers redesign jobs to adjust to the presence of skilled workers. Overnight changes in worker selection criteria are common, and training programs to adapt present and new employees to meet critical job vacancies are started and stopped on short notice. In short, employers do not know how many personnel of each type they will need in six months, let alone how many they will need in ten years. This and the reluctance of some employers to let possible competitors know of their plans create a discouraging situation with regard to forecasting the need for workers.

Vocational education's need for accurate forecasting varies according to the proportion of workers being prepared through that system. Virtually the entire supply of military pilots must come through training programs operated by the armed forces. If the need for pilots is underestimated, and the programs are kept small, the effect could be disastrous to our national defense. Similarly, if the need for pilots is overestimated, several tens of thousands of dollars will be invested in each of the pilot trainees who is not needed at the end of the training program. Instead, the program will have produced many dissatisfied officers who are not needed to fly airplanes. Production of almost the entire supply of needed workers by a single training source leads to demands from that training source for high accuracy in needs projections. High accuracy is also required if there are multiple sources of trained workers and if the graduates of each training agency are equally preferred by employers.

On the other hand, if the graduates of training system A (e.g., public school practical nurse training) are generally preferred to the graduates of training system B (e.g., private school practical nurse training), the preferred training system can tolerate vast errors in forecasting so long as it is preparing considerably less than the total number of trainees needed by employers. If the need for skilled workers has been underestimated, the shortage will be made up through OJT. If the need for workers is overestimated, the graduates of the preferred vocational program will still be able to secure employment, and personnel who have been trained in the private school will suffer. When there are multiple types of training activities for a certain occupation, and each trains less than the total number of personnel needed, the graduates of the preferred training program will be less affected by errors in forecasting than will graduates of the less preferred programs.

For the less preferred training system, however, forecasting of the need for workers is extremely critical. Moreover, the less preferred system must have knowledge of the output of the preferred system. For example, in the construction industry, apprenticeship is the preferred training program for skilled workers, so vocational programs in most construction occupations must depend both on accurate forecasting of the need for and knowledge of the apprenticeship program output. On the other hand, because vocational training is preferred over OJT in clerical occupations, correct forecasting for this group of occupations will not be critical for vocational education until output begins to be nearly as great as the total demand.

Demands for Workers

Despite the enormous difficulties involved, the Bureau of Labor Statistics, U.S. Department of Labor, prepares estimates of annual needs which extend five to ten years in the future. Two hundred forty occupations, slightly more than half of all employment in the United States, are covered. Professional and technical occupations and skilled crafts, all of which require long periods of education or training, are covered extensively. For example, estimates have been made for the annual average labor demands in occupations which cover 95 percent of employment in technical occupations, 93 percent of employment in health occupations, and 81 percent of trade and industrial occupations. However, projections of annual demand cover occupations which account for only 22 percent of employment in distributive occupations (occupations which have to deal with wholesaling, retailing, and transportation). No estimates are available for agriculture, agriculturally related occupations, or home economics related occupations, or for the numerous occupations which employ the remaining half of the labor force. In the field of distributive occupations such large occupational groupings as general merchandise sales (over three million employees), industrial marketing (over one million employees), and food distribution (one million employees) are completely omitted.

Preparation of estimates of annual need for each occupation requires that several variables be considered: (1) employment by age and sex, (2) demand for each type of product or service produced, (3) production requirements in each industry generated by this demand, (4) employment required to reach these levels of production, (5) trends in occupational requirements resulting from technological change, and (6) job openings resulting from retirements and deaths. In addition, estimates must be made of the growth and changing character of the economy, the gross national product, and the national income and its distribution. Errors in any of these estimates can result in errors in estimated annual demand for workers in an occupation. No assessments are made of shifts of workers from one occupation to another, so this introduces a further source of possible error.

Most estimates of worker need are national estimates. Even if they are correct, they may be completely misleading as a guide to local policy (10). Local demands may be far higher in one occupation and far lower in another than national estimates would suggest, and there is ample evidence that geographic mobility is not adequate to move people rapidly from an area of low demand to an area where there are many jobs. For example, there has been little success with paying people to move from areas of high unemployment to areas of low unemployment. Consequently, it seems desirable to shift away from the current policy of providing training at home and encouraging mobility after training to a policy of encouraging mobility *prior* to training. Experience in the practical nurse training field indicates that not only do trainees move prior to training, but when instruction is provided in a geographical area where jobs are available, trainee graduates tend to settle in that area.

Supply of Workers

Adequate forecasting of the need for workers requires a knowledge not only of the demand for workers of a particular type but also of the supply of such workers. Knowledge of the supply side of this equation is even more inadequate than knowledge of the demand side. Workers learn the skills necessary for success in an occupation in a variety of ways:

1. vocational education in secondary and postsecondary schools,
2. apprenticeship,
3. Comprehensive Employment and Training Act programs,
4. on-the-job training,
5. proprietary vocational schools,

6. military training,
7. correspondence schools,
8. trial and error, observation, and other informal methods.

No systematic method exists for collecting information on the output of these types of training.

Attempts are now being made to secure information on the number of graduates from in-school vocational education and Comprehensive Employment and Training Act programs. Some estimates are available on the number of apprenticeship and military technical training program graduates. However, a complicating factor is the problem of how to count dropouts from training programs. Some people drop out of a training program because they have lost interest in the occupation or they fear failure. However, a significant proportion of dropping out, particularly in adult vocational programs, is due to the fact that when sufficient levels of salable skills have been achieved, many trainees leave the program to go to work in the occupation. This has been particularly true in the Comprehensive Employment and Training Act programs. Since the goal of the program is to secure employability and these trainees drop out to go to work, the goal of the program has been achieved. Many adults who enroll in community college programs meet their personal educational goals without completing an associate degree program. Since the trainee's time is valuable, the cost effectiveness figures for dropouts who achieve employability skills before completing the program may be higher than for those who continue through graduation.

Another problem in determining the supply of people prepared to enter an occupation is the matter of quality. Most training programs produce some graduates who are not qualified. Since few fields have established quality standards for vocational education programs, the number is unknown. Moreover, the number of people considered to be unqualified for entrance to an occupation depends considerably upon the state of the labor market. If trained workers are in short supply, a person who otherwise would be considered ineligible may be employed immediately. Conversely, when the labor market is tight, only the most qualified or those who have friends or relatives in influential positions may be employed.

Occupational Shifts

Many lay people think of vocational education as being a secondary school or community college program. However, approximately half of the vocational enrollment is made up of adults who are securing training to enable them to shift from one occupation to another or to enable them to cope with changes within an occupation. All authorities agree that employees change employers frequently and that within an occupation job titles and content change quite rapidly. Most authorities are of the opinion that the rate of such change is increasing. A common statement is that an individual will hold seven "jobs" during his or her working lifetime. Unfortunately, this figure is not of much help in planning vocational education. A change in job may mean that the employee moves from one employer to another. Under this criterion, a nurse or a bricklayer may change jobs many times during a year. Yet if the knowledge, skills, and attitudes required by each employer are essentially the same, then there may in effect be great job stability. However, a steel worker may, during the course of a year's employment by one company, change occupations from yard worker to hand trucker to power trucker. The job content of these three occupations is quite different. But since one cannot normally enter employment for a steel company except as an unskilled laborer, and since promotions are based on seniority, the implications of increased rapidity of shifts from one occupation to another in the steel industry have little or no significance for vocational education designed to prepare youth for an entry job. (It may, on the other hand, have considerable implications for adult vocational education which is designed to make the transition from one occupation to another more painless.)

Proponents of nonspecialized education commonly use the statistics on job changes without recognition of their complexity and suggest that because one will change jobs frequently, preparation for an entry job is not needed. They say that our education is designed for a lifetime, while vocational education will be of value for only a few years. This argument overlooks the rate of change in all of knowledge, which seems to be expanding at a considerably greater rate than the frequency with which a person changes her or his occupation. Moreover, the same individuals who downgrade vocational education generally support education for the professions, where the rate of change is almost certainly greater than in the occupations with which vocational education is most concerned. Yet no one has suggested seriously that schools stop training people for the professions.

Slippage

Seldom do all graduates of an occupational education program enter the occupation for which they were prepared. Not all law school graduates become lawyers, and not all graduates of carpentry apprenticeships become carpenters. Indeed, information on a number of professional schools indicates that slippage may be as high as 50 percent. In the case of apprenticeship, it is very common for approximately one-third of the graduates to enter the occupation, one-third to go into supervisory and management positions, and one-third to become technicians of various types associated with the occupation. Any attempt to balance supply and demand in a particular occupational field must take this slippage into account. Unfortunately our knowledge of the amount and direction of this slippage is very limited. It seems likely, however, that slippage is accentuated when the wages which can be earned by the graduates of a particular occupational training program are higher outside the occupation than in it. Relative working conditions (other than wages) probably have a similar effect.

Meeting Society's Needs as an Educational Objective

Not all educators see the meeting of needs for workers as a desirable objective of education. Haskew and Tumlin feel, "the talents of people are now viewed as instruments of corporative welfare, as tools for advancement of mankind's triumph over nature (including human nature), as resources to be exploited fully, lest the economy collapse" (8, p. 66). While this may be the way some people view the talents of people, it is also true that the talents of people are important in each of these enterprises. These talents should be exploited fully with the goal not only of avoiding the collapse of the economy but also of providing each individual with a sense of control over her or his environment and a sense of having markedly increased individual options.

REFERENCES

1. *America's Industrial and Occupational Requirements, 1964–75.* Bureau of Labor Statistics. Washington, D.C.: U.S. Department of Labor.
2. "The American Repairman—A Vanishing Breed," *U.S. News and World Report,* September 13, 1965, p. 88.
3. Belitsky, A.H. *Private Vocational Schools and Their Students.* Cambridge, Mass.: Schenkman Publishing Co., 1969.
4. Folk, Hugh N. "The Problem of Youth Unemployment." In *The Transition from School to Work.* Princeton: Industrial Relations Section, Princeton University, 1968.
5. Eninger, Max. *The Process and Product of T. and I. High School Level Vocational Education in the U.S.* Pittsburgh: American Institute for Research, 1965.
6. Gardner, John W. *Excellence: Can We Be Equal and Excellent Too?* New York: Harper & Row, 1961.
7. Hall, Oswald, and McFarlane, Bruce. *Transition from School to Work.* Ottawa: The Queen's Printer, 1963.
8. Haskew, Laurence D., and Tumlin, Inez. "Vocational Education in the Common School." In *Vocational Education,* edited by Melvin L. Barlow. Sixty-fourth Yearbook of the National Society for the Study of Education, Part I. Chicago: University of Chicago Press, 1965.
9. Lindman, Erick L., and Kurth, Edwin L. "Dimensions of Need for Vocational Education." In *Dimensions of Educational Need,* edited by Roe Lyell Johns et al. Gainesville, Fla.: National Educational Finance Project, 1969.
10. Mangum, Garth, and Snedeker, David. *Manpower Planning for Local Labor Markets.* Salt Lake City, Utah: Olympus Publishing Co., 1964.
11. Parnes, Herbert S. et al. *Career Thresholds,* vol. 1. Columbus, Ohio: State University Center for Human Resources Research, 1969.

3

Increasing Individual Options

Many academic educators feel that vocational education decreases individual options by limiting students to one or a few occupations. Perhaps this is true in some vocational courses for some students. But for most vocational students, options are markedly increased by the availability of vocational education, and as more vocational educators accept the increasing of individual options as a basic objective, the proportion of students having multiple options will increase.

Our best information about increased options in vocational education comes from Project TALENT, which tested and followed up 5 percent of the students in United States high schools in 1961. It showed clearly that the general curriculum, which many educational philosophers *claim* offers the greatest number of options to students, really offers the least. The general curriculum allegedly prepares a student for any activity in life, and it enrolls 25 percent of the high school students in the United States. Yet this curriculum produces two-thirds of the high school dropouts, and its graduates rank behind both the college preparatory and vocational curricula in (1) proportion who go to college, (2) annual earnings, (3) job satisfaction, (4) length of unemployment, (5) frequency of unemployment, and (6) almost every other measure of success.

The Nature of Individual Options

Some people have more options than others; that is to say, they have more opportunities for choice as they go through life. Individuals with many options can choose from several places of residence, can choose several ways of spending a substantial part of their income, and can choose any one of several different occupations. People with fewer options have fewer opportunities for choice as they go through life. They may be restricted to renting a modest home or apartment, may be forced to spend a large portion of their limited income on food, shelter, and clothing, and may be forced to accept whatever employment is available by chance, for they have few salable skills.

While the process of choosing among alternatives may occasionally be difficult, it seems clear that the person who has options or choices is in a far more enviable position than the person who does not. Ideally, a person in retirement could look back over a life which was filled with options, and feel that he or she had had many opportunities for significant choices, rather than being buffeted entirely by uncontrollable forces. He or she could also look forward to further options during retirement.

Income beyond the amount required for subsistence generally increases an individual's options as does athletic ability, verbal intelligence, manipulative skill, and almost every attribute valued by society. Options are decreased by prejudice, poor education, social isolation, poor health, and many other factors. Some factors are under the control of society or of the individual, and some are not. It should be a major goal of society to strive to bring more of these factors out of the realm of chance and put them under control of individuals and groups of individuals.

The Role of Education

> There is a horrible example in history of what the Educated Society might easily become. . . . It is the destruction of one of the world's greatest and most creative civilizations, the China of the T'ang and Sung periods, by the imposition of a purely intellectual, purely analytical education on man and society, the Confucian Canon. Within a century this commitment to the purely intellectual in man destroyed what had been the world's leader in art as well as in science, in technology as well as in philosophy. We are today in a similar danger. (4, p. 93)

This type of education not only decreased individual options but destroyed a civilization. But education, properly conceived, can not only increase options, but do so more effectively than other institutions.

In the United States education appears to be the only social institution which has the increasing of individual options as a major goal. Even the family, which wants the best for its sons and daughters, often prescribes its definition of "best" in terms which severely limit the individual options of its members. Too often the remaining institutions of society work toward maintaining the occupations of the son and the daughter at the same level as the father and the mother. Even certain educators, who view the school primarily as a transmission agent for our culture, also act as a force for maintaining occupational levels at the same point from generation to generation. This view is losing ground since gradual acceptance of the revised protestant ethic (see chapter 6) has created a revolution of rising occupational expectations, and since society has turned to education as an institution which can satisfy these rising expectations.

Institutions other than education undoubtedly increase certain individual options, but in every case outside of education, the increasing of individual options is at best a secondary goal. For example, work experience in industry often increases individual options, but this is never a primary goal of industry. If an institution has the increasing of individual options as a primary goal, it should be able to achieve this goal much more consistently than could an institution where this goal is subordinate. A screwdriver can be used as a hammer, but if serious hammering is to be done, it should be done with a tool designed for this purpose.

Not all education is designed to increase individual options. Sometimes it seems to be designed to increase knowledge, as in some of the major universities. Sometimes it seems to be designed to maintain the status quo, as in occupational education programs designed to meet the needs of local employers or in "social studies" courses designed to perpetuate the existing economic, political, and religious structures. Sometimes it appears to be a bureaucracy designed to serve the needs of the incumbent bureaucrats. In education, as in other institutions, if the increasing of individual options is a subordinate rather than a primary goal, this goal is less likely to be achieved. Education which has the increasing of individual options as a major goal must also have the increasing of individual *occupational* options as an explicit goal because occupation has an enormous effect on other options.

Educational programs can be classified roughly into three general types:

1. those programs which have no occupational emphasis at all. These are generally based on the education of the past which was designed for the elite and emphasized leisure time activities and the performance of civic duties, with the implicit understanding that occupational preparation would be provided by the family business. These programs became ineffective for an increasing proportion of students as schools assumed the responsibility of education for all, but they continue in use, perhaps because they still work well for a small but influential proportion of the population.
2. separate occupational education for certain students through college preparatory programs in the high school followed by baccalaureate and graduate school programs; other students attend separate vocational schools, public and private.
3. a combination of general education and specialized education (including occupational preparation) where one reinforces the other. Occasionally the programs are deliberately designed to reinforce each other, but more commonly the reinforcement occurs in a less planned way as the individual student sees relatedness between the two types of education.

Educational theorists often see the combination of occupational and general education as being superior. Quarrels arise, however, as to the type of occupational and general education that should be provided. The principal difficulty arises in the fact that many people see specific occupational education as actually decreasing individual options. They argue that the preparation of an individual for a specific occupation inevitably ties the individual to that occupation, and even if this were the person's chosen occupation, he or she might later decide differently or the economic need for that occupation might decline, thus leaving him or her with no place to go. They argue that the school should provide a program which prepares each individual for *all* occupations since this would enhance the individual options of all students.

This argument is fallacious on two grounds. While on-the-job training by employers and education in certain proprietary schools is limited to preparing an individual for a single occupation, this rarely, if ever, is the case in public school vocational education. Instead, vocational education in the public schools prepares an individual for a family of occupations. A machine shop course prepares a student for at least two hundred different occupations in metal work. A distributive education course prepares a student for an extremely large family of occupations in wholesaling, retailing, and transportation.

Second, no educational program has yet been devised which prepares a student adequately for entrance into and progress in all occupations. Undoubtedly if such a program could be devised, and if it appeared relevant to students, educational efficiency would be raised. But the fact remains that such a program has not been devised. In its absence, many schools provide a "general curriculum" at relatively low cost, with occupational education deferred until after the end of formal schooling when an individual can be given specific occupational preparation through on-the-job training or can purchase occupational education in a proprietary school. It is a complete anomaly that those who are most vehement in their condemnation of vocational education in the school as decreasing individual options want to leave occupational education in the hands of employers who are assumed to be able to provide this education more economically. These critics point out correctly that the occupational education provided by employers often benefits only employers and hence should be paid for by employers, but they neglect the fact that when education is designed to benefit employers, it sometimes takes a form which decreases individual options of employees.

Vocational Education and Individual Options

The content of vocational education ranges from that which is specific to a particular employer or enterprise to that which is useful in almost any enterprise. An example of the former would be instruction in how to operate a unique piece of equipment found only in a particular firm and requiring skills and knowledge which are present in no other occupation. At the opposite extreme is content, for example, from clerical occupations which is present in almost every enterprise. There is general agreement that the responsibility of training for those jobs which are enterprise-specific should be placed squarely on the shoulders of the employing firm. Because of the operation of internal labor markets, a person trained on the outside for such a job would often have no opportunity to gain access to it. Moreover, because of economies of scale, training on the job would probably be the most efficient method of learning such an enterprise-specific skill. But perhaps most important, because employees cannot sell such skills elsewhere, the major benefits of training for enterprise-specific jobs clearly go to the employer. Therefore, the employer should be responsible for providing the necessary training.

Vocational education for jobs which are found in many enterprises is considerably different. First, economies of scale in training programs suggest that vocational education which is not enterprise-specific should be provided either through vocational schools, which serve a large number of employers, or in very large establishments, which have enough need for training that they can provide large enough groups of trainees to make training economical. But if a particular firm provides training which is useful outside that firm, labor turnover is almost certain to transfer some of the benefits to other firms which have not helped to finance the training. This suggests the need either for public financing of training (inside or outside the firm) or for joint financing by all firms, which could conceivably benefit from the training through shared training costs on the British Industrial Training Act model. The case for publicly conducted vocational education is strengthened by the finding of Doeringer and Piore (3) that when individual firms provided instruction in reading and writing, their employees often were taught to read only those symbols and to perform only those calculations required by their present jobs. This narrow training perhaps reduced labor force turnover, but it certainly was not in the best interest of the trainees and may even have encouraged learning habits which would later impede the worker's ability to acquire additional training. Doeringer and Piore stated that training in more general occupational skills "like literacy training, . . . tends to be excessively narrow" when provided by the enterprise "and may, therefore, yield unnecessarily high adjustment costs in the long run" (3, p. 119). They suggest that federal subsidies to employers might encourage broader training programs, but this seems unlikely unless the subsidies are contingent on the provision of broad training. A sizable federal contract with a chicken rendering plant for employee instruction in reading suggests that we should raise the further question of the competence of certain employers to provide broad educational programs.

Training for Secondary Labor Markets

It has long been recognized that jobs differ in desirability. Similarly, workers differ in their desirability to employers since they differ in age, amount of education, verbal test scores, and so on. It is easy to imagine a queue of young workers who have no vocational education and no significant work experience. If these youths were arranged in order according to their desirability to employers, and if available jobs were arranged in order according to the judgments of the potential workers as to their desirability (based on pay, opportunities for promotion, working conditions, etc.), one would expect that the most attractive workers would seek and would be employed in the most attractive jobs. In fact, this is what seems to happen. These attractive job vacancies constitute the "primary labor market."

In the "secondary labor market," which is made up of the less desirable job vacancies, no such order seems to exist. Employers spend little time screening applicants but hire almost anyone who appears at a convenient time. The relative desirability of jobs within the secondary labor market is quite uncertain in the minds of employees. Moreover, employment tends to be less secure so workers drift into and out of employment frequently, thus blurring the line between the employed and the unemployed. Workers who change jobs seldom improve their lot but end up with a job which is as low or lower on the job desirability scale as the one they had before.

An employer is likely to be involved almost entirely in the primary labor market or in the secondary labor market. However, almost every employer has a few jobs (such as manager) which are clearly in the primary labor market and a few jobs (such as custodian) which are clearly in the secondary labor market. A few employers, such as hospitals, have significant numbers of employees in each of the labor market types, e.g., physicians and hospital administrators in the primary labor market and aides and orderlies in the secondary labor market.

Federal training and employment programs (and to a certain extent, vocational education) have been placed in the unenviable position of being asked to give job training to the less desirable workers, while having their efficacy measured in terms of the proportion of these less desirable workers who secure employment. In a number of cases this has led to training for the secondary labor market because it is in this market that these less desirable workers match the availability of jobs to the satisfaction of employers. Some critics of training and employment programs and vocational education have suggested that the federal government is involved in an undesirable subsidy to the secondary labor market and has, particularly in the health fields, artificially depressed wages and working conditions by providing a flow of trained workers who are being employed at substandard wages. There is probably some truth to this argument, but the remedy is not clear. If all publicly supported training programs for health occupations were to be stopped, the cost of health care would increase dramatically, and the public would be asked to bear costs which might be far greater than it now pays for vocational training. Moreover, during the period of market adjustment, the cost in human life and suffering would be staggering.

It should be remembered that the secondary labor market varies in character from country to country and from time to time. Job vacancies for slave labor have largely been eliminated in Western industrial economies. As the availability of a well-trained labor force increases, it is possible to invest capital effectively in equipment and procedures which move more and more jobs from the secondary to the primary labor markets. This should be one of the primary goals of vocational education, for this should markedly increase individual options.

Factors Which Affect Individual Options

Career Ladders and the Internal Labor Market

A career ladder is a succession of jobs available to an individual worker with each job successively offering increased responsibility and wages and more desirable working conditions. Job career ladders may involve a few steps, e.g., apprentice carpenter, journeyman carpenter, and carpenter foreman, or many, e.g., from yard laborer in the steel industry through twenty-nine labor grades to roller. Progression through some career ladders may be accomplished in a short time, e.g., the transition from probationary assembler to assembler may take only sixty days, while the progression from medical student to psychiatrist may take twelve years or more. Because of different aptitudes, motivations, and opportunities, a given individual may progress only part way along the career ladder or may even progress through the entire range and then drop back one or two steps if he or she finds that the increased responsibilities of a job on one of the top steps are too demanding.

Successive steps in a career ladder are normally related in job content, with the lower steps being prerequisites to advancement to higher steps. This is not necessarily always the case, however, for there are often alternative routes to a particular stage in a career ladder. For example, a technician may come from the ranks of skilled workers or may enter technician status from a school vocational program, having had no experience as a skilled worker. One of the primary functions of education and of vocational education in particular is to enable the individual who completes the educational program to enter a career ladder at a higher step, and to progress further along the career ladder than would be possible without the educational background he or she has received. Some employment situations, however, are structured so that vocational education can have little effect upon the career ladder. The example most frequently cited is in the field of the health professions, where a person who receives vocational education as a practical nurse can go no further. In most states, if a person desires to be a registered nurse, the only alternative is to begin an educational program which does not take into account the person's previous training and experience. Similarly, a registered nurse has only a slightly longer career ladder, and if he or she desires to become a physician, must begin completely anew. Presumably this situation could be corrected through job redesign and changing of licensure procedures, but once having been established, it seems to be extremely difficult to change.

The internal labor market provides a completely different approach to career ladder development. In the internal labor market, a person secures employment at an "entry port." He or she then progresses to broader and broader career opportunities, based almost entirely upon seniority with that company. The amount of vocational education received before or during employment has almost no effect upon the career ladder progression. Moreover, if the firm stagnates so that retirements and expansions of production do not provide openings higher on the career ladder, he or she has no opportunity to transfer seniority to another firm which may have an almost identical career ladder structure. Indeed, the individual may find the career ladder within a single firm obstructed because the department within which he or she accumulates seniority has stagnated, while other employees with less seniority move up the career ladder in other departments within the same company.

The literature in vocational education and in career development has almost completely neglected the type of career ladder developed through internal labor market agreements and has concentrated upon career ladders free from a particular company or department in a company. Recent studies which contrast the career development of college professors who owe their loyalty to an institution rather than to a discipline are a notable exception. Further studies of this type in a variety of occupational fields should throw much more light on this pervasive problem.

Efforts of the school to increase individual options of students are of little avail if a large proportion of entry-level occupations lead to dead ends (since entry-level occupations are the only occupations open to recent graduates). Moreover, society has an obligation to provide a range of individual options to people of all ages, not just to youth. The first step in increasing individual options for all is the development of additional career ladders so that any person who enters an occupation at an entry port has opportunities to progress toward occupations which provide increased responsibilities and challenges.

The availability of career ladders is greater among large employers than small employers mainly because there are more occupational areas covered by an existing promotional scheme. But even large employers often subdivide their operations so that promotion is possible only within one department or within one technical subspecialty. Where this situation exists, the effect on career ladders is the same as if the large employer were really a series of unrelated small employers. The employee should have an opportunity to progress as far as he or she is capable within a career ladder and should also have the right to stop at any point along the career ladder without substantial penalty. In some occupations, to refuse promotion is to invite discharge or other punitive action. A full range of individual options includes an option to refuse promotion as well as the opportunity to accept one. It should also be possible to shift from one career ladder to another without excessive penalty. (Where such horizontal shifts are feasible, we say that a "career lattice" exists.) Reasons for wanting to shift from one career ladder to another may be quite diverse, ranging from physical disability to changes in interests. Another common reason is that opportunities for promotion may be blocked in one career ladder but are available in a closely related career ladder. Many people do not know these types of facts about the labor market.

Education should play two roles for adults in enabling them to move from one career ladder to another.

1. It should serve an instructional function enabling the person to utilize her or his past experience wherever this will be of value in the new career. It should provide instruction at a significantly high level so that as a person moves to a new career ladder, he or she is not forced to drop back to an entry-level wage. It should teach the realities of the labor market so that one can adapt to them or make intelligent decisions about acting to change them.
2. It should serve a validating function by certifying to prospective employers that the graduate, whether youth or adult, has the necessary skills, knowledge, and attitudes to succeed in the new career.

By providing a flow of trained and retrained individuals, education also should enable the employer to have more flexibility in redesigning jobs and families of jobs in ways which will enhance career development and individual options. The school as a part of its general education function should convey to all citizens the fact that career ladder restrictions based on race, sex, age, or religion are highly undesirable and counterproductive. Simultaneously, it should convey the message that employers and employee groups have responsibilities to all citizens and not just to themselves.

Youth Organizations in Vocational Education

The Smith-Hughes division of occupations into occupational fields has influenced the structure of youth organizations for vocational students. Thus we have organizations like the Future Farmers of America and Vocational Industrial Clubs of America. These clubs have done a great deal of good by providing opportunities for leadership development and education outside the school. It is interesting, however, that the youth organizations of vocational education appear to be more resistant to change than the vocational education programs which gave birth to them. Pitched battles have been fought over whether to change the name of FFA to indicate that it includes students interested in agricultural occupations other than farming. There have been numerous discussions as to whether or not the name Future Homemakers of America includes the wage-earning aspects of home economics.

These battles are being fought on the wrong grounds. If a major goal of vocational education is to increase individual options, and if youth organizations assist in achieving this goal, it is undesirable to exclude students of general agriculture or students of general education industrial subjects (industrial arts) from youth groups which are devoted to occupational exploration. Moreover, programs of each of these organizations should give students an opportunity to learn about occupations which are not included in the original youth group charter. Ideally there should be a national vocational education youth organization with parallel state and local school groups concerned with all of occupational life. Then if students change occupational goals, they could move from the equivalent of an intramural basketball team to an intramural football team. Youth organizations devoted to all of vocational education could more efficiently provide programs which develop skills in the commonalities of vocations as well as in their specialties.

Income and Social Class

Children of most middle class families receive considerable financial assistance as they progress through school. There are many costs associated with school which the student must pay, including costs of books, paper, pencils, art supplies, and, especially in vocational education because of the relatively high cost of instruction, charges for materials used. Moreover, the student must pay for such items as transportation to and from school, clothes which are in a style acceptable to the peer group, and minor luxuries.

In the lower class home not only may there be insufficient funds to provide for these necessities and near necessities, but there may be considerable pressure for the student to contribute to the finances of the family, so that the parents and other children may have items which they regard as necessities. Middle class families which have accepted the values of the protestant ethic are not only more likely to transmit this ethic to their children but also to accept the desirability of foregoing current pleasures themselves in order to enable their children to persevere in their education. Self-denial helps little, however, when income is very low. Modest housing, food, and clothing more than consumes the income of a family at the poverty level and leaves nothing for education. Table 3–1 shows the correlation of education and poverty. It indicates the the equation "inadequate education causes poverty" is true and reversible.

Students who need money for their own needs or for the needs of their families often try first to secure it by part-time employment. They frequently are unsuccessful in this because they lack salable skills. If we remember that an unemployed person is defined officially as a person who is looking for work but has been unable to find it, we can attach considerable significance to the finding of Parnes (8). He found that while only 52 percent of students are interested in working, in contrast to 96 percent of youth out-of-school (8, p. 50), the rate of unemployment for those in school is almost three times as high as the unemployment rate for those who have dropped out of school (8, p. 66). Obviously, both sets of figures must be considered for one alone is misleading.

TABLE 3–1. *Education and poverty*

Educational Attainment of Family Head	Percent of Families Below Poverty Level		
	All Families	White	Black
Less than 8 years	25.2	21.1	40.1
8 years	11.2	10.1	24.1
1 to 3 years high school	10.7	7.9	29.8
High school graduate	5.4	4.6	16.9
1 to 3 years college	4.4	4.0	8.9
Baccalaureate	2.0	2.0	1.1
Average	**9.7**	**7.7**	**27.8**

SOURCE: Derived from reference 9, p. 5.

If students do find work, over 15 percent work more than thirty-five hours a week, and well over half work more than fifteen hours per week (8, p. 91). This amount of work is almost certain to have detrimental effects on school achievement unless the student is well above average in verbal intelligence. The result is likely to be less interest in school and more interest in income, even though the occupation in which the student is engaged is very likely to lead to a dead end. This emphasizes the need for financial assistance which goes beyond scholarships or fellowships which pay for tuition (if this is charged) to include work-study programs and direct financial aid. After the student reaches age sixteen, the best possible solution seems to be a part-time cooperative education program which not only provides income but relates the material the student learns in school to what he or she is learning in the occupation. Federal employment and training programs have always recognized the need for financial assistance to the adult trainee.

Sex Differences

Citing experience in Canada, Hall and McFarlane have pointed out that " . . . the girl has a much greater likelihood of climbing above her parents (occupationally) than is the case for the boy" (6, p. 49).

> Over 60 percent of the boys from the families of non-manual workers are themselves employed in non-manual occupations, whereas 90 per cent of the girls with a similar background are in non-manual work. . . . two thirds of the girls whose fathers or guardians are manual workers have found work in non-manual fields, . . . (while) two-thirds of the manual workers' sons are engaged in manual occupations . . . .(6, p. 59)

Not only is this true of the world of work, but also of school.

> The school world . . . turns out to be, fundamentally, a feminine world. It provides an academic atmosphere in which girls thrive and boys fail. . . . it is a world to which girls adapt with relative ease. Boys appear to reject it, and eventually it rejects them. Moreover, the school is a feminine world in the vocational sense. It prepares them admirably for their careers in the work world . . . . Especially is this true for those who continue to university, those who prepare for school teaching and nursing, and those who enter clerical occupations. . . . our society provides much more in the way of specialized training facilities for girls than for boys. (6, p. 65)

In part, the design of educational facilities which serve girls better than boys has come about accidentally. Girls have been preferred for white-collar jobs, and the college preparatory programs of schools provide a greater degree of occupational preparation for white-collar than for manual occupations. Girls more than boys have been willing to enter lower paying occupations, and teaching has been one of these occupations. This has led to the development of teacher education programs catering largely to women and to the development of common school staffs heavily populated by women. School staffs in turn have been much more sympathetic to white-collar vocational education programs in business education and distributive education (which enroll mainly females) than they have been to blue-collar programs such as auto mechanics and machine shop (which enroll mostly males).

Project TALENT reported that over 40 percent of high school senior females said they were involved in vocational curricula, compared to less than 25 percent of males. Moreover, the girls who enrolled in vocational programs were considerably more intelligent than the males. The more intelligent males were likely to be enrolled in the college preparatory curriculum, due in part to a reverse type of discrimination in higher education. The proportion of females receiving doctorates has been declining for a long time, and many baccalaureate programs still discriminate against women. Until recently, many universities had unofficial quota systems for females, and many professional programs, e.g., veterinary medicine, were almost entirely closed to females. At present, such trends are shifting both in legal and practical terms, although the residual attitudes of sex stereotyping in occupations and vocational education are likely to continue for some time. In this sense, sex differences still assume more importance in the reinforcement of choices made by males and females than can be supported by job analyses or other types of assessments of job requirements.

Influence of Family and Friends

The Horatio Alger literature recommended to youth a means by which they could increase their occupational level. The theory expressed repeatedly by the single plot of the many Horatio Alger stories was that if you worked diligently, your merits would be recognized by a benevolent upper class, and you would receive rapid occupational advancement. This theme is still repeated constantly in literature distributed by corporations as a part of their training programs. Many managers still believe it implicitly, which is not too surprising, since they generally are satisfied with their own occupational progression. Also it is psychologically satisfying to imagine that this state of affairs has been reached through diligence and personal effort rather than through chance or education. The fact remains, however, that without the aid of society, occupational mobility would be nearly impossible. And, even with the aid of public education, the protestant ethic (and particularly the Horatio Alger version of the protestant ethic) has not worked for a large proportion of the population.

Study after study shows that securing employment depends heavily on help from family and friends. Since friends and family tend to come from the same social class, and since social class is closely related to occupation, the availability of information about an occupation or about employment opportunities tends to be restricted to those occupations and to those types of employment which are represented in the limited circle of family and friends. The type of employment received depends heavily on one's geographic setting, race, sex, and socioeconomic status. For a person in a rural area, only a very narrow range of occupational opportunities is available. There is a general belief that as transportation facilities improve, the influence of the geography of the home on occupational choice will decrease. This seems questionable. For the last three hundred years people in this country have shown a willingness to move long distances in order to find employment, but the employment is usually similar to what they left. Improved transportation just seems to cause the worker to spend weekends in expensive and time-consuming travel back to visit the area from which she or he migrated. While transportation facilities between cities have been improving, transportation within cities has not.

In the past, entry to many occupations was denied to people of certain racial or religious backgrounds or sex. Even though such discrimination is illegal, some subconscious barriers still exist. These barriers are breached most readily by individuals who possess either occupational experience or educational preparation or both.

Occupational Status and Career Counseling

A number of studies have revealed that there is a definite hierarchy of occupations; this hierarchy is not only remarkably constant over time but is also constant in the value structures of quite disparate groups of individuals. While no single factor determines whether an occupation is ranked high in status, such characteristics as high income and high educational requirements for entry are associated with "high level" occupations, while occupations which require manual effort tend to be ranked low. School counselors are quite responsive to the demands of parents and teachers and have learned that the safest course to pursue in occupational counseling is to encourage students to prepare for occupations which have parent/teacher approval. If a student is not interested in or capable of preparing for a high status occupation, such as one of the professions, counseling which strongly suggests preparation for a profession may have the effect of decreasing rather than increasing options. The schools should have a goal of providing adequate information about occupational opportunities, stressing the point that the status of an occupation is of little importance compared to job satisfaction. They should also encourage students to make occupational decisions which can be changed later if a student feels it would be desirable. Practice in decision making with regard to occupations is an essential part of the educational process.

Attitudes toward work are discussed in greater detail in chapters 6 and 8. It should be pointed out here, however, that if students learn in the elementary school that manual work is not desirable, or if they learn that work in any form is to be avoided, they have already decreased their options. Attitudes toward work begin to be learned in early childhood and are often confirmed in the elementary school. Early education should emphasize the value of work to the individual and to the society, and in the elementary school each student should learn that any socially productive occupation is noble.

Cognitive Styles

Individuals differ enormously in the ways they learn. Yet many schools still assume that everyone should be able to learn and to think in verbal terms. Even in such obvious cases as the hearing or visually handicapped student, where an important channel of learning has been cut off entirely, schools are often unwilling to adjust the means of teaching and consequently drive the student from the school. Fortunately, the number of specially trained teachers and new teaching methods for those obviously disabled students is increasing rapidly.

Less obvious but more important, at least in terms of the numbers of students affected, is the plight of people who simply do not operate well with verbal symbols. These students usually are substandard in reading ability, often because they are not interested in reading. Though most of them can read, they simply do not learn easily through reading. There is also a significant portion of the population which does not think well in terms of objects. Since the school has little to say about objects, this latter group is not handicapped greatly in school, though they may be markedly handicapped once they leave the school. We know very little about these two types of students.

The operation of these two cognitive styles can be observed in a setting where people attempt to assemble an object they purchased. Frequently, manufacturers, in order to save assembly and shipping costs, produce objects in an unassembled form and enclose instructions for assembly. The individual who does not think readily in verbal symbols or cannot read well or both is apt to discard the instructions and instead look at the parts to be assembled and at a photograph or sketch provided by the manufacturer. He or she then proceeds to put the object together. If the basic difficulty is poor reading skill, the individual may ask someone to read the directions to her or him, but this will be of little help if her or his cognitive style does not include facility with verbal symbols. Hearing the instructions will be of less value than seeing the unassembled parts and the photograph of the assembled object.

Conversely, some highly educated people who have no difficulty in reading directions have difficulty in making the transition from the verbal directions to the actual objects to be assembled. In some cases, this may be due to inadequacies in their educational background (even if they have a Ph.D.). They may not know what a flange is or may not know what a round-headed screw is. Such educational inadequacies are to be regretted, of course, but they are corrected easily through a short course in industrial nomenclature, or through the process of continuing to assemble products of a similar nature. If, however, the difficulty is that they are unable to think in terms of objects and relationships among objects, their only course may be to employ someone to assemble the object for them or to be certain that in the future they do not purchase unassembled products.

The lessons from this example are obvious. First, all students who can do so should be taught to think in terms of symbols, objects, and the relationships between symbols and objects, instead of following the pattern of traditional education which emphasizes symbols. Second, if students are having difficulty thinking in terms of symbols, they should not be shut off from education but should be provided with educational experiences which increase facility with symbols as well as increase their options within the world of objects. Similar provisions should be made for those who experience difficulty thinking in terms of objects, even though the school typically is organized so that they can experience "success." Similar comments could be made about students who have trouble working with other people or thinking in terms of other people's needs and interests or learning in situations which involve individual study. If the school is to serve all people, it must provide programs which take into account the vastly different cognitive styles of its students.

Gagné points out that a lesson on the "reflection and refraction of light" could be presented in many different ways: (1) a demonstration could be used with accompanying oral communication; (2) a chapter of programmed instruction might be assigned; (3) an assessment exercise might be conducted by the teacher to see if the required principles have been learned; (4) a motion picture sequence might be used to show an unusual example of the principles being taught; (5) a discussion of how to go about investigating a problem shown in the film could be used; or (6) the teacher might assess ability to solve problems in reflection and refraction by means of a test on ability to transfer knowledge to a new situation (5, p. 294). This long list of media and methods of instruction is not complete; for example, a laboratory exercise in the discovery or testing of the principles to be learned could be added. He says, "the real point to be made is that the use of variety of instructional modes is both feasible and potentially effective" (5, p. 294). Though correct, this statement overlooks the vital point that these methods and media of instruction are differentially effective for students. Cronbach points out that "many approaches have some success, and none works in all situations or on all students" (2, p. 352).

We know that students learn more rapidly those things which are interesting to them, and we know that student interests vary enormously from time to time and from one student to another. Moreover, students have different cognitive styles, that is, some individuals learn in considerably different ways from others. If a particular student does not learn well from a lecture, for example, we have four options.

1. We can choose another method of presenting the same material.
2. We can present material which is so interesting that he or she will learn even though the lecture method seldom teaches him or her much.
3. We can teach the student how to profit from the lecture method.
4. We can allow him or her to sit through the lecture without learning anything.

All of these possibilities except the last seem to be defensible, yet that alternative is the one most frequently used.

The laboratory method which is so common in vocational education is much more effective with certain students than with others. If students have goals which can best be met through vocational education, methods of teaching should be adapted which enable them to learn its content most effectively. Too often, vocational educators are as adamant in using laboratory methods as the history teacher is in using the lecture.

Some students will learn only if education appears to be relevant. If a subject appears relevant to the student, she or he will usually learn regardless of the method used, though perhaps less rapidly than possible with an optimum method. Because vocational education courses are elective, their teachers, administrators, and teacher educators too often rely on the strong interests of the student to substitute for inadequacies in educational planning.

Interests

It is trite to say that individual interests differ. Yet the school rarely seems to capitalize upon these differences in interests. If the goal of the school is to teach the student to read, this goal is much more likely to be reached if the reading matter is of interest to the student. Great progress has been made in adapting reading materials to fit the interests of the majority of students, but the goal seems still to have all students read the same material. It is often found that students in vocational education are exposed, for the first time, to reading materials which are interesting and important to them as individuals. The world of occupationally related literature, from the *Farm Journal* to the *Wall Street Journal* and from repair manuals for automobiles (often two inches thick for a single make and year of car) to instruction on a new surgical procedure, is probably as important to our society as the novels, essays, and poems which provide the bulk of instructional material for classroom reading programs. Yet the literature related to occupations is hardly touched in schools, even in vocational education. This is not to say that the school should avoid its responsibility to develop new interests on the part of its students. What it does say is that capitalizing on existing interests of students may be the best way of providing skills which can later lead to the development of additional interests.

Aptitudes

Individuals differ enormously in their aptitudes, but the school concentrates primarily on developing only a few of them. Athletic aptitudes are highly developed for those few students who are capable of performing on the varsity teams. Musical aptitudes for performance on band instruments and in certain types of choral groups are well developed if they are utilizable in performances which reflect credit on the school. Similarly art aptitudes are fostered on the part of those students who have proved capable of producing works of art which can grace the school or its public displays. It seems that certain types of aptitudes are not developed by the school at all. Aptitudes in troubleshooting, horticulture, child care, sales, and so on are almost totally ignored. Yet, if individual options are to be increased, these aptitudes need nourishing as much as any others. A related problem is the discovery of aptitudes. Students who have undiscovered aptitudes certainly have had their individual options decreased, even if their school has a program for developing those capabilities.

Influence of Residential Schools

For a small but significant fraction of our population a desirable educational program includes the provision of residential school facilities. Whether the educational program is a four-year college, a community college, a high school, or remedial education program, some students learn a great deal by being removed part-time from their home environment to one which provides more stimulus for learning. In some cases this is necessary just to give the student an opportunity to make decisions without constant supervision. In other cases it is necessary to provide an atmosphere which develops attitudes and values which are more acceptable to society than those which can be learned on the street or in certain homes. Examples of such schools include the Civilian Conservation Corps (CCC) of the late thirties which provided on-the-job training and useful employment in public works. More recently the Job Corps has provided an educational program of a more formal nature with heavy emphasis on occupational preparation. In all societies, the military has provided a similar type of residential training which removed students from their previous environment. Residential colleges have a similar effect. Success of any of these undertakings seems to be closely related to whether or not their primary goal has been the increasing of individual options. Where this has been the case, they have succeeded with a much larger proportion of their trainees than if the increasing of individual options had been a distinctly subordinate goal. These programs are invariably expensive, but the results achieved have often been quite economical when one considers that they have surely reduced the proportion of people who would otherwise be sent to penal institutions, exist on welfare, or become emotionally dependent upon parents. For quite different reasons, residential schools are needed in sparsely populated regions. It simply is not possible, using the techniques available today, to provide a comprehensive high school within commuting distance of students in some parts of our country. Between twelve hundred and three thousand students (estimates vary) is the minimum enrollment needed to establish a high school with adequate programs to serve all types of youth, and to do this economically. But economics is not the only concern. Many communities which now have high schools have no breadth of employment opportunities. Part-time cooperative employment for significant numbers of students in a variety of occupations is simply not possible. A residential high school in a larger and more diversified community offers education more economically, and more importantly, it can offer broader and better vocational education.

Education in Penal Institutions

It has been frequently pointed out that the proportion of inmates who return to penal institutions is extraordinarily high. One of the principal reasons for this is related to a lack of individual options for former prison inmates. Employers carefully gather employment history information and may view with suspicion any gaps which may indicate that the potential employee has been incarcerated. If some employers learn that a person has been imprisoned for any reason, they are not likely to employ the ex-convict in a position of trust. While this is sometimes an irrational decision which seeks to penalize the ex-convict further, it is in large part a rational reaction based upon an expectation that a person who has once been in prison is likely to return and hence does not warrant expenditures for training which would be justified for a potential long-term employee. Regardless of the cause, the fact that it is very difficult for an ex-convict to secure satisfactory employment is undoubtedly a major reason for recidivism.

A major factor in the realistic objections of employers to ex-convicts is found within penal educational systems. With the exception of those in some federal penitentiaries, there are few significant programs of vocational education in penal institutions. Almost all of the so-called vocational educational programs which exist in these institutions are in fact production programs aimed at providing goods and services for consumption within the institution. Thus a person who is listed as a cook-trainee is likely to be ladling out soup in the cafeteria line. In a few cases this on-the-job training produces satisfactory results. Because it is important for prisoners to have their hair cut and because the quality of these haircuts is visible to visitors, instruction in barbering (or hair dressing) is probably the best vocational program in many penal institutions.

One of the main difficulties in vocational training in prisons is financial. There have been attempts to reduce the cost by establishing on-the-job training program which produce goods which are sold to nonprofit institutions, but these are attacked by employer and employee groups as unfair competition provided by underpaid workers. One method of avoiding this problem is the work release program of such states as North Carolina, which involves more than two thousand prisoners who leave the prisons to work full-time, returning each evening or each weekend for incarceration. A second method has been proposed by Bernard Puchalski of the Iron Workers' Union. He has suggested that prisoners be paid standard wages for goods and services produced and that the states subsidize the difference between their productivity and those of trained workers, justifying these added expenditures as part of the cost of training. Both of these schemes would profit from a coordinated educational program designed along the lines of the very successful part-time cooperative programs employed in secondary schools and colleges. A major goal of an educational program in a penal institutions, as in any other educational institution, should be to increase the individual options of the students.

Learning for Mastery

Schools which have accepted the obligation of allowing all students to attend have not necessarily assumed the parallel responsibility of seeing that these students learn all the types of knowledge they need. Benjamin Bloom (1) points out that it is more common for a school to accept responsibility for *presenting* material to all students than it is to assume responsibility for seeing that all students *master* certain specified skills, knowledges, and attitudes. As a result certain students who have been exposed to twelve years of instruction in the use of the English language are performing at a level typical of the average person who has received only half as much instruction. The goal is almost always specified in terms of the number of years of instruction rather than in terms of specified skills to be mastered. This phenomenon occurs at all levels of instruction from early childhood education through college.

If the school actually assumes responsibility for mastery of certain content by all students, it will find certain students who have not learned through the traditional approach, which emphasizes the authority of the teacher as the source of educational relevance. If society does not permit the school to allow its failures to escape through dropping out or "social promotion," it will be forced to find techniques which meet the needs of each of these students. This in turn will lead to a recognition that for many students, learning will occur most efficiently when tied to the student's perception of relevance. Moreover, the school will realize that for many students, educational relevance is best perceived when the student sees that skills, knowledges, and attitudes are needed for occupational survival, and that these are taught in many different school subjects. This in turn suggests that the school should encourage identification of occupational goals at an early age, even though the goal of each student is likely to change several times during his or her school career. Moreover, it suggests that the high school or community college which denies vocational education to the half or more of the students who desire such instruction is limiting the options of those students. Proponents of the general curriculum say it is designed to increase options, but on every variable in every study it has been shown to be far less effective in this regard than the vocational curriculum or the college preparatory curriculum (which is occupationally oriented for most students).

REFERENCES

1. Bloom, Benjamin S. "Learning for Mastery." *Evaluation Comment* 1, no. 2 (May 1968): 1–3.
2. Cronbach, Lee J. *Educational Psychology.* New York: Harcourt, Brace, & World, Inc., 1954.
3. Doeringer, Peter B., and Piore, Michael J. *Internal Labor Markets and Manpower Analysis.* Lexington, Mass.: Lexington Books, 1971.
4. Drucker, Peter. "The Rise in Higher Education." In *The Revolutionary Theme in Contemporary America,* edited by Thomas R. Ford. Lexington, Ky.: University Press of Kentucky, 1965.
5. Gagné, Robert M. *The Conditions of Learning.* New York: Holt, Rinehart & Winston, Inc., 1965.
6. Hall, Oswald, and McFarlane, Bruce. *Transition from School to Work.* Ottawa: The Queen's Printer, 1963.
7. Havighurst, Robert J., and Gottlieb, David. "Youth and the Meaning of Work." In *Youth,* Seventy-fourth Yearbook of the National Society for the Study of Education, edited by Robert J. Havighurst and Philip H. Dryer. Chicago: University of Chicago Press, 1971.
8. Parnes, Herbert S. et al. *Career Thresholds,* vol. 1. Columbus, Ohio: Ohio State University Center for Human Resources Research, 1969.
9. *Poverty Continues to Decline in 1969.* Consumer Income, Current Population Reports, No. 71. Washington, D.C.: U.S. Department of Commerce, Bureau of Census, 1970.

4

Lending Intelligibility to General Education

The least understood of the three major objectives of vocational education is the one suggesting that vocational education can and should consciously interpret general education to vocational students. It has always been true that a high proportion of students in vocational education see little value in most of general education and hence have little interest in it. Many of these students, as they progress through vocational education, suddenly see the need for (and hence the value of) many general education learnings which they had rejected earlier. This process occurs naturally, usually with no help from the vocational teacher. Unfortunately, after a vocational student has seen the need for learning material which she or he failed to grasp earlier, the school is often ill-prepared or even disinterested in helping her or him learn it later. In order to discuss this process further, we need to consider what general education and vocational education are and what their relationships should be.

There are many definitions of the term *general education.* Two contrasting versions are (1) educating for leisure, usually through acquiring specific knowledges and attitudes, such as an understanding of the great books of the past, and (2) acquiring the ability (and confidence in that ability) to cope with one's environment in today's world. The definition used in this book is much closer to the latter than to the former of these, but, in addition, general education as used here means that education which is needed by *every* student. It is assumed that the general education needed by every student will be supplemented by specialized education which is needed by some students but not by others, and that the totality of general education and specialized education received by each student will enable him or her to cope successfully with the environment and to feel confident about it.

Vocational education is often thought to be antithetical to general education. Though in some types of vocational training programs, especially outside the public schools, there is indeed a separation between vocational and general education, it is assumed here that the two are complementary and necessary to each other.

In certain vocational training programs in private schools, no instruction is offered which is labeled as general education, though a considerable amount of general education does take place. Even in on-the-job training, the most specialized and nonintellectual part of vocational education, a considerable amount of general education occurs. The only conflicts which exist are personal ones among instructors, with a few general educators demanding more time for their material and some vocational educators denying the relevance of some of the school instruction labeled as general education. Perhaps a consideration of what vocational education really is will help to dispel the notion that it and general education are incompatible.

Definitions of Vocational Education Content

The most inclusive view of vocational education content sees it as that content necessary for occupational success. Under this definition, much, if not most of, general education would be included, because reading, for example, is needed for full success in every occupation. A very different definition states that vocational education content is what makes a person more competent in one occupation than in another. If vocational education is limited to this definition, it appears to be entirely specialized since that content which enables a person to succeed in more than one occupation is relegated to general education. Because we defined general education as that education needed by every student, we cannot limit vocational education to training for a single occupation. This would eliminate a large part of education which is not needed by everyone but which does help people become competent in more than one occupation. For example, typing and welding would be eliminated because they are each important in more than one occupation, but they are not needed by everyone. A better view sees vocational education content as that which helps a person to succeed occupationally but which is not needed by everyone. Under this definition, vocational and general education together cover a much larger portion of education. All that is left out is that specialized education which is nonoccupational in nature, e.g., education for a specific avocation.

No definition of vocational education is entirely satisfactory. In this book *vocational education* includes all education which makes a person more competent in one group of occupations than in another. (This part of vocational education is all specialized since it is not the same for all people.) But the content of vocational education often also includes parts of general education necessary for occupational success but neglected by the general educator. Many educators, including some vocational teachers, see vocational education as being entirely specialized. Hence they reject the latter part of the definition used in this book. However, if essential parts of general education relating to occupational success are being neglected (e.g., development of psychomotor skills, ability to work in groups, an understanding of basic materials, processes and services, and the process of choosing an occupation) and if vocational teachers believe that this material is essential, then they must include it in their programs. When general educators assume the responsibility for teaching this general vocational education content effectively, vocational educators should be willing to surrender it. So long as it is no one's responsibility or everyone's responsibility, it is unlikely to be taught.

Generalizability of Vocational Education

Some types of knowledge about work and occupational life apply to almost all jobs and are needed by almost all people. Some examples include (1) an understanding of the economics of the production of goods and services, (2) an understanding of the social security system, and (3) the ability to satisfactorily complete an application form for employment. According to our definition, this is very close to being general education. On the other hand, there are types of knowledge about occupational life which are highly specialized and may be needed by only a dozen workers in the entire world.

Two points deserve emphasis: (1) there is no sharp line dividing general and vocational education, and able educators cannot agree on exactly where such a line should be drawn; (2) the content of vocational education covers a wide range of generalizability, from content which is usable in almost every type of work to content which is applicable in only a very few situations.

Instruction on obsolete processes and products has much less generalizability than instruction on current products and processes. Some people think that since no one knows what the products and processes of the future will be, no vocational education should be offered. Actually, this is more an objection to occupational education in the professions than to preparation for other occupations since the rate of technological change in the professions is much more rapid than it is in most other occupational fields. In any case, if we refused to educate people in a field because its future content was uncertain, we would be refusing to educate anyone on any subject.

Since products change much more rapidly than processes, education about processes is more generalizable than education about products. Work behavior, work group interactions, and work attitudes change even less rapidly than processes. Thus it is likely that instruction in attitudes is more generalizable than instruction in products or processes. However, no one has discovered a way to teach work attitudes without teaching them in a setting which involves products, processes, and services.

Vocational Education as a Direct Method of Instruction

Until now we have been considering the content of vocational education; however, vocational education is also a method of instruction. Even specialized vocational education provides a vehicle for teaching general education content, and for teaching it in a far more effective way than often can be accomplished in a standard classroom. Suppose a high school or community college has several different vocational programs. One part of each program is teaching students to work together effectively. This is a general education objective since all students need to learn how to work together. Certain students can learn to work together on a science project or on an athletic team, others in repairing an automobile, designing a sales campaign, or preparing a meal. While the science project might be labeled by the school as general education, the other examples indicate how general education goals can be achieved through specialized vehicles of instruction.

The effectiveness of vocational education as a method depends on such factors as (1) teachers who are genuinely interested in the success of students, (2) goals which appear relevant to students, (3) an atmosphere of responsible freedom rather than regimentation, and (4) content that is viewed as a means to an end, not an end in itself. Vocational education has no monopoly on such factors. Other subjects, especially in the practical arts, have some or all of them, but vocational education, more than most subjects, combines these factors in a way which appeals to students who are not motivated to learn content for its own sake. If a student does love learning for learning's sake, almost any method of instruction is effective. But if he or she does not, the method of instruction and the context of content become extremely important. The evidence suggests that vocational education as a method of instruction is highly effective with many students, and the evidence is clear that far more students want vocational education than can be accepted in a program of its current size.

Vocational Education as an Indirect Method of Instruction

Vocational educators are concerned that students learn more than is taught in vocational education classes. Occupational success depends on the student learning many things taught in general education classes. Reading, writing, and basic computational skills immediately come to mind, but concepts from science, economics, government, and history are also essential. Too often these concepts are presented as though they had no occupational value, and students who have not learned to value knowledge for its own sake may simply decide that this material is not worth learning. Later, often only when they have left school, they learn that these concepts are valuable, and wish they had learned them. This leads to a common phenomenon: an adult, past the age when he or she learns most rapidly, enrolls in a basic literacy class as part of a worker training program, and grows three years in reading achievement during one year of instruction. This usually occurs because for the first time the adult sees a reason for learning to read. Such programs for adults will probably always be needed because some schools will probably always fail to serve some students. But how much richer their lives would have been if they could have been provided a reason for learning to read while they were still in school.

Vocational education provides a reason for learning basic academic skills. It lets the student know that these skills are important in life and more particularly, are important in achieving occupational goals. Too often, however, the knowledge of the importance of basic academic skills comes late in a student's school life. Most vocational education begins at age sixteen, and many schools do not offer remedial instruction in basic academic skills to students of this age. Many vocational teachers proceed to do the best they can and teach basic academic skills in the vocational classroom. This is of some help, but most vocational teachers are not well prepared for this type of instruction. If the student could have learned earlier that basic academic skills *are* important or if remedial classes could be offered concurrently with vocational education, more effective results could be achieved.

A second way vocational education achieves general education indirectly is by helping to keep students in school. Several studies show that half of high school freshman want vocational education and half want college preparatory education. The half that want college preparatory work get in,but of those who want vocational education, half are rejected and placed in the general curriculum. Project TALENT data have shown that two-thirds of high school dropouts of both sexes come from this general curriculum. Vocational education has a higher dropout rate than the college preparatory curriculum and might have a still higher rate if it enrolled those students now assigned to the general curriculum. However, when student intelligence and socioeconomic class are held constant, vocational education appears to have the lowest dropout rate of any high school curriculum.

Historical Relationships between Vocational and General Education

The history of education shows an uneasy relationship between general and vocational education. One of the best accounts of that history has been compiled by Vincent P. Lannie (5). He points out that early apprenticeship agreements in this country required the master to teach not only a useful employment but also fundamental literacy and civic and moral responsibilities. But many masters were unable to provide adequate nonvocational instruction and during the eighteenth century began to send their apprentices to evening schools for the three Rs. This is the first example in this country of the separation of vocational and academic instruction.

The decline of apprenticeship in the early nineteenth century stopped vocational instruction (other than on-the-job training) for most American youth. Formal schools confined their occupational instruction to the professions and generally were available only to children of the wealthy. Only a few visionaries like Robert Owen called for education ". . . combining mechanical and agricultural with literary and scientific instruction . . ." and ". . . making every scholar a workman and every workman a scholar . . ." (7, p. 9). Gradually this idea of combining vocational and general education grew through lyceums and mechanics institutes until it culminated in the land-grant colleges.

Economic considerations as well as the opposition of academicians made the extension of vocational education into the common schools a far more difficult matter. But during the last half of the nineteenth century a method which appeared to provide a practical solution came from Russia (5). Della Vos, an engineer, had developed a system of "instruction shops" which taught students to use common tools as they completed a graded series of exercises. Although this system was adopted first at the college level, it quickly became the basis for the manual training program in the secondary school. This appeared to bring vocational and general education at this level together again, but manual training did not really meet vocational training needs. A single educational program based on faculty psychology could not meet the nation's needs for various types of skilled manpower. Thus the cry for "real" vocational education appeared and resulted in state and federal legislation supporting more specific instruction in a limited number of occupational fields. The first step of the new vocational educators was to set up separate vocational schools. This not only had the unfortunate effect of separating general and vocational education, but it was clearly an attack upon the educational irrelevance of the literary instruction labeled *general education.* The response of leading American educators was the creation of the comprehensive high school, which was designed to serve all youth. The response of other educators, however, was to deny that vocational education had a place in the public school.

The comprehensive high school was implemented fully in very few communities, and most high schools drifted gradually in the direction of serving college-bound youth exclusively. In the late thirties this drift was reversed by the threat of the Civilian Conservation Corps and the National Youth Administration vocational schools. This awoke principals and teachers of comprehensive schools to the danger of a separate school system outside their control. They responded by developing vocational programs which were highly effective in the war effort. But following World War II, the drift away from vocational education began again, only to be reversed by the Vocational Education Acts of 1963 and 1968.

A cycle can be observed which is repeated approximately once every generation: (1) establishment of a reasonably comprehensive high school, (2) gradually decreased emphasis on vocational education, (3) establishment of separate vocational schools, and (4) the reestablishment of comprehensive high schools which emphasize vocational education. Elsewhere in this book it is pointed out that these cycles tend to coincide with the nation's needs for skilled workers. These cycles may also demonstrate two other things: (1) that many general educators think vocational education should somehow be improved in efficiency, and (2) the accuracy of the feeling many vocational educators have that general educators look down on them and try to minimize their influence.

Perhaps the basic difficulty is in implementing the concept of the comprehensive school. Too often a school bearing this name tries to meet the needs of all students simply by putting programs for all students under the same roof.

What we need is a community high school and a real community (junior) college which is not content to have competing programs under the same roof, but which ". . . fuses academic and vocational education as every-day partners" (3, p. 23). One of the first ways to make vocational and general education everyday partners is to establish instructional programs which point out to students that instruction in every class is relevant to what they are now learning and will be relevant in their lives ahead. Since we do not want to tell students an untruth, we need to make sure that all education really is relevant.

General Education and Relevance

Much of what is taught in our schools under the name of general education is not general education at all. Not all people need trigonometry and calculus, nor do all people need the most advanced courses in foreign language, industrial arts, art, music, or most other subjects currently labeled *general education* in our high schools and community colleges. However, much of the material taught is general education and is needed by everyone. Many students, however, do not see that they need it, and hence many of them lack motivation to learn some of the things they will need most. Hugh Calkins, former Chairman of the National Advisory Council on Vocational Education, described the situation very well.

> Most of those who fail to learn to figure, read, and write in our schools, fail because schooling seems to them an exercise in futility. Books which are irrelevant to their interests, classes which are oriented toward further years of schooling after the 12th grade, mathematics which seems to serve no useful purpose, do not get the attention of boys and girls brought up to solve immediate problems. The elementary grades are where vocational and technical education must begin for all students. There is where the connection between reading and employment, arithmetic and income, writing and self respect, must be made clear. To the public, these connections are obvious. The public expects that school will make them obvious to the students also. (4, p. 2)

The Calkins proposal of vocational education for all students in the elementary school raised the hackles of many educators, both academic and vocational. Vocational educators did not like it because they wanted to be sure that current programs in the secondary schools and community colleges were adequately financed before funds were diverted elsewhere. Academic educators were disturbed because they thought vocational education is always specialized education, and they felt that there was no role for specialized education in the elementary school. But Calkins, a layperson, was right, and the educators were wrong. The Calkins proposal was a forerunner of career education (see chapter 13). This program of education about occupations, the economic enterprise, and the place of work in society and in the satisfaction of human needs can, in the elementary school, develops attitudes which increase individual options, eventually help meet society's needs for workers, and simultaneously lend relevance to the rest of general education. Academic educators object that the Calkins plan and its successor, career education, neglect the fact that young students do not respond well to deferred rewards. It seems reasonable, however, to assume that the current emphasis (even in elementary school curricula) on preparation for graduate school delays rewards for most students far longer than would be required by the Calkins proposal.

Early Occupational Choice

There is a mistaken notion that early occupational education necessitates an early, irrevocable occupational choice. It is a generally accepted fact that the average age at which a person chooses an occupation has been increasing. This is almost universally viewed as a desirable trend. We rightly view with horror the days when students were forced to leave school even before the eighth grade to accept employment because the family needed added income. Traditions of other countries which require that a boy's occupation be identical to his father's are repugnant to most Americans, and yet we have gone to the opposite extreme. It has become an upper class ideal in the United States that a boy or girl should complete the baccalaureate degree before thinking about a possible occupation, and this ideal is too often being achieved.

Unfortunately, two completely different concepts have been mixed in this type of thinking. Early occupational education or even early occupational choice is very different from an early occupational decision which is unalterable. Many students do make occupational choices early. If they have made such a choice, the school and parents can and should capitalize on the fact by encouraging the student to read, write, and talk about it. Almost everything taught in the elementary school has an occupational application. Many of these applications should be pointed out to the students, and they should be encouraged to discover additional ways in which general education has value in the occupation they tentatively have chosen.

Of course it would be wrong for parents or the school to discourage students from exploring other occupational opportunities by regarding the students' early occupational choices as immutable. Parents tend to do this more overtly than teachers. The student who has said for some time that he or she wants to be an engineer may have considerable problems with parents if he or she later decides to be a plumber. The elementary school is much less directive. In most school texts there is no mention of occupations. Instead of writing about their hobbies or chores or occupational aspirations, students are required to write about what they did on their vacation, even if they did not take a vacation. Selections from literature emphasize adult upper class standards which, if they mention occupations at all, treat only the professions. In high school and beyond, however, the school becomes much more directive. If students choose a vocational curriculum, the school makes it extremely difficult for them to change from one occupational field to another, sometimes even requiring them to change schools. But often the general attitude of the schools toward occupations is that the best thing to do about vocational education would be to forget it. In forgetting it the school forfeits an enormous opportunity to capitalize on the students' interests of the moment and forces them into the strait jacket of constantly deferred gratification.

Practical Arts Instruction

Industrial arts and home economics are the only courses commonly offered below the high school level which have education about employability as a major objective. These programs are taken by a sizable majority of boys and girls. Until recently, home economics emphasized family life education for girls and completely neglected the dual role of homemaker and wage earner which is expected of a great majority of women (and more and more men). Improved curriculum materials and trained teachers are becoming available in home economics to enable junior high school programs to prepare students for this dual role and to emphasize its relationship to other general education courses.

Curriculum revision in industrial arts has in some respects gone further than home economics but in other respects not as far. Until very recently, most industrial arts programs have emphasized the production of goods and neglected the fact that this type of production is becoming less important while services are rapidly gaining importance in our economy. Nevertheless, if instruction in "the world of construction" or the "world of industry" is taught to and perceived by the students as being illustrative of a much broader world of work, a great deal can be accomplished. Certainly the revised curricula are far better than the material they replaced, which emphasized a world of leisure based on home workshops which in practice could be afforded only by the wealthy.

Most industrial arts and home economics instruction occurs at the junior high school level and above. In the past, through a process of segregation on the basis of sex, teachers of these two subjects artifically restricted the range of occupational activities with which a student could become acquainted. More recently, notable progress has been made toward restructuring home economics to include knowledge of wage earning occupations. Since the number of female wage earners continues to grow, all women, as well as men, need to understand the process by which goods and services are produced.

Industrial arts has suffered from an inadequate portrayal of the nature of industry. In its broad sense, as when we speak of the Industrial Revolution, industry includes agriculture, the distribution of goods and services, the provision of health services, and homemaking as well as the production and repair of manufactured articles. In part because John Dewey's school at the University of Chicago had certain craft instruction attached to it, and in part because certain leaders in the fields of manual training and manual arts felt rejected by vocational educators during the early part of the twentieth century, industrial arts concentrated almost entirely upon materials employed by those who produce and repair manufactured goods and used the methods of a preindustrial society. This maintained the traditions of the University of Chicago admirably, and it asserted the independence of industrial arts from vocational education, but it woefully shortchanged the general education of boys and girls by omitting major portions of our industrial society. Recent involvements in career education and emphasis on curricular revision have made marked strides toward overcoming these problems.

Business education, through its general education courses, has for many years provided a close link between general and vocational education. Personal typing is open to boys and girls alike, as are personal note taking, commercial arithmetic, and general education offerings in bookkeeping and consumer law. Business education with both general and vocational objectives was excluded from federal vocation education legislation until recently, so there has been no historical split within the field which sets one type of teacher against another.

The result has been that students in advanced vocational and business education courses are well aware of the importance of general education, and general education teachers of many types are cognizant of the needs of business education. Another result has been that business education attracts far more capable students than other types of vocational education. It is true, of course, that as a program to prepare students for white-collar occupations, business education has been more acceptable to general education teachers than have other types of vocational programs. Nevertheless, the fact that general business education courses were planned to serve as a bridge between general and vocational education seems to have been a major factor in its success. No other field of vocational education is as well accepted by employers and by general education teachers alike.

Polytechnical Education

There are two major difficulties in bridging the gap between general and vocational education. One is to make all teachers aware of the close relationships between these two aspects of education, and the second is to bring such awareness to students. Improved preservice and in-service teacher education can bridge the gap for teachers. For students there is no systematic vehicle. Industrial arts and home economics are two types of instruction which could provide this bridge for students, but we have seen that both have moved very slowly in this direction in the United States.

In Eastern Europe both the elementary and secondary schools have courses of instruction known as *polytechnical education.* The purpose of polytechnical education is to help the student " . . . to develop creative technical abilities and to inculcate a love and respect for physical labor and work" (7, p. 18). In polytechnical education courses, students learn how goods and services are produced and learn the scientific principles on which such production depends. They also learn to handle common tools and machines. Polytechnical education gives the students a broad general and technical background which helps them to select future occupations and prepares them to take an active part in technical developments of the future. Polytechnical education is regarded as desirable in its own right, but it is recognized also as an absolute prerequisite for vocational education.

Polytechnical education in Communist countries has an interesting history. Vocational education in the Russian schools had existed long before the revolution of 1917. These vocational schools were segregated by social class and were, of course, suspect by the revolutionaries. In 1917, Lenin, drawing on the ideas of Marx, ordered the substitution of the word *polytechnical* for *vocational* on the ground that the aim of schooling "is to train not specialists but people capable of doing any type of work" (8, p. 35). Despite this urging from the highest authority, Soviet educators were unable to develop a single educational program which would prepare people for any and all types of work. In many ways, early polytechnical education in the U.S.S.R. was similar to the manual training which educators in the U.S. imported from czarist Russia. Wherever it has been tried, it has been found wanting as an effective means of vocational education.

It can be, however, a good system of prevocational education. This led to the current relationship in Russia between polytechnical and vocational education in which the former emphasizes activities and knowledge important to all work, while the latter enables students to achieve their own occupational goals and to meet the needs of society.

The Physiological Basis of Polytechnical and Vocational Education

Skatkin pointed out that a combination of classroom instruction with productive work is necessary for physiological reasons.

> When identical stimuli are acting on the cerebral cortex all the time, proactive inhibition sets in, with the result that reflexes already developed become diminished, and the formation of new reflexes become difficult. This often happens when pupils are kept busy day after day only with mental work or with the same school subjects. They quickly tire, become inattentive, and start to lose the facility for understanding and assimilating the subject matter. This does not happen if different types of activity—mental work, gymnastics and sport and physical work—are intelligently alternated. (8, p. 19)

In the elementary school polytechnical program, students " . . . plant and grow flowers, vegetables and trees, run a pet's corner and take care of rabbits and birds, look after the school yards, playing fields, and the streets and squares adjacent to the schools; in the school workshops they make and repair school supplies, rebind library books, and make simple articles" (8, p. 21). In the high school, both in Russia and the United States, vocational education, physical education, and academic studies provide the alternation of types of activities which Skatkin felt important. For some reason, few educational psychologists in the United States have felt this to be an important area of investigation.

Regional Accrediting Association Attitudes

The statement is sometimes made that regional accrediting associations require that all teachers have degrees and that vocational education be de-emphasized. These statements are quite incorrect. Regional accrediting associations insist that instructors be qualified in the subject they are teaching. They are much more critical of a vocational teacher who has a baccalaureate or more and yet does not know his or her field than they are of a vocational instructor who is only a high school graduate, has been prepared to teach, and is teaching capably. These associations do insist that general education courses be a part of any vocational curriculum because they recognize that the interaction of vocational and general education is highly desirable. Accreditation teams are quite critical of schools, regardless of level, which offer only college preparatory curricula to their student body when a sizable proportion of that student body will not graduate from college. It seems clear that in this aspect, as in many others of education, the regional accrediting associations are used as excuses for not doing something that the school wishes to avoid.

Mechanisms for Eliminating Irrelevant Education

In schools, as in other bureaucracies, the bureaucrats seek to preserve their jobs. The high school teachers of Greek, Hebrew, manual training, and religion fought the introduction of English, science, and vocational education because they perceived correctly that the limited resources of the school would follow the choices of the students, and they saw that students would prefer these new subjects to the old. Many new subjects should be taught today. We need courses in the behavioral sciences, modular approaches to building specific communication skills, cooperative education, and curricula reflecting combinations of earlier and independent forms of vocational education (e.g., agribusiness).

One way of resolving these conflicts would be to let students choose and adjust the size of programs accordingly. Teachers fear such a system, however, and have gone to great lengths to insure that certain programs are required for graduation. Often they have enlisted the support of legislators who have written into law certain minimum educational requirements and have thus protected the jobs of certain teachers. Vocational educators have followed this same route and have been instrumental in securing support of legislators, governors, and state boards in protecting their field. For example, federal legislation up to 1963 specified that minimum amounts of money were to be spent on certain vocational education programs. State boards of education and of junior colleges have specified that vocational education should be allocated minimum amounts of money or staff time.

Whenever educators get outsiders to mandate minimum amounts of support for their course, they either confess that students do not want the programs they offer or that certain educators are unwilling to support their programs. The best solution might be to let students choose the subjects which appear relevant to their goals. This would force reforms and enlist the support of teachers for educational programs which point out to students the relevance of subjects which are being taught. Another alternative is to use cost-effectiveness ratios or other economic measures to decide what should be taught. Some of these economic tools are discussed in the chapter on economics. Here it should be noted that economic measures are not the only measures which should be applied. No one has a good solution to the problem of keeping education relevant. Until we find such a solution, we can help the situation by minimizing the number of required courses, maximizing the number of worthwhile elective courses, and making special efforts to insure that instruction points out to students the relevancies (and irrelevancies) which exist.

Unlike the first two major objectives of vocational education, little attention has been paid to the third major objective of lending intelligibility to general education. If something is intelligible, we know its good points and its weaknesses. Knowing these, we can move to strengthen the good and eliminate the bad. General education and vocational education each have an obligation to make themselves intelligible. Just as certain disciplines are now in the process of making vocational education more intelligible to vocational and nonvocational educators and to citizens at large, so vocational education can shed light on the purposes and accomplishments of general education. Often we need interpreters to see the import of a message. Some of this interpretation happens by accident every day in vocational education classrooms and laboratories. More and better interpretation will occur as curriculum developers, teacher educators, and teachers in vocational education set out consciously to implement the goal of lending intelligibility to general education.

REFERENCES

1. Barlow, Melvin L. *History of Industrial Education in the United States.* Peoria, Ill.: Charles A. Bennett Co., Inc., 1967.
2. Bennett, Charles A. *History of Manual and Industrial Education 1870–1917.* Peoria, Ill.: Charles A. Bennett Co., 1937.
3. Brameld, Theodore. "Reaction." In *Vocational Education: A Prospectus for Change,* edited by Carl J. Schaefer and Jacob J. Kaufman. Boston: Massachusetts Advisory Council on Education, 1967.
4. Calkins, Hugh. "What the Public Expects of Vocational-Technical Education," dedication speech. Columbus, Ohio: Center for Vocational Education Research and Leadership Development, 1969.
5. Lannie, Vincent P. "The Development of Vocational Education in America: An Historical Overview." In *Vocational Education: A Prospectus for Change,* edited by Carl J. Schaefer and Jacob J. Kaufman. Boston: Massachusetts Advisory Council on Education, 1967.
6. Mays, Arthur B. *Principles and Practices of Vocational Education.* New York: McGraw-Hill Book Company, 1948.
7. Owen, Robert D. *Working Man's Advocate* (24 April 1830). Quoted in Lannie, Vincent P., "The Development of Vocational Education in America: An Historical Overview," in *Vocational Education: A Prospectus for Change,* edited by Carl J. Schaefer and Jacob J. Kaufman. Boston: Massachusetts Advisory Council on Education, 1967.
8. Shapovalenko, S.G., ed. *Polytechnical Education in the U.S.S.R.* Paris: UNESCO, 1963.
9. Skatkin, M.N. "Marxist-Leninist Ideas of Polytechnical Education." In *Polytechnical Education in the U.S.S.R.,* edited by S.G. Shapovalenko. Paris: UNESCO, 1963.

part II

Disciplinary Foundations of Vocational Education

5

Introduction

This section on the foundations of vocational education has no pretense of being exhaustive. Rather, it is designed to call the attention of the vocational educator to a few of the numerous ways in which four disciplines, philosophy, economics, sociology, and psychology, can contribute to an understanding of our tremendously complex field. Industrial relations, administration, special education, and similar applied fields have been tapped wherever their concerns intersect those of the disciplines. Anthropology, political science and government, and even biology and the physical sciences have a potential contribution to make, but they are not discussed here because their effect to date has been less direct. History has been omitted because it is relatively well covered in most other standard texts in vocational education. This brief exposure should lead the student (and the practitioner who wants to continue to learn) to a more thorough study of at least these four disciplines.

Relatively few practitioners of the academic disciplines believe that there is a need for formal occupational education for fields other than the professions. Some of them seem to believe in occupational education only for their own speciality. Their opposition to vocational education is often due to a lack of understanding of the depth of knowledge and skill required in fields other than their own. The vocational educator should not make a similar mistake and assume that a knowledge of the disciplines can be acquired easily on the job with no formal preparation.

A discipline is a way of thinking. It provides a conceptual framework for attacking problems. It describes, defines, and classifies information. Most importantly, it provides a means of predicting outcomes and of testing these predictions. By these standards vocational education is not a discipline. At this state in our development, it is probably fortunate that we are not since we need to try a wide variety of ways of viewing and attacking the problems which face us.

The disciplines have affected vocational education in two principal ways. They have produced researchers within each discipline who have explored their own interests, have accumulated knowledge, and have disseminated it. After a long period of time, bits of this knowledge have become part of the education of most individuals and have affected decisions in vocational education. This is a very inefficient process for not only is it slow but vital bits of knowledge are not widely communicated.

Vocational education recently has begun to employ specialists from the academic disciplines to work on vocational education problems. This has been done directly in university vocational education departments, research centers, in research coordinating units in state departments of education, and it has been done indirectly through research contracts and grants. The involvement of people from the disciplines has been expanding rapidly, not only because vocational education offers them employment but also because these academicians are finding that the problems of vocational education are intrinsically interesting and challenging and offer new insights within the disciplines.

6

Philosophic Foundations

Occupational education programs may be provided to students at many different age levels, from early childhood to late adulthood, and in many different settings, from trial and error learning on the job to highly structured graduate school education. When these programs are provided in formal schools, the educational philosopher has a great deal to say about their content, methods, and goals. Most educational philosophers have chosen (rightly or wrongly) to restrict their views to the elementary and secondary schools and to higher education, but they should have something to say about occupational education which is provided by employers, unions, philanthropic or governmental groups, and private trade schools because these organizations are also involved in the process of education.

What To Teach

The most important question in educational philosophy is "What should be taught?" Economists, sociologists, psychologists, and particularly educational philosophers are concerned with this question. Obviously it is impossible to teach and to learn everything. The "explosion of knowledge" is real. So decisions have to be made and priorities established. Some material must be rejected; some must be taught to a fraction of the students; and some must be taught to all.

The key question is "What knowledge is of most value?" Today, when most philosophers pose this question, they are really asking, "What knowledge is of most value for *all* people?" (Though surely it is as important to ask "What knowledge is needed by each individual?") In Aristotle's day the question was "What should a nonslave know?" In eighteenth century England, it was "What should a gentleman know?" But ever since John Dewey revolutionized our ideas of education, the prevailing view in the United States has been that we should use education as a means of achieving the values of the American system. (Though occasionally individuals in our country who espouse extreme left-wing or right-wing views suggest that we accept Stalin's view of education as a weapon, "the effect of which depends . . . on who controls this weapon and at whom . . . it should strike" [16, p. 220].) The view of education as essential to democracy leads teachers to select course content which will enhance individual freedom and equal opportunity for educational development.

Since *all* students will live in a developing democracy, some educational philosophers believe that the school should present identical content to each student. The most persuasive case for identical content for all is presented by Broudy, Smith, and Burnett.

> . . . some ideas are more general and consequently have a greater explanatory potential than others, and some cognitive operations are more pervasive and more strategic for understanding than others. . . . there are key ideas and criteria and . . . there are indispensable symbolic and logical operations without which interpretation cannot be adequate. A curriculum which includes these ideas can make a plausible claim to be "needed" by all human beings and therefore to be studied by all of them. (1, pp. 12, 245–46)

Although Broudy and his colleagues were writing about the secondary school, they hold these same beliefs about the elementary school. So do many other educational philosophers.

However, instead of the key ideas and indispensable operations called for by these philosophers, a common curriculum has developed which is based on success in further schooling. The key ideas have become those which glorify leisure, and the indispensable operations are those which lay the groundwork for success in academic work, not necessarily occupational roles or personal/social interactions. The net result is a common curriculum for kindergarten (or even early childhood education) through the junior high school with little regard for individual differences in talent or interest. In many schools, students who cannot carry a tune are expected to sing; those who are color blind are graded on their success in mixing colors; and those who enjoy manipulating objects spend as much time in their seats as those who enjoy manipulating ideas. Each student should have a right to try these activities, the right to fail in them, and the right to persist in that failure if desired. But one should not be required to persist indefinitely in an activity which is not essential to one's life. This idea is less widely implemented than instructional enlightenment or philosophy would lead one to assume to be the case in most schools today.

A common curriculum based on success in further schooling was not what the philosophers wanted, but it is what has happened as a result of the mistaken belief that individual differences can be catered to by varying the teaching methods used, or by teaching at different levels of abstraction, depending on the intelligence of the pupil. The result is portrayed vividly in G.H. Reavis' biting satire "The Animal School," where

> . . . the duck was excellent in swimming, in fact better than his instructor; but he made only passing grades in flying and was very poor in running. . . . he had to stay after school and also drop swimming in order to practice running. . . . an abnormal eel who could swim exceedingly well and also run, climb, and fly a little had the highest average and was valedictorian. (12, p. 141)

In the high school (unlike the elementary school) the argument for identical content for all students has not been implemented. The pressures exerted by colleges and local employers who want certain content taught have been more persuasive. Only in the general curriculum do the views of educational philosophers appear to have had much weight, but those views have not had a fair trial in the general curriculum because the students who are enrolled are rejects from the college preparatory and vocational curricula. On every variable which has been measured, the results of the general curriculum have been very poor, but we do not know how much of this failure is due to an ineffective application of educational philosophy and how much must be charged to the segregation of students who are difficult to educate.

It is hard to quarrel with the Broudy, Smith, and Burnett curriculum theory as the basis for most of the content of the elementary school, and of at least the first two years of high school. Even for those students in the last two years of a secondary school vocational curriculum, they provide the rationale for a curriculum which should occupy at least half of the student's time. However, content based entirely on the demands of the next level of education, which results in "school for schooling's sake," cannot be justified. Nor can we justify content based entirely on the demands of employers.

Which Key Ideas and Skills Should Be Taught?

The first criterion imposed by the educational philosopher is that nothing should be taught in the school that will be learned adequately and efficiently in another of society's institutions. The family, the church, the place of employment, and the communications media all have educative functions. The school has too much to do to allow it to spend its valuable time in unnecessary and inefficient duplication of functions. Unfortunately, however, some families are not as effective teachers as others. Some education by employers and by communications media is designed to benefit individuals other than the student. So the school has a responsibility to all individuals who would be shortchanged by other institutions. For example, the school has the responsibility to teach consumer education because it is probably less biased than most other agencies who are also engaged in consumer education.

A second criterion for choosing content assumes that all students will have to live in a common culture and that all instruction (at least through the twelfth grade) should be based on the demands of that common culture. Certainly all students will be expected to deal with certain common cultural views, but the lower class culture is markedly different from that of the middle class. Which culture should the school choose as its ideal? Since most teachers are proponents of the middle class culture, that is the one which is most likely to be taught, though middle class teachers faced with a group of lower class students often decide not to teach certain topics on the grounds that such children couldn't possibly be expected to learn because of the disadvantaged background from which they come. While current emphasis on the importance of pluralistic cultures is likely to change this situation in the future, the majority culture (middle class) still tends to be the dominant force with regard to identifying knowledge, skills, and other behaviors that students should acquire.

A third criterion for content selection suggests that if we have a choice between teaching a concept which explains a broad aspect of the environment and one which explains only a narrow aspect, we should choose the former. The reason for this is based solely on efficiency of instruction. If a useful, broad concept can be learned in the same amount of time as a narrow concept, the general concept is obviously a better choice. Yet a concept may be so general as to be inefficient for instructional purposes. A special problem arises in teaching a general concept which really will be useful but does not appear so to the students. Students are usually asked to accept and learn such "cold storage" concepts because the teacher says they will be useful later. The younger the student, the more likely he or she is to accept and learn on the basis of faith. If the student is older, rebellious, and has had previous experiences which have lead to a mistrust of adults, he or she is more likely to demand evidence that the material is relevant. Too often, the teacher provides a justification which applies only to students planning to enter the professions.

A fourth criterion is based on the concept that each student should understand, be able to control, and be confident in the environment. Each of the organized disciplines is devoted to understanding and attempting to control a portion of the environment. Because they are well organized and have been subjected to continued refinement, they appear to be efficient vehicles of instruction. However, practitioners of the disciplines are specialists and tend to try to make specialists of their students. It is impossible for an individual to become a specialist in each of the disciplines (the typical large university has more than one hundred departments, each representing one or more disciplines). Therefore, the school must restrain this natural tendency of practitioners to recruit disciples, and during the first years of schooling must devote its time to instruction which is needed by nonspecialists. This certainly includes instruction about the importance of the world of work.

The Education of Specialists and Nonspecialists

In a democracy, all students must have enough education to enable them to understand the basic problems of society and to vote intelligently. In addition, it is a basic tenet of democracy that individuals should have the opportunity to develop fully their human talents. All citizens should be able to review their lives and feel that they have had multiple chances to explore their strengths and weaknesses, to try different paths of life, and to choose life-styles which fit their needs and talents. The school should provide many of these opportunities, but above all, it should provide students with the skills, knowledges, and attitudes which will encourage them to seek out opportunities and take advantage of them when they arise.

Citizenship demands general education (that education which is needed by all). Vocational competence and personal development demand both general education and specialized education (that education needed by some but not all). Most educational philosophers agree that the elementary school should concentrate on general education and the graduate school should concentrate on specialized education. The arguments occur with regard to the role of the secondary school, the community college, and the baccalaureate program. Those who believe that twelve or sixteen years of general education are necessary for citizenship would deny specialized schooling to anyone who drops out of the school before high school or college graduation. Thus, Broudy et al. feel free to say,

> Presumably . . . problem solving courses will come late in the school life of the pupil. This means, of course, that early dropouts may miss them altogether. This is regrettable, but then one regrets all dropouts if they occur before their learning potential is exploited to the full. There seems to be little point in giving problem solving instruction to those who have not been sufficiently motivated to master the other parts of the curriculum by which intelligent encounters with problems are made possible. (1, p. 272)

These authors do believe in specialized education, for they say, " . . . specialized training is so necessary for *everyone* that one layer of our educational system should be devoted exclusively to it rather than treating it as a substitute for, or as an orphan of, common, general education" (1, p. 182). These philosophers would deny with passion that they are elitist, but it is difficult to otherwise classify those who would deny an essential part of education to those who choose not to continue in school beyond the compulsory age of attendance. The key to their position lies in the assumption that problem solving should be postponed because other things must be learned before intelligent problem solving is possible. This assumption is questionable, for psychologists and historians have demonstrated that complex problems have been solved by people who had relatively little formal educational background.

More important, however, is the failure of many educational philosophers to recognize the value of specialized education as a motivating force for all education (perhaps because they, themselves, come from the group of students who see the pursuit of knowledge as intrinsically desirable for its own sake).

> Education is really not a series of separate little containers of knowledge, though we tend to act as if it were and thereby to establish further barriers to effective learning. A vocational objective . . . could be the vehicle to bring the containers together, to allow each student to see education in an action setting and to provide

> more flexible paths toward its attainment. . . . The current tendency to give a student initial general education, then specialization, is inappropriate on pedagogical grounds, and is at the root of the major problems in curriculum development. Nor does it fit an educational philosophy which holds that culture and vocation cannot be separated. . . . The intertwining of liberal and vocational elements in an educational program seeking to expand opportunity for a major proportion of our population is . . . a necessity. (5, pp. 8, 10, 11)

Haskew and Tumlin are even more positive.

> Occupation-labeled courses frequently are prime vehicles for achieving such outcomes as ability to handle quantitative relationships, command of problem-solving processes, and many other "prime essentials of schooling." In fact, such achievements for some pupils have proved to be impossible in the absence of occupation-centered methodology. In the second place, occupation-centering is typically used as a magnet which holds pupils in contact with so-called general education. In the third place, some vocational education reinforces much abstract learning by affording opportunities for practical application; thus helping general education make sense. (7, p. 68)

The student who chooses an occupational goal (even if that goal may later be changed) has an education "organizer" which serves as a unifying force and provides meaning to everything she or he studies. Some students can and do learn without this particular organizer, but for all students formal, specialized instruction lends further meaning to general education. Separation of general and specialized instruction into different institutions and nonconcurrent blocks of time minimizes this interaction. At the same time, it maximizes educational segregation based on social class. In every educational institution, for at least part of the time, students from all backgrounds should learn together.

Social Class Distinctions in Occupational Education

Most educational philosophers in the United States agree that occupational education should not be designed exclusively, or even primarily for potential dropouts, lower class youth, minority youth, or for students who have lower than average academic ability. To do so would create class distinctions which are inimical to a democracy. There can be no serious quarrel with this concept. Project TALENT indicated that the full range of social class and academic ability is represented in vocational education. The fact that students of lower ability and from lower class homes are significantly overrepresented in vocational education is not necessarily bad if the choice is made by the students and not by the school. It would be detrimental if the school, consciously or unconsciously, designed curricula which promoted segregation by social class. Every curriculum should be available, in fact as well as in theory, to the children of physicians and laborers, alike.

It is indefensible to accept a belief that " . . . only the hard core might well benefit in secondary school vocational education programs. . . . he (the "hard core" student) belongs in vocational education programs, and . . . we must develop programs that get at understanding responsibility and all the rest that goes with the kind of positions hard core misfits can hope to fill" (15, p. 28). Yet it is true that failure to provide effective vocational education programs which serve all youth in the schools has led to the development of the federally supported remedial programs operated outside the schools. Similarly, it is indefensible to hold that the school has an obligation to provide specialist training only for those students who plan to be professionals. Mays has been correct in pointing out that "neither the extent of education, expert knowledge, character of social service, or method of remuneration, nor any other factor appears that is common to (the professionals) but not found in other callings. One is therefore driven to the conclusion that the classification of *profession* is arbitrary, based solely upon custom or social dictum" (9, p. 9). It seems absurd to use this arbitrary classification as a basis for determining what should be taught in the schools. It seems equally absurd to hold that specialized education is appropriate for so-called high level occupations but not for those at a lower level, or that specialized education is appropriate for middle and upper class students, but not for students from the lower class.

Duality in Education

Most contemporary American educational philosophers dislike dualism intensely. One group believes that there is an essential unity in everything, and searching for it is an important task. These educational philosophers apply this reasoning to the school. They feel that surely, if they will but look hard enough, they will find a common curriculum which will meet the needs of all students. They may well be right, but this curriculum has not as yet been found. The closest approach to it is the general curriculum, a goal-less, nonvocational, noncollege preparatory program, found in most high schools. Though students in the general curriculum are between the students in the college preparatory and the vocational curricula with regard to academic aptitude and socioeconomic status, they are remarkably unsuccessful, inside and outside the school. Sixty-seven percent of the high school dropouts come from the general curriculum, though it enrolls less than a fourth of the high school students. Of those who manage to graduate, fewer go on to postsecondary education than from any other high school curriculum (3, pp. 353, 359). And 88 percent of the enrollees in Manpower Development and Training Act (MDTA) programs came from the high school general curriculum, compared with 10 percent from college preparatory, and 2 percent from vocational curricula (10, p. 29). Since MDTA was established to serve high school dropouts and the hard-core unemployed, this preponderance of enrollment from the general curriculum is perhaps understandable. But obviously the general curriculum has not been meeting the needs of the students enrolled in it.

Even if the general curriculum could be revised so that it did meet student needs, philosophers would not have solved the problem of dualism in education by setting up a common curriculum for the first twelve years of schooling and specifying that the next two to ten years of education should be devoted to specialization. This would be more dualistic than the comprehensive high school ever has been, and it contains two defects. This plan forgets that when taught concurrently, specialized and general education reinforce each other. Second, it would deny the benefits of specialized education to those students who cannot (for economic reasons) or will not (from lack of motivation) attend school from age six to twenty-six.

Another major group of educational philosophers, the pluralists, also rejects dualism. They feel that the division of the real world into artificial dichotomies such as mind vs. body, theory vs. practice, academic vs. nonacademic, and vocation vs. general is undesirable. As do most Americans, they tend to be pragmatists and value what "works well." What seems to work well in education is the provision of a variety of goals, content, and methods which can be matched with the variety of goals, abilities, and achievements which students bring to the school.

The great majority of educational administrators in the United States are pluralists and are interested in meeting the needs of all students. What they need and want are positive suggestions of ways in which this can be accomplished.

The Uses of Knowledge

Broudy, Smith, and Burnett (1) have identified four uses of knowledge: associative, replicative, interpretive, and applicative. Any bit of knowledge may be used in each of these ways, but some knowledge is more likely to be used in one way than another.

The *associative* use of knowledge occurs in such diverse fields as the appreciation of poetry and puns, scenery and scents. It is the calling to mind of knowledge by the association of one word or thought with another. The two do not have to be logically related—a product makes one think of the maker, a song makes one think of a place in which it was sung, a single word *die* makes one think of a dozen situations which have little relationship to each other. We could exist reasonably well without using knowledge associatively, but this use of knowledge gives an aesthetic richness to the use of words and other sensory images which they would not otherwise have. The more general or specialized education an individual has, the more likely he or she is to use this knowledge associatively, for one bit of knowledge calls to mind another.

Most formal schooling, both general and specialized, is concerned with the *replicative* use of knowledge. Recall of facts and use of skills in exactly the way they were taught in school is very common. "What is two plus two?" calls forth the answer, "four," in or out of school. If a particular bit of knowledge has only replicative use within the school, it is worthless. The more that material learned in school relates to life, the more it can be used replicatively. However, since the school can never foresee all the requirements of life, it must teach students more than just the replicative uses of knowledge.

The highest levels of education lead to the *interpretive* and *applicative* uses of knowledge, through which we view new situations, interpret their meaning, and choose appropriate courses of action. Problem solving, family life, troubleshooting, invention, and adaptation all require interpretation and application. Some philosophers hold that application can be done only by specialists and that it should not be a part of general education. These men would stop with interpretation. To say that general education should stop short of problem solving seems quite unrealistic, for we all need to solve problems which are unrelated to our field of specialization.

Most of vocational education (and most of general education) is devoted to the replicative uses of knowledge. Many critics of vocational education believe that it consists of nothing else. If this were true, vocational education would have little long-range utility, for the replicative use of knowledge cannot cope with changes in job content unless the worker is retrained. Actually, the only types of vocational education that stop at this level are certain on-the-job (OJT) training programs and elementary technical programs in the armed forces. In such programs, nomenclature is memorized, and rigid step-by-step procedures are mandatory. Better quality OJT and advanced level military technical education, like all of the rest of vocational education, place strong emphasis on the interpretive and applicative uses of knowledge.

Both general and vocational education need to stress the applicative and interpretive uses of knowledge more. If this is done, the associative uses of knowledge may take care of themselves. All three uses are markedly facilitated by the interaction of general and vocational education. Replicative uses of knowledge are most subject to obsolescence caused by developing technology. Fortunately, this very technology is quite efficient in retrieving knowledge for replicative use. This lessens the need to teach masses of facts, recipes, and set procedures in school.

Types of Knowledge

A classification scheme which overlaps the four uses of knowledge has been proposed by Elizabeth Macia and adapted by D.G. Lux and other staff members of the Industrial Arts Curriculum Project (9, p. 7).

1. Event or descriptive knowledge describes phenomena and the interrelationships among phenomena. The sciences are largely made up of this type of knowledge.
2. Valuational or prescriptive knowledge is concerned with whether or not something is worthwhile, good, true, or beautiful. The fine arts and humanities concern themselves principally with this area of knowledge.
3. Formal or structural knowledge is an attempt to find a structure or form for all knowledge. Formal mathematics and logic are attempts at such structures.
4. The knowledge of practice, or praxiological knowledge, covers man's ways of acting efficiently to reach the goals that he values. Instruction in all the professions and vocations must include such knowledge, and internship, plus previous or concurrent instruction in related aspects of the other basic types of knowledge.

Praxiology

The term *praxiology* comes from the Greek *praxis* meaning "a doing" or "an action." The common suffix *ology* indicates systematic study of it. Praxiology is the key to occupational education and to most other purposeful education at all levels. It must be differentiated from practice itself (*practice* is used here as a noun, not as a verb). Imitation, which is the sole content of much on-the-job training, is practice, not praxiology. Practice without praxiology will usually have adverse effects, since it is not based on theory. When the job content changes, that part of practice immediately become obsolete. If an inadvertent change in process or material occurs, the change is not self-correcting, so practice alone leads to changes which are often in an undesirable direction.

Praxiology must be based on descriptive and valuational knowledge, but it goes beyond them to search for efficiency and rationality in practice. It provides an answer to the question "Why should we follow this particular procedure?" Practice without praxiology says, "This is the procedure to follow. Don't inquire why." But praxiology goes further. It provides at least tentative answers to questions such as "What procedure should be followed if conditions of practice are changed?" "What is a rational way of deciding which of two procedures is more efficient?" "Is this procedure necessary at all?" Practice combined with praxiology leads to real skill.

The elementary and secondary schools have almost completely ignored praxiology and have stressed descriptive knowledge. Minor emphasis has been placed on valuational and structural knowledge. Praxiology has flowered in the university, with graduate programs being almost solely devoted to it. Even at the undergraduate level, engineering, education, chemistry, marketing, agriculture, nursing, and many other professional programs devote considerable time to praxiology.

Both praxiology and practice (the noun, not the verb) are examples of knowledge which is used applicatively. According to Broudy, Smith, and Burnett the applicative uses of knowledge are valuable only to specialists and should be taught outside the common school. Unfortunately, they do not distinguish between practice and praxiology and do not recognize that general education, praxiology, and practice are mutually supportive for all students. Moreover, for many students, all three must be present for effective learning to occur.

With the possible exception of a few learning handicapped students, no one in the common school should ever be taught a practice without concurrently learning the theory behind that practice. Except in time of national emergency, no student should be taught the practice and praxiology of an occupational field without being taught at nearly the same time a substantial amount of the descriptive and valuational knowledge which is part of general education. Teaching these types of knowledge concurrently leads the student to see relationships and relevances which could not otherwise be learned. Even better would be a program which was taught concurrently by teachers who *planned* their general and specialized instruction to be mutually supportive.

The comprehensive high school and the community college regularly design their vocational curricula to make sure that general education, praxiology, and practice all are taught during the school year, though they rarely make certain that their presentations are mutually supportive. Attempts to design separate schools devoted only to practice or to practice plus praxiology are educationally and socially unwise, yet many armed forces schools and industry-operated schools do just this. Segregation by educational goals is justified by the operators of these schools on the basis of efficiency, but the efficiency, if it exists at all, is short-term and often benefits the proprietor more than the student. This can be illustrated by an example from training in the armed forces. During World War II, vocational educators in the armed forces designed programs for electronics technicians which were some two years in length. They included theory of the use of electronics (praxiology), skill in design, construction, and troubleshooting (practice), plus basic science (descriptive knowledge) and communication skills (descriptive plus valuational knowledge). These programs produced excellent electronics technicians, yet the armed forces were dissatisfied because instead of reenlisting, most of the graduates were employed by private industry when their enlistments expired. This well-rounded vocational curriculum was replaced by a short instructional program which emphasized only practice and enabled the graduates to repair only one piece of equipment, using a rigidly prescribed procedure. These graduates were not desired by industry, so they were more likely to reenlist. After the soldier was thoroughly acclimated to military life, he was offered the opportunity to attend a broad electronics education program if he would agree to enlist for a period of time which would make it financially desirable for him to stay on to retirement at about age forty. Clearly the revised system was more advantageous in the short run to the armed forces, but it was less desirable for most students. The armed forces leadership has now come to believe that in the long run, this decision had adverse effects on our national defense. Much, if not most, of the vocational education offered by small employers has been dominated by similar considerations, for they also cannot afford to lose trained workers to competitors. Large corporations have offered more broad vocational education since their workers have better opportunities for promotion within the company and are therefore less likely to leave. However, few American companies can count on a lifelong commitment from all their employees to the extent that foreign companies once could. This has led American companies to provide broad vocational education only to those employees who seem most promotable.

The Concept of Vocation in Philosophy

Aristotle believed that there were two types of work: bread-labor, work for the purpose of subsistence, and leisure-work, or work which was interesting in and of itself. Slaves and serfs engaged in bread-labor because if they did not they would starve. Freemen pursued careers in government, religion, and in the arts and sciences, not to earn a living, but for the satisfaction which came from doing something interesting. Since these were the same reasons used to choose a leisure-time activity, the term *leisure-work* seemed appropriate. Bread-labor might by chance be interesting. Slaves who were artisans and teachers often enjoyed their work, but this was purely fortuitous and of little importance. The key question was "Could you stop work without economic penalty?" If the answer was "no," the work was clearly undesirable for the free citizen, even though it might be necessary for the state.

Though Paul stated that if a man will not work he shall not eat (II Thessalonians, 3, 10), the medieval church interpreted this to mean that while the natural law imposed this obligation on the human race, it did not apply to certain individuals. Thus those who engaged in religious contemplation or those who begged for the church (mendicant friars) were exempt. There was a ranking of occupations from the servile tasks of the peasant to the highest duties of the clergy. Since all vocations were assigned by God, it was futile and blasphemous to attempt to change vocations. The Reformation produced a considerable change in attitude. Partly because of the Plague, there was no longer an adequate supply of slaves or serfs to do the unpalatable but necessary tasks required by society. In this period, Luther was stating that every legitimate calling had exactly the same worth in the sight of God, though each vocation was still assigned by heaven.

The modern view of philosophy and economics toward work began with Adam Smith, who recognized that "it is not from the benevolence of the butcher, the brewer, or the baker that we expect our dinner, but from their regard to their own interest. We address ourselves, not to their humanity, but to their self-love; and never talk to them of our own necessities, but of their advantages" (14, p. 14). This was a bit too crass, however, and consequently Ruskin and Tolstoy, among others, recognized that man does not work only for economic self-interest, but because work is psychologically necessary. If you do not work, you die spiritually. Perhaps the most extreme expression of this point of view came from K.D. Ushinsky, a Russian educator: "The tangible fruits of work constitute human property; but the only source of human dignity, and at the same time of morality and happiness, is the inner spiritual, life-giving power of work itself" (17, p. 26). Most people would not accept a concept of work as the ". . . *only* source of . . . morality." Yet in his book ***Round the Bend,*** Nevil Shute, a supporter of capitalism and individualism, expounded a religion based on work, with the highest morality based on work performed accurately and conscientiously (13).

Now if work is important to human dignity, how do we find this dignity in modern life? It was relatively easy in Benjamin Franklin's day. He said, accurately, "He who hath a trade hath an estate." Back then the skilled worker performed a variety of interesting tasks and could expect to perform them for the remainder of his life, using, essentially unchanged, the knowledge he had learned as an apprentice. The growth of modern industry and business has been based on two factors which often are inimical to the dignity of workers: (1) specialization of work and (2) constant changes of work content to promote efficiency. Specialization of work decreases the variety of each worker's tasks, sometimes to the point that a single bodily movement is repeated rapidly all day long. The constant search for greater efficiency means that at least part of a worker's knowledges and skills will become obsolete. "Specialization . . . makes the development of skill possible . . . " (18, p. 161) for every worker; changes in work content make it necessary to retrain every worker periodically. Marx and Engels believed that specialization would chain each worker for life to a particular repetitive job and a particular tool, but change is so rapid now that many people do not spend even a year on the same task. Also, Engels did not foresee the rapid introduction of automation which has taken over many of the menial tasks of the past.

The dignity of work lends dignity to the worker. Conversely, "labor acquires a character of irksomeness by virtue of the indignity imputed to it" (18, p. 30). Unfortunately many schools still teach that labor, other than academic labor, is not dignified.

Elements Missing in General Education

The major group determining the school curriculum has traditionally been made up of academics, many of whom have had little or no experience outside the school. They have gone through each level of schooling and have had no employment outside the school. Their social contacts have been limited too often to people in the professions who share a similar school background. These people write textbooks, sit on curriculum committees, and, as teachers, decide what will be emphasized in classrooms. As administrators and faculty menbers, they control the reward structure in the schools. Advisory committees which attempt to suggest major changes are not reconvened. School boards are told to stick to policy decisions while the academics determine what will be taught and how. The primary influence of the student is the negative one of dropping out. The primary influence of the general public is the negative one of refusing to approve tax increases for school operation, and the general public is influenced greatly by academics who insist that the prime measure of a school's success is the proportion of graduates who enter college. As a result of this "academic incest," the school tends to value school for its own sake, to design each level of schooling to prepare for the next, and to regard anyone who drops out of school prior to completion of a doctorate as a failure. This has resulted in the elimination of a major portion of our heritage, called by Max Weber the "protestant ethic," and the substitution of a meritocracy based on school achievement. Increasing demands for educational accountability and the infusion of career education concepts into educational planning and curriculum development (and the attendant emphasis on school-community cooperation) give promise that such circumstances will change fairly dramatically during the next decade.

The Untaught Curriculum

In spite of its name, the protestant ethic had little to do with religion. The name comes from the fact that during the later phases of the Reformation, most Western peoples substantially changed their views of occupations. Christians from the time of Paul through Luther saw a calling or occupation, as something sent from heaven. In practice, a man's occupation was almost invariably the occupation of his father. But because it was felt to be heaven-sent, it would have been impious to choose a different occupation, for this would be rebellion against God. Calvin's followers had a very different view. For them, an occupation was to be chosen by the individual and to be pursued strenuously and exactingly with a sense of religious purpose. This produced capitalists and workers who were frugal and diligent and resulted in industries and businesses which were efficient beyond any level previously attained. Prior to the acceptance of the protestant ethic the proverb was "either eat well or sleep well." After its acceptance, a person could do both. The major factor in allowing a person to sleep well was a contented feeling which Weber called ". . . the irrational sense of having done his job well" (19, p. 71). Rational or not, it was a major factor in the industrial development of the West because it produced skilled and conscientious labor and management. The traditional cycle of sin, repentance, atonement, and release, which incorporated the freedom to sin again, was incompatible with the undeviating promptness, sobriety, and attention to duty which made the Industrial Revolution possible.

The concept of leisure also changed radically. Up to Calvin's time, leisure occupied all of the day which was not required for earning subsistence. For lower class workers, the working hours were long but were broken by feast days and by enforced leisure due to unemployment. For managers, "the number of business hours was very moderate, perhaps five to six a day, sometimes considerably less" (19, p. 66). After Calvin's time, leisure was seen as a voluntary absence of work which had been earned and which refreshed the worker so that when he returned to work he would perform more effectively. The goal of leisure was work, rather than the goal of work being leisure. "The old leisurely and comfortable attitude toward life gave way to a hard frugality in which some participated and came to the top" (19, p. 68). Both managers and workers were affected. The former greatly increased the rigor of their supervision, setting new quantity and quality standards, and the workers had to be trained to meet these standards.

Benjamin Franklin was the prophet of this new concept in America, and his proverbs were a major component of American education during the eighteenth and nineteenth centuries. Partly due to his influence, the protestant ethic was accepted by nearly everyone in the northern United States. After the destruction of the plantation system following the Civil War, it was accepted by majority groups everywhere in the country. In this case, the lack of European traditions was a tremendous benefit to the expanding industrial economy.

Franklin may also be regarded as the prophet of vocational education in America. Although the colleges and the public schools lagged by fifty to one hundred years, respectively, in accepting the responsibility of producing well-qualified nonprofessional workers through formal vocational education, they accepted Franklin's statements of the values of the protestant ethic early and taught them assiduously throughout the nineteenth century. Private trade schools, business, and industry taught these values and the specific skills and knowledges needed for workers and managers to put the values into practice.

During the twentieth century, society began to doubt the efficacy of the ideals of the protestant ethic. Some people interpreted these ideals to mean that personal success could and should be achieved at the expense of others. Anti-trust laws, income taxes, and other restraints were imposed in an attempt to retard the dominance of certain groups who had justified their acts in terms of the protestant ethic. More importantly, it became clear that the protestant ethic was not bringing success to a sizable portion of the population. Though some were getting rich, others were starving. Some minority groups which were quickly assimilated had no long-term difficulty. Others, such as the native Americans, Mexican-Americans, and blacks who were visually different, did not profit at all from acceptance of the protestant ethic. They could work as hard and conform as closely as possible to the ethic and still not succeed because they were stereotyped with those of their group who did not conform because they preferred their own ethic. Orientals who accepted the protestant ethic even more fully than the white majority were rejected on the ground that they worked too hard.

At the same time a series of moves was made to take religion out of the public schools. In the first half of the twentieth century most public schools were clearly Protestant. They forced students of other faiths to observe Protestant religious holidays, used Protestant religious literature, and hired Protestant teachers. (In those communities where Catholics were a strong majority, Catholic holidays, literature, and teachers were the norm.) Something needed to be done, and most schools, to avoid controversy, simply stopped teaching all values except academic ones: don't cheat on examinations, don't plagiarize, and honor thy teacher and thy principal. The protestant ethic was a casualty, not because it was religious (for American Catholics, Jews, and Protestants alike accepted it), but because it was a value, and all out-of-school values had to go. It was not an important in-school value because it had been replaced by the academic meritocracy which held that those who were low in academic aptitude were doomed to failure regardless of how hard they tried. For most students, conscientious work and other protestant ethic virtues were a necessary but not sufficient condition for school success. Yet, if you had a sufficient measure of academic aptitude, it was not even necessary to work conscientiously to obtain success in school.

The net effect is that the values of work simply are not taught in school unless the school has a program of career education. Nor are they always taught in the home. Children no longer see their parents at work, for the place of employment usually excludes visitors. No longer do children have work of their own to do, for they are likely to do as much harm as good in many mechanized homes. Even in vocational education laboratories the values of the protestant ethic are usually absent. Unless the students are enrolled in a cooperative education program, carry newspapers, live on a farm, or are involved in an interesting simulation of employment, such as Junior Achievement, they have absolutely no contact with employment or with the ethics of work. Clearly, the protestant ethic and related vocational values form the major untaught curriculum of the school.

The preceding discussion has identified two major difficulties with the traditional protestant ethic: (1) it has not worked well for those minority groups which are easily stereotyped, and (2) it has been used by certain individuals to justify personal advancement at the expense of others. The latter can be disposed of by identifying it as a perversion of the ideal, but education must teach that such perversions exist and should be dealt with firmly by society.

The problem of the "visible" minority groups, however, is more difficult. There are those who say that if a portion of a minority group does not value work, it would be morally wrong for the schools to impose such a value on them. But the schools do not impose the value. It is society which values work, and it is one of the major tasks of the school to prepare students to survive and achieve in society. It is the most blatant hypocrisy to teach students that they can hold any values they please, and then to throw those students into a competitive world which gives them a choice between accepting its work values or having a marginal economic and social existence. It is perfectly acceptable for the school to work to change society's values, but it is not acceptable for the school to lie to its students by telling them that as long as they conform to the academic values, they may hold any values they like outside of school.

In spite of the fact that schools do not teach it, the vast majority of people in our society still believe in the ideal person of the protestant ethic: a person who works diligently, enjoys the work and does not let unrelated activities distract him or her from it, and saves money and goods for tomorrow, even if it means self-denial today.

During the depression of the thirties, when 25 percent of the labor force was unemployed, it was apparent that this ideal was not working. But today most people have forgotten the Depression, or regard it as temporary aberration due to the greed of stock market speculators who were not following the ideals of the ethic. The only real modification in this ideal since Weber stated it in 1904 has been the acceptance of the view that for a few (but very few) individuals chance can cause disadvantage and the addition of the portion of the Hippocratic oath which enjoins one from doing harm. The major group which does not accept this revised protestant ethic is the lower-lower class, for whom the protestant ethic has not worked. But the lower-lower class is decreasing rapidly in size. The other classes in society accept the revised protestant ethic as readily as the merchant aristocracy of one hundred years ago accepted the original version, and for the same reason—it makes one feel good to be able to attribute one's success to his or her own merits, rather than to chance or to other factors over which he or she has no control. This suggests that contrary to the views of alienated youth the protestant ethic is not disappearing but is as strong as ever, outside the schools.

Work and Leisure

Thomas Green (6) has drawn a sharp distinction between *work* and *labor.* He feels that labor is futile because we labor in order to use up what has been produced and thus add nothing of consequence to society. Work, on the other hand, is a "quest for potency" which allows us to express our individuality. To find the place where our actions can have real consequences is the only means for discovering who we really are, and only in a leisure society can we maximize the opportunities for every person to find work. Schools do not prepare students for work and leisure but rather prepare them for labor. Recognition of the futility of such preparation is a major cause of alienation between students and schools (6).

Until recently, most people felt we were well on the road to the leisure society valued so highly by Green. The popular literature assured us that every year people worked less and had more time for leisure. Thus work was seen as becoming less important, and education to enable people to enjoy this new leisure appeared to be more and more essential. Automation was seen as a force which would immediately decrease the work week, and eventually would result in only a small proportion of people needing to work at all.

One of the foremost authorities on leisure, De Grazia, agrees that the time actually spent at work is decreasing, but, after adding up all of people's non-leisure activities, concludes, "never before have so many Americans had so little time to call their own" (4, p. 64). Data from the United States Bureau of Labor Statistics have shown clearly that for the last few decades, even the time actually spent at work has been increasing (from forty to forty-three hours per week on the average). It is also very probable that automation has increased the amount of time spent in work and work-related activities. Automation and other changes in work structure have decreased the proportion of unskilled workers (in part because these jobs are most easily automated) and increased the proportion of technicians and professionals. Unskilled workers have always had the greatest amount of leisure time, and professionals have had the least. These changes do not eliminate the need for education for effective use of leisure time, but it is clear that this need is not increasing as rapidly as the need for education to cope with increased work demands.

The reasons why leisure time is not increasing rapidly are complex, but among the more important reasons are that most workers would rather have more pay than more time off, and many workers feel that their job is the only interesting and purposeful activity in which they engage.

Whatever the reasons, "the vast majority of employed men say that they would go on working even if they inherited enough money to live comfortably without working" (2).

Philosophers would understand leisure much more fully if they paid attention to what economists call "transfer payments." Such payments are made from one person or group to another for some reason other than to buy goods or services. Much of today's leisure comes from transfer payments; for example, most people who are in jail as well as those who receive pensions, aid to dependent children, or scholarships are being paid by others to engage in leisure or unpaid work. It may be a bit less apparent, but the 10 percent of the Athenians who were citizens in the time of Aristotle were being supported by transfer payments from the 90 percent who were noncitizens, and who were paid little or nothing for their work. The bread-labor of slaves paid for the leisure-work of Aristotle, and this amounted to a transfer payment because the slave did not expect to get much in the way of goods or services in return.

It is, of course, possible for people to produce enough goods and services to pay for their own leisure. As skill increases our productivity more and more, we can afford to pay not only for our own leisure but for the leisure of others. What seems indefensible is to require one to pay for another's leisure when he or she has little or none of his or her own. This, indeed, is one definition of slavery. Vocational education and other programs of human development have as a goal minimizing the necessity of net transfer payments to the person who has been educated, and maximizing the possibility that this person can aid others without sacrificing his or her own opportunity for a full life.

Summary

General education is that education needed by all students. (In practice, the education *given* to all students includes much which is not general education.) In addition to being valuable for citizenship, it provides the *basis* for personal and occupational development of the individual. Thus, some general education should precede specialized education (which is not the same for all individuals). General education and specialized education reinforce each other. Hence they should be taught concurrently during the latter part of an individual's schooling. Most of the content of specialized occupational education should focus on knowledge of the practice and the theory of practice (praxiology) required by one or more occupations.

Unfortunately, specialized occupational education is offered so late in the formal school that few dropouts from high school receive any of it. Yet many educational philosophers favor further postponement of all specialized education until postsecondary education. This would ensure that the majority of students would not get specialized occupational education in school. This postponement must not be allowed to occur until the vast majority of students are able to avail themselves of postsecondary education. Nor can the postponement be justified if a vital part of a student's education is delayed to be used as bait to force him or her to stay in school and to keep him or her off the labor market.

In addition to specialized occupational education, the school has an obligation to provide general occupational education for all students. This education should begin early and should emphasize the importance of vocations in life and the values of work to humanity and to society.

The major untaught curriculum of the school has to do with values, especially the values of work as they affect life. The protestant ethic, which formed a major portion of the content of elementary and secondary school education in the United States during the eighteenth and nineteenth centuries, has been discarded by the school along with most other values. All that remain are the academic values which deal with relationships between students and teachers. Though the protestant ethic has not worked well for visible minority groups, it is accepted in slightly revised form by the vast majority of our society and is likely to continue to be accepted as we work to make society better. The worst possible course for schools to take would be to teach students that the values held by society are unimportant and can be discarded with impunity.

Youth who have been taught that work is unimportant and that the protestant ethic is passé are in for a rude shock when they leave the sheltered world of the school and enter the real world of work. Education which differentiates between labor and work and which prepares the student for work is desirable as a way of reducing alienation. In the final analysis, however, education which leads to effective work is necessary simply because work is essential to the survival of society. A society without labor (in Green's sense) is conceivable, but a society without work is not.

REFERENCES

1. Broudy, Harry S.; Smith, B.O.; and Burnett, Joe R. *Democracy and Excellence in American Secondary Education.* Chicago: Rand McNally & Company, 1964.
2. *Changing Schedules of Work: Patterns and Implications.* Washington, D.C.: U.S. Department of Labor, PB 219177, 1974.
3. Combs, Janet, and Cooley, W.W. "Dropouts in High School and After School." *American Educational Research Journal* 5, no. 3:343–63.
4. DeGrazia, Sebastian. *Of Time, Work, and Leisure.* New York: Anchor Books, Doubleday & Company, Inc., 1964.
5. Feldman, Marvin J. *Making Education Relevant.* New York: Ford Foundation, 1966.
6. Green, Thomas F. *Work, Leisure and the American Schools.* New York: Random House, Inc., 1968.
7. Haskew, L.D., and Tumlin, Inez. "Vocational Education in the Common School." In *Vocational Education,* edited by M.L. Barlow. Chicago: University of Chicago Press, 1965.
8. Hook, Sidney. "John Dewey's 'Democracy and Education'." *New York University Education Quarterly* 5, no. 3:26–29.
9. Lux, Donald G. et al. *A Rationale and Structure for Industrial Arts Subject Matter.* Industrial Arts Curriculum Project Series C-002. Columbus, Ohio: The Ohio State University, 1966.
10. Pucel, David J. *Variables Related to MDTA Trainee Employment Success in Minnesota.* Minneapolis: Department of Industrial Education, University of Minnesota, 1968.
11. Ray, Elizabeth M. "Social and Philosophical Framework in Vocational, Technical, and Practical Arts Education." *Review of Educational Research,* edited by J. Moss, Jr. 38, no. 4:309–325.
12. Reavis, George H. "The Animal School." *Educational Forum* 17 (January 1953).

13. Shute, Nevil. *Round the Bend.* New York: Ballantine Books, Inc., 1951.
14. Smith, Adam. *Wealth of Nations.* Book I. New York: Modern Library, Inc., 1958.
15. Stadt, Ronald. "Man and Technology in Secondary School Curriculum." *Journal of Industrial Teacher Education* 6, no. 2:21–30.
16. Stalin, Joseph. *Nochal'naya Shkola,* 1946. Translated by Maurice J. Shore in *Soviet Education.* New York: Philosophical Library, Inc., 1947.
17. Ushinski, K.D. *Collected Works,* vol. 2. Moscow R.S.F.S.R.: Academy of Pedagogical Sciences, 1948. Translated by S.G. Shapovalenko, ed., in *Polytechnical Education in the U.S.S.R.* Paris: UNESCO, 1963.
18. Veblen, Thorstein. *The Theory of the Leisure Class.* New York: The New American Library of World Literature, Mentor Edition, 1953.
19. Weber, Max. *The Protestant Ethic and the Spirit of Capitalism.* Translated by Talcott Parsons. New York: Charles Scribner's Sons, 1958.

BUREAU OF EMPLOYMENT SERVICES
OHIO

7

Economic Foundations

Economics helps to identify ". . . the most efficient ways of utilizing available human, natural, and capital resources to fill the needs and achieve the objectives of society" (14, p. 5). All of these resources are scarce, and often they could be used in alternative ways. Occupational education is that program designed to develop people (our human resources) to use natural and capital resources wisely and to participate fully and efficiently as productive members of society. Obviously economics and occupational education are related in important ways.

The Economic Revolution and Vocational Education

In the United States there have been three great stages of economic history: (1) the agrarian stage in which natural resources were the critical determinant of wealth, (2) the industrial era when the accumulation and use of capital were the keys to economic growth, and (3) an emerging postindustrial economy in which human resources are rising to prime importance (14, p. 5). Vocational education began during the second of these three phases, so it was natural that it concentrated on meeting the needs of employers who had to have trained people in order to utilize their capital efficiently. In this type of economy, human resources development was clearly subordinate to the short-term needs of the labor market. When employers had an immediate need for skilled workers, vocational education flourished. When their needs were temporarily met, vocational education was expected to lie dormant, regardless of the people who needed vocational education to develop to their fullest potential.

This short-term approach neglected the need for long-range forecasting of labor market demands. It neglected the role of vocational education in motivating general education learnings. And, worst of all, it neglected the fact that human resources are perishable. Minerals, if undeveloped, wait indefinitely without deterioration. Machines may obsolesce but if protected from the elements do not physically deteriorate from disuse. On the other hand, human beings, if undeveloped, neglected, or underutilized, continue to get older and less able to learn rapidly. Moreover, the attitudes of humans change as they become accustomed to a subsidized existence instead of to meaningful work.

In 1963 Congress recognized that vocational education needed to shift its goals to fit the needs of phase three of the economic revolution. These new goals emphasized development of human potential and the employment needs of people, regardless of short-term labor market needs. (Long-term shifts in labor market needs still have to be considered, however, for no one wants to prepare people for occupations in which additional workers will not be needed.) The net effect has been a sizable expansion in occupational education—in numbers of people served, in types of people served, and in breadth of programs offered.

The smallest change has occurred in the proportion of people served. Since the twenties approximately 25 percent of secondary school students have taken vocational education courses, with the percentage by states ranging from 10 to over 50 percent. High school enrollments in vocational education are likely to increase markedly only as the general curriculum is discontinued school by school. In postsecondary education, however, enrollments have increased significantly, with most of the increase occurring in technical education programs.

The most pronounced shift has been in types of people to be served. The Smith-Hughes Act of 1917 specified that vocational education students must be able to profit from the instruction offered. The instruction offered was designed to meet the needs of local employers who needed skilled workers. Students who were not able to meet employer's standards were excluded, regardless of the students' personal needs. Blacks, Indians, Mexican-Americans, the handicapped, and students who scored low on employment screening tests have all been excluded at times from certain vocational education courses on the grounds that they could not profit from the instruction offered.

The new vocational education views the world differently. It would not exclude any students but would design courses and curricula to make sure that each student could profit from the instruction offered. It would be inclusive rather than exclusive. Coincident with this change is a new flexibility in hiring standards and worker utilization by employers, with new opportunities for the disadvantaged appearing every day. Barriers still remain, but the vocational educator has even less justification now for saying that certain individuals should not receive vocational education because they would be unemployable.

Equally important as we move from the second to the third stage of economic history is the increase in breadth of vocational education. Originally designed to meet the short-term needs of the local employer, the early occupational education programs were narrow, specific, and sometimes nontransferable. With the shift in goals to human resource development, vocational education emphasizes transferability of skill and knowledge and strives to provide opportunities for geographic and occupational mobility. While vocational education was shifting its goals, economists were developing methods of stabilizing the economy and minimizing the rapid changes in general employment levels which had been common. With a relatively stable economy, the differences between short-term and long-term labor market needs have decreased. This helps the economist and the vocational educator to concentrate on long-range forecasting and preparation of people for long-range needs.

Economists' Contributions to Vocational Education

Vocational education frequently has been criticized for training people for occupations that no longer exist. This is not an accurate statement since we know of no occupation which has disappeared entirely. The criticism really implies one or both of these questions:

1. Is vocational education preparing more people than can be absorbed into a given occupational field?
2. Would vocational education be more efficient if it decreased certain of its expenditures or increased other types of expenditures?

These are economic questions, and the vocational educator needs to have the help of economists to answer them. In order to be of help economists need pertinent data. Decisions as to what data are pertinent must be made jointly by vocational educators and economists. Then the data must be collected and analyzed on a continuing basis. This process is in its infancy in vocational education. One of the first requirements is for vocational educators to acquire economic literacy and for economists to acquire literacy in vocational education. Only then can they talk to each other.

The first question asked previously concerns the number of people that should be prepared to enter a particular occupational field. To decide whether or not vocational education is preparing more people than can be absorbed into a given occupational field, four basic types of data are needed:

1. How many new entrants to the occupation will be needed to meet expected expansions or contractions in the labor market, how many new entrants will be needed to replace workers who die, retire, or shift to a different occupational field, and what training will they need to compete successfully?
2. What proportion of the people trained to enter an occupation actually do enter it, either immediately or later in life?
3. What are the types and amounts of retraining needed if we are to use our capital and natural resources wisely?
4. How many people are completing all types of vocational education programs in this occupational field?

Let us consider each of these questions more fully.

1. How many new entrants to the occupation are needed to meet expected expansions or contractions in the labor market and how many new entrants will be needed to replace workers who will die, retire, or shift to a different occupational field? The latter part of this question looks at the *replacement* part of the worker demand picture, but the two parts of the question are interrelated. The replacement workers can come from two different sources. If the demand in an occupational field is expanding, they must come principally from new entrants to the occupational field. These new entrants may be youth who enter the occupation or older workers who are retrained to allow them to change occupations. But if the total demand for workers in the occupation is decreasing, replacements can come, in part at least, from people presently in the occupation. For example, suppose that in an occupational field which employs ten thousand workers, one thousand are needed annually as replacements for those who die, retire, or shift to other occupations. If total demand is unchanged, vocational education (of all types) needs to supply one thousand workers per year. But if the total demand expands 5 percent to 10,500 workers, vocational education needs to supply one thousand workers as replacements plus five hundred workers to meet expansion needs. Thus a 5 percent increase in total demand results in a 50 percent increase in the supply needed from vocational education.

If fifty vocational teachers can prepare the one thousand workers needed for normal replacement demand, and if five of these teachers usually resign, retire, or die each year, only five new teachers are needed annually. But a 5 percent increase in total demand calls for these five teachers plus twenty-five new teachers to prepare five hundred additional workers. Thus a 5 percent increase in the demand for workers results in a 500 percent increase in the demand for vocational teachers. Because many vocational teachers are drawn from the ranks of workers, the situation is even worse. When we most need teachers, we also most need workers, so wages go up, and it is impossible to recruit teachers. Moreover, some teachers will return to their former, nonteaching occupation because of its higher wages.

If total demand for workers *decreases,* the situation is reversed dramatically. Using the same example of ten thousand workers, with one thousand needed annually for replacements, a 5 percent decrease in total demand drops the need for vocational graduates to five hundred each year. This cuts the total number of teachers needed to twenty-five. But we have fifty teachers who have been supplying the normal replacement demand of one thousand workers. Five of these teachers leave the field, and five are trained to replace them, but we have a 50 percent surplus of teachers as a result of a 5 percent decrease in demand for workers. The economist calls this phenomenon *acceleration.* This simple example illustrates graphically why vocational education historically has followed a "boom or bust" cycle of expansion or contraction. Only the fact that most in-school vocational programs have trained 20 percent or less of the new entrants to the labor market has saved us from grave difficulty. Obviously, the nearer vocational education comes to providing the entire supply of new workers in a given occupational field, the greater the importance of the acceleration principle in vocational education planning.

The new philosophy of vocational education which calls for the best possible development of people, rather than meeting short-term labor market demands, should aid greatly in reducing the effects of acceleration. Programs which meet the needs of people must take long-term labor market demands into account. The labor economist must be responsible for determining long-term labor market needs, and the vocational educator must use this information in decision-making at the national, state, and local level. The only attempt at the national level to do this forecasting systematically and regularly has been published by the United States Department of Labor as the *Occupational Outlook Handbook.* It covers some seven hundred occupational fields and attempts to forecast moderate or sharp increases or decreases in demand for workers (both for replacements and for expansions in total demand). While these forecasts have been criticized sharply by economists, they seem sufficiently accurate for most vocational education planning. In any case, the *Handbook* summarizes the best available information. A new edition of the *Handbook* is prepared every two years. Between editions, the *Occupational Outlook Quarterly* provides current information. The *Handbook* has a good record of success in forecasting general magnitudes and directions of occupational change, though it has been conservative in estimating needs in new fields. It is, of course, of little value in determining the needs of a particular locality. Attempts to forecast the amounts of training which will be needed by each type of worker are no more satisfactory than projections of quantitative demand.

2. What proportion of the people trained to enter an occupational field actually do enter it, either immediately or later in life? It is very rare for all trainees to enter employment in the occupational field for which they were trained. This is as true of the education of lawyers and engineers as it is of barbers and stenographers. As a greater proportion of trainees enter their field of specialization, the more closely the number of trainees will approach the number of new entrants who are needed. This proportion varies widely by occupational field, from 67 percent for agriculture, to 92 percent for health occupations (24, p. 31). If 80 percent of the ten thousand students who are prepared to be automobile mechanics actually work in this field, it is the eight thousand rather than ten thousand students who must be considered when we make a decision as to whether or not we are educating too many people to be automobile mechanics.

3. What are the types and amounts of retraining needed if we are to use capital and natural resources wisely? This is the question asked most frequently by training directors of large corporations. They need to plan training programs within the company and purchase educational services outside the company (both for their present employees and new recruits who are inadequately trained). They must consider not only the needs of their own firm but also of competing firms. Small competitors usually do little formal training and therefore will try to recruit employees from the large firm. However, the small firm may have a much better OJT program than the large firm, where jobs are often far more specialized. This may cause the large firm to recruit from the small one.

The planning of retraining programs is still in its early stages. Most such training is in response to an immediate need, when a new product, process, or service has been introduced, and management suddenly discovers that it has an insufficient number of trained employees to cope with the change. This leads to a crash program of retraining. For example, the armed forces periodically install new weapons systems. It takes several years to develop such a new system, but it also takes time to design a training program, install it, and produce retrained personnel. Ideally, the trained personnel ought to be available at the same time the new product or process is introduced. In practice, however, the new product or process is introduced, and by trial and error we determine what sorts of personnel are required to handle it. Only then is a training program planned. This traditional method works reasonably well when the product or process is introduced gradually, but it proves difficult when it is desirable to introduce the new procedures simultaneously throughout the organization.

As we gain experience in planning retraining programs on the basis of prototype products (rather than on the basis of experience in the field), we can shorten the lag between the introduction of new products, processes, and services and the availability of trained personnel to deal with them. The necessity for simulation in the training of personnel for space exploration requires the development of procedures for reducing this lag to near zero.

A second type of retraining is designed to cope with recurring problems which have not been solved by earlier training efforts. A typical example is the almost continuous retraining of first-line supervision. The tasks of the first-line supervisor change, but not rapidly. Much of their retraining is an effort to solve a long-term problem, for example in human relations, which earlier training programs tried and failed to solve. Whether the supervisor failed to learn the first time or no longer uses what he or she learned, retraining seems to be constantly necessary.

Still a third type of retraining is designed, not by the employer, but in response to demands from potential trainees. Schill, in his study of technicians in Illinois, found that a large majority of the technicians had acquired some postsecondary education (20, p. 35). His subsequent analysis revealed that most of these technicians had sought out courses which they thought would be useful to them in their careers and had avoided courses which did not appear to be immediately useful. The majority was not interested in degrees or formal curricula. Many adult education students in secondary schools and community colleges have a similar orientation. This would suggest that educational programs should allow the consumers of education to make choices of courses they feel they need in a free marketplace, without tie-in sales which require them to take undesired courses as prerequisites. More likely, as Associate in Arts degrees acquire more currency in the marketplace, A.A. students, like B.S. students, will accept undesired courses in order to get the valuable degree. We need to employ the methods of the economist to learn more about the role of the educational consumer in a free marketplace.

4. How many people are completing vocational education programs in an occupational field? Few data are available on the number of vocational graduates in the country as a whole, though some states are beginning to collect such information. This information is of course readily available at the local level, but unfortunately it has a limited value for local program planning because of actual and potential worker mobility. Assuming that this information will be more widely available at the state or national level in the future, we must recognize that our knowledge will still not be perfect since graduates of poor programs will be listed along with graduates of excellent programs. Moreover, especially in adult programs, students often leave to take excellent jobs without bothering to graduate. A third problem with data on graduates is that adult vocational education programs are often not designed to enable people to enter employment in a particular field, but rather to be more efficient workers in their present occupation. This results in a more effective worker pool, but the trainees cannot be counted as additions to the labor supply. Another problem is that some vocational graduates do not intend to enter the occupational field for which they were prepared. For example, some students take a vocational automechanics couse simply because they like cars as a hobby.

Vocational educators do need (1) to know how many people are completing vocational education programs at each competency level, (2) to be able to differentiate between new entrants and those who have been upgraded in skills and knowledge, and (3) to identify those who have no intention of accepting employment in the field for which they were trained. Obviously, these data must cover *all* vocational education, not just that which is federally reimbursed. The entire supply of trained workers must be counted, evaluated, and considered in planning. The private sector and public vocational education need these data for planning. Most vocational educators assume that someone else will collect the information. To date this assumption has proved to be unfounded.

The evidence provided in the above answers suggests that no field of vocational education is preparing too many people for today's labor market, though we probably come close to it in two or three occupations. This does not mean, however, that we are spending our funds in vocational education most wisely or that vastly increased investment might yield equal returns or that our priorities are correct.

The second question posed at the beginning of this chapter asked, "would vocational education be more efficient if it decreased certain of its expenditures or increased other types of expenditures?" The obvious answer to this question is "yes." But before we can know *how* to increase efficiency in education, we need answers to at least some of the following questions:

1. In what types of education do society and individual students get the best return on their investment of time and money?
2. What is the interaction among student ability, social class, and motivation, as they affect the costs and the effectiveness of various types of educational programs?

3. How much time is required for the graduates of a vocational program to adapt to the techniques of the contemporary productive enterprise?

Let us consider each of these questions in detail.

1. The economist believes that each individual and society should review each major expenditure they make to decide if the money could better be spent elsewhere. Assuming that the individual has full information and is free to act, he or she almost always will make the best choice. In many cases, the two assumptions are untenable, so the economist is interested in increasing freedom to act and in providing information which enables better choices to be made. The economist's usual operational definition of *better* is in terms of earnings per additional dollar invested. The present crude estimates indicate that one dollar invested by society in elementary education yields over 20 percent per year (mostly in increased earnings by the former student). Probably an additional million dollars invested would have a yield nearly as great. But still more dollars spent in the same way are unlikely to yield at as high a rate as the original investment.

A dollar invested in high school education does not pay as large a return as a dollar invested in elementary school education. Part of the reason is that students who attend high school are assumed to be losing money which they could be earning if they were not in school. But the return on money invested in high school education is still far higher than is obtained by investments in many fields presently supported by government or individuals (25, pp. 4–9).

Calculations of rates of return on high school education have assumed that one high school curriculum is as valuable as another. This is certainly not true. So economists have decided to concentrate on studies of rates of return to vocational education because its monetary goals seem clearer than those for either the general or the college preparatory curriculum. Even within vocational education, it is likely that some courses of study yield greater rates of return than others. Failure to take this into account tends to cause the results of studies on vocational education to be inconclusive. Most such studies, however, find that vocational graduates get jobs faster, earn more money per hour, and are employed more hours per year than comparable graduates of other curricula. (Possibly they take jobs away from graduates of other curricula rather than reducing total unemployment, though we are not sure of this.) But vocational education generally costs more than other curricula. The ratio of costs to benefits (both expressed in dollars) is a key economic measure and inevitably will be used more and more in decision making in vocational education. A newer and more promising technique, cost-effectiveness analysis, compares costs with measures of effectiveness which do not necessarily have to be stated in terms of dollars and asks which of several alternatives would produce the best results.

Warmbrod (25) lists a number of cost-benefit and cost-effectiveness studies. The more recent and more refined studies generally show more favorable results for vocational education than did the earlier exploratory studies. It may be accidental, but the studies which show the lowest rates of returns for vocational education are concentrated in the highly industrialized northeast portion of the

United States. Highest rates of return (both in absolute terms, and relative to other types of educational investment) seem to be found in studies conducted in industrially developing portions of the country (pp. 10–34).

Fortunately we are past the time when economists seriously asked, "How do graduates and dropouts from various educational programs differ in lifetime earnings?" By consulting census data they found the number of years of education and the amount of income possessed by different individuals and concluded that X years of education produced Y income. This led to statements such as "a high school diploma is worth Z dollars." They neglected to take into account the effect of socioeconomic level which leads a millionaire's son to go to college and to also have a high income after college graduation, while the child of an unskilled laborer will probably quit school early and have a low income. Such analyses also overlook the influence of ability and motivation, yet "long education causes high income" has been adopted into the conventional wisdom along with the belief that while vocational education may give a student a head start, the general curriculum or college preparatory student will soon pass him or her in earnings. As nearly as can be determined, this belief is not supported by a single study in which the effects of socioeconomic level were controlled.

2. We have very little information on the interaction of ability, social class, and motivation, as they affect the cost and the effectiveness of various types of educational programs. We know that the higher a student's ability, social class, and motivation, the longer he or she will stay in school. Since attendance in school is closely related to lifetime earnings, these three variables are probably also related to earnings. We also know that in all parts of the country (1) the college preparatory program attracts students with the highest verbal ability, (2) the general curriculum attracts the second most able, and (3) the vocational curriculum gets students with the lowest verbal ability. These curricula are in exactly the same order with regard to the average social class of their students. (See chapter 15 for further data.) We do not know their order with regard to the various types of motivations.

Based on this information, it is predictable that of those students who do not go on to college, high school graduates of the vocational curriculum would earn less than graduates of the other curricula. We do not have data on lifetime earnings, but several studies agree that for the one to nine years on which we do have information, vocational graduates earn more. It seems likely, however, that over a lifetime, as a person acquires additional vocational education on the job, or through evening schools, the effect of his or her high school or college education (vocational or general) will become less a factor in earnings, and verbal ability and social class will become more important in determining earnings.

Obviously it is difficult to decide which of the three educational programs is most effective when they have very different types of students. Instead, what we need are studies which tell us what types of education are needed for each type of student. The economist would ask which program provides the desired outcome for a particular type of student at the lowest cost or which program provides the greatest amount of the desired outcome for a particular type of student, holding cost constant.

Sometimes question B is phrased: "Given a choice among graduates or dropouts from different educational programs (e.g., vocational, general, college preparatory, public, private) which will employers choose?" It is obvious that this question cannot be answered without taking into account the background of the students being compared. The sociologist is interested in noting that corporation presidents answer this question very differently from personnel interviewers and supervisors, but the economist is more interested in who is actually employed.

We have almost no data on the relative effectiveness of public and private schools, and our data on effectiveness by level of education (high school, college, and adult) and by types of educational environment (in-school, cooperative, or in-plant) are hopelessly muddled by differences in student characteristics. It does little good to note that placement rates (in the occupation for which trained) run about 20 percent higher for cooperative education graduates than for in-school vocational graduates when we are reasonably sure that cooperative education students are more carefully screened for admission and retention than are the in-school students.

3. How much time is required for the graduate of a vocational program to adapt to the techniques of a contemporary industrial enterprise? The charge is frequently made that vocational education provides instruction on obsolete processes using outmoded equipment. Obviously this charge is incorrect with regard to cooperative education, where a major part of the instruction is provided in employment. It may be true, however, in many in-school vocational programs. The principal reason for this is that updating equipment costs a great deal of money. Obsolescence may be more apparent than real, however. The economically oriented vocational instructor, if allowed to do so, often uses scarce resources to purchase items that will most improve the instruction being provided. When an old piece of equipment is used for *basic* instruction and as a simulator for more complicated equipment, it may be a better instructional device, and a better investment, than a newer, more expensive tool.

Economics can help to make such investment decisions if we can determine the costs of instructional equipment and their effect on institutional outcomes. Economists will have to decide whether or not this would be a wise investment of time, however, in view of Eninger's findings. He showed that less than 10 percent of the trade and industrial education high school graduates found that the tools and equipment at work were "very much different" from those in school. (Trade and industrial education is more frequently criticized than other vocational programs for the obsolescence of its equipment.) More than three times as many graduates, however, found that the work *methods* were "very much different" (7, p. 25).

Economists are not very impressed by this sort of evidence. They want to know the economic effect of various types of educational obsolescence (planned or not), and we do not have these data. If we had them, it is likely that they would show that the most damaging type is that of obsolescence of the instructor. It is the instructor who makes the majority of the educational decisions which affect the economic future of the students.

Economies of Scale

There is an optimum size for any organization which produces goods or services. Below or above this optimum size, the price or quality of the services rendered will be less satisfactory. The small school cannot afford to offer a large variety of curricula or services because there would be too few students to attend the classes or use the services, causing the cost per student to be very high.

Similarly, the small employer cannot afford to employ a training director or a supervisor of apprentices because the cost per trainee would be too high.

Within limits, the way we organize to provide goods or services can change the optimum size of the organization. A small school in a diversified community can provide a broad range of vocational education by using cooperative education programs instead of laboratory-based programs. Or it may join with other nearby schools to establish an area vocational education program. The small employer can reduce the training cost of each apprentice by cooperating with other employers and employee groups in a joint-apprenticeship program. However, when the size is so low that it is impossible to provide needed services, the only solution is to increase the size of the organization.

"There is a great deal of evidence to indicate that school districts need at least two thousand high school pupils (not necessarily in one school) to organize effective and economical programs of education in all fields, including vocational education" (16, p. 10). In the United States, only some two thousand of the thirteen thousand school districts which operate high schools have two thousand or more high school students. McLure's estimate seems conservative, for few high school units with less than three thousand students actually operate broadly comprehensive schools. But even if he has been correct, three actions would appear to be necessary to achieve necessary economies of scale: (1) a great deal of secondary school consolidation, (2) establishment of residential schools where students are widely dispersed geographically, and (3) changes in the organization of schools to allow diversified curricula to be offered in medium-sized schools. The formation of intermediate school districts to provide services which cannot be offered by small schools is an example of such an organizational change.

The Internal Labor Market

Every institution makes a distinction between the employment rights and opportunities of those people employed in its various units and the rights of outsiders. This distinction is recognized by both the employer and the employee in an attempt to separate sharply the jobs contained within the employing unit (the internal labor market) and those jobs and job-holders which are outside.

Classical economic theory recognizes only the external labor market and assumes that workers are free to move from one company to another if there is a job vacancy and if they are qualified to fill the vacancy. Doeringer and Piore point out that this is not correct. "There are hiring jobs or entry ports into these internal labor markets. These are the job classifications that employers list with the employment services and in help-wanted ads, or fill through informal recruitment. They are the points at which employers reach out into the labor market to bring workers into the plant" (6, p. 9).

These entry ports are more numerous in some industries than in others—". . . in industries such as steel, petroleum, and chemicals, well-defined promotion sequences and tall promotion ladders are found; a worker is hired as a yard laborer or other unskilled worker, and, through a series of promotions over a period of time, works up into the semiskilled, and often skilled, production and maintenance jobs in the plant" (6, p. 9). This type of closed internal labor market, with almost all recruitment of blue-collar workers occurring in the unskilled jobs at the bottom of the employment ladder, is most characteristic of large employment units which have a heavy capital investment per worker. Thus, they are large enough and rich enough to provide the large amount of training required as workers move from one job to another. For example, Western Electric reported that 95 percent of their blue-collar workers are employed at the first two grade levels and that within any one-year period, half of the employees will have changed job classifications once (6, p. 29).

In sharp contrast, ". . . in men's apparel and in many shoe and textile plants, there is an open structure, so that practically every production job is a hiring classification" (6, p. 9). Most seasonal industries have similar open internal labor markets. The open labor market is most often associated with industries which have a low capital investment per worker, small unit size, seasonal operations, or weak employee organizations.

When there is a tight labor market for skilled workers (too few skilled workers in relationship to the number of employment opportunities for skilled workers), the number of entry ports in closed internal labor markets tends to increase. Very little is known about the mechanisms of or reasons for this change. Possibly the employer fears that turnover rate of skilled employees will increase and so protects the company by hiring and stockpiling skilled employees from outside the closed labor market. At the same time, during a tight labor market, the employees may be more willing to allow additional entrants from outside because they know that the existence of a tight external labor market increases their own options for employment outside the closed internal market.

In theory, the closed internal labor market should protect the employer from skill shortages caused by tight labor markets since all recruitment is at the unskilled level. In practice, however, the most highly skilled employees can leave a firm which has a closed internal labor market to accept employment with a firm which has an open internal labor market. Since the closed internal labor market restricts recruitment of skilled workers from vocational education or other firms, the employer is faced with greatly expanded training costs in order to upgrade present employees.

The closing of entry ports invariably increases the value of the internal labor market to existing employees. Hence, the closing of entry ports tends to be irreversible and to lead to major labor conflicts if management attempts to fill job vacancies from outside the firm which previously had been filled from the ranks of current employees. Repeatedly during a tightening labor market, standards for employment are reduced: (1) acceptable test scores are lowered, (2) educational requirements are reduced, and (3) unfavorable job history elements are accepted more freely. Reduced hiring standards, unlike changes in recruiting and screening procedures, are usually accompanied by increased training costs and higher production costs which are occasioned by decreased aptitude for learning, increased cost of supervision, and decreased product quality.

The Closed Internal Labor Market

In a closed internal labor market, all jobs are filled by employees who enter the company through a single (usually unskilled) job classification. Through a process of transfer or upgrading, they fill all blue-collar jobs. The primary factor in deciding whether or not a person is eligible for upgrading is seniority. A variation of the closed internal labor market exists where a variety of low-skill hiring classifications exist with titles such as assembler, sweeper, cleaner, hand-trucker. Workers from these entry level jobs workers are promoted on the basis of seniority to semiskilled and even highly skilled production jobs. On the other hand, they may not be eligible for the highly skilled maintenance and repair jobs which are filled either by promotion of apprentices or by hiring fully skilled workers. Clerical jobs often have a variety of entry ports, depending upon the skills newly hired employees bring to the establishment.

The key to the existence of an open internal labor market seems to lie in the availability of personnel with transferable skills. If skilled employees cannot be recruited from other companies or from vocational schools, a closed internal labor market seems to be inevitable. If adequate vocational training is available, it tends to promote the existence of an open internal labor market. However, the existence of relatively high unemployment rates in a particular occupational field can lead employee groups to insist on a closed internal labor market.

The efficiency of a closed internal labor market depends substantially upon the degree to which each job in a promotional ladder requires skills dependent upon experience and training received in lower level jobs. Where jobs require skills that are essentially independent of jobs lower in the hierarchy, the closed internal labor market is quite inefficient, for the full costs of training must be incurred by the employer each time the worker is promoted or reassigned. If a company is expanding rapidly, has high rates of turnover, or has sharp seasonal changes in labor force, the inefficiencies of the closed internal labor market make it difficult for a company to remain profitable because of the high training costs involved.

Effects on Recruitment

If a company hires almost all of its blue-collar workers at the unskilled job level, it expects that seniority will give these workers a right to fill from ten to thirty successively higher skilled and higher paid jobs during their working life. Consequently it will attempt to employ workers who have high intelligence, good human relations skills, and who will have a loyalty to the employer rather than to an occupational field. People who have these characteristics can be trained and retrained rapidly and will not be interested in the short-term advantages which might be gained by shifting employment from one company to another. In short, an employer looks for an employee who will spend a lifetime working for one institution. The parallels with traditional Japanese industrial recruitment and training are striking (13).

Recruitment into closed internal labor markets has tended to penalize people from low income and minority groups. The employer is concerned not only with whether the new employee can perform satisfactorily at the entry port job, but also whether he or she will be able to perform satisfactorily the higher level jobs to which he or she will be entitled by increasing seniority. Stereotypes associated with minority groups are a serious barrier to employability in a firm with closed internal labor market.

The Internal Labor Market and Vocational Education

Where there is a closed internal labor market, relationships between the employer and vocational education are substantially altered. Since the employer assumes full responsibility for the vocational training necessary to upgrade present employees to fill better positions in the company, he or she is faced with a "make or buy" decision. That is, the employer may decide to conduct the training "in-house" or to purchase it from an outside vendor. The outside vendor may be a public vocational educational system, a private trade school, the manufacturer of certain equipment which is installed in the employer's plant, or any other group which can provide adequate training. The employees will usually be paid for the time they spend in training, and the organization providing the training will have no control over who is admitted to the program. Whether the employer purchases training or provides it in-house, the content of the training will be designed to make the employees competent to perform a job to which they are already entitled by seniority.

In an open internal labor market, however, vocational training, whether public or private, will attempt to provide salable skills and knowledges in various levels of occupations. The trainees will forego earnings (though they may receive stipends from public sources as a means of encouraging them to take training in order to reduce welfare costs). Those who complete training satisfactorily will seek employment at whatever skill level they have achieved. Adult workers will enroll in part-time classes designed to upgrade their skills in the expectation that these additional skills will enable them to obtain higher level jobs. (In a closed market few adults attend such classes since the possession of additional skills does not provide the seniority necessary for higher level jobs.)

Specificity of Skills

Gary Becker identified a range of training from the very specific ". . . that has no effect on the productivity of trainees that would be useful in other firms" (2,

p. 18) to the very general, which increases productivity by the same amount in all firms. He said that specific training should be provided by the employer, while it would be appropriate for society to provide general training. An example of general training would be instruction in how to read.

While the content of a particular hour or day of training may be quite specific, no training program for an individual is completely specific. Even training for a job which is performed in only one firm by one individual would teach a person certain knowledges and attitudes with regard to punctuality, quality control, and so on, which would be of value in many firms. Of course different types of training vary tremendously in their general usefulness across firms. It should be pointed out, however, that Becker's use of the terms *specific* and *general* is markedly different from their typical use in education. Training in typing, which would be considered quite specific by most educators, would be regarded as general by Becker since typing skills are useful in many firms.

As a guide to deciding whether or not a public agency should provide a given type of training, Becker's definition is far more useful than the one commonly used by educators. If training is useful in only one or two firms, it is more difficult to justify public expenditures of funds than if the trainees were able to use their skills in many firms. The educator's definition of *general* suggests that education should be reserved for nonoccupational activities such as citizenship, leisure, and physical well-being, which are common to all citizens, and should exclude activities related to employment since there is no common type of employment.

It is a basic technological principle that the greater the number of tasks a machine can perform, the less efficient it is in the performance of any one of these tasks. Industrial engineers tend to assume that this same principle applies to people: the greater the number of tasks a person is trained to perform, the less efficient he or she will be in the performance of any one of them. The application of this concept to machines and people results in the designing of machines and jobs to make them more enterprise-specific since each enterprise is interested in reducing its costs through increased efficiency. However, standardized equipment is generally cheaper because (1) it can be produced in larger quantities than specialized equipment, (2) it has standardized parts available which reduce repair and maintenance costs, and (3) its general utility makes it more adaptable to changes in product specifications. Similarly, broadly trained people can (1) be produced effectively through courses designed to meet the needs of a group rather than an individual, (2) be recruited from one type of employment to another, and (3) adapt more readily to changes in product demand.

Therefore educators must try to strike a balance between programs which are so general as to have little or no occupational value and programs which are so specific as to decrease the options available to the graduate. Job designers must also strive for this balance between job content which is amost entirely specific to a particular business enterprise and job content which is so broad as to be inefficient.

Jacob Stern has suggested that the more "volatile" the technology, the more general the training for that technology should be (21, p. 60ff). This is justified on the grounds that a volatile technology is changing rapidly; hence training should be general in order to avoid rapid obsolescence. In a relatively stable occupation, however, more specific training could be justified because its utility would continue longer. This analysis assumes that in a rapidly changing technology, specific concepts change more rapidly than general ones. While this assumption sounds reasonable, it is possible that the most rapid changes occur at a level somewhere between the most general and the most specific. If one looks at instructional programs in new occupational areas (which often are changing rapidly), Stern's principle is regularly violated. Because no instructional materials are available, the instructor of a new course uses catalogs, operating manuals, and personal experience to teach a mass of specific skills which are not bound together by generalizations. At the same time, because few courses are available for the new occupational field, the remainder of the student's program is made up of standard courses which appear to be most relevant. Thus the student is exposed to extremes of specificity and generality with no intermediate subject matter to serve as a bridge between the two. When instruction for an occupation has become widespread, a market exists for instructional material which bridges this gap. The combination of a market and adequate writing time results in publications designed to fill this need.

Planning to Meet Needs for Workers

The most serious employment problems arise when there is a serious discrepancy between supply of and demand for trained workers. Most of this book is concerned with factors which affect the supply side of this equation, but variables which affect demand are also important and need to be understood by the vocational teacher and student. Economists have worked much more intensively on problems of demand than on problems of supply. Indeed, many economists have held that supply automatically adjusts to demand. There is some truth in this statement, for humans are adaptable. It is also true that demand adapts to supply as employers change their hiring requirements in loose or in tight labor markets, and as machine designers and industrial engineers adapt tools and processes to the labor available. The long continued increase in youth unemployment would indicate that neither supply nor demand has succeeded well in adapting to the other.

The government attempts to alleviate the employment problems caused by the action or inaction of other parts of society, but the government has other demands which it must meet.

> Governments need a basis of comparison for allocating among competing demands. One kind of comparison . . . is between broad categories—the manpower program as against all other government activities. The result of that comparison presumably influences the size of the entire manpower program in the total of government budgets. A second type of comparison is between different elements within the manpower program. That comparison should influence the allocation of manpower funds among the various functions and activities, such as forecasting, information analysis and distribution, testing,

counseling, employer contacts, the matching of applicants and job vacancies, different types of training, sheltered workshops, and job creation efforts (12, p. 172)

Some of the factors which must be taken into account in reaching these decisions are outlined below.

Geographic Mobility of Employers

If the demand for skilled workers in a given location greatly exceeds the expected future supply, the employer may decide to move or select a new location for expansion. In choosing a new site, the employer will be concerned about the availability of productive employees. The governors of several states have wooed employers with promises of vocational training programs to meet their needs. This has been assailed by certain economists as counterproductive from a national point of view (though they admit it may be good from the state's point of view). If a state decides to increase the demand for workers to counter widespread unemployment or underemployment in that state, and if the employer moves from a locality where demand for workers greatly exceeds supply, the use of federal vocational education funds will probably be justified. What cannot be justified on a national basis is for one underdeveloped state to steal employers from another underdeveloped state (22, p. 138ff).

Geographic Mobility of Employees

As in the case of employer mobility, geographic mobility of employees affects both supply and demand in the sending and receiving localities. Social, racial, age, and sex discrimination have reduced worker mobility. Increased general education and vocational education tend to promote mobility of the individual who has the education. Increases in hiring standards (whether justified or not) usually call for increased general or vocational education and thus decrease the mobility of that part of the labor force which cannot meet these demands. Clearly, the national trend is toward expansion of opportunities in occupations which require long periods of education or training (professions and skilled work) and relative declines in demand for most occupations which can be learned in a short time (unskilled labor). Without a corresponding increase in training opportunities, these increased hiring standards will reduce worker mobility.

Desirable and Undesirable Geographic Mobility

Economists usually think of increased geographic mobility as being desirable since many of their analyses assume that workers are free to move to accept improved working conditions. At some point, however, worker mobility becomes wasteful. Employee turnover is expensive to the employer. This expense increases if the new employee has come from a different occupation and thus must be completely retrained. A capable employee is often destined for increased responsibilities, so if he or she leaves, the employer loses not only that person's value in the present job but also his or her potential value in the new one.

Mobility may be costly to the sending and receiving community. People leaving nondepressed areas are likely to be the most able inhabitants, thus bleeding the sending community of needed talent. People leaving depressed areas may be the most able of the unskilled, depriving that group of leadership, and may still be a liability to the receiving community because of their inability to cope with urban problems.

Mobility can be very costly for employees. They may lose pension rights, seniority rights, and vacation rights. Costs are incurred in the moving process. But sometimes workers have no choice. If they are laid off, fired, or forced out by job dissatisfaction, they must look elsewhere. (It is odd that if a worker's income is high enough, society pays some of these costs through income tax exemptions. But if the worker pays no income tax, an exemption from a portion of the tax is of no value. The lower the worker's income, the less help society will provide toward meeting the costs of moving.)

Vocational education graduates are regularly reported to have higher job satisfaction, higher earnings, and less change of occupation than comparable graduates of other school curricula. Yet, if their training is in demand, they have greater opportunities to move. Therefore, vocational education graduates are in a position to avoid forced mobility and to accept mobility based on informed choice. Usually forced mobility is undesirable, and mobility based on informed choice is desirable.

Increased general and vocational education provides the *option* for increased geographic mobility. But if adequate employment possibilities exist in the community where the student finished vocational training, she or he will have lower geographic mobility than less well trained individuals who must move in order to find suitable employment. This seems to be self-evident, but it is contrary to the conventional wisdom which states that the more specialized training an individual has received, the more likely she or he is to move to find employment. It is still true, of course, that the more specialized a trainee is, the harder it is to find exactly the right job at home.

Firm-specific Skills and Knowledges

Almost every job contains a few elements which are unique to the company in which the job is performed, e.g., a special form which must be used for reports, a word which has a special meaning in that company, or even a secret process. A few jobs have a high proportion of content which is specific to one firm. If an employee had only skills and knowledges which were firm-specific, mobility outside that firm (and perhaps even within the firm) would be quite low, for he or she would not have skills which are salable on a broad market. Firm-specific skills and knowledges should seldom be taught outside the firm in which they will be used. By definition they are useful only to those who plan to continue working for a particular company, so they are not suitable for vocational instruction for a group of individuals, some of whom will seek employment elsewhere.

We know very little about the proportion of either firm-specific or general skills and knowledges present in various occupations. Presumably the professions have a high amount of general skills and knowledges and a low amount of firm-specific content. The same is probably true of the work of carpenters. In contrast, semiskilled workers and the people who supervise them probably have a low amount of general knowledge and a high amount of firm-specific knowledge.

There are three major costs incurred by an employer when a worker is replaced: (1) the cost of persuading applicants to apply for a job, (2) the cost of determining whether or not to employ a particular candidate, and (3) the cost of training to bring the new or promoted worker up to the performance level of the person being replaced. A major factor in determining these costs is the degree of firm-specificity in the job. As firm-specificity increases, the possibility decreases that workers who have the needed skills will be available. This lack of availability increases all three types of costs, particularly the cost of training.

People who think vocational education is the sole responsibility of the employer assume that job success is due almost entirely to firm-specific content. Vocational educators, however, assume that firm-specific content is relatively unimportant, and can best be learned after mastery of generalizable content from both general and vocational education. Both ideas are probably correct, depending upon the occupation. Where job success depends almost entirely on firm-specific content, the employer should have the responsibility for specific vocational education. It is to the company's advantage to provide it, since it can employ workers who will have low mobility, which will lower the turnover costs. This is not to say that the employer will want to provide firm-specific training if the schools can be persuaded to provide it satisfactorily.

A common problem occurs when a large employer in a small community serves on an advisory committee to a vocational education program. If a decision needs to be made as to what type of hardware should be purchased for instruction, the employer will probably recommend a product or process which is used in his (her) firm. That product or process may be used by other firms as well, but to the extent that its use is not universal, students trained to use it will have their mobility restricted. The decision should be based on the cost-effectiveness of each possible choice, rather than on whether or not the product or process is used by a local employer.

If economists were interested in costs and effectiveness *within* vocational education, they could provide information which would help to make such decisions. To date, however, they have been more concerned with *external* efficiency, that is, the returns to society and to the individual on completion of a particular program.

Unrealistic Hiring Standards

When there are too many workers, employers frequently increase hiring standards beyond those actually required by the job. During the depression of the thirties, people with college degrees were hired to drive buses, and high school graduates were willing to accept employment as unskilled workers. When the depression ended, there was a mass exodus from such jobs, and companies vowed never again to make the mistake of setting unrealistic hiring standards. But during the seventies it happened again. High school graduation, no record of arrests, and an unbroken record of employment came to be required for many jobs which did not really need these qualifications. Part of the problem of increased hiring standards, however, has been created by agreements to promote workers on the basis of seniority. For example, the typical bargaining agreement in the steel industry calls for all new workers to be employed in unskilled jobs. As the workers acquire seniority, they have the opportunity for promotion to more and more responsible positions. This causes management to seek new employees who are promotable and to demand qualifications which fit the jobs to which the worker might eventually be promoted, rather than standards which fit the jobs for which the workers are being employed initially (18). Even in the face of legal sanctions, such unrealistic hiring standards are often a not too subtle means of discrimination based on race, sex, age, or social class. If a company does not want to hire certain individuals, it can design hiring standards which will make it impossible for them to be accepted. For example, employers intent on discriminating on the basis of sex may require that all new employees be able to lift eighty pounds even though most jobs require lifting no more than twenty-five. Similar mechanisms are also used to set minimum and maximum ages regardless of the job to be performed.

Specialization of Workers

Since the start of the Industrial Revolution, the classic way of meeting increased demands for workers has been to redesign the job or occupation, usually by splitting it into fragments which can be learned quickly and can be performed routinely. This allows lowered hiring standards and less training, decreases the pay per worker, and increases the output per worker. Assuming that these changes result in decreased cost per unit produced, they are all desirable in the eyes of the traditional economist. Decreasing the content of the job works quite well for some workers, especially for those who do not find such jobs boring. It works reasonably well for workers who have no salable skills, for they have no other options and usually are willing to accept boring jobs during a period of emergency. Naturally this traditional method does not work well in the long run for workers who are bored by repetition, and who have enough skills to allow them to seek better paying or more satisfying employment.

There is an interesting and vitally important relationship between the school curriculum and employers' efforts to design jobs to utilize the available workers. Some graduates of the high school general curriculum and those graduates of the college preparatory curriculum who do not go to college may actually be sought for certain types of employment because they have higher verbal intelligence scores than dropouts or graduates of the vocational curricula. But because they rarely have salable skills, they are placed on routine jobs which do not demand expensive training from the employer. Because they are relatively intelligent they find these jobs boring. It is a complete anomaly that two curricula which purport to be liberating insure that certain of their graduates are enslaved by the lack of relevance of their preparation. In contrast, the graduates of the high school vocational curriculum (regardless of whether or not they go to college) and those graduates of the college preparatory curriculum who do go on to college (if they thus acquire salable skills) have markedly higher job satisfaction.

Probably as the average level of education increases, workers will be less content with specialization which results in boring jobs which require little training. This suggests that jobs should be designed to have content which offers more variety, but this would force the employer to (1) recruit workers who have adequate vocational education or (2) increase the amount of training offered to workers. Since small employers do not benefit from the economies of scale available to large employers, they find training programs to be extraordinarily expensive. Increased demands for employer-sponsored training either force small employers out of business or cause them to recruit trained workers from large companies. Large companies, of course, frequently lure trained workers from small companies because small companies are less mechanized and their workers are less specialized. Stealing a worker often costs a company less than training one. The costs to society incurred when a small company fails because it has lost trained workers may be quite high, however. In the United States, vocational education often acts as a subsidy to the small employer, unlike European countries, where government requires all employers, regardless of size, to share most of the costs of training for their industry.

Substitution of Workers

Another method of changing the demand for employees is to substitute one kind of worker for another. Technicians may be used in place of engineers, licensed practical nurses in place of registered nurses, and typists may replace stenographers. This interchangeability is not complete, of course. Technicians know how to do things that engineers do not, and vice versa. Moreover, because of legal and traditional restrictions, engineers are permitted to do things that technicians are not permitted to do (even though they are perfectly capable of doing them), and some engineers refuse to do things which they feel are beneath them.

A very common method of substituting one kind of worker for another is to lure certain types of workers from a declining industry to an expanding industry. The workers most sought are those who have directly transferable skills, e.g., pipe welders in a shipyard can go to work with very little retraining as pipe welders in the construction industry. The more retraining required, the less likely the employee will be sought.

Who Should Receive Vocational Education?

One of the principal arguments for vocational education and worker training is that for many years there have been shortages of workers (especially at the technician, white-collar, and professional levels) at the same time when there has been a large group of unemployed and underemployed individuals (especially among the unskilled). The assumption is that if we had adequate vocational education, the surplus of unemployed and underemployed persons could be trained to eliminate the shortage of high level employees. But most of the unemployed and underemployed unskilled workers would need from four to ten years of general and vocational education to qualify for the majority of the chronically vacant high level jobs. This indicates that it would be impractical to solve the problem of shortages of workers by simply retraining the unskilled and the unemployed for the vacant high level jobs. It simply is not economically feasible to provide the complete reeducation which is needed.

Two courses of action are possible, and both are being used. First, unskilled workers could easily be converted to semiskilled workers, and semiskilled workers could be retrained as skilled workers, etc., through each level of the occupational ladder. This necessitates retraining a high proportion of the labor force. The second course of action is to train a high proportion of youth for high level jobs, sending only the dropouts to lower level employment. If employed exclusively, this method would make the plight of the older worker even worse, by preempting employment opportunities to which he or she might be promoted. Labor unions and large companies concentrate on the first of these methods. In-school vocational, technical, and professional education concentrate on the latter.

Many Comprehensive Employment and Training Act programs have the fatal defect of preparing minority group members for entry level employment but making no provisions for upgrading the workers who currently hold these jobs. This leads to a pileup at the bottom rungs of the occupational ladder. Some large companies will themselves do this upgrading job in order to protect their relationships with their present workers, but small companies lack the means to do this upgrading. The availability of two socially antagonistic competitors for one semiskilled job can only lead to sharp conflict. This conflict is almost certain to be sharp during periods of economic recession. CETA programs cannot be criticized severely for creating this problem, for they have been placed in the same position that other parts of vocational education were in for fifty years. They are limited, in practice, to training for skills which are needed immediately in the geographic area in which the training is given. Unlike vocational education, they have been restricted to short-term training, both by a typical institutional training period of less than a year and by heavy pressure for immediate results. The heavy concentration of CETA on training for entry level jobs is the result.

The Roles of the Economist and the Manager in Decision Making

A few educators hold a belief that all education is good regardless of its costs, but this view is not held by most people who control the purse strings. There are many more good ways to spend money than there is money to be spent, so decisions have to be made about allocation of our scarce resources. In educational decision making, "failure to take . . . cost-benefit factors into account *explicitly* means that they are considered *implicitly* on a set of assumptions unknown to the decision maker" (11, p. 17).

Outside the field of economics, economists usually do not make decisions. Rather, they provide information which allows others to make better decisions. Managers have to make decisions. Some are easy; others are difficult. In some cases, the type of decision made is relatively unimportant; what is important is that *some* decision be made. In other cases, the nature of the decision is crucially important; the life or death of an organization or the occupational liberation or enslavement of an individual may depend on the quality of the decision made. Most decisions fall between these two extremes. To aid managers in better decision making, various management information systems have been developed. All operate on the general principle of providing needed data in a form and at a time which helps decision making become more simple and more rational. Many of them allow the manager to divide important and difficult decisions into a series of less difficult steps. Most of them provide for corrective information (feedback) to inform the manager when decisions are wrong and need to be changed.

The need for management information systems in vocational education became obvious in 1963 and critical in 1968. Prior to 1963, the federal and state governments acted as conduits for the distribution of funds under relatively rigid rules and in noninterchangeable categories. Line-item budgeting was the rule. The Vocational Education Act of 1963 loosened these restrictions, however, and the amendments of 1968 removed all subject-matter categories and mandated local and state planning for allocation of the still scarce resources of vocational education. This necessitated decision making which was far more difficult and important than any made in the past.

Management information systems are developing very rapidly but at the present time the most useful techniques appear to be those called Program Planning and Budgeting Systems (PPBS). They are a group of closely related systems which emphasize management information, theoretical models, analyses of possible economic and noneconomic results of different tentative decisions, and cost-effectiveness analysis of the actual results of the decisions made. Every vocational education administrator should be able to understand and use these systems or the improved systems which inevitably will replace them. Borgen and Davis (3) have shown simple but effective ways of using PPBS in vocational education.

Economic Knowledge Needed by Vocational Education Students and Teachers

Quite aside from the question of whether or not a government should make an investment in a vocational education program, or an individual should make an investment of time (foregone earnings) and money in taking such a program, is the question of what economic content should be presented in a vocational education curriculum. This question is particularly pertinent since most high schools offer no economics instruction to the non-college-bound. Until all high schools recognize that economics is a vital part of general education and until sufficient numbers of economic teachers can be trained, some other action must be taken.

> To be adequately prepared for employment, the vocational student must come to the labor market armed with a general understanding of the workings, values, and institutions of the American economy, the information and wisdom for occupational choice, a motivation to produce, and the ability to do so. All of these need not be provided by vocational teachers, but it is the responsibility of vocational leadership to see that the requisite knowledge is obtained. (14, p. 6)

Home economics and business teachers have been developing instructional programs in consumer education, which necessarily involves considerable economic education. If they collaborated more with the few social studies teachers trained in economics to prepare instructional materials, if vocational education made instruction in economics a requirement for completion of the curriculum, and if vocational teachers emphasized the application of economics in their regular courses, perhaps we could meet Mangum's challenge. The only other way of providing economic knowledge in high school is to ask the vocational teacher to provide it. This alternative is not attractive, for once we decide what economic content should be taught, we need to find ways for the vocational teachers to learn it. Most vocational teachers have had little contact with the study of economics, and except for a few in business education, none are prepared to teach it. Fortunately, this difficult situation need not exist in vocational and technical curricula in community colleges since economics teachers are usually available and presumably can offer the economic instruction needed.

REFERENCES

1. *Acquisition of Skills.* Research Program on the Training of Skilled Manpower, Report No. 4. Ottawa: The Queen's Printer, 1960.
2. Becker, Gary S. *Human Capital.* New York: Columbia University Press, 1964.
3. Borgen, Joseph, and Davis, Dwight. *Planning, Implementing, and Evaluating Career Preparation Programs.* Bloomington, Ill.: McKnight Publishing Co., 1974.
4. Combs, Janet, and Cooley, W.W. "Dropouts: In High School and After School." *American Educational Research Journal* 5, no. 3:343–63.
5. Corazini, A.V. "The Decision to Invest in Vocational Education: An Analysis of Costs and Benefits." *Vocational Education* (Supplement to *Journal of Human Resources*) 3 (1968):88–120.
6. Doeringer, Peter B., and Piore, Michael J. *Internal Labor Markets and Manpower Analysis.* Lexington, Mass.: Lexington Books, 1971.
7. Eninger, Max W. *The Process and Product of T. & I. High School Level Vocational Education in the United States.* Pittsburgh: American Institute of Research, 1965.
8. Evans, Rupert N.; Agler, Linda Sonna; and Phillips, William Y. "Economic Rationale for Human Resource Investment." In *Developing the Nation's Work Force,* edited by Merle E. Strong. Washington, D.C.: American Vocational Association, 1975, pp. 293–312.

9. *Formal Occupational Training of Adult Workers.* Manpower/Automation Research Monograph No. 2. Washington, D.C.: U.S. Department of Labor, 1964.
10. Hovey, Harold A. *Techniques for Evaluating Government Programs.* New York: Frederick A. Praeger, Inc., 1968.
11. Kaufman, Jacob. "The Role of Economics in the Training of Leaders in the Field of Vocational and Technical Education." In *The Advanced Degree and Vocational-Technical Education,* edited by J.L. O'Brien. New Brunswick, N.J.: Rutgers University Press, 1966.
12. Lester, Richard A. *Manpower Planning in a Free Society.* Princeton, N.J.: Princeton University Press, 1966.
13. Levine, Solomon B. *Industrial Relations in Post-War Japan.* Urbana, Ill.: University of Illinois Press, 1958.
14. Mangum, Garth L. *The Economic Education of Vocational Educators.* Columbus, Ohio: The Center for Research in Vocational and Technical Education, 1969.
15. McGivney, Joseph H., and Nelson, William C. *Programming, Planning, Budgeting Systems for Educators,* vol. I. Columbus, Ohio: The Center for Research in Vocational and Technical Education, 1969.
16. McLure, William. "The Future of Vocational and Technical Education." *Bulletin of the National Association of Secondary School Principals* 35, no. 262 (1961):7–12.
17. *Occupational Outlook Handbook.* Washington, D.C.: U.S. Department of Labor, 1968.
18. Piore, Michael J. "Management Reactions to Changed Conditions." In *Work Force Adjustments in Private Industry,* edited by J.T. Dunlop. Manpower/Automation Research Monograph No. 7. Washington, D.C.: U.S. Department of Labor, 1968.
19. Piore, Michael J. "On-The-Job Training and Adjustment to Technological Change." *Journal of Human Resources* 3, no. 4 (Fall 1968):435–49.
20. Schill, William. *Curricula Content for Six Technologies.* Urbana, Ill.: University of Illinois Press, 1965.
21. Stern, Jacob. "Conceptual Models to Analyze Occupations for Educational Purposes." In *Guidelines and Supportive Papers for Planning and Conducting Short-term Teacher Education Activities,* edited by Lewis D. Holloway. Iowa City: University of Iowa, 1970.
22. Stromsdorfer, Ernest W. "Aspects of Geographic and Occupational Mobility." In *Manpower Information for Vocational Planning,* edited by Robert C. Young. Columbus, Ohio: The Center for Vocational and Technical Education, The Ohio State University, 1969.
23. Veblen, Thorstein. *The Theory of the Leisure Class.* New York: The New American Library of World Literature, Mentor Edition, 1953.
24. *Vocational Education: The Bridge Between Man and His Work.* Washington, D.C.: General report of the Advisory Council on Vocational Education, Superintendent of Documents No. FS 5.280:80052, 1968.
25. Warmbrod, J. Robert. *Review and Synthesis of Research in the Economics of Vocational-Technical Education.* Columbus, Ohio: ERIC Clearinghouse, The Center for Vocational and Technical Education, 1968.

8

Sociological Foundations

Industrial sociology is an important area within the discipline of sociology which provides new ways of thinking about work behavior. Industrial sociologists feel that ". . . work behavior is social behavior and, as such, may be one of the most fulfilling and enriching experiences of life" (12, p. xii). Sociologists who study industry do not restrict themselves to factories or manufacturing but are concerned with all types of work and the social context in which work is performed. Thus, "an office, a sales organization, a hospital, a school, a day nursery, a window-washing company, and a farm which sells its products are all industries" (12, p. xii) because they are all organized to assist in the performance of work. Industrial sociologists are also interested in the effect of social forces and social activities on work, the worker, and work organizations. They feel that these are so interdependent that a change in one is certain to affect the others. Obviously they have much the same breadth of interest as have career educators. Increasingly, the knowledge accumulated by sociologists is affecting both the practice and the philosophy of vocational education and the relationships of vocational education with the remainder of education. Entwistle (6) offers particularly compelling reasons for the inclusion of vocational education in the public schools.

The Roles of Work and Work Groups in Society

According to sociologists, work is a goal-directed group activity. Even the solitary writer must interact with other workers with related goals. For the group to function effectively, there must be a division of labor, with technically competent individuals and a set of rules which governs the relationship of each worker to the group. This organization may be set up by the group itself or imposed by a bureaucracy. Since the work group is relatively cohesive and often resents direction from outside, most changes come from within the group. In addition to meeting the needs of society for its products or services, a work group provides an opportunity for the worker to get rewards from association with others. It protects the worker-members from outsiders; it provides a channel of communication (through the grapevine) that prevents surprise; it reassures the workers of their personal worth; and it controls the workers' behavior to protect them from injury by outside forces. The work group defines work in all its dimensions, provides status for the worker, and determines the values and merits of his or her work.

To a large extent, work determines how much money workers receive, where they will live, what kind of recreation they will enjoy, who they will meet socially, and those whom they will avoid meeting. Eighty percent of the labor force say they would work even if they did not need the income because it keeps them occupied and healthy. Without it they would feel lost, useless, and bored. This does not mean that work is alway pleasurable. In order to meet the goals of the work group, individuals must subordinate some of their own goals either willingly or because they find it necessary in order to receive subsistence. Major conflicts arise when an individual worker is torn between loyalties to two different groups, for example, between the work group and a group based on another common ground. Professionals find similar conflicts between loyalties to their colleagues and to their clients or students (6, pp. 1–30; 12, pp. 1–4; 11, pp. 1–14).

Less than 15 percent of workers in the United States are self-employed. Over 85 percent work in some type of organization. Organizations are more or less bureaucratic, with small businesses being least so and government and the military being highly bureaucratized. The dominant characteristic of an industrial society is the pervasive role of the large, bureaucratic work unit. While 90 percent of the business firms have less than twenty employees, these firms employ only 25 percent of the labor force. Well over a third of workers are employed by firms which have one thousand or more employees. Since these proportions have changed little during the last fifty years, vocational education is needed for self-employment and for employment in both large and small organizations. Because few firms with less than a thousand employees have the necessary economy of scale to permit them to provide formal training to their employees, we should be particularly concerned about vocational education for the majority of workers who are and will be employed by such companies.

The Effect of Industrialization on the Labor Force

As a country becomes more highly developed (that is, as it develops more effective work organizations), it passes through a sequence of steps which affects its occupational structure, its types of work organizations, its communities, and its entire cultural value structure. This sequence applies also to those portions of a country (such as Appalachia) which have been late in moving toward industrialization. It may also apply to female workers.

The best description of the social process of industrialization comes not from industrial sociology, but from four labor economists. One of the questions they asked was "How is an industrial work force recruited and settled into industrial life?" (7, p. 7). This is obviously a key question in vocational education. Though they were not able to answer the question fully, they answered it in part by identifying four stages of commitment on the part of the labor force (7, p. 145).

1. Uncommitted workers take employment for a specific, temporary purpose. The need to raise money for taxes, to tide the family over a period of famine or low agricultural prices, or to support a habit. Since they plan to stay in industrial employment only for the time necessary to get money for a particular purpose, they are not interested in vocational training and usually are employed in unskilled work. If they have some skills, they are generally not interested in upgrading or replacing them with other skills. These workers have a high turnover rate which is costly, and their employment can only be justified if no other workers can be found or if very low wage rates can be paid.

2. Semicommitted workers are torn between two ways of life. They expect to spend a sizable portion of their lives in industrial employment but really prefer to live in their home communities, where they would be engaged in subsistence agriculture (farming which provides money only for bare necessities). In the United States, if they live in a city, they often drive long distances on weekends to maintain ties with the home community, or (if they work close to home) they farm and hold industrial employment simultaneously. The economist usually interprets part-time farming as a desire for more income, but the sociologist sees it as a lack of full commitment to industrial employment and as an attempt to keep a foot in both industrial employment and in the traditional social environment. If the worker can make enough money to support a family through nonindustrial employment, he or she often will leave industry, returning only when economic conditions force a return. Since the worker does not thoroughly enjoy industrial employment, he or she often takes full advantage of sick leaves and takes holidays on every possible occasion.

3. Generally committed workers no longer have strong ties with nonindustrial life. They see themselves as permanent members of an industrial work force, usually in an urban area. Since they must sell their labor to survive, and since they have relatively few skills to sell, they are dependent on a changing job market. They tend to seek security through a labor organization and expect it to persuade the employer to provide retraining if their skills become obsolete.

4. There are two types of specifically committed workers: the enterprise-committed and the occupation-committed. Both are permanent members of the industrial work force.

In Germany and Japan (and, some sociologists feel, increasingly in the United States), large numbers of workers are tied to a particular work organization. Their turnover rate is low because they expect to spend their entire life with one employer. When asked, "What do you do?" they tend to say, "I work at Monsanto," or "I am in the office at Caterpillar Tractor." Large corporations and industrial-type labor unions encourage such company affiliation through pension plans and seniority rights which guarantee a career ladder of varying length to the enterprise-committed employees. A major difference, however, between America and Japan is that in the former the worker tends to identify with the employing organization only when his or her own work denies him or her significant status.

A quite different type of committed employee is tied to a particular occupation. A large proportion of the work force in Great Britain and the United States is made up of occupation-committed workers. A high proportion of professionals, semiprofessionals and skilled workers feel no compunction about leaving a particular employer if opportunities in their occupation appear to be better with another employer. If they are represented by a labor union, it tends to be of the craft type rather than an industrial union. The turnover rate for this type of committed worker may be high if one looks at employment by company, but it tends to be low in terms of the occupation because the worker keeps the same occupation when moving from employer to employer.

The more highly developed the economy in a particular geographic area, the higher the proportion of committed workers. Companies with sophisticated and expensive equipment cannot afford the high turnover and high rates of absenteeism which are characteristic of the less committed worker. Because committed workers are more frequently found in cities and rich agricultural areas, companies tend to expand in such areas rather than in poorer areas. At the same time, in industrialized areas, employers, unions, schools, and families all exert pressure to convert uncommitted workers into committed workers. This pressure from homes and schools is likely to be much lower in less industrialized localities. Indeed, the local value structure may be such that full work commitment is discouraged. These factors hasten the industrialization process in the already industrialized areas and retard it in less industrialized sections.

The evidence is not clear as to whether the enterprise-committed worker or the occupation-committed worker will predominate in mature industrial cultures. Large employers are more frequently found in mature industrial economies. The formation of large enterprises seems to favor the enterprise-committed worker since a large corporation provides greater stability of employment and a wider range of career opportunities within the corporation than does a small company. On the other hand, the requirement of a high degree of worker skill and specialized education seems to lead to occupational commitment. Increasing demands for education and skill are also characteristic of mature industrial economies. In Japan the evidence indicates that the result is a gradually decreasing enterprise commitment and an increasing occupational commitment.

Judged by these standards, it would appear that the plumber has an enterprise commitment rather than an occupational commitment. However the enterprise to which the plumber is committed is the union rather than the plumbing contractor. If the union insists on apprenticeship as the major path to employment in the occupation (most unions do not) and determines which people will be available for employment on a particular type of job, that union assumes many of the characteristics of an enterprise.

Vocational education in American schools has been concerned primarily with developing occupation-committed workers. In-plant training has been concerned primarily with developing enterprise-committed workers. Comprehensive Employment and Training Act programs are aimed at less fully committed workers, but the planners of these programs have not been consistent in deciding whether their goal is to persuade workers to adopt an occupational or an enterprise commitment.

The future of vocational education in the schools is certain to be influenced by the type of commitment which becomes predominant. If occupational commitment becomes the norm, vocational education in the school is likely to expand rapidly, and training offered by employers is likely to be restricted to the training needed to help the employee adjust to the *unique* problems of the work situation (plus training to compensate for the inadequacies of the vocational education that the employee received in the schools). On the other hand, if enterprise commitment becomes the norm, there is need for much less vocational education in the schools, for workers are likely to enter employment at the unskilled level and be trained and retrained by the employer each time the worker's seniority allows entrance to a higher level job.

In the meantime, vocational education is likely to continue to concentrate on these occupations for which occupational commitment is the norm (such as machinist, nurse, and typist) and to avoid involvement in educational programs for types of employment where enterprise commitment is common (such as the steel industry, the automotive industry, and the meat packing industry). Though there are many individual exceptions, it appears that people with low occupational competency are likely to be loyal to the enterprise, while those with high occupational competency have first loyalty to their occupation. The latter will exhibit loyalty to the enterprise only if it gives them greater opportunities within their occupation than does a competing enterprise. Therefore if vocational education succeeds in raising occupational competency, it will also raise the level of occupational commitment.

Table 8–1 indicates demographic factors which are increased or decreased by full industrialization. It suggests a number of changes in the subject matter, clientele, and geographic site for reallocation of vocational education resources.

Social Class and Work

Social class is most often characterized as upper, middle, and lower, or working. These three categories are sometimes further subdivided into upper-upper, lower-upper, upper-middle, lower-middle, and so on. The divisions between classes are not sharp, but people in each class tend to have different values and behavior. Social class is closely related to occupation. Indeed, "most

TABLE 8–1. *Effects of full industrialization of importance to vocational education*

Increases	Decreases
Proportion of the population which is working for pay	Amount of sickness
Proportion of women working for pay	Proportion of workers in agriculture and manufacturing
Average size of the work organization	Proportion of young and old workers
Proportion of workers who provide services	Proportion of unskilled workers
Amount produced per worker in agriculture and manufacturing	Proportion of education devoted to the classics
Amount of general and vocational education	
Geographical and occupational mobility	
Proportion of people in cities	
Expenditures for transportation	
Length of life	
Amount of leisure for young and old people	

students of social class behavior agree that . . . (as) a single measure of the overall complex of class behavior, . . . a scale of occupations is clearly the most efficient instrument to use" (12, p. 96).

Managers and professionals tend to be upper class or upper middle class. Skilled workers, semiprofessionals, small proprietors, and white-collar workers most frequently are lower middle class. Semiskilled workers are frequently upper lower class, and those people who work only when they choose to do so are usually lower lower class. The higher the social class, the higher the income, education, material possessions, and status. In some countries, movement from one social class to another is an extremely slow and difficult process. It is not easy even in the United States. Upward movement usually occurs as a result of increased education, though seniority in large firms is becoming more and more important as a route to higher level occupations. Downward movement can occur because of technological change, economic failure of the employer, or continued failure of the worker to perform job duties satisfactorily.

Vocational education is most concerned with occupations which lead people to lower middle class status. Upper and upper middle class occupations are usually associated with college degrees, and while a relatively high proportion of vocational graduates go on to college, vocational educators tend to ignore the demonstrated value of their programs to motivate people to want increased education. Vocational education for youth is most frequently designed to provide *entry* to lower middle class occupations. Vocational education for adults is most concerned with combatting technological change and other factors which tend to reduce the occupational level of the worker and with providing this education before substantial dislocation has occurred. Comprehensive Employment and Training Act (CETA) programs, on the other hand, have concentrated on lower and lower middle class entry occupations for people over age eighteen and on providing help to the dislocated or underemployed adult only after he or she is in serious straits.

Since lower class occupations are likely to be in decreasing demand or to have relatively low wage scales, it is understandable that vocational education prepares few people to enter them. However, the demonstrated ability of vocational education to increase a student's social class (especially from lower to middle class) is too frequently overlooked by teachers. Most vocational educators are middle class and given a choice between a lower class student and a middle class student, they usually give preference to the latter. But the lower class student needs vocational education much more than does the middle class student, for family status and community resources tend to assure the middle class student entry into a middle class job. The success of Skills Centers (CETA) and Opportunities Industrialization Centers (private) proves clearly that significant numbers of lower class people are interested in and can profit from vocational education.

Income, Class, and Occupation

Since most middle class parents desire their children to move to white-collar or professional occupations and since little is done to prepare lower class youth for high level manual occupations, there is a shortage of skilled manual workers. This shortage is compounded by the high costs of apprenticeship, which have led employers (often with the assistance of unions) to keep apprenticeship opportunities so scarce that they do not begin to meet replacement demands in skilled occupations.

A shortage of workers in any field leads in the long run to increased wages. Wages for many skilled manual occupations are now higher than for occupations which traditionally have paid more and have had higher status. In some cities, street cleaners earn twenty thousand dollars a year, and husband-wife truck drivers may earn fifty thousand. Moreover, working conditions in high status occupations often are not good. Pressures are severe, with mental health difficulties being highly correlated with occupational level (the correlation is 0.85 according to Clark [2]). Heart attacks and ulcers are more frequent. Hours are longer. Though farmers work the most, averaging fifty-two hours per week, managers, proprietors, and professional and technical workers are close behind. Laborers and private household workers have the most leisure (or underemployment).

In spite of the free time they provide, working conditions in lower class occupations are not good either. Unemployment is highest in lower class occupations and decreases sharply as status of the occupation increases. Freedom from unemployment seems to be nearly as important as income in determining the status of an occupation. All in all, medium status occupations seem to offer the best working conditions.

Table 8–2 lists factors associated with low occupational status which have been identified by industrial sociologists. These factors are classified according to the extent to which it appears the schools can modify them directly. Obviously the schools can have substantial *indirect* effects on the items in the two left-hand columns, for example, by persuading the community that sex and race are not desirable as determinants of occupational status. If the school fails to act in the areas where it can make a sizeable difference, direct or indirect, it is clearly delinquent.

TABLE 8–2. *Factors associated with low occupational status*

Not Directly Modifiable by Schools	*Modifiable to a Certain Extent by Schools*	*Readily Modifiable by Schools*
Female sex Minority race Youth or old age High unemployment Low wages Low fringe benefits Decreasing employment opportunities Low governmental regulation Low education of parents Low occupational status of parents Low social status of parents Low seniority Low savings High physical exertion	Low geographic mobility No union Low intelligence Low independence Low optimism about the future Low aspirations for their children Low loyalty to occupation Low loyalty to employer Low loyalty to fellow-workers Poor health Poor diet	Low educational attainment Low occupational skill and knowledge Low awareness of occupational opportunities Little understanding of effects of absenteeism, productivity, promptness, etc.

Careers and Unemployment

Economists traditionally have excluded students and homemakers from their analyses on the ground that they were not productively employed. Industrial sociologists, however, have included them on the ground that their work is productive even though it does not result in monetary income. Until recently neither discipline has been particularly concerned about people who are neither working nor looking for a job. Illustrative of their lack of concern is the fact that even today an unemployed person is defined as one who is looking for a job but cannot find it. A person who is not looking for employment is not unemployed; he or she is just not counted.

Sociologists and psychologists identify five phases in work life: (1) preparatory (usually in school), (2) initial (first employment), (3) trial (a period of job changing as the worker tries to find work which is attractive), (4) stable (usually the longest period, when there are relatively few changes in occupation), and (5) retirement. Most unemployment occurs during the initial and trial stages. It is also relatively high among people who have been forced into retirement but have not accepted this retirement either because they cannot afford to do so or because they want to work for other reasons. Both types of unemployment have been increasing in the United States, but we know considerably more about youth unemployment than about unemployment of older people.

Youth Unemployment

Youth unemployment in the United States has been increasing steadily for at least forty years, if it is measured in relationship to general unemployment. In the mid 1970s youth unemployment (ages fourteen to nineteen) was about three times as high as general unemployment (22 percent versus 7 percent). No other industrialized country has such a high rate of youth unemployment. Both sex and race strongly affect youth unemployment. For example, female, black youths of ages eighteen to twenty have an unemployment rate of over 35 percent. Graduates of high school vocational programs have unemployment rates below 7 percent and markedly below the rates for graduates of the general curriculum or the college preparatory curriculum (currently over 18 percent for those who do not go to college). Even high school dropouts have greater earnings than and the same amount of unemployment at age eighteen as high school graduates from nonvocational curricula who do not go to college (3). For some unknown reason, however, almost all of the youth secure regular employment by age twenty-five. This is true whether or not they have received vocational training after leaving high school.

The high rate of youth unemployment has been blamed on many factors, including the federal minimum wage, alienation, and laws governing work in hazardous occupations. None of these, however, adequately explains the long-term rise in youth unemployment, for it has continued to go up regardless of changes in any of these factors. Vocational education, (including apprenticeships) and college attendance are the only readily modifiable factors which seem to decrease youth unemployment effectively.

Cyclical and Seasonal Unemployment

"The greatest menace to stable career patterns is cyclical and seasonal unemployment" (11, p. 601). We have seen that unskilled and semiskilled workers are hardest hit by unemployment. Not only is the total need for unskilled and semiskilled workers decreasing, but because the learning period for such jobs is very short (often a matter of hours or weeks) almost anyone can replace such a worker on short notice. Since individuals who have higher level skills are difficult to replace, they are usually kept in employment for short periods of time when they are not really needed. The unskilled or semiskilled, however, frequently are dismissed immediately when there is a cyclical or seasonal decrease in demand.

Technological Unemployment

Technological unemployment results from changes in occupational content or in the numbers of people needed in an occupation as a result of the introduction of new products or processes. If the company's business continues to be economically strong, it often assumes responsibility for retraining some of the displaced workers (sometimes being forced to do so by a labor union). But if the employer goes out of business, the workers have no recourse. In any case, a marked change due to technological innovation creates severe problems of adjustment for the worker. Society can help people make these adjustments by providing retraining programs, which are a vital part of vocational education.

Physical and Emotional Disability

By inheritance, or more frequently through accidents of the environment, people acquire physical and emotional disabilities which can disrupt a career. Vocational rehabilitation programs are very effective remedies for such disabilities. These programs include diagnosis of the problem, treatment (including provision of artificial limbs, psychiatric help, and counseling), vocational training or retraining, placement, and follow-up.

Retirement

One test of the importance of work in our lives is found in the activities of retired people. Less than 20 percent of males drawing social security retired to enjoy leisure. Almost three-fourths of the retirements were involuntary: either the employer retires the worker or he or she is forced to retire by poor health. "Most . . . returned to work whenever their health permitted it, and they could obtain employment" (14, p. 3). With increasing social security benefits, retirement is slightly more palatable. Studies during the forties and fifties found less than 6 percent retiring to enjoy leisure and almost 90 percent being retired involuntarily.

Restriction on Job Entry

Formal or informal restrictions of many types keep certain people from entering most prestigious occupations. Some restrictions are imposed by the teaching-learning process itself: the length of training time required to enter many professions discourages some potential entrants. The four or more years required to complete most apprenticeships also keeps people out. Other people are eliminated by requirements of good high school grades, high test scores, or absence of criminal records. If these restrictions help to insure successful completion of the training program or success on the job, they may be justified. If they do not have a relationship to occupational success, they should be removed. For youth, the most exasperating requirement is that they must have had previous experience in the work to be performed. One cannot get experience without working, and one is not allowed to work without experience. It is this barrier that vocational education most successfully removes.

Women and Work

Of every ten women, nine work for pay at some time during their lives, and the average length of time they work is twenty-five years. Over half of the working women are married, and two-thirds are in white-collar jobs. All of these figures have increased very rapidly, many of them threefold in the last fifty years. Employment of women in clerical jobs has increased sevenfold during this same period. In contrast, the proportion of women who work in domestic service has dropped from 28 to 5 percent (8, p. 52; 12, pp. xiii, 61). These changes have come about in part because of cultural changes which make it permissible for women to work. Another important factor is the increased vocational competence of female high school graduates. By far the majority are in business and commercial programs. This undoubtedly is related to the fact that 70 percent of the female high school graduates who do not go to college are working in clerical occupations. Nevertheless, women still do not have nearly as many opportunities for occupational choice as do men. Half of all women workers are in eight occupations, and 75 percent are in only twenty occupations. Half of the women workers are in occupations where 75 percent of the workers are women. Compared to men, only a third as many women belong to unions, and they are far less likely to be supervisors or skilled workers. (8, p. 52 ff.)

The high proportion of women who work outside the home causes problems in the home. While the culture permits women to work for pay, it also expects them to continue most of their responsibilities for work in the home. When their children are young, many women stop work outside the home. This is due in part to the increased work load imposed by the young children and in part to pressure from society, which feels that the woman should give children her full attention at least until they begin school. But additional children also bring additional financial burdens, and a second paycheck is usually needed by the family. This leads many women to endure a period of combined work for pay and child care for which they are not at all prepared. Even without young children in the home, the task of the married female worker is enormous. She still is expected to carry two jobs simultaneously and to subordinate her career ambitions to those of her husband. This suggests that both men and women need vocational education not only for wage earning, but for the dual role of wage earner and homemaker. This requires substantial changes in traditional homemaking courses, and these changes are occurring very slowly since many such courses still assume that the woman will not be employed outside the home. Until our culture changes further, vocational education for many women should be for wage-earning occupations that are available in almost every community. Otherwise, if the wife moves with her husband, she may be forced to accept employment in unskilled work which will contribute little to the family income or to her own personal satisfaction.

Learning on the Job

Sociologists are very interested in how outsiders become members of existing groups. Before a person can become a member of a work group, he or she must acquire both technical and social skills. Effective vocational education will provide part of each, but those skills which are unique to a particular work group can only be learned on the job. Obsolete vocational instruction may actually hamper graduates as they seek to be accepted by the group. Vocational educators are well aware of the need for up-to-date technical skills, including knowledge of time-saving shortcuts and methods of working safely. But they often overlook the need to provide instruction in social skills.

The most common method of teaching these social skills on-the-job is through *horseplay*. The new worker is told to perform an impossible task, is sent for a nonexistent tool, or made to look foolish in some other way, which convinces him or her that acceptance by the group is highly desirable. The worker is taught what constitutes a good day's work and is expected to do neither more nor less, learns which people have views acceptable to the group, which must be listened to politely, but then ignored, and which must be pointedly ignored. He or she learns those to whom to speak frankly and those to be mislead. Very often there are only subtle clues to identify a correct action, but the penalties of an incorrect action are swift and often severe. All of this instruction is informal, unplanned, and very time-consuming. This explains in large part why learning an occupation on-the-job frequently takes many years. It also helps to explain why so many studies show that "getting along with others" is at least as important as having technical skills. And it helps to explain why high scores on personality tests have little relationship to job success. If the new worker is lucky, he or she will be taken in hand by an older worker who plays the part of parent and teacher and accelerates the learning of social skills necessary for group acceptance. This is done through direct instruction, rather than through the more common method of trial, error, and punishment.

The vocational teacher, like the all too rare parent-like fellow employee, can smooth the path of the new graduate by providing direct instruction in the social skills of work in a particular occupational field. Since the vocational graduate may go to work in any one of a variety of groups, he or she will have to learn on-the-job the characteristics of a particular group. But a very large part of the social skills of work are common throughout an occupational field and can be learned in advance.

As was pointed out earlier, most vocational course content concentrates exclusively on technical skills and pays little attention to the social skills of work. Even if the course outline includes provision for teaching social skills, it is almost essential that the teacher have recent, direct personal contact with the occupation in order to provide effective instruction in these skills. Many clues to correct social action in the work group are so subtle that a person who does not know them intimately may teach incorrectly. Fortunately, work social groups are quite similar to student social groups in the vocational education laboratory, and students can and do learn from each other. Many of these learnings cannot take place, however, in the standard classroom. It is very likely that much of the effectiveness of preparatory vocational education is due to the setting provided for learning group social skills. This setting is rarely provided in nonvocational curricula.

Job Satisfaction

The extent to which workers are satisfied with their jobs varies strikingly by occupation. The higher the prestige of the job, the greater the satisfaction usually reported by the workers. But most workers are satisfied in even the least prestigious jobs. For example, the typical semiskilled worker finds a rhythm to the work which is very satisfying. It is fortunate that people like different types of jobs, or the work of the world would never get done. There is a tendency for professional workers (who do most of the writing about jobs) either to romanticize less glamorous work or, more frequently, to assume that because the writer would not like repetitive work, no one else would like it either. Such writers frequently make the mistake of comparing the typical worker of today with the artist-craftsman of medieval times. It would be more accurate to compare the job satisfactions of today's employee with the 90 percent of medieval workers who were serfs.

Most people like jobs best if they have little direct supervision and have contact both on and off the job with other people in the same line of work. The least satisfied workers are those in service occupations and those managers who work for others. The dissatisfaction of managers is so great (31 percent) that it results in job satisfaction for all white-collar workers being lower than that for blue-collar workers. This is in marked contrast to the high job satisfaction for professionals, sales personnel, and skilled and semiskilled workers (13, pp. 191–98). The best explanation of this comes from Crozier (4) who found that managers had low job satisfaction because they were not in a position to control their own destiny or to affect the direction of their work group. This contradicts the conventional wisdom which sees managers as having great power and considerable satisfaction from the use of this power.

Ethnic and religious orientation is strongly related to work attitudes (15, p. 25), and job satisfaction is related to school curriculum. All studies report graduates of the high school vocational curricula to have higher job satisfaction than graduates of other curricula who do not go on to college. The most likely reason for this was also noted by Crozier (4, pp. 100–11). He found that in a highly bureaucratic work organization the maintenance workers had high job satisfaction, with production workers being less satisfied, and supervisors being most dissatisfied. He attributed this to the fact that bureaucracy sharply limits the decision-making opportunities of all except the technically trained. In a factory where the chief value is to keep the product flow moving, the technically trained personnel are the only ones who have options. While they are under heavy pressure to restore production from a broken down production line, they know they are needed, and all other employees recognize their importance. Bureaucrats are not the only people who defer to technically trained workers. Homemakers and deans treat plumbers and professors with kid gloves. Vocational education provides technical competence. It seems likely that as the world of work becomes increasingly complex, technical competence is going to be increasingly valued, and this will lead to continued high job satisfaction.

REFERENCES

1. Bendix, Rinehard. *Work and Authority in Industry.* New York: John Wiley & Sons, Inc., 1956.
2. Clark, Robert E. "Psychosis, Income and Occupational Prestige." *American Journal of Sociology* 54 (March 1949):433–40.
3. Combs, Janet, and Cooley, William W. "Dropouts: In High School and After School." *American Educational Research Journal* 5, no. 3:343–63.

4. Crozier, Michael. *The Bureaucratic Phenomenon.* Chicago: The University of Chicago Press, 1964.
5. DeGrazia, Sebastian. *Of Time, Work and Leisure.* New York: Anchor Books, Doubleday & Company, Inc., 1964.
6. Entwistle, Harold. *Education, Work and Leisure.* New York: Humanities Press, 1970.
7. Kerr, Clark et al. *Industrialism and Industrial Man.* New York: Oxford University Press, Galaxy Edition, 1964.
8. Levitan, Sar, and Johnston, William. *Work Is Here To Stay, Alas.* Salt Lake City: Olympus Publishing Co., 1973.
9. Lipset, Seymour M. et al. "Job Plans and Entry into the Labor Market." *Social Forces* 33 (1955):224–32.
10. Lipset, Seymour M., and Bendix, Reinhard. "Social Mobility and Occupational Career Plans." *American Journal of Sociology* 57 (1952):366–74, 494–504.
11. Mays, Arthur B. *Principles and Practices of Vocational Education.* New York: McGraw-Hill Book Company, 1948.
12. Miller, Delbert, and Form, William. *Industrial Sociology.* New York: Harper & Row, Publishers, 1964.
13. Morse, Nancy C., and Weiss, R.S. "The Function and Meaning of Work and the Job." *American Sociological Review* 20 (1955):191–98.
14. Wentworth, Edna C. *Employment After Retirement.* Washington, D.C.: U.S. Government Printing Office, HEW 68-5, 1968.
15. *Youth and the Meaning of Work.* Washington, D.C.: U.S. Department of Labor, Manpower Research Monograph No. 32, 1974.

Psychological Foundations

The educational philosopher is most concerned about what should be taught, but the psychologist is concerned with *how* it should be taught if everyone is to learn and how to determine what has and has not been learned. Knowledge is seldom acquired by presenting the student with a great mass of information, even if it is important information. And if the knowledge is not learned and retained, education has not taken place. These statements sound trite, but a large proportion of high school and college teachers act as if all that they need to do is to lecture, and learning will automatically take place. Vocational educators seldom make this mistake, though they may err in the opposite direction and overteach by insisting on repetition which goes on well after the concept or skill has been thoroughly learned. Either type of error leads to educational inefficiency. The psychologist offers help in improving the efficiency of both teaching and learning by pointing out the importance of the process of instruction and the need for adaptation to the learner's individual characteristics.

The Process of Learning

Perhaps the best statement of the relationship of psychology to teaching and learning is provided by Cronbach (3, pp. 3–28). Psychology gives the teacher new viewpoints which help him or her to (1) design instruction which is most likely to aid each student's learning, (2) determine whether learning has occurred, and (3) redesign instruction to ensure that learning occurs. Gagné has defined learning as ". . . a change in human disposition or capability, which can be retained, and which is not simply ascribable to the process of growth" (5, p. 5). We decide whether or not learning has occurred by observing changes in behavior before and after the student has been taught (by a teacher or by a situation likely to promote learning). Teachers often think of learning only in terms of improved performance, but poor performance can also be learned, and much of learning affects interests and values, which in turn can affect performance. Interests, values, and performance are closely related, with changes in any one of these having sharp effects on the others. We are more interested in and value more highly those areas in which we perform well. This seems to be a prime reason why students who regularly fail in academic subjects often take a completely different attitude toward school after success in vocational education.

We learn through our senses (including our kinesthetic sense) and thus modify the chains of nerve activity in our central nervous system. This leads to a changed pattern of muscle action in response to future stimuli. This pattern of action is called *behavior,* and the effects of behavior are called *performance.* Most experimental study of the learning process has been done on animals, especially rats. This has led to great emphasis on trial-and-error learning and conditioned response learning. Both are very important for rats but relatively unimportant in human learning. The first serious work on human learning was the study of how we learn nonsense syllables, which were used because they were not known before the experiment began, while syllables like JIG or NAN probably would have been known by some but not all students. If some students had had this prior knowledge, it would have been difficult to determine how much had been learned during the experiment.

A great deal is now known about how we learn nonsense syllables. Unfortunately, this type of learning is relatively unimportant in real life, and we now know that the way we learn *meaningful* material is very different from the way we learn nonsense material (3). Regardless of the learning conditions, meaningful material is always learned faster and retained longer than nonsense material. Many teachers overlook the fact that material which appears meaningful to them may seem nonsensical to the student. In this case, it is learned slowly and retained for only a short time, just as is material which appears to be nonsense to both teacher and learner. One of the chief values of vocational education is the fact that it can change material which some students consider nonsense into relevant and meaningful material.

The generalization that meaningful material is more easily learned than nonsense material is about the only generalization that can be made about all types of learning, though psychologists, like educational philosophers, have been searching for a single pattern to explain a wide variety of events. (It has been stated that learning requires readiness, motivation, and that one type of learning affects another, but it appears that these are only different ways of expressing the desirability of meaningfulness.)

It is the job of the teacher to provide the external conditions which facilitate learning. This sounds simple, but it is not, for these conditions are different for each learner and must be modified, even for a single student, with each new learning acquired by that student. The conditions are also different for each type of learning. The discovery of this fact by Gagné (5) made a major contribution to the psychology of learning. He identified eight types of learning, ranging from responses to signals to complex problem solving, and he specified the conditions of learning for each type. If a person attempts to teach concepts, principles, and problem solving in the same way he or she teaches signal learning, stimulus-response learning, chaining, and other simple types of learning, the results will not be good. The student will probably learn the *words* which state the concept but will not learn the real meaning of the concept. "Words facilitate the development of concepts only when the ideas they represent are understood. Verbalization without understanding is likely to hinder the learning of concepts. . . . The ability to verbalize a concept is not a guarantee that the learner can apply or relate the concept and language" (10, p. 10). Too often teachers accept the words instead of being certain that the concept itself has been learned.

It has long been known that people forget certain simple types of learning quickly but remember quite well the more complex types of learning. The reason is that those people who really learn the more complex types of content do this because that content is meaningful. On the other hand, the simple types of learning can be acquired by almost everyone, but unless they are meaningful or used often, they are forgotten.

Gagné (5, p. 96) points out that *chains* (sequences) of motor behavior are not forgotten easily and can be relearned very rapidly. He cites examples of swimming, bicycle riding, and playing a musical instrument. Similar motor chains form a major portion of the content of many vocational courses, e.g., typing, manipulating a welding torch, making biscuits or a buttonhole. Many educational philosophers advocate postponing specific vocational education until just prior to the time it will be used on the ground that much of its content is apt to be forgotten. Similarly the evidence from psychology suggests that it would be appropriate to postpone instruction on specific factual information until just before the student is going to use it.

Active Participation

Occasionally a person can learn a complex sequence of responses such as typing by trial and error. More often he or she learns imperfectly, after a long period of time, and the bad habits acquired can interfere with later learning of more efficient methods. The learning of skills usually occurs more efficiently if the learner sees a demonstration of the skill from a teacher or from a film prior to performing the action. The more complex the skill to be learned, the more important it is to have competent instruction to accompany practice.

Knowledge of Results

If students know how well they are doing and what the strong and weak points of their performances are two beneficial results occur: they spend time learning those things that really count and their motivation for learning is increased because they know they are not wasting time. Knowledge of results works best when it is immediate rather than delayed, and it is most important when the students set goals for themselves which are difficult to achieve (8).

Vocational education laboratories and cooperative education training stations offer a variety of opportunities for feedback (knowledge of results which leads to corrective action). But the typical vocational education lecture or discussion provides as little immediate feedback as the typical academic class, often because the instructor is unaware of its importance.

Vocational education has an advantage over many subject matter fields, however, because its goals are clear to the student and are related to the real world. It seems reasonable that knowledge of results would likely be of little benefit unless the subject matter appears important to the student or unless he or she is one of those people who find feedback useful because they see learning as a game which is important for its own sake.

Individual Differences

Perhaps the greatest contribution of psychology has been its study of individual differences—the ways in which individuals differ from each other. Other disciplines accept the fact of individual differences but often proceed to treat all members of a group as if they were the same. Even educators do this, though they ought to know better. Individuals differ in a large variety of ways: in social class, intelligence, motivation, maturation, physical characteristics, and so on. Since the ability to learn is noticeably affected by most of these factors, one would expect that educators would be experts in identifying these differences and in providing a learning environment which makes the most of them. Unfortunately, however, we know surprisingly little about how individual differences and learning affect each other. Until psychology can tell us more about this process, the safest course of action seems to be to provide a wide variety of teaching-learning opportunities in the hope that one or more of them will be effective for each individual.

The academic subjects have in common a very high emphasis on verbal ability. They are usually taught in ways which emphasize memorization, verbal fluency (including reading skill), interest in knowledge for its own sake, and postponement of rewards. The classroom setting, in which they are most often taught, rewards those who sit still, pay attention to symbols (rather than to objects), and have a long span of attention. Some students do very well with these tasks in these settings; others do not.

Laboratory courses are effective with some students who do not learn well in a classroom. Nonacademic courses such as art, music, physical education, industrial arts, and vocational education emphasize environments for learning which are markedly different from the academic classroom or laboratory. Equally important is the fact that they emphasize learning tasks which are attractive to some students who are not at all successful in their academic courses.

Some students, of course, enjoy and excel in almost any learning task in any school setting, for great abilities in one area tend to be accompanied by great abilities in many other areas. We are all familiar with the athlete who is an "A" student in music, the practical arts, and academic studies. Poor nutrition and some types of brain damage hamper performance in most types of learning. But a large proportion of students fall between these two extremes. They learn some things well, but not others. They may have physical problems (color blindness, slow maturation, low metabolic rates) which interfere with some types of learning, but not with others, or have special interests and motivations which cause them to succeed in some fields but fail in others. Even worse is a school which offers a narrow program which rewards only those students who excel in verbal learning, who enjoy working with symbols instead of with people or things, and who work well in the classroom setting. The fully comprehensive school provides a variety of paths to school success and capitalizes on individual differences rather than trying to force all individuals into a common mold.

Social Class and Learning in the School

We have discovered that social class in one of the most important individual differences affecting school learning. "In the United States, [during the nineteenth century] . . . the public schools quickly became the common school, attended by representatives of all classes . . . excluding only those upper-class children in private schools, those poor who went to no schools, and Indians and Southern Negroes, who were without schools." (2, p. 9). In most other countries, however, there have been two parallel systems of education, one designed for lower class students, and the other attended by upper class and middle class children. This situation continues to the present day, though reformers of education in most countries recognize that it is undesirable and often view the American comprehensive school as an ideal.

One of the goals for a dual school system is ". . . that of maintaining the existing social order—a system . . . designed to prevent a wholesale challenge by the children of the working class to the positions held for children of the middle [and upper] classes (2, p. 10). The truly comprehensive high school rejects this goal and substitutes for it a goal of opportunity for vertical social mobility. It attempts to achieve this goal by two means: (1) exposure to and choice from a variety of school curricula which have different social class outcomes, and (2) contact with students from a variety of social classes, with the expectation that students will learn from one another that social classes exist and that upward social mobility is usually desirable. Obviously, a school which offers a narrow range of curricula cannot use the first of these methods, and a school which is segregated by social class cannot use the second.

The desirability of giving students a choice from a broad range of curricula has long been recognized in this country, but the undesirability of segregation on the basis of social class has only recently been recognized. The most complete documentation of the effects of segregation by social class came about by accident. Coleman (2) set out to discover the effects of low levels of school expenditures and high proportions of inexperienced teachers on the achievement of black students. He found that these had much smaller effects than he had thought, but he found that schools which had a heavy majority of students from low socioeconomic levels almost invariably had low achievement levels, even when other variables were held equal. Project TALENT data showed that while students of every social class are enrolled in vocational education, lower class students predominate. The establishment of separate schools for vocational education therefore tends to mean establishment of schools which segregate students by social class. This, in turn, is almost certain to result in lowered achievement.

Intelligence

> . . . the word "intelligence" has *two* valuable meanings. One is (A) an *innate potential,* the capacity for development, a fully innate property that amounts to the possession of a good brain and a good neural metabolism. The second is (B) the functioning of a brain in which development has gone on. . . . There are then two determinants of intellectual growth: a *completely necessary* innate potential (intelligence A), and a *completely necessary* stimulating environment. It is not to the point to ask which is most important . . . given a perfect environment, the inherited constitution will set the pace; given the heredity of a genius, the environment will do so. (6, pp. 294, 302)

Intelligence tests measure A and B combined and are not able to separate the two factors which determine test results. Moreover, the intelligence test "only purports to measure verbal ability and to predict school performance—not ability or performance in the mechanical and social areas" (1, p. 59). Indeed, the only reason such tests are successful in predicting school performance is that almost all school activities emphasize verbal ability.

For many years psychologists felt that the hereditary aspects of intelligence were all important. They noted that intelligence test scores were relatively constant throughout school careers and attributed this to the influence of innate potential. They neglected to note that each child's environment changed little during his or her school career. More recently it has been found that the intelligence test scores of children of immigrants were much higher than the test scores of their mothers and fathers. Assuming adequate nutrition, the scores should have been about the same. It has also been found that very young children from poor homes gain considerably in measured intelligence when they are placed in a stimulating school environment at an early age. This has led to the conclusion that

> The IQ can be trusted as an index of intelligence A only when the social background of the (people) compared are identical; and this adds up to the proposition that we cannot in any rigorous sense measure a (person's) innate endowment, for no two social backgrounds are identical. . . . Intelligence in sense B is a different matter. We know, beyond dispute, that the adolescent with generally low intelligence-test scores, whether Negro, poor white American, or foreigner, is a poor prospect for college training, or training as a mechanic, or Army officer, or dress designer. . . . To be a bank manager, an airline pilot, a mathematician, a secretary, or a surgeon requires a certain common conceptual development that must occur in this or a closely related culture, and in childhood mainly; and intelligence tests on the whole

can provide a rather good index of the extent to which that development has occurred. (6, pp. 300–301)

Vocational education is, of course, much less interested in intelligence A than in B, for it can have no effect on the former. Its effects on the latter are probably minimal. Early childhood education offers promise of modifying B, but vocational education comes too late in life to change intelligence appreciably. Because intelligence is measured by tests which are largely verbal, it has even less chance of changing *measured* intelligence. This leaves vocational education with the necessity of living with the intelligence its clients bring to it, but this acceptance of intelligence can be done in one of two ways. The first way is to screen potential students out on the basis of intelligence test scores. There are three methods of accomplishing this screening.

1. If there are more applicants for a vocational education program than can be accommodated, intelligence test scores are sometimes used, together with other factors such as previous grades, to screen out the less able. This results in a reputation for a program with high standards of admission and increases the proportion of graduates eagerly sought by employers.
2. A slightly more sophisticated use of intelligence tests is commonly employed in training within business and industry. On the basis of past experience, it is often found that trainees who score above a certain level on intelligence tests have relatively high turnover and accident rates (possibly due to boredom). On the other hand, trainees who score below a certain level are less likely to complete the training program successfully. This leads to selecting trainees whose test scores fall in a band between high and low scores.
3. A related use of intelligence test scores is found in an organization which must accept trainees having a broad range of intelligence and must supply specified numbers of vocational graduates in each of a variety of occupations. On the basis of past experience, we determine which programs require very high scores for successful completion and which can be completed successfully by trainees with lower intelligence test scores. Test scores are then used to distribute the available trainees among the vocational programs, with each program being geared to turn out the required number of graduates. Similar techniques are followed in countries with rather fully planned economies.

These uses of intelligence test scores can be justified if the goal of the vocational program is to produce trained workers to meet labor market needs. They are not justified if the goal is to enhance individual options. Instead, potential trainees should be counseled on the basis of the probability of their success in the occupation chosen. If trainees decide that they want to pursue a vocational program even though they have only a 20 percent chance of success in the occupational field, they should be permitted to do so, for they might be among the twenty in a hundred who would succeed.

The screening of potential vocational education students on the basis of intelligence test scores should be approached with care, for there is little relationship between intelligence and occupational success. This is not to say that intelligence is not important in vocational success. There are three ways in which it is important: (1) for each occupation there is probably a minimum intelligence level below which success is unlikely (but above which intelligence has little effect on success), (2) promotability is enhanced by intelligence, and (3) intelligence is most clearly related to success in occupations requiring verbal skill (but even here the relationship is not close). The basic mistake, which is too often made, is to assume that because the *average* intelligence varies widely between occupations, the *minimum* intelligence required for success is the same as the average. Obviously this is not true.

A second and more satisfying way for the vocational educator to live with the relatively fixed intelligence of students is to recognize that no one begins to approach the limits which his or her intelligence sets for his or her ability to learn. Sound education can enable the individual to approach this limit much more closely than possible without this learning environment.

Motivation

Psychologists agree that motivation is extremely important in determining what an individual will or will not learn. But despite intense study, they have produced surprisingly little that aids the teacher either in recognizing existing motivations (so that teaching can be structured to capitalize on these motivations) or in changing motivations (so that a student will want to learn essential ideas and skills). Perhaps the most helpful ideas have come from Abraham Maslow who has suggested that there is a hierarchy of human needs, with each of the lower level needs having to be satisfied before a need at a higher level is effective in motivating a person to want to learn. From low to high, he lists needs as: (1) physiological, (2) safety, (3) belongingness and love, (4) importance, respect, self-esteem, and independence, and (5) information, understanding, beauty, and self-actualization (9, p. 80).

Most schooling assumes that the first four of these needs have been met outside the school and that every individual is therefore ready for learning based on needs for information, understanding, beauty, and self-actualization. This assumption may be true for many middle or upper class students for the moment, but many students are concerned about the future. They wonder what type of education will satisfy their physiological needs when their parents no longer provide financial support. Preparation for a vocation will meet their physiological needs and satisfy needs for safety, belongingness, importance, respect, self-esteem, and independence as well. With some prospect of these needs being satisfied through vocational education or through college preparatory education, they are in a position to begin to be concerned about their higher needs.

The future is not all that concerns students. While they are in school, many students, especially those from lower class homes and homes with one or more parents absent, have unmet needs within Maslow's first four categories and hence cannot be motivated by the fifth category. Indeed, some students even have unmet physiological needs, for they are hungry, tired, poorly clothed, and inadequately housed. Such students are likely to view academic schooling in particular as being irrelevant. On the other hand, vocational education, especially cooperative education with its pay for useful work performed, offers a way to meet certain physiological needs; its small classes and work teams offer a sense of importance and belongingness; its emphasis on nonverbal content provides respect and self-esteem for the student with poor verbal skills, and its individualized instruction provides independence. With these needs met, the student may be ready for both vocational and nonvocational instruction designed to provide information, understanding, beauty, and self-actualization.

The need for safety (as Maslow defines it) is the only primary need to which vocational education does not make substantial contributions. Vocational education segregated by social class may indeed heighten the student's concern for personal safety, because it may put a student into an environment where threats to his or her safety from lower class students are much more common.

Two ways in which the school can modify the motivations of its students are by allowing the student to receive (at least for part of each day) instruction which appears relevant to needs and by providing extrinsic rewards for desired behavior. Properly designed vocational education appears relevant in its own right, and as the student learns that basic skills are required in the world of work, vocational education lends relevance to the study of basic skills. Both of these provide intrinsic motivation. The study of operant conditioning has emphasized the importance of extrinsic motivation and has suggested ways in which it can be provided in the school. There are moral questions which inhibit teachers from using operant conditioning extensively to modify student motivations and behavior. Vocational education is relatively unique in providing both intrinsic motivation and a considerable amount of perfectly natural extrinsic motivation through such rewards as the take-home project, pay (in cooperative education programs), rank in the student personnel structure, and awards by out-of-school organizations.

Physical Maturation

We know very little about the relationship of physical maturation to performance in vocational education. We do know that adolescent girls mature physically about two years sooner than boys. We also know that girls perform better than boys in general education and in the few areas of vocational education which encourage co-education. Fuzak (4, p. 53) found a high correlation between physical maturity, as measured by hand dynamometer scores and boys' success in performance tests in junior high school industrial arts. We do not know whether this relationship holds for girls and for other types of subject matter, nor do we know whether it holds in the senior high school and junior college. Since a few boys (though almost no girls) are still physically immature at age eighteen, it seems likely that physical maturity might be a factor in vocational education success. Certainly we need more information on these points.

If physical maturation is important for both sexes and for a broad variety of subject matter, the typical organization of a vocational education program would seem to be particularly unfortunate. Usually, vocational education, like history, is presented in chronological order. Those skills and processes discovered first are taught first. This means that skills requiring a high degree of manipulative dexterity are taught early in the course, while the operation of machines, which requires less manipulative skill, is taught later. If physical maturation is important to success, this order should be reversed.

Physical Characteristics

The ability to see small details, distinguish colors, hear high pitched sounds, lift heavy weights, be able to stand or sit for long periods of time, and other physical characteristics are important to success in certain occupations. Individual differences in these characteristics are rarely measured before enrollment in vocational education courses. So it is possible, for example, for a student who is partially color-blind to complete a year of instruction in printing and to be dismissed from the program as unsuitable without knowing what caused the difficulty in matching colors. Each student should be informed about any physical characteristics which will be handicapping in an occupation and be advised of the probability that the handicap will be serious.

Personnel Selection

The traditional way of selecting students and employees is the interview. More than fifty years ago psychologists proved that this is an unreliable means of choosing people. Even worse, it gives complete freedom to the interviewer's biases. All the applicant knows after most interviews is whether or not he or she has been selected; there is no indication of why. Consequently, interviews have been criticized because they were used easily to exclude people of a particular race, sex, age, or religion. Nevertheless, interviews continue to be used for personnel selection purposes, in part because they are quick and cheap since interviewers have confidence that their own judgment is sound (even if they admit that other interviewers are inaccurate) and in part because of legal problems in the use of selection devices other than interviews.

The principal legal problem with using tests and personal records for personnel selection is that each test used must have validity. In other words, the people who score well on that test must be shown to be the best performers on the task for which they are being selected. This seems to be a reasonable criterion, but many of the tests used cannot meet it.

Tests may be roughly classified as aptitude and achievement tests, interest tests or inventories, personality and attitude tests or inventories, and proficiency tests. All of them have definite weaknesses. Aptitude can only be measured in terms of ability to achieve success on the test which is used. This in turn is based on past experience in the culture for which the test was built. Consequently, test results usually underestimate the ability of an individual who comes from a different culture. Interest test results are influenced by factors surrounding the testing situation. Applicants for a clerical job who take an interest test are likely to show higher clerical interests than they would if they were applying for a scientific job. Personality and attitude test results are seldom related to success on the job, in spite of the often repeated claim that personality is a major factor in job success. Proficiency tests are difficult to administer if proficiency involves skills which cannot be measured with paper and pencil. Despite these difficulties tests can be very useful, especially in two situations: (1) where a *group* is being screened for admission to training or to work and (2) where an *individual* is sincerely interested in learning more about personal interests, strengths, and weaknesses.

Screening for Admission

If more people have applied than can be accepted for training or for employment, some method must be used for rejecting some and accepting others. Interviews, past records of success in similar situations, and test results are the most frequent devices used. A test which has relatively poor predictive ability (predictive validity) may still be useful in improving the batting average of the person who must decide who will be employed. Gross errors can be made in individual cases, but if the proportion of successful employees is increased by use of test results, the person is likely to continue using these tests.

The problem of the vocational teacher and counselor is more difficult. They must be concerned about both the accepted and rejected individuals. Most tests having sufficient predictive validity for use with groups are not sufficiently accurate to provide assurance that each individual student is being treated fairly. Usually all that can be said is that test results indicate the *probability* of success or failure in a particular training program.

The decision as to what should be maximized by the process of selection of trainees is extremely important but is rarely considered. The success of a vocational education program is usually measured in terms of the success of the graduates. To maximize the success of graduates, the only students who should be admitted to the program are those who do not need the program. This technique has been used for years in some colleges; only those students are admitted as freshmen who already have the knowledge possessed by graduates of most colleges. This type of screening procedure assures the graduates' success even if the educational program adds nothing to their competence. Similarly, in vocational education some programs admit only students who have abilities and attitudes which virtually guarantee success in employment, even if the vocational program does nothing for them. From an educational standpoint, this type of evaluation and student selection is unacceptable. "Value added by education" should be the criterion of the program's success, and students should be selected who will gain most from the program, regardless of the level at which they start. We still know little about methods of selecting those who will profit most from instruction, and this must continue to be given high research priority in psychology and vocational education.

Student Interests, Strengths, and Weaknesses

Fortunately, more is known about counseling students who want to learn about themselves. Here the emphasis is on helping the individual to help him/herself. The first step is to help each individual to understand his or her interests and abilities. Interest tests are more useful in this situation than in screening for admission because the individual is free of immediate pressures. If the students have definite vocational goals in mind, tests can be selected to include their probability of success. If they do not have definite vocational goals, their interests can form the basis for selecting educational experiences which will help them explore occupations related to those interests.

The process of counseling individual students requires skill which is achieved only after specific training. The vocational teacher can, of course, provide answers to questions which lie within his or her field of expertise. Perhaps the best advice which psychologists provide to the untrained vocational counselor is to avoid telling people what occupations they should or should not enter. The vocational teacher can best work in cooperation with trained counselors, where occupational knowledge and knowledge acquired about the students can supplement their skills in counseling. Such cooperation assumes that the teacher has some familiarity with counseling techniques and also assumes the availability of fully trained counselors. Too often the ratio of students to counselors is so high and the availability of *well-trained* counselors so low that even the students who ask for assistance cannot be accommodated. Hopefully the expansion of career education programs will help to increase the availability of capable counselors to aid all teachers in providing aid to students and to help all students to understand themselves better.

REFERENCES

1. Ausubel, David P. *Psychological Aspects of Curriculum Evaluation.* Paper presented to the National Seminar for Vocational Education Research. Washington, D.C.: National Science Teachers Association, 1964.
2. Coleman, James S. "The Concept of Equality of Educational Opportunity." *Harvard Educational Review* 38 (1968):1–22.
3. Cronbach, Lee J. *Educational Psychology,* 2d ed. New York: Harcourt, Brace & World, Inc., 1963.
4. Fuzak, John A. *The Role of Physical Maturation in Determining the Ability of Junior High School Boys to Perform Complex Finger Coordinative Activities in Industrial Arts, and an Index to Level of Ability.* Chicago: American Technical Society, 1958.
5. Gagné, Robert M. *The Conditions of Learning.* New York: Holt, Rinehart & Winston, Inc., 1965.
6. Hebb, Donald O. *The Organization of Behavior.* New York: John Wiley & Sons, Inc., 1949.
7. Klausmeier, Herbert J. "Psychomotor Abilities and Skills." In *Learning and Human Abilities.* New York: Harper & Row, Publishers, 1961.
8. Locke, E.A. "A Closer Look at Level of Aspiration as a Training Procedure." *Journal of Applied Psychology* 50 (1966):417–20.
9. Maslow, Abraham H. *Motivation and Personalty.* New York: Harper & Row, Publishers, 1954.
10. NSTA Curriculum Committee. *Theory into Action.* Washington, D.C.: National Science Teachers Association, 1964.

part III

Structural Foundations of Vocational Education

10

Introduction

Vocational development is a field of study which draws upon the social science disciplines. It serves as the basis for vocational guidance and career education, which, together, can form the foundation of vocational education. Historically, of course, vocational education preceded each of the three because in its early days vocational education was coping empirically with immediate problems that had to be solved with or without a theoretical base. Consequently, until perhaps the 1950s, vocational education contributed more to an understanding of vocational development than it received in return. Such a relationship is by no means rare. Practice often precedes and guides theory. As theory becomes more structured, however, it points out inconsistencies in practice and makes it more rational. Before vocational educators can be guided by these principles they must understand them. This understanding leads to improved practice and, in turn, to improvements in theory.

Vocational development attempts to predict and explain vocational behavior. Vocational guidance uses the principles of vocational development to help individuals learn to make wise occupational choices. Vocational guidance can be and is provided by many sorts of people, including parents, peers, and educational personnel of all types, but it is best provided by people who have been prepared for this role and who are allowed time to provide it. It can be provided through individual or group counseling, through work experience, and as a part of formal instruction.

Career education attempts to structure the process of vocational guidance by providing systematic ways of helping people to become aware of and to explore their own interests and talents and the settings in which work is to be performed. Career education goes beyond vocational guidance by providing career preparation.

In its broadest sense, vocational education is identical to career preparation, but in the narrower sense used in this book vocational education is a part of career preparation. Although vocational education is not concerned directly with preparing people for the twenty percent of paid work which is considered professional, vocational educators must be aware of the problems and methods of professional education. Not only are many of these problems and methods similar to those encountered by vocational educators, but the two fields increasingly exchange students.

Vocational educators also need to understand the principles of career awareness and career exploration. Ideally all students should have received instruction in these two parts of career education prior to entering vocational education, so vocational educators should be aware of what these students have learned previously. Even under the best conditions, however, many students will enroll in vocational education needing substantial additional opportunities for career awareness and exploration. This can be provided by the vocational educator. Changes in individual interests and aptitudes combined with changes in the world of work will make further career awareness and exploration activities a continuing necessity for most adults. The vocational teacher is often the best person to meet these adult needs.

When we add all these reasons to the fact that many schools expect vocational educators to assume leadership roles in career education, it is apparent why vocational educators need a firm grounding in vocational development, vocational guidance, and career education. Together, these three fields increasingly provide the structural foundations for vocational education.

GUIDANCE AND COUNSELING

11

Vocational Development

The term *vocational development* (frequently used interchangably with the term *career development*) embraces a body of speculation and research which attempts to understand and describe such areas of vocational behavior as the relationship of different kinds of self-characteristics to success in different kinds of learning or work tasks, on what bases people choose occupations, factors affecting different choice-making styles, family and social elements affecting one's understanding and use of information, or exploratory experiences as a basis for planning or occupational preparation. In essence, vocational development includes a comprehensive set of areas and questions pertinent to why vocational behavior is different among individuals, how it comes to be that way, and the importance of such behavior in people's lives. Borow has described vocational development theory and research as "a search for the psychological meaning of vocationally relevant acts (including the exploratory behavior of youth) and of work itself in the human experience" (2).

Because of the complexity of the approaches to describing vocational development, it is useful to separate them into their major emphases for discussion purposes. We will examine five approaches, which typically are labeled *trait-and-factor, decision, sociological, need-drive,* and *developmental.*

Trait-and-Factor Approaches

The trait-and-factor approach is probably most familiar to the vocational educator. Actually this approach is not focused on development but on identifying and describing the factors by which people differ and the degree to which these factors are important in learning or in job performance.

The logic of this approach is that individuals can be conceived of as being comprised of a constellation of traits, e.g., aptitudes, interests, values, psychomotor abilities, energy levels, temperaments, which can be observed and measured. The assumption is that these patterns of personal traits are more or less unique to each individual. The further assumption is that the individual, if he or she understands the personal characteristics possessed, can order these in some priority ranking and choose in accordance with them.

Trait-and-factor approches also assume that different occupations or learning situations can be described in terms of their unique requirements for different combinations or "quantities" of these individual characteristics. In essence, different occupational or educational options can be profiled in terms of those levels of individual behaviors or potential behaviors which are essential to performing whatever is required in such situations. The information used is that which comes from such sources as trade competency examinations, job analysis, occupational aptitude profiles, or work sampling.

Finally, trait-and-factor approaches assume that occupational choice is primarily a function of matching the person's profile of characteristics with that set of occupational or educational requirements most closely related to it. The prediction is that the closer the congruency between the individual characteristics and the requirements of occupational or educational options available, the more likely it is that adjustment and success will result.

Trait-and-factor approaches have been a mainstay of many vocational guidance and employment selection systems since the turn of the twentieth century. They have spurred the development of tests and inventories to assess individual characteristics, the use of occupational information, the creation of predictive systems for assessing the weights or importance of individual traits in the accomplishment of different occupational tasks, and the establishment of counseling systems.

Even though the trait-and-factor approach has had considerable influence on American educational and occupational thought, many critics believe it to be too simplistic and too deterministic. Specifically, many theorists contend that a major limitation of the trait-and-factor approach is its implied assumption that either personal traits or environmental requirements are constant and unchangeable. Some adherents of the trait-and-factor approach tend to behave as though an assessment of an individual's traits at a specific point in life is predictive of all future observations; however, such a position does not take into account the amount of change possible in a person or in educational and occupational requirements over time. Extending the point further, considering individual traits as "fixed effects" tends to underestimate the degree to which many such traits are learned or the degree to which they are latent unless triggered through encouragement and other social stimuli.

Finally, matching individuals and jobs on the basis of an observable fit is seen as overly deterministic unless the person involved is an active participant in the choice. Frequently, one finds that what appears to be the best fit is not valued by the person involved and thus success and adjustment do not result. In such instances, it is not a matter of which is the best literal fit between an individual's characteristics and the requirements of different alternatives but rather how the available choices accord with the particular person's assessments of what such a fit should be.

Regardless of the criticisms or the limitations of the trait-and-factor approach, the informational base about people and the options available to them which this approach requires is an exceedingly important influence upon vocational development. Virtually all of the approaches to vocational development include trait-and-factor information, but the emphases they give to its use vary markedly.

Decision Theory Approaches

Focused somewhat more upon the process of decision making than upon the importance of individual traits or occupational trait requirements, decision approaches have evolved from an original base in economics. The assumption is made that one chooses an educational or occupational goal that will maximize one's gain and minimize one's chance of loss. Obviously what each person values or considers gain or loss is likely to be different in degree and kind. The gain or loss is not confined to money but can be anything of value to a particular person. A given occupation or an educational opportunity might be considered as a means of achieving many different possibilities—among them greater prestige, security, social mobility, leisure time—when compared to another course of action.

The specific notion of a decision approach is that an individual has several possible "alternatives," or courses of action among which to choose. In each of these alternatives certain events can occur. These events have different values to the individual and different likelihoods of occurrence which can be estimated. If each possible event is multiplied by its value to the person and its probability of happening, the person can determine the alternative which is likely to have the greater sum of value to him or her (10).

The expectation in decision theory is that individuals can be helped to choose more rationally by predicting the outcomes of each alternative available as well as the uncertainty and risk each involve. Such a position acknowledges, however, that decision making is based largely on subjective grounds, on what the individual's perceptions of events and alternatives are rather than on what some form of test data or another person would say they are. Given such circumstances, it has become an accepted principle that the kind of information one has and the way he or she uses it will affect decision outcomes.

Bross (4) has argued that information is the required fuel for the decision maker. He suggests that the process of deciding requires a "predictive system" (determining possible alternative actions, outcomes, and probabilities), a "value system" (determining the desirability associated with outcomes) and a "decision criterion" (leading to integration and selection of an appropriate action). Clarke, Gelatt, and Levine (6) contend that the two requirements of good decision making are adequate information and an effective way of analyzing, organizing, and synthesizing this information in order to arrive at a choice. They further suggest that bringing these requirements together means that the individual needs appropriate information in terms of (1) possible alternative actions, (2) possible outcomes of the various actions, (3) the relationships between actions and outcomes, and (4) the individual's relative preference for the different outcomes likely to occur.

The individual's interpretation of different actions and outcomes present at a choice-point involves two other concepts typically included in decision approaches. First is the matter of risk-taking style. People differ in their willingness to cope with ambiguity or uncertainty of outcomes. Some people prefer the security of knowing what they will be paid and that they are likely to have a permanent position rather than the possibility of greater rewards and the unknowns of variety and tenuousness. Second is the matter of investment. Emphasized in this notion is the fact that any choice requires both tangible and intangible investments by the chooser, e.g., capital, prestige, time, tuition, union dues, deferred gratification, which can be deliberately considered and valued.

Finally, decision approaches stress the importance of personal values in choice. Unlike a simple translation of the fit between traits and occupational requirements as the major structure of decision making, the decision approach advocates an active assessment by the individual of the odds faced in any alternative. Such a deliberation is seen as placing personal values at the heart of decision making. Decision making includes the identifying and the defining of one's values: what they are and what they are not, where they appear and where they do not appear (12).

Sociological Approaches

Vocational development theorists have increasingly analyzed risk-taking styles, value differences, information availability, and characteristics of people doing different types of work from a sociological perspective. Such a view is concerned with the nature of the transactions a chooser, or a worker, has with his or her personal environment, e.g., family, community, social class, and the belief systems or values they present.

Borow (3) has identified a number of areas which relate to occupational choice and adjustment and which are essentially sociological in emphasis. They include socioeconomic status, occupational prestige, level of aspiration, level of occupational choice, differences among rural-urban groups, institutional pressures, the influence of parents and other significant people, cultural deprivation, outside work experience, and social trends. Lipsett (13) has observed that the following social factors interact directly with vocational development: social class membership, home influences, school climate, community values, pressure groups, and role perceptions.

A sociological view of vocational development suggests that the narrowness or the breadth of the individual's culture or social class boundaries has much to do with the choices a person is likely to consider, make, or implement. In a sense, the social structure can be seen as a percolator and filter of the kinds of information that gets to individuals occupying different social strata. Basically, the encouragement and the information the poor receive in relation to educational opportunity or occupational alternatives is simply different from that obtained by the middle or upper socioeconomic classes. The sources of information, the models of successful accomplishment of different choices, and the subtle forms of reinforcement to value one goal rather than another vary throughout the continuum of socioeconomic advantagement in the society. Similar differences exist for males and females. While many efforts are being generated to modify these situations, the fact remains that such differences in information and encouragement affect choice making and subsequent work adjustment.

LoCascio (14) has studied continuity-discontinuity in vocational development among many different populations. He described vocational development as continuous, delayed, or impaired based on the richness of one's behavioral repertoire and the incorporation of learning. His findings indicate that the vocational development of those labeled as *disadvantaged* is more likely to be delayed or impaired than is that of their more favored contemporaries. Studies of Appalachian poor whites, inner-city poor blacks and Hispanics, and rural disadvantaged American Indians largely support LoCascio's findings.

It seems clear that if one is to understand the functioning of any given individual's psychological characteristics—traits—it is important to consider the characteristics of the social grouping in which he or she has been born and reared. It is the social context which influences the self-image, the ranking of the personal traits one is likely to use in work, and the alternatives one is likely to know about or consider appropriate.

Thus the sociological perspective addresses the nub of subjective probability mentioned in the previous section on decision approaches. The vocational and, indeed, life preferences of people across social and economic class lines may be similar, but their expectations of being able to achieve such preferences are likely to differ. The individual raised in an environment which does not support planfulnes or commitment to long-range goals or provide knowledge of how to cope effectively with the environment is going to have different aspirations and experience vocational development of a different character from that individual who experiences none of these limitations.

Need-Drive Approaches

Need-drive perspectives on vocational development would contend that occupational choice is a means of satisfying personal needs. Thus, such approaches stress the role of intrinsic psychological motivation in occupational choice more than do the other approaches described thus far. In particular, they contrast with the trait-and-factor approach, which emphasizes observable and measurable behavior (rather than inferred states), to explain the motivations of people to behave as they do.

Advocates of need-drive approaches include the psychoanalytic and self-theorists as well as personality theorists less clearly defined. Perhaps the major assumption of these approaches is that because of differences in personaltiy structure, individuals develop specific needs and seek satisfaction of these needs through occupational choices. It is further assumed that different occupational or, indeed, curricular areas are populated by people of different need or personality type.

A prominent characteristic of need-drive approaches to occupational choice or vocational development is their use of classifications of personality types or needs and the relating of these to gratifications available in different occupations or educational options. Depending upon the particular orientation of the theorist, such classifications have several different emphases.

Those theorists who view vocational behavior through a psychoanalytic lens tend to view work as a sublimation or socially acceptable channeling of specific gratifications remaining from unresolved early problems in psychosexual development. Summarizing the writings of several psychoanalytic writers, Zaccaria (22, p. 29) has suggested connections between need levels and occupations which are socially acceptable, as in the following examples:

Need or Motivational Pattern	*Occupation*
Sadomasochism	Surgeon or butcher
Voyeurism	Photographer
Domination	Teacher
Exhibition	Actor

People of the psychoanalytic persuasion would argue that adult vocations are sought for their instinctual gratifications as need for these is developed in early childhood, particularly the first six years of life.

Partially psychoanalytic and partially self-theory in origin is the need-drive perspective of Anne Roe (16). Her work has three specific aspects that are worthy of note. First, she has adapted the theory of prepotent needs developed by Abraham Maslow to vocational behavior. Maslow (15) arranged human needs into a hierarchy in which he contended that under equal deprivation the lower order, more primitive needs would influence behavior more than the higher order needs. Put somewhat differently, the emergence of higher order needs is contingent upon the relative satisfaction of the lower order needs. In effect this means that if individuals are not sure of where the next meal is coming from, they are likely to choose occupations which will satisfy their physiological needs and their need for a sense of security rather than seek gratification of needs further up the hierarchy. On the other hand, if people can take for granted that lower order needs will be satisfied routinely, they are freer to take risks and seek belongingness, self-esteem, information, beauty, and other higher order psychological gratifications. The hierarchy proposed by Maslow begins with the highest order need, self-actualization, and descends to the most primitive, physiological:

Need for self-actualization
Need for beauty
Need for understanding
Need for information
Need for importance, self-esteem, respect, independence
Need for belongingness and love
Need for safety
Physiological needs (shelter, food, drink). (5)

A second dimension of Roe's work is an emphasis on the effect of child-rearing practices upon adult orientations to or away from people and things. Basically, she speculated that child-rearing environments that were overprotecting, democratic, or rejecting had a tendency to shape the kinds of interactions people have with other people—toward them or not toward them—and with things. These interactions in turn were seen as manifested in adult life in the interest patterns by which people select an occupational family. Thus, if you come from an overprotecting family background, you are likely to seek gratification in work from close relationships with other people, possibly in entertainment or social work. On the other hand, if your child-rearing environment was a rejecting one, it is likely that you will seek adult vocational gratifications in occupations emphasizing work with things. This line of logic led to the third aspect of her work which was a field-and-level conception of occupational families. This conception antedates the current orientation to cluster approaches but has much in common with it.

Specifically, Roe's field-and-level structure was composed of eight fields across a horizontal axis. They included **I** Service, **II** Business Contact, **III** Organization, **IV** Technology, **V** Outdoor, **VI** Science, **VII** General Culture, and **VIII** Arts and Entertainment. Groups I, II, III, VII, and VIII are seen as primarily oriented to people, and groups IV, V, and VI are oriented principally to things. It is assumed that the major variable affecting choice of a group is interest and that the latter is an adult residual of early childhood experiences. On the vertical axis are cited six levels of responsibility, training, or education. They include **1.** Professional and Managerial I, **2.** Professional and Managerial II, **3.** Semiprofessional, small business, **4.** Skilled, **5.** Semiskilled, **6.** Unskilled. It is assumed that the level attained is a function of genetic endowment as reflected in intelligence, education attained, and capability for responsibility.

The need-drive approaches discussed thus far indicate that occupational choices are made in response to some form of self-classification, either conscious or not. Thus, the searching for and the choosing of occupations is an attempt to affirm a personal behavioral style.

Holland's approach (11) gives major and explicit emphasis to behavioral style or personality type. It is assumed that as a result of the interaction between heredity and environment, the individual develops a hierarchy of habitual or preferred methods for dealing with social and environmental tasks; these preferences come together as her or his behavioral style. It is further assumed that this behavioral style, or modal personal orientation, can be described in relation to one of six personality categories: artistic, conventional, enterprising, investigative, realistic, or social. Regardless of how the individual's modal personal orientation can be classified, the theory then holds that the person will seek occupations or educational settings which satisfy and are compatible with the hierarchy of preferences.

Because people gravitate to settings where others are seen as sharing one's values and interests in regard to work activity, leisure time, and so on, occupations or educational units tend to attract different kinds of people. Consequently, some of them tend to be "loaded" with a particular emphasis, e.g., realistic rather than enterprising or artistic instead of conventional type individuals. Thus, it is possible to think about occupations and curricula in education as being classifiable into the same six categories used to describe personality types: artistic, conventional, enterprising, investigative, realistic, and social. The underlying premise of this approach is that people of a particular personality type seek out those educational or occupational opportunities in which they can be themselves. Changing career patterns, occupational or educational maladjustments, and other similar choice or adjustment difficulties would be explained by suggesting that people who have certain patterns of preferences or certain behavioral styles achieve in some occupations and not in others. According to this view, the function of occupational choice is to match, as congruently as possible, the personal style and the characteristics of the work or educational setting.

Developmental Approaches

In each of the four preceding perspectives, there is an implied assumption that people are better suited for one job or a cluster of jobs than all of the other possibilities. In essence, the need-drive and trait-and-factor approaches attempt to classify the bases on which such differences in fit might be identified. The decision theory approaches speak somewhat more directly to the characteristics of the choice process itself. The sociological approaches address primarily the environmental circumstances which relate to continuity and discontinuity in vocational development. None of these four types of approaches, however, focus very directly on the characteristics of vocational development over time.

As compared with the approaches just described, the developmental approaches are more comprehensive and more attentive to the sequencing and longitudinal character of vocational development. Indeed, until these emphases began surfacing in the early 1950s the primary concern of researchers and theorists was upon occupational choice as an act which occurred at a particular point in time. The primary questions were (1) What individual traits would predict whether or not a particular choice was appropriate? or (2) Why do people choose different occupations?

The developmental approaches changed the focus of concern from occupational choice as an act to occupational choice as a process. In so doing, it became obvious that choice was not confined to a certain period of life. Indeed, people focusing on the *process* of vocational development began to see it as having roots in the early life of the child extending throughout one's life span and changing in response to institutional and social pressures.

Eli Ginzberg and his colleagues (8) laid the base for current conceptions of vocational development as a longitudinal process. They asserted that "occupational choice is a developmental process: it is not a single decision, but a series of decisions made over a period of years. Each step in the process has a meaningful relation to those which precede and follow it" (8, p. 185).

Using the process concept as their organizing premise, Ginzberg et al. identified a series of life stages in which certain tasks ultimately related to choice are faced by preadolescents and adolescents. These stages were labeled *fantasy, tentative,* and *realistic,* and each of these was in turn broken into substages. For example, the tentative period is divided into interest, capacity, value, and transition substages which emerge sequentially. These in turn are followed by the realistic stage which is broken into exploration and crystallization substages. The basic point is that as children, preadolescents, and adolescents cope with the tasks, the self-insights, and the information about alternatives available to them in these different life periods, there is a constant compromising between wishes and possibilities. This synthesizing and compromising process in turn defines and narrows the range of choices a particular individual is likely to consider.

While Ginzberg et al. speculated about the whole of the lifespan in relation to vocational development, their work principally focused upon the periods from birth to the early twenties which culminate in the initial vocational choices. In addition to the staging phenomena related to vocational development, Ginzberg et al. also identified four sets of factors which interplay to influence vocational choice. They include individual values, emotional factors, the amount and kind of education, and the impact of reality imposed by environmental pressures.

Closely related conceptually to this early work of Ginzberg and his associates is the continuing work of Donald Super and his various colleagues. Their career pattern study examined the vocational behavior of a group of ninth-grade boys who were followed from the early 1950s until they entered their late thirties. This study has provided the major pool of data from which Super's vast productivity has flowed. It is fair to observe that this work has received the most continuous attention, stimulated the most research, and is the most comprehensive of the developmental approaches which have arisen in recent decades.

Super's approach has attempted to integrate insights from differential, developmental, social, and phenomenological psychology to explain vocational behavior (18). As such it embraces many of the concepts from the trait-and-factor, sociological, need-drive approaches into a more organized whole.

Super has used the staging phenomena described by Ginzberg et al. as well as earlier perspectives developed by Buehler (5) to create a structure incorporating the whole of the lifespan. This structure is composed of five stages: *growth* (from birth to approximately 14 years of age), *exploration* (ages 14 to 25), *establishment* (ages 25 to 45), *maintenance* (ages 45 to 60), and *decline* (age 60 on). Each of these stages is divided into substages comprised of developmental tasks necessary to the individual's achieving and maintaining vocational maturity. For example, the developmental tasks with which people must deal in the exploratory state and early establishment stage include

crystallizing a vocational preference,
specifying it,
implementing it,
stabilizing in the chosen vocation,
consolidating one's status,
advancing in the occupation.

In adolescence, crystallizing, specifying, and implementing a vocational preference are major tasks which individuals must face and are tasks with which education must help them deal. According to Super's approach, these developmental tasks need to be broken down further into the behaviors and the attitudes of which they are comprised.

It is not possible to deal with these behaviors, attitudes, and stages in depth here. However, the important point is that Super views the person's evolving vocational maturity in relationship to how the person is mastering the developmental tasks appropriate in different life stages. If the person experiences a lack of information or reality-testing experiences at a particular stage, he or she is not likely to be able to cope with certain later developmental tasks and thus the person's vocational maturity may be impaired or delayed. Such people may prematurely close off consideration of training opportunities or occupational choices because of a lack of self-knowledge, planning, or an array of other possibilities. Super's research has demonstrated that the levels of vocational maturity attained at grade nine and at grade twelve are predictive of the levels of vocational success in young adulthood (17). Thus, such things as possession of occupational information, information about training and education required in a preferred occupation, and planning and interest maturity while the person is in the secondary school are related to whether one stablizes or flounders in one's occupational life in the mid-twenties and beyond.

The key construct which weaves throughout Super's research and theory is the importance of the development and implementation of the self-concept. The assumption is that the individual chooses an occupation which will allow him or her to function in a way that is consistent with a self-picture. Indeed there is some evidence that occupational choice is made in some cases not only to affirm and actualize a presently held self-concept but also to provide an opportunity to actualize an ideal self-concept (21). In any case, a comprehensive literature has grown since the 1950s linking the person's view of self with the way he or she views occupations, educational opportunities, and life-styles.

According to a vocational development view, the self-concept, in effect, represents a shaper of and a trigger for individual behavior. As such, it becomes obvious that vocational education must attend not only to helping students understand and acquire occupational skills and information about differences among occupations but also to help them to learn to view themselves realistically. Just as one can suffer from distorted information about occupational characteristics or training requirements for entry into occupations, one can also suffer from unrealistic estimates of one's ability and from vague understandings of personal values and preferences.

Before leaving developmental perspectives, it is important to note other theorists and researchers who have made important contributions in this realm. Among the most prominent are Tiedeman and O'Hara and Gribbons and Lohnes.

Tiedeman and O'Hara (20), individually and together, have validated many of Super's concepts on the staging of vocational development. They have also significantly extended our insights into particular components of this development. Specifically, they have studied the intersection of anticipation of an occupational choice and actual induction into the occupation chosen. They have identified the stages of the occupational induction process as composed of social induction, reformation, and integration. According to them, the individual comes to the occupation with a set of ideas about what it will be like to work in that occupation. These ideas have evolved through the stages of anticipation, exploration, crystallization, choice,and clarification. The question is whether these ideas are congruent with the reality of the occupation when the person is inducted into it. Expectations and realities are never totally congruent so there is always some give-and-take between the individual and the environment (these involve the processes of reformation and integration). The individual modifies her or his self-concept to accommodate job expectations, and the job tends to bend to the individual's style. If these demands are not too dramatic, induction is successful. If, on the other hand, induction requires accommodations beyond the limits of the individual's tolerance or beyond those permitted by the self-concept, the process of exploration and anticipation will likely be reinstituted as the individual moves toward occupational change (20).

Other highlights of Tiedeman and O'Hara's perspectives include an emphasis on vocational development as a continuing process of differentiating ego identity. They have used Erikson's model of psychosocial crises encountered at various developmental stages (7) as an explanation for differences in vocational development. They have also indicated that individual personality is shaped by career choices and by the individual's conformity to the norms and values of individuals already established within the vocational setting chosen. Thus there is a stress in this view upon the intimate interaction of the self-concept and the career concept as they develop over time through many small decisions.

Gribbons and Lohnes (9) have been occupied with a longitudinal study designed to clarify what behaviors comprise *readiness for vocational planning* in adolescence. They have identified eight variables which correlate to a high degree with postsecondary vocational development, field and level of occupation two years after high school, and career adjustment. These variables (9, pp. 15–16) have the following emphases (in paraphrased form):

Variable 1. Awareness of personal characteristics—abilities, interests, values—in relation to curricular choices as well as the relationships of different curricula choices to occupational choices.

Variable 2. Awareness of personal characteristics and educational requirements in relation to occupational choice.

Variable 3. Ability to accurately identify personal strengths and weaknesses relating to educational and vocational choices.

Variable 4. The accuracy of one's self-estimates of ability in comparision to levels of actual achievement.

Variable 5. The evidence used by a person for self-appraisal.
Variable 6. Awareness of interests and their relation to choice options.
Variable 7. Awareness of values and their relation to occupational choices.
Variable 8. Willingness to take responsibility for one's choices.

Summary

Vocational development is a fabric of many threads. It is composed of factors in the individual's environment which convey values and encouragement differently about the many educational and occupational options a person might consider. It is also composed of the degree to which one incorporates these beliefs about oneself and about one's options into a composite self-picture. Thus vocational development is a process of learning about oneself, one's choice options, and both as they are viewed by others.

Such perspectives indicate that vocational educators have a responsibility to assure that occupational task skill development is taught in ways which aid students to attain a sense of personal competence to use occupational skills effectively and simultaneously in ways which allow them to meet personal needs for identity and self-worth.

REFERENCES

1. Bordin, E.S.; Nachman, Barbara; and Segal, S.J. "An Articulated Framework for Voca-Development. *Journal of Counseling Psychology* 10(1963):107–116.
2. Borow, H. "Vocational Development Research: Some Problems of Logical and Experimental Form." *Personnel and Guidance Journal* 40(1961):21–25.
3. Borow, H. "The Development of Motives and Roles." In *Review of Child Development Research: Volume 2,* edited by L.W. Hoffman and M.L. Hoffman. New York: Russell Sage Foundation, 1966.
4. Bross, I.D. *Design for Decision.* New York: MacMillan Company, 1953.
5. Buehler, Charlotte. *Der Menschliche Lebenslau als Psychologiches Problem.* Leipzig: Hirzel, 1933.
6. Clarke, R.; Gelatt, H.B., and Levine, L. "A Decision-Making Paradigm for Local Guidance Research." *Personnel and Guidance Journal* 44(1965):40–51.
7. Erikson, E.H. *Childhood and Society,* 2d ed. New York: W.W. Norton, 1963.
8. Ginzberg, E.; Ginsburg, S.W.; Axelrod, S.; and Herma, J.R. *Occupational Choice: An Approach to a General Theory.* New York: Columbia University Press, 1951.
9. Gribbons, W.D., and Lohnes, P.R. *Emerging Careers.* New York: Teachers College Press, Columbia University, 1968.
10. Hills, J.R. "Decision Theory and College Choice." *Personnel and Guidance Journal* 43 (1964):17–22.
11. Holland, J.L. *The Psychology of Vocational Choice.* Waltham, Mass.: Blaisdell, 1966.
12. Katz, M. *Decisions and Values: A Rationale for Secondary School Counselors.* New York: College Entrance Examination Board, 1963.
13. Lipsett, L. "Social Factors in Vocational Development." *Personnel and Guidance Journal* 40(1962):432–37.

14. LoCascio, R. "Continuity and Discontinuity in Vocational Development Theory." *Personnel and Guidance Journal* 46(1967):32–36.

15. Maslow, A.H. *Motivation and Personality.* New York: Harper and Row, 1954.

16. Roe, Anne. *The Psychology of Occupations.* New York: John Wiley and Sons, 1956.

17. Super, D.E. "The Natural History of a Study of Lives and of Vocations." *Perspectives on Education* 2(1969):13–22.

18. ______ "Vocational Development Theory: Persons, Positions, and Processes." *The Counseling Psychologist* 1 (1969):2–9.

19. Super, D.E.; Starishevsky, R.; Matlin, N.; and Jordaan, J.P. *Career Development: Self-concept Theory.* New York: College Entrance Examination Board, 1963.

20. Tiedeman, D.V., and O'Hara, R.P. *Career Development: Choice and Adjustment.* New York: College Entrance Examination Board, 1963.

21. Wheeler, C.L., and Carnes, E.F. "Relationships among Self-Concepts, Ideal Self-Concepts, and Stereotypes of Probable and Ideal Vocational Choices. *Journal of Counseling Psychology* 15(1968):530–35.

22. Zaccaria, J. *Theories of Occupational Choice and Vocational Development.* Guidance Monograph Series IV. Boston: Houghton Mifflin, 1970.

12

Vocational Guidance

Vocational guidance and vocational education have had a strong interrelationship since the beginning of the twentieth century. That relationship has been based on the assumption that vocational guidance could help people make wise occupational choices and that vocational education could help them prepare for what they had chosen. Both vocational guidance and vocational education have become increasingly professionalized and dependent upon their own technologies. In the process the original partnership has suffered from periodic growing pains. This chapter will provide a historical overview of the evolution of vocational guidance in America, including the changing definitions of vocational guidance. Following this introduction, the philosophical principles and assumptions on which vocational guidance rests will be identified, current perspectives on vocational guidance will be explored, and the major categories of vocational guidance techniques will be discussed.

Vocational Guidance: Some History

Conventional wisdom assigns the beginnings of vocational guidance in America to the first decade of the twentieth century. This was the middle stage of the Industrial Revolution in the United States, a period of heavy immigration and a

Portions of this section have been adapted from Edwin L. Herr, *Guidance and Counseling, Vocational Education, Research and Development,* a paper prepared for the National Research Council's Committee on Vocational Education Research and Development. Washington, D.C., March 1975.

time when adequate education for children and effective placement of people into our rapidly growing industrial complex were becoming social imperatives.

As a part of a network of social reform efforts generated by the problems of economic and personal welfare current at the time, rudimentary forms of vocational guidance had spontaneous birth in several parts of the country almost simultaneously. However, it was the work of Frank Parsons in Boston which received the major share of credit for founding vocational guidance in America.

Parsons received this distinction because of the posthumous publication of his book *Choosing a Vocation* in 1909. In it was a clear formulation as to how one might assist another in choosing an occupation. This book and the techniques elaborated were really extensions of work Parsons had been conducting with adolescents since about 1895 in an effort to help them identify, or diagnose, their capabilities and choose jobs in which reasonable chances of success could be expected.

Parsons's formulation consisted of three steps.

> First, a clear understanding of yourself, aptitudes, abilities, interests, resources, limitations, and other qualities. Second, a knowledge of the requirements and conditions of success, advantages and disadvantages, compensation, opportunities, and prospects in different lines of work. Third, true reasoning on the relations of these two groups of facts. (8, p. 5)

This schema defined the elements of what has been known since as an actuarial, or trait-and-factor, approach to counseling or to vocational guidance.

From 1909 until the present, Parsons's formulation has spurred research and developmental efforts flowing from his first two steps. The first step has stimulated efforts to identify and measure individual characteristics, particularly through the use of various types of tests. The second step has stimulated attention to the acquisition and use of occupational information. Together, the use of tests and information with clients has had a continuing effect upon vocational guidance practices (15).

History of Relationships with Vocational Education

As the industrialization of the United States escalated during the late 1800s, criticisms that public education was too bookish, too elitist, and unrelated to the actualities of life became frequent and strong. This kind of reformist flavor gave at least partial impetus to guidance and counseling, but it also affected vocational education.

Vocational education in tax-supported schools began at the college level with the passage of the Morrill Act in 1862. This created land-grant colleges and gave emphasis to the professionalization of agricultural education. By 1876, Morrill, among others, was recommending the support of practical, manual, and industrial education, one function of which was to distribute migrants among the occupations and industries needing their labor.

While others spoke of the economic and practical values of vocational education, Dewey believed that such education also served exploration goals and was an opportunity for workers to learn of the social and cultural background of their vocation as well as the skills involved. That idea was echoed and extended by others concerned not only about vocational training per se but also about the needs to attend to the civic and the vocational intelligence of young workers.

Stephens has contended that

> to many leaders of the vocational reform movement . . . it was apparent that vocational education was but the first part of a package of needed educational reforms. They argued that a school curriculum and educational goals that mirrored the occupational structure created merely a platform and impetus for launching youth into the world of work. What was clearly needed to consummate the launch were guidance mechanisms that would insure their safe and efficient arrival on the job. Without guidance experts it was argued, other efforts at reform would be aborted. . . . Therefore, in the name of social and economic efficiency, the argument continued, the youth who had been carefully trained would also have to be carefully counseled into a suitable occupational niche. (9, p. 81)

During the first decades of the twentieth century, vocational guidance tended to emphasize a "tryout-through-training" approach with much emphasis placed upon occupational information. The information available was highly objective, only minimally related to the psychological appraisal of the individual, and delivered through counseling which was essentially directive and consisted primarily of advice giving (7).

Following World War I, however, vocational guidance and vocational education lost their initial partnership. The demise of this relationship rests, at least partially, with the unwillingness of the National Education Association (NEA) to view vocational education and vocational guidance as parts of a unity. In 1918 the NEA accepted a craft rather than a technical training emphasis in vocational education and a conception of guidance for education rather than a conception of vocational guidance for jobs (9).

Through the 1930s, 1940s, and 1950s vocational guidance gradually became the province of school counselors (guidance counselors) whose functions tended to broaden and change as various educational movements came into prominence, e.g., progressive education, life adjustment education. Vocational guidance was part of the repertoire of school counselors but by no means the central focus of their activity. At the same time, vocational educators continued to provide vocational guidance but to a restricted clientele, one principally composed of students taking vocational education courses and as such a relatively small portion of the total student population. In one sense, two independent approaches to vocational guidance arose in the 1920s and the 1930s: that provided by school counselors (guidance and counseling) and the other provided by vocational educators and by specialists employed by the U.S. Department of Labor.

During the 1920s, '30s and '40s, vocational guidance as practiced by school counselors became increasingly responsive to several forces. One force was the growing knowledge of individual differences, the awareness of personality dynamics in vocational choice and work adjustment, and the general influence of a psychological approach to vocational guidance. A second force, also psychologically related, was a growing developmental view of the individual. A third force tended to challenge the information-giving role of vocational guidance (or to be more correct, guidance and counseling), advocating instead therapeutic treatment or psychotherapy as the processes of choice.

Most of the economic and social events during the 1940s and '50s tended to turn school counselors away from a vocational guidance to an educational guidance focus as their major operational priority. The massive growth in higher education precipitated by the return of millions of veterans from World War II, abetted by the educational benefits of the G.I. Bill, as well as a rising belief among many that a college education was attainable to the masses and a sure pathway to dignity and affluence caused guidance and counseling practitioners to be absorbed in guidance for educational choice rather than for work choice. During much of this period, college was seen as an end in itself—its vocational implications were not typically viewed with priority concern. These social trends were given further impetus by the Russian launching of Sputnik in 1957. The American educational enterprise was brought under intense analysis and seen as wanting by many verbal and influential critics. Charges of lack of substantive rigor in the sciences and of lack of attention to the academically gifted were rife.

In 1958 the National Defense Education Act was promulgated to offset such criticisms. Among its provisions was the support for and training of counselors to identify (through testing) and nurture the gifted and talented vis-à-vis further education, particularly in the hard sciences. Perceived manpower needs for scientifically educated people caused school counselors to move further toward an educational rather than an occupational focus. The latter was not really precluded, but it took second seat to the social priority of having school counselors help students select and prepare for college. As historical events unfolded, however, the 1960s contained the conditions for a possible convergence in the views of guidance and counseling personnel and vocational educators relative to vocational guidance.

The early 1960s saw a spate of antipoverty programs focus upon the occupational preparation of the disadvantaged, the out-of-school and out-of-work youth, the unemployed and the underemployed. Many of these programs failed because they tended to focus upon meeting the needs of the labor market rather than the needs of individuals. As this realization dawned upon decision-makers and legislators, significant manpower policy shifts began to emerge. Policies took on an affective quality as well as a performance-based one. Emphases in legislation and in program operations began to shift from a prime concern on developing a competent person (as defined by occupational requirements) to a greater accentuation on developing a sense of personal competence (as defined by technical skills as well as individual capability to choose and plan) (3).

These trends were reflected in legislation dealing with nonschool and with school agencies. For example, the Manpower Development and Training Act of 1962 introduced the importance of providing counseling and placement activities as major components of its programs. More specifically, however, the Vocational Education Act of 1963 and the Amendments of 1968 reaffirmed the reciprocal needs of vocational education and vocational guidance for each other with which the century began.

Such an interrelation was expressed by Law, a prominent vocational educator, in his appraisal of the Vocational Education Act Amendments of 1968 when he stated:

> 1. Career guidance and orientation is needed by everyone.
> 2. Vocational guidance needs a regular place in the school curriculum.
> 3. There can be no satisfactory program of vocational guidance without vocational education. (6, pp. 27–28)

He further contended:

> If the vocational guidance program were longitudinal, a continuing process, as it has been described in career development theory, there would be an ample opportunity for an individualized program. From a common core of group activity, individual students would move toward the development of occupational knowledge, concept of self, and vocational competence in any variety of ways, largely determined by each person's qualities and drives. (6, pp. 27–28)

Law's observations in 1969 signalled many of the current emphases in vocational guidance. In sum, they include a growing conceptual base in career/vocational development theory underlying vocational guidance practice, longitudinal and developmental activities focused upon assisting students and adults clarify and plan for self-understanding, the interaction of educational and occupational choices, and the implications of these for a range of life options. These emphases and the specific activities which represent the tools of the vocational guidance counselor will be discussed later. Presently, some definitions are in order.

Definitions of Vocational Guidance

History (and the increase in knowledge which accompanies it) has a tendency to reshape definitions of education or of other social processes. So it is with vocational guidance.

Since the impetus for Parsons's early formulation of vocational guidance was the need to distribute the large number of immigrants arriving in the eastern parts of America throughout an expanding industrial structure, the original emphasis was on "matching" person and job. Operationally the assumptions were that individuals could be described in terms of the traits they possessed (e.g., aptitudes, skills, interests), that each occupation could be described in terms of the combinations of these traits it required, and that fitting the individual's pattern of traits to the occupation which most clearly required that specific pattern of traits would result in a meaningful and longlasting choice.

Parsons's model was concerned primarily with what the person could do rather than what he or she preferred to do or valued doing; analyzing one's interests and values or fostering freedom of choice on the part of the person are relatively recent emphases in vocational guidance. The prime question for most of the history of vocational guidance in this country has been what can the person do and where is there an occupational requirement for that skill?

By 1937 the National Vocational Guidance Association had adopted a definition of vocational guidance which began to broaden Parsons's model, although this was more implicit than explicit. Vocational guidance was said to be "the process of assisting the individual to choose an occupation, prepare for it, enter upon it and progress in it" (2). Inherent in this definition of vocational guidance was a concern for active and deliberate choice among occupational possibilities, considering and deciding among educational pathways to such occupational goals (including but not limited to vocational education), and receiving vocational guidance support during the period of work adjustment. This definition of vocational guidance began to form the base for vocational guidance to be seen as more than one or two sessions in which an individual is matched to whatever is available. Instead vocational guidance was to be seen as enabling the person in the process of choice, as learning how to choose. It also opened up the relationship between choosing an occupation and choosing the best educational method to prepare for it. In essence, it included educational guidance as a part of vocational guidance.

Notions that the person needs to be helped to learn how to choose, to choose on the basis of all relevant personal characteristics, rather than simply aptitudes and performance, and that choice is a process rather than an event were really sharpened in 1951. At that time the National Vocational Guidance Association's definition of vocational guidance was revised. The new definition of vocational guidance, proposed by Donald Super and adopted by the Association, was "the process of helping a person to develop and accept an integrated and adequate picture of himself and of his role in the world of work, to test this concept against reality, and to convert it into a reality, with satisfaction to himself and benefit to society" (10).

The 1951 National Vocational Guidance Association definition substantially and irrevocably changed the perspective of vocational guidance from one concerned with matching person and job to one which has a significant psychological content. It blends the personal, educational, and vocational aspects of vocational guidance into a unified whole. Most importantly, it emphasizes self-understanding and self-acceptance as the basis upon which to evaluate the occupational and educational alternatives available to the individual.

Subtly, but certainly, the 1951 definition of vocational guidance shifted the emphasis of vocational guidance from the needs of the occupational structure to the needs of the individual and in the process espoused individual freedom of choice. Such a view is propounded in Thompson's statement of rationale for vocational guidance.

> As a necessary service in a democratic society based on individual freedom of choice, vocational guidance has the function of helping individuals make more effective de-

cisions and plan throughout the long-term process of their vocational development by facilitating a clearer understanding of themselves and their roles in the role of work. (12, p. 535)

The most recent twist among the ever-widening definitions of vocational guidance is substitution of the term *career guidance.* This term emphasizes that choices of education and of occupation are parts of a broader and lifelong pattern of interacting choices making up a career, a life-style. In this perspective, career guidance includes consideration of leisure activities, distant as well as immediate or intermediate choices, personal values, the kinds of personal themes one's choices should serve, and the development of decision-making skill.

In sum, advocates of career guidance argue that the importance of career or vocational guidance lies with its facilitation of the process of career or vocational development (see chapter 11). Thus it must aggressively help people learn decision-making skills and how to identify and use information important to understanding themselves and their options rather than simply serving a remedial function after their decision-making skills are confused or they are suffering from occupational maladjustment.

Current Assumptions about Vocational Guidance

Philosophically, a number of principles underlie the practice of vocational guidance. Among them are the following:

—The strength of the nation rests, in part, upon natural differences in individual talents and upon the freedom of each individual to develop these talents in a unique way. (13)
—Freedom to choose one's life work is basic to our democratic society and is necessary to the fullest possible growth of individuals. (13)
—Individual differences relevant to vocational selection are both necessary and desirable. (14)
—There is a place for every person in the vocational structure of our nation. (14)
—Having job skills as well as planning and decision-making skills provides personal dignity and a sense of one's power to affect the future. (14)
—Individuals must develop greater awareness of the values society places on different talents and the relative demands for these talents. (13)
—The selection of an occupation and/or a career is a part of and influenced by the maturation process. (14)
—Because of the complexity of options available, most people need special help in identifying and acting upon decisions to be made. (13)
—Preservation of the individual's integrity disavows any type of prescriptive career guidance which commits the individual to particular directions. (13)
—The theory underlying career development is consonant with these fundamental democratic values. (13)
—Career development can be described in terms of learning tasks that are important at each stage of development. (13)
—It is possible to identify the attitudes, knowledge, and skills that make up career development. Thus, it is possible to identify career development objectives to direct the emphases necessary to a vocational guidance program. (14)

—Among the elements which students or adults need to acquire as part of their career development are

a. Awareness of the need to choose
b. Awareness of factors to consider in formulating a vocational preference
c. Use of resources
d. Awareness of contingencies which may affect vocational goals
e. Differentiation of interests and values
f. Awareness of present-future relationships
g. Possession of information on a preferred occupation
h. Planning for a preferred occupation. (11)

These assumptions about the importance and the general content of vocational guidance have been translated into specific objectives to which program elements are joined. These objectives take many forms and will not be elaborated here. Suffice it to say, however, that both the intent and methodology of vocational guidance are being sharpened and developed. Thus, rather than vocational guidance being comprised of a series of isolated techniques randomly provided to students or adults, these are being systematically merged into programs designed to affect specific attitudes, understandings, and behaviors in their consumers.

The Practice of Vocational Guidance

In many ways current conceptions of vocational guidance are efforts to develop technologies of counseling. In truth there is no one current approach to vocational guidance; there are several. Crites (1) has identified these under the rubric of *career counseling* (a subtle but growing nomenclature which may have more palatable connotations for some than *vocational guidance* but still addresses the same domain). Several approaches have been described.

1. *Trait-and-Factor.* Although there are refinements in assessment devices and the quality of information, this approach still reflects the essence of the original Parsonian model of vocational guidance. Emphasis is placed on diagnosis of the students or clients presenting problems. This process involves extensive data collection about the attitudes, interests, aptitudes, family background, work history, and other characteristics of the counselee by the counselor. This material is converted by the counselor into a set of interpretations about possible future actions the student or client might take. The client is helped to sort these actions out or match them with available alternatives and then to act upon some choice among them.
2. *Client-Centered.* This approach, which is essentially the counseling paradigm of Carl Rogers, argues that if a client becomes well-adjusted psychologically, then he or she will be able to solve whatever career problems are encountered without specifically attending to them in career counseling. This approach to counseling primarily emphasizes the quality of the relationship between the counselor (as defined by creating conditions of congruence, understanding, acceptance) and the client as the major variable in freeing the

client to become actualized, be able to make choices, gain in self-understanding, and so on. Little importance and, indeed, some negative connotations are attached to testing or the use of information during counseling except as these are clearly desired by the client. If occupational information is used, it must follow certain client-centered principles. Among them are

1) occupational information is introduced into the counseling process when there is a recognized need for it on the part of the client;
2) occupational information is not used to manipulate or influence the client;
3) the most objective way to provide occupational information, and a way which maximizes client initiative and responsibility, is to encourage the client to obtain the information from original sources, that is publications, employers, and people engaged in occupations;
4) the client's attitudes and feelings about occupations and jobs must be allowed expression and be dealt with therapeutically.

3. *Psychodynamic.* Fundamentally an application of psychoanalytic (Freudian and Neo-Freudian) conceptions of humanity and use of diagnostic categories flowing from such a theoretical base, this approach to career counseling emphasizes counselor interpretations of the roots of client decision-making problems. Various diagnostic and testing strategies are used. Occupational information is used which primarily emphasizes the need-gratifying qualities of different forms of work. This approach is also a matching person and job approach but uses personal psychodynamic needs and potential occupational gratifications as the basis rather than the more common conception of interests, aptitudes, and occupational requirements.
4. *Developmental Career Counseling.* This approach, stemming from the theoretical basis of Super's career development approach, stresses the thematic nature of personal behavior in viewing possible future actions. Diagnosis is conceived in terms of understanding the patterns of behavior the person has displayed in the past and what these may mean for future behavior. An emphasis is upon counseling the client for planfulness, readiness for choice. The process involves reality-testing information which the person has assembled about himself or herself and about various options under consideration. It is assumed that people are both rational and emotional and that career counseling must provide an opportunity for both to be displayed and considered. Questions such as the following represent much of the direction of this approach to counseling.

   What sort of person do I think I am? How do I feel about myself as I think I am? What sort of person would I like to be? What are my values and needs? What are my aptitudes and interests? What outlets are there for me with my needs, values, interests, and aptitudes?

   Testing, problem appraisal, interviewing, occupational information are each used interactively to facilitate the outcomes of this approach.
5. *Behavioral.* Theoretically based in learning theory, behavioral career counseling uses such techniques as counselor reinforcement of desired client responses, social modeling and vicarious learning, desensitization, and dis-

crimination learning to assist counselees achieve certain specified goals. Diagnosis in this approach is less related to the use of standard measurements and more concerned with analyzing the characteristics of the individual's environmental interactions to identify behavioral cues and reinforcers. In addressing themselves to vocational problems, behavioral career counselors are likely to analyze quite specifically the behavioral deficits of the client and to create conditions or experiences which will provide appropriate learned responses or skills. This specific analysis of client needs vis-à-vis some set of goals extends to the use of occupational information and its potential for helping the client learn specific concepts or experience certain material important to goal attainment.

A variation in behavioral approaches to counseling called *systematic vocational counseling,* has been identified by Herr, Horan, and Baker (15) Table 12–1 illustrates the counselor behavior, necessary conditions, and criteria for successful performance by which such an approach can be conceived.

As indicated previously, these approaches to career counseling are in some fashion embedded in a program of counselor acitivities which go beyond the one-to-one interaction of counselor and client. The development of planned experiences in didactic or simulated modes to teach clients certain information about themselves or occupational alternatives or skills in decision making or values clarification has become reasonably commonplace. Consultation about student development or employability by counselors with teachers, employers, and others, the use of group processes in vocational guidance, the use of simulation and gaming, as well as computer-based systems of information retrieval and analysis, each represent other current emphases in the provision of vocational guidance by guidance and counseling professionals. The next section will address more specifically the techniques typically incorporated in a program of vocational guidance.

Techniques Used in a Vocational Guidance Program

Regardless of the philosophical or theoretical perspective embraced, a vocational guidance program consists of many parts. Ideally each should be related to specific objectives to be served by the program and by a particular technique. In general, the following techniques would be those most frequently used.

Individual Counseling

Although the problems to be explored and the self-understanding pertinent to vocational guidance can be generally classified, their precise emphases differ greatly from person to person. Thus, a one-to-one relationship (individual counseling) is frequently necessary between the vocational guidance practitioner (counselor) and students or clients so that the latter can personalize the implications of information they have, determine the information they need, identify the content of choices available to them, evaluate alternatives, clarify their values, develop decision-making skills, or cope with other such dilemmas.

TABLE 12–1. *Sequential counselor behaviors in systematic vocational counseling*

Counselor Behavior	Necessary Conditions	Criteria for Successful Performance
1. Counselor defines the purpose of counseling and the roles of the counselor and student.	At the outset of the initial interview (unless the student discusses personal concerns immediately, then before the end of the initial interview).	Definitions should correspond to a predetermined standard.
2. Counselor helps the client define the problem via specific counseling skills.	During the initial interview and in as many subsequent interviews as are required.	The problem is defined when the student so indicates. E.g., "Yes, that's it" or "You really do understand me!"
If the problem is one of vocational choice then the following counselor behaviors ought to ensue. Other kinds of student problems may require different types of counselor activity.		
3. Counselor determines if vocational choice is the primary concern. (e.g., "It seems that although you have a lot of things on your mind, you're mainly interested in coming to some sort of vocational decision.")	After the student has expressed all he or she cares to concerning the problem or reason for seeking counseling.	The student responds in an affirmative manner.
4. Counselor explains the decision-making paradigm. (e.g., "Arriving at a good vocational decision means that we have to look at all the alternatives, then weigh them in the light of information about you and the advantages and disadvantages of each course of action. I can't make the decision for you, but together we can arrive at and implement one.")	Immediately following Counselor Behavior 3.	The student indicates that he or she understands the process.
5. Counselor explains the preparatory behaviors needed to make a good decision (i.e., provides an overview of the counselor behaviors depicted below).	Immediately following Counselor Behavior 4.	The student states that he or she understands the process.
6. Counselor determines if the student has sufficient motivation (e.g., "How do you feel about proceeding along these lines?")	Usually after Counselor Behavior 5. May be repeated after subsequent counselor behaviors.	The student indicates willingness to proceed. (If the student hesitates, or is unwilling to proceed, then recycle to Counselor Behavior 2 or terminate.)
7. Counselor asks the student to identify all possible alternatives which come to mind.	The alternatives may be identified in the interview and/or as a between-interviews assignment.	The student compiles a complete list of alternatives (oral or written).
8. Counselor identifies any additional alternatives which come to his mind and are ethically appropriate.	Counselor exhibits this behavior only if criterion for number 7 is considered to be inadequate by either the counselor or the student.	A joint list of alternatives is compiled.
9. Counselor assembles all relevant information about the student (e.g., test scores, academic performance, vocational experience and interests) from records and/or from student inquiry.	This information may be gathered during the interview or, if not immediately available, between interviews.	All existing relevant information about the student is available for discussion.

Table 12–1 (continued)

Counselor Behavior	Necessary Conditions	Criteria for Successful Performance
10. Counselor assembles additional information about the student (e.g., schedules further testing).	Counselor exhibits this behavior only if the criterion for number 9 is considered to be inadequate by the counselor.	All relevant information is compiled.
11. Counselor presents to the student any information about the student relevant to the potential vocational decision (e.g., predictive statements derived from expectancy tables).	Immediately following Counselor Behaviors 9 and/or 10.	The student indicates understanding of this information.
12. Counselor requests that the student identify the advantages and disadvantages of the alternatives which have been identified.	During the interview (in the context of counselor-student discussion) and/or as a between-interviews assignment.	The student provides a set of such statements.
13. Counselor identifies any additional advantages and disadvantages which come to his mind.	Counselor exhibits this behavior only if the criterion for number 12 is considered to be inadequate by either the counselor or the student.	A joint list of such statements is compiled.
14. Counselor asks the student to evaluate the alternatives. (e.g., "In terms of what we know about you and the various alternatives, which alternatives seem most promising?")	Immediately following Counselor Behaviors 12 and/or 13.	The student rank orders the alternatives from most to least preferred.
15. Counselor helps the student obtain additional information about the most promising alternative(s). (e.g., verbally reinforces the student for reading about the prospective profession(s) and talking to members of the prospective profession(s); may also schedule modeling or simulation experiences for the student to participate in.	The additional information is usually accumulated outside of the counseling interview.	The student gathers this information or participates in the scheduled experiences.
16. Counselor helps the student implement the most promising alternative.	Immediately following Counselor Behavior 15.	A tentative course of action is selected and tried out.
17. Counselor determines if the selected alternatives is satisfactory.	Immediately following Counselor Behavior 16.	The student reports that he is happy with the decision. (If not, recycle to Counselor Behavior 16, [next most promising alternative].)
18. Counselor terminates the counseling relationship.	Immediately following Counselor Behavior 17.	The student has learned the decision-making paradigm and is able to engage in independent action. (5)

SOURCE: From E.L. Herr, J.J. Horan, and S.J. Baker, "Clarifying the Counseling Mystique," Table 2, *American Vocational Journal* 484 (April 1973):68.

There are hundreds of definitions of counseling. They offer many variations on a central theme which essentially is as follows:

> Counseling is a purposeful relationship between a counselor and a client (student) in which processes used vary with the nature of the client's needs and in which the

counselor and client collaborate to facilitate self-clarification, decision making, planning, and action by the client.

The basic content of counseling, and in the larger sense vocational guidance, are the choice possibilities which society permits an individual to consider as these are defined by age, particular setting, economic and psychological circumstance. Vocational guidance does not coerce people into making specific choices but rather provides them the opportunity to learn and/or to make choices which are free and informed and in accordance with their personal values.

Group Processes of Vocational Guidance

The one-to-one relationship is not the only technique employed to facilitate the exploration and choice described above. Group processes will also be valuable adjuncts to individual counseling. Such experiences have various purposes. Herr and Cramer (4) have identified several reasons for implementing group approaches.

1. *Information Dissemination.* Providing and clarifying for students or adults information about personal, occupational, educational alternatives available to them and the ways by which such information can be obtained and processed for personal purposes.
2. *Persuasion.* Motivation to consider the importance of personal options, that choice is available, etc.
3. *Teaching.* While much of choice-making and planning is emotional and not really susceptible to a teaching approach, much of vocational guidance and clarification of personal alternatives rests on a cognitive base and is appropriately treated in this manner.
4. *Practice.* Fundamentally, group processes of guidance are opportunities to test in simulated ways one's own characteristics in relation to different possibilities for action. Through role playing, case studies, selected audio-visual devices, discussion, resource people, an opportunity can be created for students to project themselves figuratively into a given situation and analyze how they, personally, would feel in that situation.
5. *Attitude Development.* Although most attitudes are learned within family and peer groups, group guidance processes represent an important tool to discuss and clarify vocational attitudes and values as well as self-understanding.
6. *Counseling.* Groups can be used to provide a secure and supportive environment in which developmental growth and the emotional characteristics of personal and vocational dilemmas can be assessed and acted upon.
7. *Exploration.* Groups can use the presence and security of several people at similar developmental levels to stimulate exploration or to provide feedback and mutual analysis of exploratory experiences.

Obviously, these seven purposes are not mutually exclusive but rather represent emphases, sometimes acting together, which group processes of vocational guidance can serve.

Appraisal

Sometimes considered synonymous with testing, *appraisal* is a somewhat broader term referring to the analysis of personal characteristics—aptitudes, interests, values, temperaments—as well as the ways they might be modified or strengthened in relation to various options available to the person. Appraisal sometimes deals with an analysis of predictor variables pertinent to some choice or more broadly with an analysis of the viability of goals held by the person. Appraisal data include previous achievement and behavior patterns as well as the more commonly understood use of tests related to educational and vocational decisions, e.g., General Aptitude Test Battery, Ohio Vocational Interest Survey, The Bennett Test of Mechanical Comprehension.

Information Retrieval

Throughout the vocational guidance process, accurate and relevant information is the fuel necessary to effective decision making; thus it is a central element of a vocational guidance program. There are many sources of information to which the counselor will have occasion to turn in individual counseling or in the group processes of vocational guidance. The source used will depend upon the purpose to be achieved and the readiness or the educational level of the student or adult to be served. Sources such as the *Occupational Outlook Handbook* and the *Dictionary of Occupational Titles* (Bureau of Labor Statistics, U.S. Department of Labor) are excellent starting points from which to obtain information about the occupational structure, specific occupations and requirements, or the relationship of vocational education courses to occupational alternatives. Depending upon the needs of the student or adult, however, it may be more useful to turn to the wide variety of commercial or professional printed or audio-visual material designed to explore different personal, social, occupational, or educational domains.

It is typically necessary to use appraisal or other forms of information first to help the client gain a personal frame of reference from which can be evaluated information about the personal, educational, or occupational options available.

Environmental Treatment

Vocational guidance practitioners have increasingly been implored to help to change the environments of their clients to make them more psychologically wholesome and supportive. In that sense, vocational guidance practitioners treat not only their individual clients but also the environmental characteristics affecting them. In some instances, this means that the vocational guidance person should be a source of information about the needs of a student or adult to aid the development of an educational program for that person; in other cases, counselors should stimulate the school to create educational experiences which comprehensively respond to the range of human talent rather than only some small sample of it (e.g., abstract verbal ability, numerical reasoning); in still other instances, counselors and vocational educators need to communicate with and assist employers in bringing about realistic employment requirements.

Remediation and/or Development

The five categories of techniques used in vocational guidance are used in two ways. First, they are used for remedial purposes when a particular person's career development is somehow blocked, the individual is in conflict, or the person's behavioral repertoire is inadequate to resolve the choice-making dilemma he or she is facing. A remedial approach to vocational guidance takes place after a person already gives evidence of experiencing a problem which he or she cannot resolve or cope with effectively. Second, these techniques are used for developmental purposes. Increasingly, vocational guidance efforts are being focused on helping students and adults acquire self-understanding, exploratory and decision-making skills, knowledge of ways to sort out available educational and occupational alternatives, job application and employability skills before they are required. In a sense, vocational guidance is conceived of as facilitating the acquisition of survival skills known to be necessary in a complex society in an effort to counter the need for remediation later in the life of clients.

It is probable that for a long time to come vocational guidance programs will need a combination of remedial and developmental emphases. The proportion of energy devoted to each will depend upon the kind of clients being served, the setting, and the resources available. In general, however, the developmental emphasis will likely grow as the favored treatment for school populations for the foreseeable future. This suggests a need for a return to the type of partnership between vocational education and vocational guidance which existed in the early days of both fields.

REFERENCES

1. Crites, J.O. "Career Counseling: A Review of Major Approaches." *The Counseling Psychologist* 4, no. 3 (1974):3–23.
2. ———. *Vocational Psychology.* New York: McGraw-Hill, 1969.
3. Herr, Edwin L. "Manpower Policies, Vocational Guidance, and Career Development." In *Vocational Guidance and Human Development,* edited by Edwin L. Herr. Boston: Houghton Mifflin, 1974.
4. Herr, E.L., and Cramer, S.H. *Vocational Guidance and Career Development in the Schools: Toward a Systems Approach.* Boston: Houghton Mifflin, 1972.
5. Herr, E.L.; Horan, J.J.; and Baker, S.B. "Clarifying the Counseling Mystique." *American Vocational Journal* 484 (April 1973):66–68.
6. Law, G.F. "Vocational Curriculum: A Regular Place for Guidance." *American Vocational Journal* 44 (1969):27–28, 60.
7. Miller, C.H. "Historical and Recent Perspectives on Work and Vocational Guidance." In *Career Guidance for a New Age,* edited by Henry Borow. Boston: Houghton Mifflin, 1973.
8. Parsons, F. *Choosing a Vocation.* Boston: Houghton Mifflin, 1909.
9. Stephens, W.R. *Social Reform and the Origins of Vocational Guidance.* Washington, D.C.: National Vocational Guidance Association, 1970.

10. Super, D.E. "Vocational Adjustment: Implementing a Self-Concept." *Occupations* 30 (1951):88–92.

11. Super, D.E.; Starishevsky, R.; Matlin, N., and Jordaan, J.P. *Career Development: Self-Concept Theory.* New York: College Entrance Examination Board, 1963.

12. Thompson, Albert S. "A Rationale for Vocational Guidance." *Personnel and Guidance Journal* 32(1954):535.

13. United States House of Representatives. Introduction. The Career Guidance and Counseling Act of 1975. Washington, D.C.: The Committee on Elementary, Secondary, and Vocational Education, 1975.

14. Walton, L.E. "The Scope and Function of Vocational Guidance." *Educational Outlook* 31, no. 4 (May 1957):119–28.

15. Williamson, E.G. "An Historical Perspective of the Vocational Guidance Movement." *Personnel and Guidance Journal* 52(May 1964):854–59.

SONY
SONY

13

Career Education and Vocational Education

This chapter addresses two common but contradictory assumptions: (1) that career education and vocational education are two phrases describing the same educational program and (2) that career education will replace vocational education because the former is newer and better. Neither of these assumptions is correct. Instead vocational education is an integral and necessary part of career education, and career education is a logical and desirable extension of educational response to trends in society which earlier created and continue to modify vocational education. But they are not the same, and an examination of their similarities and differences is in order.

The easiest way to describe the relationship between career education and vocational education is to point out that all of the latter is part of the former. But this is only part of the story. Governmental support of vocational education began in the United States before World War I, long before career education had been named. At that time, a coordinated educational program to meet the career needs of all people simply was not salable, though a number of capable people, such as John Dewey, tried. Part of the problem was that faculty psychology was dominant; there was little knowledge of personal development or career development, and little was known of the effects of segregation by race, sex, and socioeconomic status.

The result was that public school, tax-supported vocational education was instituted as a group of programs designed to prepare people for jobs below the

---

This chapter is based on Rupert N. Evans, *Career Education and Vocational Education: Similarities and Contrasts.* Washington, D.C.: U.S. Department of Health, Education and Welfare, Office of Education Monographs on Career Education, 1975.

professional level. These programs were philosophically and often physically separate from the remainder of the school. Students who desired to attend college were excluded on the not unreasonable assumption that schools would use their own resources for the college-bound, so federal funds for their aid were not as necessary. Despite this limitation to "lower level" jobs, vocational education was an enormous step forward because it met the needs of many students who otherwise almost certainly would have dropped out of a school designed solely for those who intended to go on to college.

What Is Career Education?

The term *career education* was first used by U.S. Commissioner of Education James Allen in 1970 (1, p. 268). It was described and popularized by Allen's successor, Sidney P. Marland, who undoubtedly deserves credit as the father of the movement.

Dr. Marland refused to define career education precisely, leaving that to local and state initiative. If an official federal definition had been proposed at that time, it is likely that much effort would have been expended in attacking and defending it rather than in building career education programs. Instead Marland suggested the need for

1. more emphasis on vocational education, as the core of career education, and less on the general curriculum,
2. each person to exit from the high school prepared for either continuing education or productive work,
3. education for and about work, using a variety of delivery systems (which he called models), and
4. increasing the career options open to individuals.

The authority of Marland's position as well as the timeliness of his ideas encouraged many people to begin working on career education in all parts of the country. Almost every state and many local schools adopted a definition of career education, and many of them began programs. While the definitions and programs had differences, it is obvious that most of them were influenced by the Hoyt definition in *Career Education: What It Is and How To Do It* (8), which in turn grew out of research on vocational development. Virtually every program included the phases of awareness, exploration, and preparation, and almost every definition included the following:

1. Career education is concerned with education for work, both paid and unpaid.
2. Awareness and exploration of self is as important as and must be related to awareness and exploration of the world of work.
3. A major goal is to increase the career options available to individuals and to make work possible, meaningful, and satisfying for everyone.

4. Because attitudes are formed early in life, career education should begin with the first year of school (or earlier, in the home), and because individuals and the nature of work change, career education must continue throughout life.
5. The program must involve the entire community and all parts of the school program.

Almost every program began to try to develop awareness of the world of work in the elementary school, exploration in the junior high school, and preparation in the senior high school. (Unfortunately, some career educators assumed that each of these three phases ended at the school level in which it began instead of recognizing that each continues throughout life.) Few career education programs, in spite of their rhetoric about serving all people, made any provision for adults, either through educational assistance in maintaining career competence or by recognizing that many adults need educational assistance to further career awareness, exploration, and preparation for changed careers. At the same time, secondary school vocational education continued a trend of concentrating more and more on school-aged youth and less and less on meeting adult needs.

Almost every program adopted some method of grouping activities in the world of work into some ten to fifteen clusters of similar jobs in order to ensure that no major portions of the world of work were omitted, and presumably in order to make learning more efficient by promoting the study of similar products or services at the same time. Almost every system of clustering grouped together jobs ranging from unskilled to managerial and professional so that the student who studied *construction,* for example, would be exposed to a wide range of occupational levels and could learn the advantages and disadvantages of each. This appeared to be sound, but most clusters suffered from overlap which, for example, led to the study of clerical jobs in every cluster. A few programs used the clusters of people, data, things, and at least one program (American College Testing Service) added ideas to the previous three. This type of clustering was based on studies of actual jobs and careers rather than depending on logical grouping which may or may not have been closely related to the ways in which people really think about themselves in relation to careers.

Although career education has used as few as three and as many as fifteen clusters to classify the entire world of work, vocational education has used a larger number of clusters to represent the subprofessional occupations with which it is concerned. The recent trend in vocational education definitely is toward use of a smaller number of (and hence broader) clusters. This trend, however, is in sharp contrast to the situation which existed when federal support for vocational education was initiated.

At the turn of the century, schools were employing nearly the ultimate in clustering. Faculty psychology was in vogue, and in accord with its dictates, the two basic groups of school programs trained the mind and the hand. Manual training purported to prepare students for any nonprofessional occupation. It did not produce the desired results, and federally supported vocational education was substituted for it. These early vocational programs went to the opposite extreme, under the assumption that it was necessary to have separate educational programs for each job title. Thus there were separate programs for tool grinders, wheat farmers, and hundreds of other specialized job titles.

Because even the largest school could offer specialized programs for only a small proportion of the more than 20,000 job titles, there was a gradual movement toward grouping similar job titles and developing a vocational program for these groups of jobs. This led to broader programs such as machine shop and production agriculture. The grouping of job titles progressed slowly, however, because of fears that this was a return to the discredited manual training concept.

The most recent clustering system in vocational education was developed by Dr. David Fretwell (10, p. 190–205). Nineteen clusters are used, but one of these is a miscellaneous category which includes less than 5 percent of vocational education students. These clusters can be used in two ways: for data collection and for instruction. If used for instruction, a student receives a program designed to prepare him/her for employment in any job in the cluster. The majority of the clusters are used for instruction in most parts of the country, e.g., marketing, food service, and electricity-electronics. Other clusters, e.g., metals, construction, and health, are used for instruction in only a few states. Every state, however, can use these clusters for data collection. Each cluster can be subdivided into specialized programs if the local school feels that instruction covering the entire cluster would be so broad as to decrease its utility. The state can then add data from all of the specialized programs in a cluster for reporting enrollments, costs, and so on. This clustering system almost certainly will increase the uniformity of vocational education programming and data reporting.

The degree of uniformity of program which has been achieved independently in career education across the country is remarkable, particularly considering that there was no one charged with career education leadership in the U.S. Office of Education until 1974. Occasionally one still hears remarks that career education will never amount to anything until it has a single definition upon which everyone agrees. This type of assertion implies that because there are slightly different definitions of secondary education in use that therefore secondary education is hampered significantly. Whether or not this is the case is not at all clear.

What is clear is that anyone who has the opportunity to read the career education literature or to visit a number of career education programs will find similar goals and activities underway throughout the nation. Misunderstanding of career education tends to come from those who have not read the literature or visited programs.

The rapidity of development of career education is particularly surprising because for the first four years of its life, career education received very little federal money, and what it did receive was taken from monies appropriated for vocational education.

Changes in Vocational Education

Vocational education began to receive federal funds more than 50 years ago because of a feeling that the local and state controlled schools were placing almost their entire emphasis on preparing an elite group of students for college and little or no emphasis on preparing the majority of students for the kinds of work needed by society. Three types of programs were subsidized by the new legislation: agriculture, home economics, and trades and industries. The first of these emphasized entrepreneurship, the second stressed nonpaid work in the home, and the third prepared people for employment in factories and repair shops.

The next half century saw a number of gradual shifts in the types of programs which were supported.

1. More occupational fields were included.
2. There was more and more stress on employability and less on entrepreneurship.
3. Paid work was emphasized and nonpaid work (e.g., homemaking) de-emphasized.
4. More emphasis was placed on programs in postsecondary schools for full-time students and less on programs designed for adults who were occasional students.
5. Part-time cooperative programs (school-supervised employment in business and industry) increased markedly.

The late sixties and early seventies produced a series of research results which changed vocational education significantly and laid the groundwork for career education.

1. People with no salable skills have greater difficulties in the labor market than those who have skills of almost any variety.
2. Because unskilled jobs are usually the easiest to automate, the average level of knowledge and skill required by jobs continues to increase.
3. Socioeconomic segregation has greater adverse educational effects than does even racial segregation.
4. The school curriculum in which a student is enrolled is related to the student's race, sex, socioeconomic status, and verbal ability. Measures of educational effectiveness of the various curricula which do not control for these variables are very misleading.
5. Handicapped youth learn less when they are segregated than when they have both special assistance and exposure to regular classes. Segregation appears to have a greater negative effect on the learning of attitudes and cognitive skills than on the learning of manual skills, but vocational education involves all three types of learning.
6. We have been unable to develop effective methods of forecasting local employment needs for even a ten-year period, but students and their parents know what types of vocational education they want. If given a choice, they

appear to choose wisely in the long run. A program which does not have acceptance from both students and parents will disappear because of low enrollment.

7. The student who drops out of school (physically or mentally) does so in large part because he or she sees school as being personally irrelevant.
8. The old notion of a career requiring continued promotion until a person reaches a level of incompetence with its accompanying frustration is beginning to be replaced by the concept that a career should lead to greater and greater personal satisfaction, even if this means a shift to a different career ladder or a step down the career ladder.

Not all of these research results have been incorporated in all vocational education programs, but enough people accept them to affect markedly the formation of new vocational education programs. The blend of new and continuing programs has increased until now about one-third of high school graduates and community college students have access to vocational education of some type. The proportion of students enrolling in college preparatory and college transfer curricula is static and the general curriculum is contracting. Vocational education is growing in enrollment; so if one uses the criterion of consumer acceptance, it is succeeding. Many vocational educators believe that career education programs in the elementary and junior high schools will increase this acceptance of vocational education by students and parents. It would appear that this same assumption leads some nonvocational teachers to be wary of career education because they fear it will decrease emphasis on preparation for college. Many parents, especially those in minority groups, have similar fears. This is discussed further in the section on "people served."

Awareness and Exploration Phases of Career Education

Many vocational educators who have not had contact with career education programs in the elementary and junior high schools assume that career awareness and exploration are simple matters which can be handled by a course or two taught by vocational educators in high school. Several things are wrong with this attitude.

1. Attitudes are learned early in life, and attitudes toward work are difficult to change by the time a student has reached high school age.
2. A course (or even two courses) is not a very effective way of teaching people to become aware of or to explore the world of work. Thousands of students during the 1920s suffered through "occupations" courses which consisted of the teacher reading long lists of job descriptions, pay scales, and job entry requirements. This type of course cannot substitute for observation, simulation and discussion which are best spread over several years and are best presented in relationship to other types of school learnings.
3. The vocational educator is not necessarily the best person to teach career awareness and exploration. As a specialist in one part of career preparation, he or she is apt to seek recruits for that specialty and may have little patience

with those who are not interested in or qualified for that specialty. And, because nonprofessional careers are emphasized in vocational education, the vocational educator may be suspect of not giving adequate attention to professional careers. As with academic teachers and guidance counselors, vocational educators need special training to do the best possible job of helping students to develop career awareness and to explore a wide variety of careers.

Preparation Phase of Career Education

Because vocational education constitutes an indispensable part of the preparation phase of career education, an understanding of this phase is necessary to an understanding of the relationship of vocational and career education. Awareness and exploration precede preparation, the phase in which students or adults

1. acquire career decision-making skills, work-seeking skills, and work evaluation skills;
2. perfect skills in communication, computation, and human relations which are needed by everyone; and
3. acquire additional salable skills which apply more to some types of work than to others.

The preparation phase of career education can be (and once was) conducted entirely on the job. However, there has been a continuing trend toward a combination of preparation in school with training on the job. This combination may be done *sequentially* (as is the case when a person goes to engineering school for four years and follows this with two years of experience on the job or *concurrently* (as in a part-time cooperative education program, in which the student engages in alternating periods of study and work under the supervision of the school). Both the sequential and the concurrent methods of instruction are usually accompanied by a certain amount of general education while the person is in school. (Most commonly, 50 percent of the school time in any one school year is spent in general education and 50 percent in specialized instruction).

The length of the in-school preparation phase varies considerably from one type of career to another. For convenience, careers can be divided into four categories of length of specialized in-school preparation:

1. professional—40 to 100 semester hours spread over 4 to 7 years of full-time schooling, usually in a university.
2. technical—30 to 45 semester hours spread over 2 years of full-time schooling, usually in a community college.
3. vocational, skilled—20 to 35 semester hours in 1 year of full-time schooling, usually in a community college, or approximately the same amount of instruction (4 to 6 Carnegie Units) spread over 2 to 4 years of high school.
4. vocational, specialized—one day to 6 months of intensive instruction, usually offered to adults by high schools, proprietary schools (e.g., trade and business schools), community colleges, or universities. Specialized preparation is

usually completed by people already employed and hence provides few additional entrants to the labor force.

When one studies the data on the percentage of people employed in various types of occupations and the proportion of students in different types of occupational education programs, some interesting comparisons emerge (see figure 13–1). Professional preparation is useful for about 20 percent of the labor market and is completed by about 20 percent of students; technical preparation is useful for about 15 percent of the labor market, but less than 10 percent of students complete it; and vocational preparation is useful for about 40 percent of the labor market, but less than 30 percent of students complete it, and about one-third of its graduates go on to technical or professional preparation instead of going immediately to employment.

FIGURE 13–1. *Types of school-based career preparation (estimated percentages)*

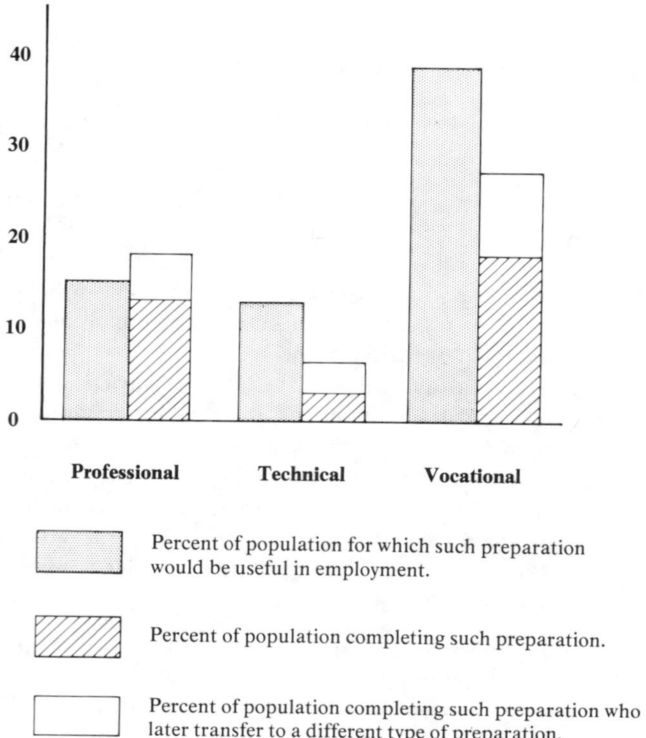

There are no in-school programs preparing people for job entry to approximately 20 percent of the careers in the labor market, and about 50 percent of new entrants to the labor force have not participated in career preparation programs of any type.

It is a common assumption that vocational education is synonymous with the career preparation phase of career education. This assumption is not quite accurate. Vocational education is concerned with preparation for the large numbers of vocational and technical careers which are nonprofessional and require less than a college degree for entrance, but which require more knowledge and skill than is possessed by the typical high school graduate from the general curriculum.

Career preparation includes (but vocational education usually omits):

1. preparation for the professions and for similar careers requiring a baccalaureate for entry (about 20 percent of the labor force);
2. preparation for nonpaid work such as homemaking (once a full-fledged part of vocational education, but now half-in, half-out due to evaluation specialists who convinced Congress that placement of vocational graduates in homemaking was equivalent to unemployment) and volunteer work. (Both of these major types of work are, of course, outside the paid labor force.); and
3. education which is needed for more effective involvement in all types of work, e.g., work-seeking skills, personal and work evaluation skills, and knowledge of how work is organized and carried out (preparation for all work inside and outside the labor force).

It is a common mistake to say that the vocational education curriculum prepares people for 80 percent of the jobs, while the college preparatory curriculum in the secondary school prepares people for only 20 percent of the jobs. It would be more accurate to say that at least 50 percent of high school students are not now prepared for work of any type and that traditional programs of vocational education designed to prepare people for skilled occupations are unlikely to meet this need. Career education programs which emphasize preparation for nonpaid work and preparation which is useful for all types of work offer real promise of meeting some of the needs of this 50 percent.

It might be assumed that there would be no conflict between vocational educators and other career educators with regard to career preparation programs in the high school and community college. Unfortunately, this is not always true. The greatest conflict appears to arise between career educators and the coordinators of part-time cooperative education (co-op) programs. Co-op coordinators arrange and supervise employment for students and provide an educational link between the half of the student's time spent at work and the half-time spent in school (see chapter 17). Such programs rarely serve more than 10 percent of the school population, and in order to get participation which is this extensive, the co-op coordinators work night and day to find willing and able employers with whom they can work. A coordinator will do nearly anything to preserve a good "training station." But along comes career education with blithe promises of providing work experience for everyone, and very often the first reaction of the co-op coordinator is fear of the loss of training stations, and, more basically, a fear that unsupervised work experience will destroy cooperative education, which many people feel is the best method vocational education uses. The more knowledgeable coordinators cite statistics of 73 percent unemployment among unsupervised work experience students in one eastern state during the early 1970s.

Other conflicts are certain to arise as high schools begin to expand their career education beyond what they have been doing in vocational education.

These conflicts will not be resolved simply by castigating vocational educators as being resistant to change. They were, after all, in career education before it had that name, and they do know some things which have worked and some things that have not. The co-op coordinators, for example, can supply excellent suggestions on a variety of methods of working with the business and industrial community. And perhaps they are right that unsupervised work experience programs are far from what they might be.

Youth Clubs as a Means of Career Exploration and Preparation

Almost two million high school and postsecondary school vocational education students participate in five youth organizations. The oldest and largest of these organizations are the Future Farmers of America and the Future Homemakers of America. All five of the groups are organized to parallel the traditional vocational programs of agriculture, business, distributive education, homemaking, and trades and industries. The closest major parallel in the health occupations field is the Student Nurses Association, though an organization of health occupations is being developed. In each organization a vocational teacher is usually the club adult advisor.

These clubs hold local, regional, and national conferences, and most of them conduct competitive contests in a wide variety of activities and publish materials for student use. Their principal emphasis is on development of leadership skills, and the results are impressive. Their state and national officers are perhaps the best spokespeople for vocational education in the Congress and before business and industry groups.

There are also youth organizations for high school youth who wish to explore one or more of several professions. Future Teachers of America, Junior Engineering Technical Society, and Junior Academy of Science are three large national groups. There are national or local counterparts in journalism, music, theater, and many other professions. The adult sponsor may be a local teacher or practitioner who has expertise in the field with which the club is concerned.

At first glance it might appear that vocational and preprofessional youth groups might have similar goals, but this is not the case, in spite of the fact that their programs are remarkably alike. Vocational youth groups usually require that the student member be enrolled in the related vocational program. This, in turn, means that the student has made at least a nominal career choice and is in the preparation phase of career education. Consequently, the club program emphasizes proficiency in, rather than exploration of, careers. In contrast, the students in preprofessional youth groups are encouraged to explore more widely (but only within the professions represented by the club charter), and there usually is an open-entry, open-exit membership policy unrelated to the student's major field of study.

The undisputed value of youth clubs in developing attitudes and leadership skills leads one to inquire why there are so few career education clubs, or at least prevocational clubs. Such groups could play a major role in developing career awareness and assisting with career exploration. Some industrial arts and home economics clubs play this role, but most seem to have avocational goals.

The youth groups with the most extensive career exploration programs usually are operated outside the schools. Explorers (formerly Explorer Scouts) have an extremely well-developed career exploration program which encompasses all types of careers. Somewhat less extensive exploration is offered by 4-H Clubs and by Junior Achievement.

Career Education and Vocational Guidance

Vocational guidance can be provided by many types of people in many types of settings. School counselors who have been prepared specifically to offer vocational guidance should be the most effective single group of people in filling this function in schools. However, there are far too few such people, and they have too many other duties to allow them to meet the need without help. Consequently, peers, parents, the media, government agencies, and many other types of individuals and groups have provided certain vocational guidance functions, more or less effectively, usually outside of the school. The major untapped group within the school has been the various types of classroom teachers.

A major goal of career education is to involve classroom teachers more frequently and more effectively in positively influencing the vocational development of students. Typically this requires teachers to employ guidance activities. The reason for such teacher involvement is simply that there are, and probably always will be, far more classroom teachers than there are guidance personnel. An even more important reason for involving classroom teachers, however, is the fact that studies of vocational development have emphasized that such development is a long process closely related to other types of learning. Classroom teachers ought to be (and most are) concerned with all types of learning. Moreover, they work with groups of students for long periods of time, while counselors usually have only brief encounters with any one student or group of students. Because vocational development is a lengthy process, rather than a single act, the classroom teacher, who is in contact with the student every day, is better situated to deal with the information-giving and subject-related aspects of vocational guidance than any other person in the school. Such experiences tend to stimulate personal assessment and other forms of exploration. A side benefit is that as the classroom teacher develops the student's ability to make more effective career plans, the student sees more relevance to the other things the classroom teacher desires to teach.

But career education goes beyond involvement of classroom teachers in guidance functions. Many of the written materials used in career education encourage and give practice to the student in providing self-help in solving personal vocational guidance problems. Parents, peers, employer, and employee groups are involved in a wide variety of activities which help all of the participants to teach each other and to learn from each other.

All of this activity can facilitate the work of the professional guidance counselor. Students who have had exposure to career education come to the counselor with much preliminary work done: they have thought about themselves and their plans, and they know what questions to ask. In a school which has a planned career education program, the counselor is assisted by a much wider range of guidance-oriented library resources to which students can be referred, and computer-assisted occupational information searches are more likely to be made available. The increased demand for adequate vocational guidance often leads to the employment of additional professional guidance staff and to freeing existing staff from clerical and other nonguidance functions. Another result of the increased demand for vocational guidance services is that counselors are led to experiment with group guidance activities. Many, but not all guidance activities can be provided far more efficiently to groups than to individuals. By experimentation and further training, the counselor learns which group activities are most successful.

Perhaps the greatest effect of career education on vocational guidance is to stress that everyone in society can provide certain elements of it and that everyone in the school, the home, and the place of employment should assume certain guidance responsibilities. One of the most important tasks of career education is to use effectively the talents of such diverse groups.

The possible benefits of broadened responsibility for vocational guidance carry with them a danger: what is everybody's business is nobody's business. Planning and evaluation of the career education system must assess the potential and actual contribution of each group in carrying out the guidance functions. Concurrently, it must be assured that those who provide guidance do it in terms of careers rather than in terms of the first job (or, in the case of adults, the next job). To some people, vocational guidance has been concerned primarily with one job at a time. Career education demands, and most counselors have emphasized, the need for continuous assessment, by the individual of himself or herself and of the environment as the person's career progresses. More than the next job needs to be taken into account. Also involved are intermediate and future goal setting, decision-making skill development, educational planning, life-style and leisure value clarification. Because vocational guidance can be and sometimes is assumed to relate only to a single job, it might well be replaced by the term *career guidance*. The concept, however, is more important than the term used to describe it.

Goals of Vocational Education and Career Preparation

Vocational education and the preparation phase of career education have precisely the same goals of:

1. meeting society's needs for workers,
2. increasing individual options related to work, and
3. conveying knowledge of the relevance of general education in work.

Because the goal of meeting the needs of society for workers was the initial goal of vocational education, it is sometimes believed by nonvocational educators to be its sole goal. Equally bad is the belief that career education has this as its sole goal.

Vocational education has been hampered continually in achieving its goal of increasing individual options by systems of evaluation which measure its effectiveness in terms of the percentage of graduates placed on jobs in the field for which they were "trained." This type of evaluation counts as a failure the realization by a student that the type of career for which he or she is being prepared is unlikely to be personally satisfying, and that a shift to a different type of career is therefore desirable. Most educators agree that far from being a failure, such realization represents a success.

Awareness of self inevitably will be enhanced by high quality vocational education. Exploration of the world of work is included in every vocational program, but sometimes the range of exploration allowed is not great. Evaluation of the vocational education phase of career education should include measurement of the effects of awareness and exploration as well as the results of preparation. The career education concept should make such a broadened evaluation more readily acceptable to labor economists and academicians who in the past have seen only one goal for vocational education.

The process of helping students to find work which is meaningful and satisfying is not aided by evaluation procedures which reward schools for restricting student placement to the small number of vocations for which the school has established specific training programs, or for restricting admission to students who are so highly qualified that they are placeable with or without training. The evaluation should be made, first, in terms of the proportion of former students who secured paid and unpaid work, and, second, in terms of the proportion who found their work satisfying and meaningful.

Even more difficult to understand is the type of evaluation which counts it as a failure of vocational education if a student continues her or his education rather than immediately going to work after graduation. In the early days of vocational education such an evaluation might have been justifiable to prevent school administrators from using federal vocational funds as a subsidy for college preparatory classes, but now such evaluation can only serve to limit student options.

People Served by Vocational Education and Career Education

Career education is designed to serve all of the people. In contrast, vocational education has tended to serve those high school students who are low in verbal ability *and* have low socioeconomic status (3). In the postsecondary school it serves those who are low in verbal ability *or* are low in socioeconomic status (5). Those who are low in both rarely attend postsecondary schools. Those who are high in both tend to go to four-year colleges and universities. Clearly, vocational education does not serve all.

The most obvious difference between career education and vocational education is in the minimum age of individuals served. Career education may begin in early childhood; vocational education usually begins about age 16. It seldom or never begins below age 14, and the average age of entry to vocational education has been increasing ever since its inception.

Vocational education is usually thought of as a program for males, but slightly more than half (55%) of its enrollment is female. Sex stereotypes in enrollment parallel those in the world of work, with business education, health occupations, and home economics having female students and teachers almost exclusively. Agriculture and trade and industrial education are as solidly male.

Some spokespeople for minority groups see vocational education as a means of teaching which destroys opportunities for higher education for minority students, by providing another rationale for "tracking" students. This may be true in certain communities, but in the nation as a whole minorities are neither overrepresented nor underrepresented in the vocational education student body. They are underrepresented, however, in the teaching staff and in certain higher level technical education programs.

Problems in the Relationship of Career and Vocational Education

Career education has had its greatest success in the elementary school. It now appears that its introduction into junior high schools is well under way, but in high schools there is little to be seen of career education except for vocational education. This can be explained in a variety of ways, most of which are based on misconception.

1. Some people feel that vocational education and the preparation phase of career education are synonymous, so if their high school has the former, they feel that the latter is accomplished.
2. Parents want career education to be available in high school but don't necessarily want their children to enroll in it, especially not in its career preparation phase.
3. The curriculum in high school is mandated by colleges and by accrediting associations.
4. High school teachers who accept career education goals feel that little can be done until awareness and exploration activities are well under way in the lower grades.
5. Some of the high school teachers who accept career education goals know that they have only a limited awareness of the vast range of career options existing in the world of work and are uncomfortable with the thought that they will be involved in preparing students for careers with which they are unfamiliar.
6. Some people who accept awareness and exploration of careers as legitimate school activities feel that preparation is the job of private trade schools or employers rather than of the schools.

The true reasons need to be identified and means found to cope with them. A career education program which is full blown only until it reaches the preparation stage cannot long survive if it then becomes a program only for those who are low in verbal ability and low in socioeconomic status.

Career education obtained its initial financing and leadership from vocational education. In the U.S. Office of Education it is difficult to identify more than a handful of people involved in career education who did not come from vocational education. In other parts of government, however, the reverse is true: it is hard to find more than a handful of people who understand what vocational education is or who see its vital role in career education.

One former official of the Department of Health, Education and Welfare set career education back several years by trying to equate career education with all education. Two results were apparent: career education began to be diluted, because it had diffuse goals and fears of educators were heightened because they saw this as a move by career educators to take over all of education. Education has several key goals which are important in their own right and are only tangentially related to career education. Careers are important and deserve the attention of the school, but they are not and should not be the sole concern of the school. Every part of the school has something to contribute to career education, but every part of the school also has concerns outside of career education.

This mistake of stating that all of education is career education must not be repeated, and the only way to be sure to avoid it is to develop leadership, especially from the fields of career development, educational administration, learning resource management, special education, and vocational education to work with subject matter specialists in building a complete program of career education (9). Internships in active career education programs along with graduate work in career education would make a useful and attractive package for leadership development. Leadership can no longer be allowed to rest solely with vocational educators and vocational guidance personnel.

Career education is needed as much in postsecondary and adult education as in the common schools, and programs aimed at enhancing career awareness and exploration are needed as much as career preparation. Ideally, a career education program which extends from early childhood through adulthood would be planned by all agencies concerned. It is obvious, however, that it is easier to plan around a single K-12 school system than to develop plans which involve several K-12 school systems plus one or more postsecondary institutions, public or private. To overcome such obstacles to coordinated action, incentives should be provided to encourage joint planning which brings together educational institutions of various levels, Comprehensive Education and Training Act (CETA) agencies, and the various adult education agencies.

Summary

This chapter has examined some of the similarities and contrasts between vocational education and the remainder of career education with the goal of a better understanding of both. It has indicated ways in which the older, more specialized field of vocational education is an essential part of the newer, broader, concept of career education. The fact that these two programs must rely on each other will not prevent their having conflicting views, due in part to their different genesis, goals, and types of people served.

Both educators and evaluators of education should recognize that career education is now faced with a dilemma which many vocational educators have been unwilling to recognize: that it is extremely difficult to prepare workers who are both conformists and change agents. How can one be both satisfied with one's job and eager to change its content? How can one learn to have good human relations and at the same time be pushing other humans to change age-old problems in the work place?

Career education has begun to be important enough to attract critics. One of the criticisms is that it is designed to produce docile workers for the military-industrial complex. It would appear, however, that even modest programs of career awareness, exploration, and preparation are likely to decrease docility by affording both blue collar and white collar workers new ways of looking at work as well as new opportunities for mobility. If this is true, one can expect soon to hear cries from other critics that career education is producing people who expect too much from their work. Steering a course between these two groups of critics will be difficult, but it is better than using education to perpetuate the notion that work is necessarily bad and fit only for slaves. Career education and vocational education share the goal of making work possible, meaningful, and satisfying for everyone.

REFERENCES

1. Bailey, Larry J., and Stadt, Ronald. *Career Education: New Approaches to Human Development.* Bloomington, Ill.: McKnight Publishing Company, 1973.
2. Bezdek, Roger H. "Education and Training Requirements for Scientists and Engineers." *Journal of Continuing Education and Training* 3, no. 3–4 (Winter-Spring 1974):311–25.
3. Evans, Rupert N., and Galloway, Joel D. "Verbal Ability and Socioeconomic Status of 9th and 12th Grade College Preparatory, General, and Vocational Students." *The Journal of Human Resources* 8 (1):1973.
4. Evans, Rupert N. et al. *Career Education in the Middle/Junior High School.* Salt Lake City, Utah: Olympus Publishing Company, 1974.
5. Evans, Rupert N., and Jackson, Truman. *Socioeconomic Status and Verbal Ability of Post-Secondary Vocational Students.* Forthcoming.
6. Hoyt, Kenneth B. *Career Education, Vocational Education and Occupational Education: An Approach to Defining Differences.* Columbus, Ohio: Center for Vocational Education, The Ohio State University, 1974.
7. ______. *Career Education: Strategies and Dilemmas.* Columbus, Ohio: State Directors of Vocational Education Leadership Seminar, Center for Vocational Education, The Ohio State University, 1974. Mimeographed.
8. Hoyt, Kenneth B. et al. *Career Education, What It Is and How To Do It,* 2d ed. Salt Lake City, Utah: Olympus Publishing Company, 1974.

9. Hoyt, Kenneth B. et al. *Career Education in the High School.* Salt Lake City, Utah: Olympus Publishing Company, 1976.

10. Lee, Arthur M., and Sartin, Robert. *Learning a Living Across the Nation,* vol. 2. Flagstaff, Ariz.: Northern Arizona University, 1973.

11. National Association of State Directors of Vocational Education. *Position Paper on Career Education.* Las Vegas, Nev.: The Association, 1971.

12. National Advisory Council on Vocational Education. *A National Policy on Career Education.* Eighth Report. Washington, D.C.: The Council, 1974.

13. Scoville, James G. *The Job Content of the U.S. Economy, 1940–1970.* New York: McGraw-Hill Book Company, 1969.

part IV

Organization of Vocational Education

14

Introduction

Vocational education is provided by many agencies in our society. Public schools and employers undoubtedly provide much more such education than do other groups, but almost every institution incorporates some vocational education activities so that it may operate more effectively.

Considerably more information is available about vocational education conducted by the public schools than by other institutions of society. Moreover, public schools are more amenable to control by society than are most of the other institutions which have large programs of vocational education. Consequently, this section concentrates more heavily on the public school portion of vocational education than on its other parts.

Issues in the Organization of Vocational Education

Client-centered versus Institution-centered Vocational Education

In one sense, all vocational education is concerned both with meeting the needs of its students and with meeting the needs of the institution providing the instructional program. Nevertheless, the balance between these concerns is quite different from one institution to another.

If the potential student has complete freedom to participate or not participate, the vocational education program is likely to be client-centered. Examples of such programs are found in community colleges and in private, proprietary vocational schools. Unless these programs meet student needs, they are out of business.

Vocational education conducted by the military and by other employers is likely to be designed to meet the needs of the institution. These programs are rarely elective because a group of rewards and punishments strongly encourages participation by employees who have been selected to attend.

Secondary school programs tend to be in an intermediate position. Pressures to attend secondary school are very real, and the student may have few choices among school programs. The broader the range of choices the student has, the more likely that the program will be designed to meet the needs of the student rather than the needs of the teacher or the school. Competition aids the student; monopoly aids the institution.

On-the-Job versus Formal Classroom-Laboratory Instruction

It is often assumed that employers provide vocational education through on-the-job (OJT) instruction, while public schools use formal classroom-laboratory instruction. This distinction is becoming less and less accurate. As chapter 18 indicates, employers provide an increasing amount of their vocational education in classrooms and in laboratories such as vestibule schools. Many large employers have established formal schools for their employees and customers. At the same time, public schools are increasing their use of on-the-job instruction through part-time cooperative education, work experience, work-study, and simulated or actual production within the school.

On-the-job and formal classroom-laboratory instruction are settings within which instruction can be accomplished. The choice of setting is not so much a function of the institution providing the instruction as it is a function of the task to be taught. Instruction on how to use a typewriter is invariably done in a classroom-laboratory setting rather than on-the-job. Teaching students to operate expensive, one-of-a-kind equipment is usually done on-the-job.

As work acquires a larger and larger component of theory, instruction in how to perform that work is more and more likely to be taught in a classroom-laboratory setting. Physicians and lawyers were trained on-the-job during the nineteenth century, but as their work acquired a greater and greater component of theory, classroom and laboratory instruction became a necessity, and on-the-job training was used for later phases of instruction. This same trend may be observed in almost every occupation which has a sizable theoretical content.

The balance of theory and practice is not the only variable affecting the setting within which vocational education can be provided most effectively. Twenty-four variables have been identified as affecting the choice of setting (1). Among the variables which indicate that a classroom-laboratory setting will be most effective are large numbers of people to be trained, high levels of danger resulting from the actions of untrained personnel, and unwillingness of incumbent workers to instruct newcomers. Conversely, if equipment is expensive and quickly becomes obsolete, if large amounts of materials are required, or if key conditions of the work place cannot be simulated in the classroom or laboratory, the best setting for instruction is likely to be on-the-job. Clearly, however, the trend is toward offering a higher proportion of vocational education through a combination of classroom-laboratory instruction and on-the-job training, with less and less reliance on OJT as the sole setting for instruction.

Job Conformity versus Job Reform as Goals of Education

Traditionally, Americans have expected the educational system to prepare people to exist comfortably in the existing society. At the same time the influential critics of education have charged education with failure to revolutionize the society or even to change it markedly. Most educators would like to prepare people who can enjoy life as it is but at the same time can perceive areas of life in which change is needed and are willing and able to work for such change. Almost invariably, however, the principal emphasis is placed on conformity because society controls the schools, and society is more interested in educating conformists than it is in educating even a small number of revolutionaries.

All education has the dilemma of the need to prepare people both to exist comfortably in society and to change or even to revolutionize that society. The same dilemma exists in career education, but especially in its vocational education phase. A frequently stated objective of vocational education is to enable the graduate to succeed in a given line of work. Success is usually measured in terms of the employer's satisfaction with the graduate and less frequently in terms of the worker's satisfaction with the job. Both of these evaluative measures encourage educational programs which stress learning to "get along with others," "practice good human relations," and learning not to "rock the boat."

But at the same time there is societal dissatisfaction with job structure. Vocational education is seen as a means of promoting job enlargement, eliminating discrimination based on sex or race, changing the distribution of national income by finding jobs for the poor, and eliminating socioeconomic barriers to career mobility.

It should be clear that a vocational education program whose graduates enjoy their work and are experts at getting along and not rocking the boat is unlikely to produce many graduates who will push employers or fellow employees for costly improvements in job safety or major changes in job content, promotion patterns, or job assignments. Nor would the vocational education program which graduated large numbers of male homemakers or black electricians (at a time when there was substantial discrimination against such people in society) be likely to have a record of 100 percent placement of graduates in productive work or to have a record of high job satisfaction on the part of its graduates.

A case in point is the limited role of females in vocational education. Although more females than males are enrolled in vocational programs, more than half of the females are being educated in only one area—home economics—and about one third are studying office occupations. Part of this segregation is due to actions of educators and part of it is due to attitudes of potential enrollees. Vocational education is being pressured by recent federal legislation to increase the mobility of both sexes across educational and employment barriers. It appears that social scientists and Congress are more concerned about nonsexist vocational education than are employers and employees whose major concern is for continuity in their present occupations (4).

There is no known method of preparing a person simultaneously to conform to the expectations of the job market and to revolutionize the job market. Employers tend to emphasize the former and social scientists, the latter, while most vocational educators try to meet both objectives in part. This allows both employers and social scientists to charge that vocational education has failed.

It is rare for an institution deliberately to prepare people to reform it. Just as it is unlikely for education to set out to prepare people to reform schools, so it is unlikely for employers to plan educational programs for its employees which will lead to significant reforms in the work place. Both schools and employers will seek improved efficiency in their own operations through an evolutionary process. Revolutionary reforms are more likely to come from outside, rather than inside the institution, so it is conceivable that employers and consumers can reform schools (for example, by encouraging career education) and that vocational education can reform the work place by preparing workers who are able and willing to question existing work practices. The symbiotic relationship between vocational education and work suggests, however, that neither can be changed without affecting the other.

These three issues suggest that some institutions are more likely than others to provide client-centered vocational education, that some tasks are better taught in classroom-laboratory settings than on-the-job, and that the ability to teach a suitable balance of job conformity and job reform is affected by the groups which provide, control, and evaluate vocational education. All three of these issues have a bearing on the ways in which vocational education is organized.

Finance

Funds for public school vocational education come from federal, state, and local taxes. The mean (average) expenditure per student per year was $262.00 in 1971, of which $43.00 came from the federal government and 5 times as much ($219.00) came from state and local governments (3, vol. I, pp. 341, 358). This ratio is typical, though it decreases briefly after a major increase in federal appropriations due to a lag in state and local financing.

Relative costs by level were highest for postsecondary instruction during this same period ($534.00), followed by secondary level instruction ($300.00), and adult instruction ($75.00) (3, vol. I, pp. 358–67). This relationship has existed for many years, partly because the relative pay of instructors at each level follows the same order, but more importantly because this is also the order of the number of hours of instruction per student per year (adult students attend only a few hours per year, and secondary school vocational students spend a smaller proportion of their school time in vocational studies than do postsecondary students).

Expenditures differ markedly from state to state. At the secondary school level the state which spends the most per pupil per year spends almost fourteen times as much as the state which spends the least. At the postsecondary level, the range is 52 to 1 (3, vol. I, pp. 358–74). Those states which earmark funds for vocational education spend more per student than those that do not, but an even more important variable seems to be the attitude of the state officials toward encouraging vocational education at a particular level and toward increasing the number of programs eligible for reimbursement. If these officials are unsympathetic toward postsecondary schools, they tend to allocate little money per student to such schools. If they believe that existing programs should receive funds rather than new programs, the latter will be shortchanged, at least until additional funds are made available. Meanwhile, in other states, every new program means a cut in funds for existing programs.

The typical state financing program for public schools uses the number of students as a key variable. Schools which are increasing in enrollment are given more money, while those which have declining enrollment receive less and less. Too often, however, this is not the case in vocational education. Federal funds are allocated to states on the basis of their population and wealth, rather than on the basis of the number of students in vocational education. Similarly, state funds are often appropriated as a flat amount, and a large increase in vocational education enrollment results in less money per student.

Enrollment

The proportion of the population served by public school vocational education programs increased 110 percent from 1961 to 1971. Slightly over 2 percent of the total population of the nation was enrolled in 1961 as compared with 4.4 percent in 1971. By far the greatest proportion in both years was enrolled in secondary school programs (3, vol. I, p. 54), but the greatest growth rate was in postsecondary programs.

TABLE 14–1. *Enrollment in public school vocational education (1970–71) compared with population (1970)*

Age	Population in Millions	Level	Enrollment in Millions	Percent Enrolled
All	203.2	All	9.0	4.4
15–19	19.3	Secondary	5.0	26.3
20–24	16.8	Postsecondary	1.1	6.6
25–64	91.6	Adult	2.8	3.1

SOURCE: Adapted from Arthur M. Lee, *Learning a Living across the Nation*, vol. I (Flagstaff, Ariz.: Northern Arizona University, Project Baseline, 1972 and 1973), pp. 159–71.

Does not include territories

The three subject areas which have the highest enrollments are consumer education and homemaking, office occupations, and trade and industrial, but the areas which show the greatest percentage of growth during the past five years are health occupations and occupational home economics (3, vol. I, pp. 90–95). The greatest numerical growth during this period has come in trade and industrial education.

TABLE 14–2. *Enrollment in public school vocational education by subject field, 1961–72*

Subject Field	1961 Enrollment in Thousands	Percentage	1972 Enrollment in Thousands	Percentage
Total	3,856	100	10,053	100
Agriculture	805	20.9	864	8.6
Distributive Education	306	7.9	634	6.3
Health Occupations	47	1.2	334	3.3
Consumer and Homemaking	1,610	41.8	2,582	25.7
Occupational Home Economics	NA	NA	266	2.6
Office Occupations	NA	NA	2,341	23.3
Technical Education	123	3.2	335	3.3
Trade and Industrial	964	25	2,368	23.6
Other	NA	NA	327	3.3

SOURCE: Adapted from Arthur M. Lee, *Learning a Living across the Nation,* vol. II (Flagstaff, Ariz.: Northern Arizona University, Project Baseline, 1972 and 1973), p. 86.

A more modern and useful way of reporting vocational education enrollments uses nineteen clusters. These clusters group vocational education programs which teach certain competencies in common (2). Project Baseline is the only source of information on enrollments in these clusters.

TABLE 14–3. *Enrollment in public school vocational education by cluster, 1972*

Cluster	Percent of Enrollment
Accounting	3.3
Agriculture	6.5
Child Care	2.1
Clerical	6.1
Clothing	4.7
Construction	4.0
Drafting	1.4
Electricity-Electronics	3.5
Food Service	3.5
Forest Products	.2
Graphics	.7
Health	3.3
Home Economics	19.1
Industrial Mechanics	7.4
Marketing	5.5
Metals	2.9
Secretarial	11.5
Service	5.2
Miscellaneous	4.3
Total	100.00

SOURCE: Adapted from Arthur M. Lee, *Learning a Living across the Nation,* vol. II (Flagstaff, Ariz.: Northern Arizona University, Project Baseline, 1972 and 1973), pp. 190–212.

A comparison of tables 14–2 and 14–3 shows that the Oregon cluster system divides the traditional fields of vocational education into more homogeneous subject fields. Office occupations, trades and industries, and consumer and homemaking are particularly affected.

In contrast to the extensive information about enrollments, much less is known about completions. In 1972, twenty-two states reported completions in relationship to projected labor demands. These figures included early school leavers who had marketable skills as well as those who had graduated from vocational education programs. A few states recorded more completions in a few subject areas than could be absorbed by the expected labor force demands, but for all of the reporting states combined, the supply (completions) fell well short of the expected demand in every subject area. Distributive education showed the greatest discrepancy, with supply amounting to less than 20 percent of expected demand. The highest percentage reported was in office occupations, with supply amounting to almost 53 percent of expected demand (3, vol. II, p. 184).

These figures are helpful but not definitive. Not only do they omit more than half of the country (there are no reports from the largest states), but they assume that all of those people prepared to enter a field of work will do so. When corrections are made for known placements in a given field of work, it would appear that occupational homemaking and distributive education are filling about 10 percent of projected labor demand and that the fields which come closest to filling demand, technical education and office occupations, are placing students who fill about 25 percent of projected demand (3, vol. II, p. 188). These are substantial figures in terms of questions as to whether or not vocational education is helping to meet the employment needs of the nation. On the other hand, they certainly lend no support to contentions that public school vocational education is producing far more people in some fields than can be employed. The fact remains, however, that these data, which are the best available, are not as extensive or accurate as they should be.

REFERENCES

1. Evans, Rupert N.; Holter, Arne; and Stern, Marilyn Cheney, "Criteria for Determining Whether Competency Should Be Taught On-the-Job or in a Formal Technical Course." *Journal of Vocational Education Research.* In press.
2. Fretwell, David. *Vocational Education Occupations.* Salem, Ore.: Oregon Department of Education, Division of Vocational Education, 1970.
3. Lee, Arthur M. *Learning a Living Across the Nation,* Vol. I and II, Flagstaff, Ariz.: Northern Arizona University, Project Baseline, 1972 and 1973.
4. Roby, Pamela A. *Vocational Education and Women.* Santa Cruz, Cal.: University of California-Santa Cruz. Unpublished paper prepared for the National Academy of Sciences Committee on Vocational Research and Development, 1974.

HYDRA-POWER DRIVE
1600

15

Vocational Education in Secondary Schools

There is virtually no vocational education (instruction in occupational-task specific skills) in American schools below the ninth grade. The little that exists is found in large city schools for the chronic truants and other students who for some reason have not secured enough academic credits to admit them to secondary schools, in spite of the fact that they have reached secondary school age. Little has been written about these programs and little is known about them outside the walls of the institution in which they are conducted.

There are three basic reasons for the fact that vocational education usually begins in the high school.

1. Vocational education is understood by most educators to be highly specialized and hence not an appropriate part of the general education programs of the elementary school and junior high school.
2. Specialized vocational education is best offered close to the time a person will use this education in employment. It is almost impossible for a person to secure meaningful employment before age sixteen, two years after the typical student leaves the eighth grade.
3. There are few examples of integrated curriculum plans which bridge the gap between elementary and secondary schools. Thus, even pre-vocational education is nearly non-existent below the ninth grade. (Fortunately, career education is beginning to change this).

Curricula

There are three principal curricula in high schools in the United States. The college preparatory curriculum enrolls amost 50 percent of the male students and 35–40 percent of the females; the general curriculum enrolls almost 25 percent of the males and 20 percent of the females, and the vocational curriculum enrolls about 25 percent of the males and from 40 to 45 percent of the females (9, pp. 5–11, E–2). These figures were based on Project TALENT questionnaires which asked high school seniors to state the curricula in which they were enrolled. Typical USOE figures show 40 percent of secondary education students taking vocational education courses and 28 percent of high school graduates completing vocational curricula. The percent of secondary school students taking a vocational class during any one year varies by state from 21 percent to almost 80 percent. Generally, the lowest percentages of enrollment are found in the Midwest and Northeast (13, vol. II, p. 49). These also are the sections of the country which are growing least rapidly in employment and in population, but we do not know if there is a cause-and-effect relationship.

The definitions provided for the curricula by Project TALENT were realistic. The general curriculum ". . . does not necessarily prepare you either for college or for work, but consists of courses required for graduation plus subjects that you like." The college preparatory program gives you ". . . the training and credits needed to work toward a regular Bachelor's degree in college." Project TALENT subdivided the vocational curriculum into commercial or business (". . . prepares you to work in an office"), vocational (". . . prepares you to work in a shop or factory, or to enter a trade school, or become an apprentice"), and agriculture (no definition) (9, pp. 5–11).

The course content of these three curricula has more similarities than differences. In most schools half of the program is identical for all three. When tracking is done in this general education half of the program, it tends to be done on the basis of the student's academic ability level rather than on the basis of the curriculum in which the student is enrolled.

The remaining half of the program for the general curriculum is usually made up of electives. Vocational and college preparatory students are required to take additional courses especially in communications, scientific, and mathematics areas, and have fewer electives. The typical vocational program requires that no more than one-fourth of the time in high school be spent in courses designed to prepare a student for a sizable family of occupations.

Enrollments and Graduates

In 1971 through 1972 approximately three-fourths of the secondary schools offered vocational education (13, vol. II, p. 50). This figure is somewhat misleading, since a school was counted if it offered only one class in vocational education. Even so, one state reported that more than half its high schools had no vocational education. Many small high schools offered vocational education only in agriculture and home economics (and in beginning typing and industrial arts, which often have vocational value). Total enrollment in federally reimbursed secondary school vocational education reached five and a half million in this period (13, vol. II, p. 47). This was almost twice as many students as were enrolled ten years earlier, but it should be remembered that during this same period the total enrollment in secondary schools increased by over thirty percent, largely due to changes in the birth rate.

If you ask people past the age of high school attendance about their secondary school vocational training, you get reports such as those shown in table 15–1.

TABLE 5–1

Vocational Courses	*Males*	*Females*
Typing	37%	73%
Bookkeeping	16	40
Home Economics		75
Shorthand		40
Agriculture	24	
Carpentry	30	
Machine Shop	30	
Metal Working	30	
Took a Vocational Curriculum		
Graduates	38	50
Dropouts	30	30

SOURCE: From Garth Mangum, "Second Chance in the Transition from School to Work," in *Transition from School to Work* (Princeton, N.J.: Princeton University, 1968), p. 242.

Information on the actual number of graduates from secondary school vocational education programs is very inadequate. Data for 1970–1971 show 998, 238 completions (13, vol I, p. 61), of whom 26 percent were continuing their education, 51 percent were available for work, and the status of 23 percent was unknown. Of those available for work, approximately 65 percent were employed in the occupational field for which they were prepared, or in a closely related field of employment.

These figures sound respectable, but if they are analysed more closely, they are not as useful as they appear to be. With five million enrollments, why were there only a million completions? Perhaps the major reason is that enrollments counted those who took even one vocational class, while completions counted only those who completed a program (usually a sequence of classes). Why do placement rates (which average 65 percent) vary from 100 percent in one state to 7.5 percent in another? What happened to the "status unknown" completers? Why is the rate of continuation in education four times as high in some states as in others? Unfortunately, we are still looking for the answers to these questions.

Characteristics of Students

Except for the few exceptions noted below, data are not available on characteristics of students enrolled in each of the fields of secondary school vocational education. Lacking this desirable information, we can only look at the known characteristics of vocational students as a group. Obviously these data are quite incomplete.

1. Sex. Vocational education is generally assumed to be a curriculum for males. However, existing data from such sources as Project TALENT show that approximately 60 percent of vocational education students in the secondary school are female (9, pp. 5–11).

USOE shows 55 percent of vocational enrollment to be female (13, vol I., p. 269), but these figures include postsecondary and adult enrollments. Project TALENT data also show that over 85 percent of the female students who told Project TALENT that they were enrolled in vocational curricula specified that they were in commercial or business curricula. Much of this instruction is not yet counted by USOE. On the other hand, students enrolled in homemaking who are counted by USOE were forced by the form of Project TALENT questions to indicate that they were in the general curriculum. A more recent study has indicated that the percentage of males enrolled in home economics classes has increased from 2.5 percent in 1968 to 15 percent in 1974 (18).

2. Academic aptitude. Female vocational students are not only more numerous than male vocational students, but they have on the average markedly higher academic aptitude. Nevertheless, each curriculum has significant numbers of male and female students at every decile of academic aptitude (9, p. E–2). For males, the heaviest enrollment in vocational courses comes from students who are at the fortieth percentile of academic ability. These students average two vocational courses (four semesters) in four years. Students in the lowest percentile of ability averaged less than one and a half year-long courses, but even students in the ninetieth percentile and above usually took one such course.

For females the pattern was similar. Those in the top and bottom percentiles of academic ability averaged two semesters of commercial subjects, while the remaining students averaged four semesters (9, p. E–4).

Data have indicated that vocational students have considerably greater ability in visual reasoning than in other abilities measured (10, p. 18). Since even visual reasoning test items required reading ability and since both white and nonwhite vocational students were relatively low in English ability as measured by these tests, it is likely that actual visual reasoning ability has been underestimated.

3. Age. It is very odd that no data are available on age of secondary school vocational students, for they could easily be collected. It is well known that relatively few fourteen- and fifteen-year-olds are enrolled. Vocational enrollment increases rapidly from age sixteen to high school graduation, because the remaining vocational education programs enroll students primarily for the last year or two years of high school (13, vol. II., p. 4).

Since the largest number of students drop out of high school at age sixteen, most dropouts have not been exposed to vocational education. Yet 70 percent of the male and 90 percent of the female dropouts report having had one or more vocational courses (14, p. 244). Presumably they are counting the often required junior high school courses in industrial arts and home economics, plus beginning typing.

4. Dropouts. Combs and Cooley (6) reported that 51 percent of freshmen who later dropped out of high school wanted a vocational education curriculum, but only 23 percent were admitted to one. In contrast, 48 percent of freshmen who later completed high school (but did not go on to college) wanted vocational education, and 43 percent got it. At the time of leaving school, 67 percent of the dropouts were in the general curriculum, 4 percent in the college preparatory curriculum, and 23 percent in a vocational curriculum. Comparable figures for those who graduated from high school but did not attend college were 36 percent, 14 percent, and 43 percent. (These figures do not add to 100 percent since some dropouts said they were in other curricula.)

5. Minority. Parnes found that 12 percent of white males fourteen to seventeen years of age who were in school were enrolled in vocational and commercial curricula as compared with 15 percent of black males (15, p. 26). The big difference, however, was in the other two curricula, with 24 percent of the blacks and 46 percent of the whites being in the college preparatory curriculum, and 61 percent of the blacks and 42 percent of the whites in the general curriculum. (Enrollment in the vocational curriculum was almost certainly understated because Parnes did not include eighteen-year-olds, who are much more likely than fourteen- to seventeen-year-olds to have vocational education available to them.) Project Baseline reported vocational education enrollments at all levels being comprised of 16.6 percent blacks, 6.1 percent Spanish surname, 1.0 percent Orientals, .8 percent American Indians, and 75.5 percent all others (13, vol II., p. 371). Of those males fourteen to twenty-four years old who had not completed high school and were not enrolled in school, 47 percent of the whites but only 25 percent of the blacks had obtained "vocational preparation outside regular school" (15, p. 23). Presumably this was through Manpower Development and Training Act programs and through training provided as a part of private employment.

Schaefer and Kaufman found that while black graduates of all curricula earned less than white graduates, the comparative disadvantage of black vocational graduates was less (17, p. 78). Almost one-third of nonwhite vocational graduates were employed as nonfarm laborers five years after high school graduation, but only about half as high a proportion of white vocational graduates were nonfarm laborers at a comparable stage in their careers. The proportion of nonwhite vocational graduates who were farm workers was approximately three times as high as for white vocational graduates in spite of the fact that few nonwhites enrolled in vocational agriculture.

Eninger found that black graduates of trade and industrial vocational curricula took twice as long as whites to find employment and were half as likely to secure employment in the occupation for which trained. Blacks were less likely than whites to get help from the school in job placement, and relied more frequently on friends and relatives. They had less job security, less job satisfaction, and lower earnings (though not lower hourly wages) than whites. Black graduates of vocational education programs were more likely to get higher education than whites who graduated from this curriculum (7, p. 19). Only 7 percent of Eninger's usable questionnaires came from nonwhites. It is likely that the plight of nonwhite vocational graduates has improved in the past few years, but to what extent is not known. The overall rate of youth unemployment for blacks remains far higher than for whites.

6. Socioeconomic. Schaefer and Kaufman found that the fathers of over half of the vocational students (both male and female) were employed as laborers or craftsmen-foremen, while one-third of the fathers of college preparatory students were in these occupational groups. College preparatory students were twice as likely as vocational students to have fathers employed as professionals (17, pp. 74, 76). Using fathers' occupations as a measure of socioeconomic status, it is clear that from low to high the ranking of curricula is vocational, general, and college preparatory, with each being approximately equally spaced along the continuum.

7. Student attitudes toward college. Tillery and Donovan (21) indicated repeatedly that high school juniors who expect to dropout, to graduate from high school, or to graduate from junior college or postsecondary vocational school all have similar attitudes, and have quite different attitudes from students who expect to graduate from four-year colleges. For example, the males in the former group most frequently chose shop, drafting, and industrial arts as their most interesting subjects, while females chose business, commercial, and secretarial subjects. Males expecting to earn baccalaureate degrees chose science, social studies, and history, while females chose English and speech (20, p. 58). Three-fourths of the former group wanted to be in occupations other than the professions. For potential baccalaureates three-fourths chose the professions (21, p. 132). Potential four-year college graduates chose majors spread widely through the professional fields. Less than 4 percent of males and 8 percent of females would have chosen liberal arts as a major regardless of their expected level of educational attainment (21, p. 142). All types of students agreed by a large majority that college is a place where you prepare for a job (21, p. 94).

8. Attendance in postsecondary education. Schaefer and Kaufman in their study of Massachusetts youth have presented the only data available on college-going rates for all of the major secondary school curricula. They found that 35 percent of vocational graduates and 41 percent of college preparatory graduates enrolled in postsecondary education. In marked contrast, only 9 percent of the graduates of the general curriculum went on to school (17, p. 68). USOE figures have indicated that nationwide, 23 percent of secondary school vocational curriculum graduates continued full time in higher education (22, p. 31). Since the Massachusetts study included part-time enrollments but USOE did not, there may not be a sizable discrepancy between the two figures.

Parnes was forced to collect his data in terms of census age groupings, rather than in terms of schooling completed. He found that for black males age twenty to twenty-four, those who had taken the general curriculum in high school were least likely to be in college, while those from the college preparatory curriculum were most likely to be in college. For white males, age twenty to twenty-four, he obtained lower results for the vocational curriculum. College preparatory was high, with general and vocational curricula sending only 8 percent each to college (15, p. 44).

In the Schaefer and Kaufman study 51 percent of those males who took work at public technical institutes or junior colleges were graduates of the vocational curriculum, but 59 percent of the females were from the college preparatory curriculum. Seventy-six percent of those who were enrolled in company-sponsored training programs were vocational graduates as compared with 12 percent from each of the other two high school curricula. Fifty-one percent of the males and 62 percent of the females who took work at private trade schools were college preparatory graduates as compared with 35 percent from vocational curricula and 10 percent from the general curricula (17, p. 69).

9. Status of vocational education in the eyes of the students. It has often been reported that vocational curricula have low status in high school. Schaefer and Kaufman reported that 33 percent of the high school graduates of the vocational curriculum felt that they had been looked down upon because of the course they took (as compared with 38 percent of the graduates of the general curriculum and only 7 percent of the college preparatory graduates). At the same time 77 percent and 87 percent of the vocational and college preparatory graduates would suggest that a young person starting high school follow their path. But only 39 percent of the general curriculum graduates would recommend it (17, p. 66). Even more striking is the fact that several U.S. Labor Department studies reported that 95 percent of high school graduates said they had one or more vocational courses in school before they graduated (14, p. 244). Since no such enrollment is possible, one can conclude that some of these people either saw nonvocational courses as vocational or invented courses. In either case, graduates would seem to be investing vocational education with considerable status.

10. Placement. During the past twenty years, placement of vocational curriculum graduates has been as low as 60 percent and as high as 80 percent, calculated as the percent of those available for employment who were placed in occupations closely related to the field of training (22, p. 31). As would be expected, placement rates tend to be high in times of labor shortage and lower in times of labor surplus. Schaefer and Kaufman indicated that the secondary school was four times as likely to help find a job for vocational graduates as for graduates of other curricula (16, p. 66). The higher the level of education sought by high school juniors, the higher the desire for a job which allowed them to create something original; the lower the level of education sought, the more emphasis on a job which provided plenty of leisure (21, p. 138).

One year after the graduation of their high school class, among students who do not go to college, vocational graduates are earning the most money per year, followed by dropouts. Last in earnings come graduates of the college preparatory and general curricula (5, p. 352). Schaefer and Kaufman reported the same relationship among graduates and found that it continued to exist for the first three jobs held. Indeed, the wage of the college preparatory graduate who did not go to college declined relative to the graduates of the other curricula by the time of the third job (16, p. 75). This seems to indicate that while the secondary school college preparatory curriculum adequately prepares a student for college, it does not prepare one for employment success without college.

11. Earnings. All studies of earnings of vocational graduates who do not go to college have indicated that they earn more per year than graduates of general curricula or college preparatory curricula who do not go to college. However, one study showed college preparatory students earning slightly more per hour than vocational students eleven years after graduation. At two and six years after graduation, the vocational students were ahead in hourly earnings (7, p. 36). Almost all studies of earnings of high school graduates from different curricula considerably understate the true difference in amount of earnings. Most studies report hourly or weekly pay, but since vocational graduates are employed a considerably greater portion of each year, the yearly earnings of vocational graduates are considerably understated. Since vocational graduates work approximately 7 percent more of each year than graduates of academic programs (7, p. 33) their weekly or hourly earnings should be increased by this much to provide comparable yearly wages.

In many studies, a second factor which understates the earnings of vocational graduates grows out of the fact that vocational students have lower academic ability and lower socioeconomic status than nonvocational students. Since earnings are related to both of these factors, a fair comparison of earnings by school curriculum should match students who have similar academic ability and socioeconomic status. This is borne out by a comparison of earnings when either ability or socioeconomic status are held constant. The difference obviously would be greater if *both* were held constant.

Clearly the vocational students of high ability and high socioeconomic status have particularly impressive earnings. Unfortunately, they are few in number. It is worth noting that earnings of students in commercial curricula are little affected by student ability.

Tracking in Vocational Education

In the early 1960s Project TALENT provided the first firm evidence that vocational students in the secondary school have lower socioeconomic status and lower verbal ability than students in the other two high school curricula. Two quite different explanations for this fact can be advanced: the school *assigns* such students to vocational education, or students *choose* vocational education based on their own past experience or because of the desires of their parents. Similar explanations can be used to explain why enrollment in certain vocational programs is predominantly female (e.g., home economics and office occupations) or male (e.g., agriculture and trade and industrial education). Bowen (3) provided the first test of these alternate hypotheses by asking teachers to assign 48 "students" to vocational or college preparatory classes on the basis of simulated student records. Stereotyped assignments on the basis of sex were particularly obvious, but racial stereotypes did not appear. Students whose "records" showed high grades or high socioeconomic status were most frequently assigned to college preparatory classes. The roles of parents and students in choosing curricula remain to be explored, but it seems likely that teachers play a role in assigning students on the basis of sex, grades, and socioeconomic status.

Separate Vocational Schools

No information has been found which indicates that vocational programs in separate vocational schools are in any way superior to vocational programs operated in comprehensive high schools. This might be due to inadequate information, but it is worth noting that, in large cities at least, the dropout rate from separate vocational high schools appears to be markedly higher than for comprehensive high schools. The Schrieber study found that the holding power of all large city high schools was 71 percent while that of vocational schools was only 51 percent (18, pp. 28, 35). In view of the fact that dropout rates from general curricula are so much higher nationally than dropout rates from the vocational curricula, these data cast grave doubt on the desirability of maintaining separate vocational schools.

Every study of costs indicates that per pupil costs are higher in separate vocational schools than they are in academic high schools. This could be due to the fact that vocational education in any type of school costs more than nonvocational education, but one study conducted by the American Institute for Research showed average costs of nonvocational and vocational programs in comprehensive schools running about the same per pupil while per pupil costs in vocational schools were approximately one-third higher. Most of the added costs for programs in vocational schools appeared to be due to smaller class size, resulting from the operation of a greater variety of vocational education programs than is offered in the typical comprehensive high school. In contrast, Stromsdorfer, who studied both comprehensive and separate high schools, found vocational education costs to be approximately 50 percent higher than the costs of nonvocational instruction. Major factors in this difference in costs were not only the smaller size of vocational classes but also higher equipment costs and higher salaries of teachers (20, p. 31). While the lack of data is unfortunate, the information which is available suggests that separate vocational schools have higher costs, higher dropout rates, and seem to promote socioeconomic segregation. They may be justified, however, in an area where high schools are too small to be comprehensive.

Shared Time Instruction

Very few parochial secondary schools have offered substantial amounts of vocational education. This is due not only to their difficult financial situation but also to the fact that all federal and most state assistance to vocational education has been limited to programs which were under public control. There is an increasing tendency toward the development of *shared time* programs which allow students to receive religious instruction plus certain academic courses in the parochial school. They then move to classes under public control for vocational education and certain other school subjects which have not been operated effectively in parochial schools. The net result is almost certain to be a sharp increase in the occupational competence of sizable groups of youths who up until now have not had access to vocational education.

REFERENCES

1. American Institute for Research. *An Analysis of Cost and Performance Factors for the Operation and Administration of Vocational Programs for Secondary Schools.* Pittsburgh: American Institute for Research, 1967.
2. American Vocational Association. *The Advisory Committee and Vocational Education.* Washington, D.C.: American Vocational Association, 1969.
3. Bowen, Ella. *Factors Related to Teacher Assignment of Students to School Curricula.* Urbana, Ill.: University of Illinois, unpublished doctoral dissertation, 1975.
4. Burt, Samuel M. *Industry and Community Leaders in Education—The State Advisory Councils on Vocational Education.* Kalamazoo, Mich.: W.E. Upjohn Institute for Employment Research, 1969.
5. ______. *Industry and Vocational-Technical Education.* New York: McGraw-Hill Book Company, 1967.
6. Combs, Janet, and Cooley, W.W. "Dropouts: In High School and After School." *American Educational Research Journal,* 5, no 3:343–63.
7. Eninger, Max W. *The Process and Product of T. and I. High School Level Vocational Education in the United States.* Pittsburgh: American Institute for Research, 1965.
8. Evans, Rupert N. "School for Schooling's Sake." *Transition from School to Work.* Princeton, N.J.: Industrial Relations Section, Princeton University, 1968.
9. Flanagan, John et al. *The American High School Student.* Pittsburgh: University of Pittsburgh, Project TALENT Office, 1964.
10. Froomkin, J. *An Analysis of Vocational Education in our Secondary Schools.* Unpublished. Washington, D.C.: U.S. Office of Education, Office of Program Planning and Evaluation, 1967.
11. Hamlin, Herbert M. *Citizen Participation and Local Policy Making for Public Education,* rev. ed. Urbana, Ill.: College of Education, University of Illinois, 1960.
12. King, Sam W. *Organization and Effective Use of Advisory Committees.* Washington, D.C.: U.S. Department of Health, Education and Welfare, Vocational Division, Bulletin No. 288 O.E.-84009, 1960.
13. Lee, Arthur M. *Learning a Living across the Nation,* vol. 1 and 2. Flagstaff, Ariz.: Northern Arizona University, Project Baseline, 1972 and 1973.
14. Mangum, Garth. "Second Chance in the Transition from School to Work." *Transition from School to Work.* Princeton, N.J.: Industrial Relations Section, Princeton University, 1968.
15. Parnes, Herbert S. et al. *Career Thresholds,* vol. 1. Columbus, Ohio: Ohio State University Center for Human Resources Research, 1969.
16. *Projections of Educational Statistics to 1975–76.* Washington, D.C.: U.S. Government Printing Office, Catalog No. FS 5.210:100030-66, 1966.

17. Schaefer, Carl J., and Kaufman, Jacob. *Occupational Education in Massachusetts.* Boston: Massachusetts Advisory Council on Education, 1968.

18. "*Scholastic's* Report on Youth Concerns, Values, Convictions." *Phi Delta Kappan* 56, no. 3 (November 1974):227.

19. Sinks, Thomas A., and Hess, J.E., eds. *Knowledge for What? The Purposes of Junior High School Education.* Danville, Ill.: The Interstate Printers and Publishers, Inc., 1969.

20. Stromsdorfer, Ernst W. *A Developmental Program for an Economic Evaluation of Vocational Education in Pennsylvania.* State College, Pa.: Pennsylvania State University, 1966.

21. Tillery, Dale et al. *A Study of Student Decision Making and Its Outcomes: SCOPE, Grade Eleven Profile, 1968 Questionnaire, Selected Items.* New York: College Entrance Examination Board, 1969.

22. *Vocational Education: The Bridge Between Man and His Work.* Washington, D.C.: General report of the Advisory Council on Vocational Education, Document No. FS 5.1280:80052, 1968.

23. Vocational and Technical Education, Selected Statistical Tables, Fiscal Year 1973. Washington, D.C.: U.S. Department of Health, Education and Welfare, Office of Education, Division of Vocational and Technical Education Information No. III, 1974.

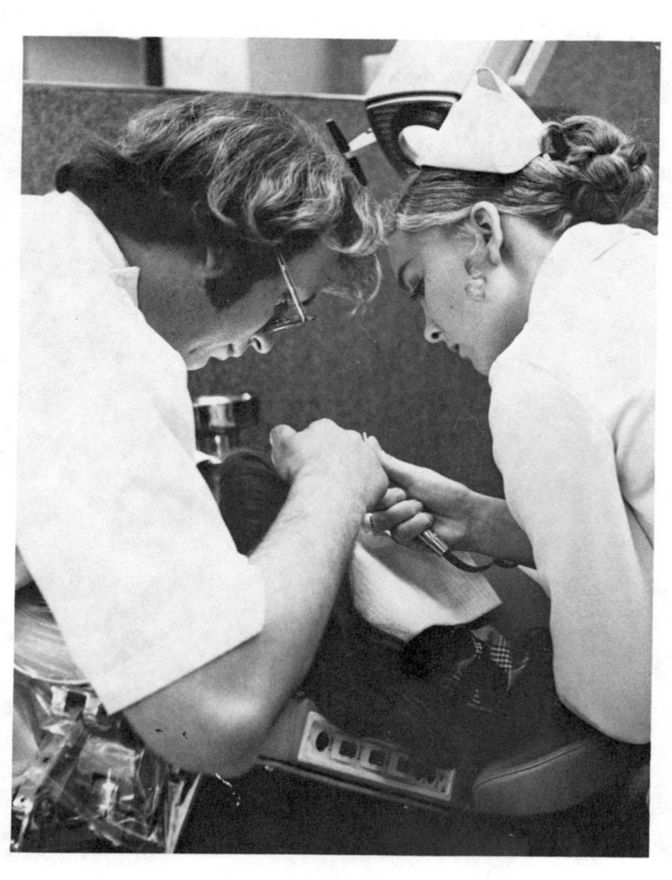

16

Vocational Education in Postsecondary Schools

Although community colleges have been in existence for over fifty years, the predominant pattern for public education until recent years has been elementary schools, junior high schools, high schools, and colleges and universities. Vocational education in this structure was concentrated almost entirely at the secondary school level, while occupational education in colleges and universities was confined almost exclusively to the professions. Increasing educational demands of a number of subprofessional occupations led to an obvious need for vocational education beyond the high school. For many years this need was either ignored or filled by private schools, most of which were designed to make a profit. This private school involvement in technical education (as the more sophisticated part of vocational education is often called) has been growing rapidly in recent years. But vocational education of all types in public postsecondary schools has been growing even more rapidly, and a high proportion of community colleges have been sold to taxpayers on the basis that they can provide significant amounts of vocational and technical instruction. Federal legislation has strongly supported vocational education in these institutions by earmarking a portion of federal vocational funds for postsecondary education.

Introducing Vocational Education into an Academic Community College

Despite the fact that community (junior) colleges usually are sold to voters on the basis that they will offer significant programs in the three fields of vocational education, college transfer education, and terminal general education, the first program offered is usually designed for college transfer students. In part, this is due to demand from students who come from families which are influential in the community. An equally important factor is the effect of limited finances and limited space. College transfer programs frequently can be offered at considerably less cost per student than vocational programs, and the amount of specialized space required is normally much lower. Since new community colleges are usually started before their buildings are constructed and before adequate revenues are available, it is quite common for the school to begin with a college transfer program. Naturally the president selects a staff which is competent to offer college transfer programs and is interested in and believes in the college transfer program at the community college level.

After several years of operation, new buildings are secured, and the financial condition of the college permits expansion to include vocational-technical programs and general terminal programs. By this time, however, the existing faculty has established committees which must approve new courses; counselors have been employed who are interested primarily in college transfer programs; buildings have been built to accommodate college transfer programs; and the institution is well on the road to becoming strictly a junior college. In this atmosphere, the president, board of trustees, or some state agency attempts to mandate the development of a meaningful vocational education program. Typically, a confrontation takes place, and a compromise is reached which allows the development of technical education programs that are closely allied to the physical sciences and mathematics. Other vocational education programs are excluded on the ground that they are too low level to deserve college credit.

This situation is exacerbated by feelings of insecurity on the part of some members of community college staffs. They feel inferior in qualifications, working conditions, and status to staff in the public colleges and universities which have been in operation for many years (though they may not be at all inferior in salary). This induces the so-called ghetto complex which causes them to try to be even more pure academically than the colleges and universities. Many technical educators support the views of their academic colleagues for essentially the same reasons. The upshot is that the community college may serve the prejudices of the staff which was hired when the college began instead of serving the needs of the community.

A similar problem exists at the state level. Federal earmarking of funds for postsecondary vocational education came about because some states either had little postsecondary education or because state officials chose not to spend much money on vocational education offered at this level. In 1970 and 1971, five states had less than 5 percent of their vocational education enrollment at the postsecondary level, while three states had more than 25 percent at this level (14, vol. I, p. 32).

Technical Education

Many of the early educational programs for technicians were designed for the field of engineering technology. This has led to the mistaken idea that technical education is a type of education for certain engineering technologies. Now, however, there is general agreement that technical education is a level of education instead of a type of education and that occupational education for the highest levels of subprofessionals in any occupational field is the proper province of technical education. Unfortunately, when some technical educators use the term *level of education,* they mean that technical education is the only type of vocational education which should be permitted in the postsecondary school. This has the effect of denying the lower levels of vocational education to students who came from high schools which did not offer adequate vocational programs, as well as denying them to individuals who decided after leaving high school that they needed vocational education.

Equally undesirable is the attempt to restrict high schools from offering technical education courses which prepare students to enter technical occupations or from offering upgrading courses for adult technicians. This has led to the curious anomaly of certain technical educators' denying that instruction in drafting can be technical education, simply because drafting often is taught in the secondary schools.

Technical education is indeed a level of education, but this refers to the fact that certain occupations require higher levels of education, rather than to the necessity for offering technical education only in postsecondary schools. Indeed the level of education required for many occupations demands a technical education program which begins in the high school and continues for two or more years beyond.

Coordination of Vocational Education Programs

Many students who wish to enroll in vocational education programs in the postsecondary school have had no previous vocational education courses. Often they are graduates of a college preparatory curriculum, either because the type of vocational education they wanted was not offered by their high school or because they discovered relatively late in their high school career that they were interested in preparation for an occupation outside the professions. It is only right that these individuals should be able to secure the type of vocational education they need in a community college or technical institute.

At the same time, however, we find students who have acquired an excellent secondary school background in a vocational field who desire further vocational education in a postsecondary school. Too frequently they are given no credit for this earlier instruction and are forced to repeat courses they completed successfully in the high school. The best, practical solution to this problem seems to be for the postsecondary school to administer proficiency examinations which would allow the student to establish credit in a postsecondary school course regardless of the way in which he or she acquired the necessary knowledge and skill to pass the examination. Some students would have acquired this skill in secondary schools, some through work experience, and some through private proprietary school instruction. The automatic awarding of credit as a result of completing a secondary school course seems to be unacceptable to most postsecondary school instructors. Community colleges expect senior colleges to award credit automatically for courses completed in the community college, but they seem to be unwilling to consider a similar arrangement with the high school.

Ideally, the curricula of the secondary and postsecondary schools should be arranged to complement each other. Then the student who made a decision prior to high school graduation to enter the higher levels of an occupational field could have a program which began in the high school, flowed without interruption into the community college, and, if he or she decided to go further, could lead naturally into a baccalaureate or even a graduate school program in that occupational field. Such an integrated system of occupational education assumes a career ladder extending from the bottom to the top of an occupational field. More importantly, it assumes that instructional personnel in all levels of education have respect for each other and are willing to work together for the good of the student.

Community Colleges and Technical Institutes

At the postsecondary school level, the community college theoretically is the rough analog of the comprehensive secondary school, while the technical institute is roughly comparable to the separate vocational high school. An examination of programs actually offered, however, reveals surprisingly minor differences. The technical institute usually has a broader array of vocational curricula, a smaller proportion of college transfer courses, more elaborate laboratories for vocational education, and a higher proportion of students pursuing subprofessional vocational goals. The technical institute is most often headed by a person who has specialized in vocational education; the president of a community college almost always has been associated with college transfer programs. Both institutions send students on to college and directly into employment. Indeed, other than the difference in name, the chief difference seems to be in relative emphasis on curricula. The technical institute emphasizes vocational and technical curricula, and the community college emphasizes college transfer curricula, but neither is devoted exclusively to its principal interest.

Vocational Offerings of Four-Year Institutions

Increasingly, vocational education is being offered by baccalaureate-granting colleges and universities. Martin reported that 40 percent of the 282 colleges and universities he surveyed offered less-than-baccalaureate level vocational programs (15, p. 7).

Vocational education legislation has prohibited the use of federal vocational education funds for occupational education at the baccalaureate level or above. This has not deterred a large number of colleges and universities from offering occupational education programs which would be eligible for federal aid if they were offered in the high school or community college. By extending the period of training from two to four years and by offering a baccalaureate upon completion of the program, they have been able to substitute tuition payments and state aid for the relatively modest federal funds available for less-than-baccalaureate degree programs. A few such programs in engineering technology were reported by Defore and Foecke (6). Most of the growth in engineering technology baccalaureate programs has occurred in institutions which do not offer baccalaureate programs in engineering. It is possible in some cases that these really are engineering programs in disguise. Whether or not this is the case, it appears that graduates are being employed as engineers by companies who disagree with the trend in baccalaureate engineering education in the prestige institutions to eliminate almost all references to technology and to concentrate instead on science and mathematics. Whatever the cause, the effect is very clear. Four-year technology programs are growing rapidly and offer serious competition to two-year technician training programs and to standard engineering programs.

Motivation for four-year institutions to offer technician training is varied. In some cases, strong support from a key executive or board member has led to the establishment of the program. In other cases, entire state university systems have begun two-year technology programs as a means of delaying or preventing the establishment of state-supported comprehensive community colleges. Four-year technician training programs frequently are offered by former teacher-training colleges which desire a broadened curriculum and are prevented from establishing engineering colleges by the opposition of existing engineering schools.

Curriculum Development in Postsecondary Education

Curriculum development in all of vocational education has been plagued by battles between subject matter specialists and administrators. The former attempt to get approval of specialized courses while the latter attempt to consolidate classes to reduce high costs caused by small enrollments. In these battles, the needs of the student are often forgotten. Traditional studies of curriculum content have looked at individual occupations after the educational requirements of the occupation have been determined by means of occupational analysis (9), activities of employed workers (5), opinions of occupationally competent people (14), opinions of supervisors or occupational specialists (21), or the teachers of the occupation (16). The items of content thus identified were combined more or less logically into courses, and the courses were fitted into a one, two, three, or four-year academic calendar. This procedure has invariably resulted in unique occupational education courses for each occupational field. Too often, the only common elements in these specialized programs have been the general education requirements of the institution offering the curricula.

Schill and Arnold (18) developed a method for determining logically the areas of instruction which are common and unique to different occupational programs. They looked at three technologies: chemical, electrical-electronic, and mechanical, and by asking technicians whether or not certain competencies were needed in their specific occupation, they found that certain areas of instruction were unique to these three technologies and to each of their three combinations (electro-mechanical, electro-chemical, and chemical-mechanical). In addition, however, they found surprisingly large areas of instruction which were common to all of these six technological fields. The methodology they used would seem to be applicable to all of vocational education and could result in elimination of much undesirable duplication of instruction.

Student Characteristics

We know considerably less about vocational students in postsecondary education than we do about high school students in vocational curricula. Graney pointed out that there is little but speculation about the technical student, but that even the speculation ". . . deals less with the subject of what technical students are than what they ought to be" (10, p. 88). Most studies of postsecondary education students have been concerned with criteria for admitting students and hence have been concerned with predictions of success in different curricula. These studies have been of little value since they seem uniformly to find that high socioeconomic status, high secondary school grades, and high ability and achievement test scores are good indicators of success in all of postsecondary education. The implication seems to be that if students who score low on each of these criteria can be kept out, all will be well. This may make the task of the college instructor simpler, but it is hardly an answer for the student who ranks low in one or more of these characteristics.

Much more useful findings have been those of Taylor and Hecker (20) and of Hakanson (11). Both of these studies indicated that students who do not succeed in the first postsecondary curriculum in which they enroll are likely to withdraw from college rather than to transfer to another curriculum. For example, Hakanson found that only 14 percent of the students who withdrew from college transfer programs enrolled in occupational education curricula. Almost all of the remainder dropped out of school. This finding suggests that community colleges should have both vocational and technical curricula available in the same occupational fields, so that students who are unable to succeed in a technical curriculum can move to a related vocational curriculum without having to change objectives sharply. For example, a student who has insurmountable difficulty in a two-year mechanical design technology curriculum should be able to transfer to the one-year vocational drafting curriculum, which has related occupational goals but does not require such high mathematics achievement. Hakanson's findings also suggested that adequate counseling at the time of enrollment may be more important than has been thought and may be even more important than counseling after the student has begun his or her studies.

This wedding of the student to the curriculum he or she desires may also explain why such a high proportion of high school freshmen who wish to be enrolled in vocational education drop out of high school when they are instead assigned to the general curriculum. The dearth of follow-up studies on the postsecondary vocational education graduates and dropouts was shown in the Sharp and Krasnegor study (19) which reviewed more than forty follow-up studies of vocational education students. No national or regional follow-up studies for people trained in technical institutes and community colleges could be found, and indeed there are very few such studies even at the local level. The work of Hoyt (12) has provided a great deal of information with regard to students both in public and private postsecondary education institutions.

Most students who have both high grades in school and high socioeconomic status will attend a university rather than a community college. Few students who are low on both characteristics attend any type of postsecondary school. This appears to explain the phenomenon of postsecondary vocational education students having low grades and high socioeconomic status or high grades and low socioeconomic status. Indeed, these students form the only population known in which grades and socioeconomic status are correlated negatively. This suggests that postsecondary vocational education may have two distinctly different student groups: one made up of children of professional workers, characterized by poor reading ability and conflicts with parents about their occupational goals, and the other group made up of children of manual and semiskilled workers who read well but have occupational goals similar to those of their parents. If this is true, different curriculum materials and vocational counseling would be needed for each group (7).

Enrollments in Postsecondary Vocational Technical Education

Less than 15 percent of enrollment in vocational and technical education comes at the postsecondary school level. This figure is misleading, however, because it does not show the very rapid growth of postsecondary enrollments in this field; it does not indicate the relative proportion of time spent by the student in vocational and technical programs; nor does it show the considerable differences by field of specialization. In 1960, there were only 93,000 reimbursed postsecondary enrollments in vocational and technical education. By 1965, this figure had more than doubled to 207,000, and it doubled again in 1966. By 1970, enrollments were almost five times those of 1965 (14, vol. II, p. 82) and 100 percent increases may be expected each five years until 1985. Enrollments give an inadequate picture of the amount of instructional time and effort. Secondary school students spend from one-fourth to one-third of their school time in vocational education, while adults may be enrolled only a few hours per week and a few weeks per year. In contrast, postsecondary students usually spend over half of their school time in vocational and technical instruction during the one or two years they typically are enrolled in the program.

By far the largest enrollments in postsecondary vocational and technical education are in programs designed to prepare students for work in offices and other commercial fields. Programs designed to prepare people for skilled occupations in industry and the construction trades and for technical occupations are large and rapidly growing. Preparation for home economics and agricultural occupations stands in sharp contrast. While these form the bulk of enrollment in secondary schools, they are by far the smallest in postsecondary education. Education for technical occupations in agriculture, however, is increasing rapidly in enrollment. Another program, which is rapidly increasing in size though relatively small in enrollment as yet, is distributive education. Almost all vocational education for the health occupations is conducted at the postsecondary school level, though high schools are beginning to offer limited opportunities in this field.

Data on those completing postsecondary vocational education are even more fragmentary than data on high school completions. A major reason for this is the tendency of older vocational students to take only those courses or portions of courses needed for employability. Thus the student often feels that he or she has completed a program while the school records show that additional work must be done before the program has been completed. The definition of who is a dropout and who is a completer becomes very tenuous. At any given time, the placement rates for graduates of postsecondary vocational education programs are higher than those for graduates of high school level vocational programs. In 1973, the figures were 79.2 and 62.1 percent, respectively, placed full-time in the occupation for which they were prepared (22, p. 50). Unemployment rates are considerably lower than those for graduates of other curricula in every comparison which has been made.

Competition between Secondary and Postsecondary Schools for Adult Education Enrollments

It has been noted that when a community college and a high school offer comparable adult education courses at the same time in the same locality, enrollments in the program offered by the postsecondary institution tend to increase while enrollments in programs offered by the high school decrease. This may be an indication of the relative status of the two types of institutions, for some adults would much prefer to be able to say, "I am going over to the college for a course this evening," rather than, "I am going to the high school" for the same course. This difference in status offers the postsecondary school an opportunity to attract adults who will not attend adult education programs offered by a secondary school either because they hold the high school in low esteem or because of past individual problems with a secondary school. At the same time, it offers an opportunity for the secondary-school educator to build highly desirable programs of adult education for people who may feel that college programs would be too advanced or too difficult for them.

Conflicts between secondary and postsecondary institutions operating adult education programs in the same community seem almost inevitable. A combination of cooperative planning, joint advertising, and careful evaluation can (1) minimize undesirable conflicts which destroy public goodwill, (2) allow replacement of programs which are not meeting the needs of the community, and (3) develop programs which meet the needs of adults who previously have not been served. The adult and continuing education programs of several community colleges have proven an ideal method of high school and college cooperation. Coordinators from each high school in the college district are employed part-time by the college and develop programs which meet community needs regardless of the level of instruction.

Non-High School Graduates in Postsecondary Schools

A number of community colleges have established programs which accept students who are not high school graduates. These programs range from remedial efforts, where an attempt is made to give the equivalent of high school instruction to high school dropouts, to an occasional program which accepts each student where he or she is and moves as far with the student as is possible. When the land grant universities were established immediately after the Civil War, many of them followed the same course of action. They set up preparatory schools for certain students and adopted a philosophy that instruction which met the needs of the students was far better than instruction which met the prevailing eastern college notion of excellence. Most baccalaureate-granting institutions discarded this philosophy long ago, but it has been picked up in part by certain community colleges, and a few have put it fully into effect.

REFERENCES

1. American Institute for Research. *An Analysis of Cost and Performance Factors of the Operation and Administration of Vocational Programs for Secondary Schools.* Pittsburgh: American Institute for Research, 1967.
2. American Vocational Association. *The Advisory Committee and Vocational Education.* Washington, D.C.: American Vocational Association, 1969.
3. Brick, Michael. *An Analysis of Selected Business and Technology Programs in High Schools and in Two Year Colleges and Institutes of New York State with a View toward Initiating Articulation.* New York: Center for Urban Education, 1967. (ERIC ED 012791)
4. Burt, Samuel M. *Industry and Vocational-Technical Education.* New York: McGraw-Hill Book Company, 1967.
5. Christal, Raymond E. "Implications of Air Force Occupational Research for Curriculum Design." In *Process and Technique of Vocational Curriculum Development,* edited by Brandon B. Smith and Jerome Moss, Jr. Minneapolis: Minnesota Research Coordinating Unit for Vocational Education, University of Minnesota, 1970.
6. Defore, Jesse J. "An Evaluation of Baccalaureate Programs in Engineering Technology." Harold A. Foecke. "Four-Year Engineering Technology Programs in Perspective." Both in *Trends in Engineering Technician Enrollments and Graduates,* edited by John D. Aden. New York: Engineering Manpower Commission, 1967. (ERIC ED 014298)
7. Evans, Rupert N., and Jackson, Truman. "Verbal Ability, Grades, and Socioeconomic Status of Students in Secondary and Postsecondary Curricula." In press.
8. Froomkin, Joseph. *An Analysis of Vocational Education in Our Secondary Schools.* Unpublished. Washington, D.C.: U.S. Office of Education, Office of Program Planning and Evaluation, 1967.

9. Fryklund, Verne. *Trade and Job Analysis.* Milwaukee: The Bruce Publishing Co., 1947.
10. Graney, Maurice. *The Technical Institute.* New York: The Center for Applied Research in Education, 1964.
11. Hakanson, John W. *Selected Characteristics, Socio-Economic Status, and Levels of Attainment of Students in Public Junior College Occupation-Centered Education.* Berkeley, Calif.: University of California School of Education, 1967. (ERIC ED 013644)
12. Hoyt, Kenneth B. "The Specialty Oriented Student Research Program: A Five-Year Report." *Vocational Guidance Quarterly* 16 (March 1968):169–76.
13. Kinsinger, Robert E., and Ratner, Muriel. *Technicians for the Health Field—A Community College Health Career Study Program.* Albany, N.Y.: New York State Education Department, 1966. (ERIC ED 011198)
14. Lee, Arthur M. *Learning a Living across the Nation.* Volumes I and II. Flagstaff, Ariz.: Northern Arizona University, Project Baseline, 1972 and 1973.
15. Martin, Robert R. *Technical Education: Less-Than-Baccalaureate Level Programs in Higher Education.* Richmond, Ky.: Eastern Kentucky University, 1968. (ERIC ED 019069)
16. North Carolina State Board of Education. *Court Reporting in Business Technology.* Raleigh, N.C.: State Board of Education, 1966. (ERIC ED 013944)
17. Schill, William J. *Concurrent Work-Education Programs in the Fifty States.* Unpublished final report on USOE project 6-2851. Urbana, Ill.: Bureau of Educational Research, University of Illinois, 1967.
18. Schill, William J., and Arnold, Joseph P. *Curricula Content for Six Technologies.* Urbana, Ill.: University of Illinois Press, 1965.
19. Sharp, Laure M., and Krasnegor, Rebecca. *The Use of Follow-up Studies in the Evaluation of Vocational Education.* Washington, D.C.: Bureau of Social Science Research, 1966. (ERIC ED 010072)
20. Taylor, Ronald G., and Hecker, Donald L. *Interest and Intellectual Indices Related to Successful and Nonsuccessful Male College Students in Technical and Associate Degree Programs.* Big Rapids, Mich.: Ferris State College, 1967. (ERIC ED 021127)
21. Vasek, Richard J. *A Comparative Analysis of Electronic Content in Public Post-High School Technical Institutes and Electronic Technology Requirements of Industry.* State College, Miss.: Mississippi State University, 1967. (ERIC ED 015302)
22. *Vocational and Technical Education Selected Statistical Tables, Fiscal Year 1973.* Washington, D.C.: U.S. Department of Health, Education and Welfare, Office of Education, Vocational Education Information No. III, 1974.

AIR

17

Cooperative Programs

Although the sharing of time between education and work is sometimes thought to be a new idea, it had its origins in England in the nineteenth century when children employed in factories were required to attend schools on a half-time basis. Factory children learned as much as ordinary children, though they received instruction for only half as long each day. The report of the Inspectors of Factories for 31 October 1865, states,

> The reason of it is, I think, obvious. The labour of half a day is sufficient physical employment for a child. . . . The change to school for the other half, and the interest taken . . . in new ideas . . . produces rest . . . whilst the discipline of labour carried into the school, absorbs all that time which a child at school from morning to night loses, in its vain efforts to relieve itself from the fatigues of school monotony (1, p. 107)

The available records do not indicate whether the school instruction was related to what was being learned on the job—probably it was not.

Over fifty years ago the University of Cincinnati decided that engineers could be better educated if they spent part of their school career in employment and if the school program could be related to the things that the student had learned on the job. Twenty years later secondary schools in the South—perennially faced with low school budgets—made a virtue of necessity by adapting the cooperative education plan for high school students.

Despite strong opposition from vocational educators in the forties and early fifties, the program grew in secondary school enrollment from zero in 1930 to

117,000 in 1965–66 (10, p. 32) and to 312,000 in 1971–72 (6, vol. II, p. 52). Some 2,500 of the 18,000 high school districts had 4,800 such programs in 1965–66. The number is certainly higher now, but no one knows how much higher.

The Advisory Council on Vocational Education, which was established to evaluate the implementation of the Vocational Education Act of 1963, stated flatly that cooperative education had the best record of all vocational programs in terms of the proportion of students placed in the occupation for which they were trained. Studies of the economics of vocational education have shown higher rates of return on investment in cooperative programs than in other types of vocational education. (Capital costs for the school are lower, and since the student is receiving wages for the on-the-job portion of the program, the costs for the individual are lower.)

Congress has responded to this evidence by earmarking funds for cooperative education programs and by authorizing the use of vocational education funds to reimburse employers for the excess costs they incur through cooperation in the programs—a provision which strengthens employer support. Until Congress acted, the emphasis placed on cooperative education varied greatly from state to state. As late as 1966, one state reported only one such program, but in 1972 all states had more than 1.5 percent of their secondary school vocational education enrollments in cooperative education. The average was over 8 percent, and one state reached 48.9 percent (15, Vol. II, p. 52). It is difficult to understand the reasons for some states having twenty-five times as high a percentage of their enrollment in cooperative education as do a few other states.

Schill, in his study of cooperative work education (CWE), found that definitions of it were nearly identical in most states. Yet he found virtually no relationship between prevalence of the programs and various measures of state wealth or unemployment. The only reasonable explanation seemed to be that boards of vocational education in some states promoted cooperative work education programs, while in other states they were apathetic to CWE or opposed to it (10).

Cooperative work education involves cooperative arrangements between the school and employers, enabling students to receive part-time vocational instruction in the school and on-the-job training through part-time employment. The primary goal of CWE is to prepare the student for gainful employment. Cooperative work education should be sharply distinguished from work-study programs where the goal is to provide economic assistance which will allow the student to remain in school. The work provided seldom is relevant to the student's occupational goal. Work-study students undoubtedly learn some things on the job that are a valuable part of their education since any employment experience has some general educational value. The work-study program, however, lacks the structured and conscious relationship between work experience and educational goals that is the major strength of cooperative work education programs (7, pp. 119–20).

Cooperative work education goes under a variety of names. Distributive education (DE), office occupations (OO), part-time industrial cooperative education, and diversified occupations (DO) are some of the more common titles used for the federally funded programs. *Vocational cooperative programs* is a common generic title.

Schill (10) found, however, that almost half of the schools operating CWE programs did not receive federal vocational education financial support for them. Little is known about the programs except that they included special CWE for mentally handicapped students, vocational rehabilitation programs, business education programs which the state chose not to recognize, and programs in wealthy school districts which chose not to ask for reimbursement.

CWE is suitable for all fields of vocational education but is much more utilized for some types of occupations than for others. Cooperative distributive education has well over one third of the enrollment in federally reimbursed CWE programs and almost twice the enrollment of the next largest subject field. Health occupations programs have clinical experience requirements which are in many ways analogous to CWE requirements. These are not counted as CWE because there may not be a regular alternation between the in-school and on-the-job portions of health occupations education.

CWE invariably has a teacher-coordinator who advises students, identifies suitable training stations for them, teaches a class in the school which is closely related to the student's experience on the job, and evaluates the learning which occurs. He or she also builds better community relationships, adjusts all difficulties which arise in maintaining equitable relationships among parents, students, employers, unions, and sometimes runs evening classes to teach the on-the-job trainers (specified experienced fellow employees of the student) how better to teach the student.

Everyone who has studied the CWE program agrees that well-prepared and able coordinators are the key to successful program operation. Ability to plan in advance, initiative, outgoing personality, and organizational skills are basic requirements. It is clear that successful coordinators are rapidly becoming the backbone of a new leadership for all types of vocational education programs at state and local levels.

Larger schools tend to operate multiple CWE programs with each coordinator specializing in a particular family of occupations. A typical large school may have a distributive education coordinator, a coordinator of office occupations, a coordinator of industrial occupations, and so on. In many states, smaller schools are encouraged to operate CWE programs under a single coordinator who is responsible for a broad range of occupations most frequently entitled diversified occupations (DO).

Advantages of Cooperative Work Education

Quick adaptability to changes in labor market demands characterizes CWE programs. By contrast, vocational education based on school-operated laboratories can become quite out of tune with labor market demands, partly because most vocational teachers are prepared to offer instruction in only a relatively small family of occupations. If teachers have tenure and cannot be retrained, the school has little flexibility in dropping outdated programs. Since CWE uses instructors on the job and since openings for training stations are closely related to opportunities for full-time employment of graduates,CWE is quickly responsive to changes in the labor market. Moreover, training stations are most easily obtained in fields with the greatest labor shortages, and the coordinator is therefore more likely to use such stations.

The CWE program needs lower capital investment in space and equipment than does instruction in the school laboratory. CWE, indeed, requires little more equipment or space in the school than is called for in first-rate classroom instruction in any subject. Highly specialized equipment which may quickly become obsolete cannot be afforded in the typical school vocational program but will be provided on the job because of production demands.

Cooperative work education stimulates desirable attitudes toward work. Work atmosphere is extremely difficult to reproduce outside of a real work situation, and the importance of promptness and regular attendance at work are much more demonstrable on the job than in school. Moreover, because of the difficulty of marketing goods and services produced within school laboratories, it is also extremely difficult in laboratory-based programs to develop realistic attitudes toward speed, quality, and efficiency.

A student who performs effectively in CWE is very likely to stay on in full-time employment after completing the school program. The employer knows the student's strengths and weaknesses, and the student has had ample opportunity to determine whether or not he or she likes and can succeed in a particular field of work and with that particular employer. As a result, typical placement rates are more than 80 percent in the occuation for which the student is trained.

If a suitable training station is available, cooperative education can be offered in a given occupational field for a small group or even for an individual. Other types of vocational education require at least ten students in a given occupational field before the program can be operated economically.

Overcoming Problems in Cooperative Work Education

CWE programs are not readily adaptable to some communities—those which are so small as to have a narrow range of available training stations, those which have declining populations, or those in which most employment is found in occupations which have little future. Cooperative programs are difficult to operate in establishments that have strong agreements with employees. If the employer has agreed that no new people will be employed until all previous workers have been recalled, there will be times when CWE programs cannot operate in the establishment. If there is a tradition of employing only the relatives or friends of present workers, CWE will be sharply restricted for most students.

No figures are available as to the proportion of CWE programs operated in nonunion or small establishments, but it is believed to be relatively high (except in times of very low unemployment). Many CWE coordinators, however, have found it possible to negotiate bona fide apprenticeship agreements for CWE students. This arrangement eliminates many of the problems inherent in typical seniority provisions.

The number of students who could profit from CWE programs in any community is determined very largely by the births which occurred there sixteen to eighteen years earlier. On the other hand, the number who can be accommodated in the program is determined in large part by the number of available employment opportunities at a particular time. Even minor economic recessions badly hamper CWE programs. In large cities, especially, it is not at all uncommon for each coordinator to have three or four students laid off and returned to the school for full-time study several times during the school year. This requires the establishment of new sections of in-school vocational courses, the overcrowding of existing sections, or (worst of all) placing the student in several successive study hall periods.

In medium sized communities, there is often a closer relationship between the school and employer. Layoffs there are not such a severe problem since the employer frequently recognizes the injustice to the student who is dropped and the burden that such layoffs place on the school. But even in small communities, prolonged economic recession inevitably will result in sharp curtailment in CWE enrollment. In such periods, rapid response to labor market demands appears as a disadvantage rather than an advantage for CWE.

Many problems posed by CWE programs can be overcome through careful planning and education of the school and community. A primary difficulty up to now has been the shortage of qualified teacher-coordinators. Congress has appropriated substantial funds for the development of teachers and other leadership personnel for vocational education. A portion of these funds has been used for training coordinators, but the turnover rate has been high as coordinators have become administrators or have left the public schools for more lucrative private employment.

CWE has often been opposed by teachers who are accustomed to teaching in school laboratory programs and who are afraid that development of CWE will rob them of their students. Some schools have overcome this by restricting CWE to occupations that are not taught in school laboratories. Other schools have assigned students to vocational programs in laboratories until their last semester or last year of school and have used laboratory instructors as part-time teacher-coordinators. Still others have required the permission of the laboratory instructor before a student can be assigned to CWE in the occupation which the laboratory instructor teaches.

The traditional vocational education program has suffered from an attempt to turn out a year's supply of new full-time employees during a single month. Naturally, there are not enough jobs to go around each June. Similarly, CWE has suffered from trying to find suitable training stations for all CWE students in a single month (September). Both problems could be eased by laboratory instruction which prepares students in advance of placement in CWE programs. The most able students would be available for CWE placement early in the school year; less able students would continue in the school laboratory for longer periods. This arrangement could tend to spread the need for job placements more evenly over the calendar year (4). Some schools now conduct the CWE program on a twelve-month basis. While this helps to hold a training station open by meeting the needs of the employer year round, graduation in June is still common.

Cooperative work education has often been opposed by individuals who think instruction must be given solely inside school walls. Every administrator who has operated a CWE program has had protesting calls from both teachers and laypeople who do not understand why a faculty member should be off the school premises during school hours. The only solution to this problem seems to be a continuing program to educate the public about the rationale for CWE. In spite of such problems, Experience-based Career Education (EBCE) programs have been particularly effective in obtaining public involvement in their CWE emphases for students in a very wide range of occupations.

CWE programs may be affected by wage hours restrictions and youth employment safety regulations. The states which have tried hard to do so, however, have generally been successful in getting exceptions to state laws and to state administrative rulings. These exceptions allow special consideration for CWE students with regard to wages, hours, safety regulations, and other restrictions designed to protect youth from exploitation. The basic rationale is that through the teacher-coordinator the school makes certain that the student is involved in a bona fide education program and is not being exploited.

Some vocational educators in state offices make clear their opposition to CWE. Fortunately, these people have declined rapidly in number and in influence. It is still common, however, for states to have restrictive regulations prohibiting coordination which extends across two or more of the traditional fields of vocational education. This eliminates many occupations from CWE—for example, sales training for industrial supplies which cuts across distributive education and trade and industrial education. Some states have solved this problem by assigning the coordination to the teacher most competent to handle the major portion of the occupation. An equally oppressive regulation excludes from CWE those occupations which require less than two years for the "average worker" to learn. By definition, half of all students are below average in their ability to learn, so the two-year rule is really meaningless. All socially desirable occupations should be available to students through CWE. In some states still another type of arbitrary regulation excludes certain occupations, such as radio announcing, because they have not been a part of traditional vocational education, even though they clearly meet all the criteria for inclusion.

Special difficulties are involved in the operation of cooperative programs in large cities. Travel time for teacher-coordinators is one problem since it is rarely possible to restrict students to employment in a particular geographic sector of the city. Other problems include a greater preponderance of employers who have tight seniority restrictions and a number of teachers who feel that the working day ends promptly at three-thirty in the afternoon unless they are paid at overtime rates. Despite all obstacles many large city school systems are operating CWE programs successfully. Other large city systems can best learn from these established programs how to develop cooperative programs of their own.

No one knows why CWE is much more prevalent in secondary schools and in four-year colleges than it is in junior and community colleges. Perhaps the ghetto syndrome is at work. Yet there are many valid reasons why CWE should be more successful in junior colleges than in secondary schools or universities. Certain community colleges have installed CWE in each of their vocational and technical fields of instruction. Cooperative work education has had to compete with work-study which does not require the school to employ a teacher-coordinator or provide an organized educational program related to the students' work. Hence the educational costs are lower than for CWE. At the same time special appropriations have been available for work-study programs. This has led some school districts unwisely to adopt work-study programs which are not as educationally defensible but which require less local financial support. There is no reason why work-study funds cannot be used for CWE. Certainly the results would be educationally superior. It is to be hoped that Congress will gradually phase out support for work-study in favor of additional support for CWE.

Cooperative programs have been hampered by a shortage of adequate instructional material of three basic types: (1) material for the general vocational instruction which applies to all of the occupations supervised by a particular coordinator, (2) materials directly related to each of these occupations, and (3) material which is suitable for developing on-the-job trainers. Very high priority should be given to the development of instructional materials for the three phases of CWE.

In common with all vocational education, CWE suffers from that aspect of our culture which places a low value on employment in nonprofessional occupations. Most parents want their children to go to college because they believe this is the path to professional employment. They should be told that CWE does not block entrance to college any more than does any other type of vocational education. Indeed, many colleges give priority to students who have demonstrated that they are willing to work to get further education. Nevertheless, the primary goal of CWE should be to enable the student to get satisfactory, gainful employment upon completion of the program.

Some economists promise a long-term solution to the cultural values problem. They hold that as the supply of nonprofessional but vocationally trained employees continues to decrease relative to demand, wages for this type of employment will rise until people will reverse their attitudes. This wage change has already taken effect in many technical occupations where graduates of two-year programs are now employed at salaries higher than are paid to holders of masters' degrees in many other fields.

A shortage of training stations caused by high costs to the employer has often discouraged efforts to develop CWE programs. No one denies that CWE training is costly to the employer. We have assumed that employers could recover added costs through having a better supply of well-trained workers or that they should contribute the added costs because of their sense of social responsibility. If CWE is to expand rapidly, it is unrealistic to expect employers to assume costs above those normally incurred in the training of other new employees. Actually a good case can be made for full payment to the employer of all the costs of training a CWE student. This is being done in some CETA training programs.

Nevertheless, it would appear feasible at this stage to take only the step of paying for the added costs of CWE training. This type of payment was authorized by the Vocational Education Amendments of 1968. It certainly would make no sense to spend two hundred dollars in applying for and substantiating added costs of training which amount to only three hundred dollars. The principal quality control should be certification by the school that the training program outline has been followed meticulously.

As is true of many other educational innovations, cooperative work education has been slow to gain acceptance. The research results make it plain that in the typical American community with a reasonable level of economic activity, CWE is a highly desirable vocational program. It offers instruction in occupations that cannot be touched by any other type of vocational education. On the other hand, CWE will not replace all in-school vocational instruction because of its sensitivity to short-term economic fluctuations, transportation difficulties in large cities, opposition from certain groups of employees, and age restrictions on employment in certain fields.

REFERENCES

1. Baker, Robert. *Reports of the Inspectors of Factories for the Half Year Ending 31st October 1865.* Cataloged under *British Parliamentary Papers,* 24, 1866.
2. Cohen, Alan J., and Frankel, Steven M. *Data Analysis Report: An Assessment of School-Supervised Work Education Programs.* Santa Monica, Calif.: System Development Corporation, 1973. Technical Memorandum 5195/001/00.
3. Evans, Rupert, N. "Cooperative Education—Advantages, Disadvantages and Factors in Program Development." *American Vocational Journal,* 44, no. 5 (1969):19–22, 58.
4. Evans, Rupert N. "Training Time and Placement Time in Vocational Education." *American Vocational Journal,* 45, no. 3 (1970):16–18.
5. Evans, Rupert N. et al. *Education for Employment.* Ann Arbor: Institute of Labor and Industrial Relations, University of Michigan, 1969.
6. Lee, Arthur M. *Learning a Living across the Nation,* vol. I and II. Flagstaff, Ariz.: Northern Arizona University, Project Baseline, 1972 and 1973.
7. Levitan, Sar A., and Mangum, Garth L. *Federal Training and Work Programs in the Sixties.* Ann Arbor: Institute of Labor and Industrial Relations, University of Michigan, 1969.
8. Mangum, Garth L. "Second Chance in the Transition from School to Work." In *Transition from School to Work.* Princeton: Industrial Relations Section, Princeton University, 1968.
9. Meyer, Warren G.; Crawford, Lucy C.; and Klaurens, Mary K. *Coordination in Cooperative Vocational Education.* Columbus, Ohio: Charles E. Merrill Publishing Co., 1975.
10. Schill, William J. *Concurrent Work-Education Programs in the Fifty States.* Urbana, Ill.: Bureau of Educational Research, University of Illinois, 1967. (ERIC ED 021049)

18

Employer and Employee Groups

Vocational training conducted as a part of employment is most commonly sponsored by employers, though many apprenticeship programs and a relatively small amount of training provided to employed skilled workers are often sponsored by labor and management groups such as joint apprenticeship councils.

> The immediate objective is utility, whether it be the most effective methods of selling, the most approved processes of production, or just getting along with co-workers. But often there is idealism too, and a profound belief in education as a way of life. . . . nevertheless, these broader concepts are usually by-products—not ends in themselves. (2, p. 9)

"Manufacturers will do as little or as much training as they need to produce their product and sell it on a competitive market—no more or no less" (12, p. 29). While certain employers undoubtedly do more training than would be required by their short-run needs, and indeed some companies provide training for disadvantaged workers (though they hold a belief that it is more of a service to the community than to themselves), the fact remains that the great majority of training offered by employers is limited to their immediate needs. It is a truism in industrial training that when corporate profits decline, the training department is almost invariably hard hit by economy measures and may be eliminated entirely. Moreover, there is a close relationship between the state of the labor market for different types of employees and the amount of training provided to these types of employees.

Belman and Bliek (1) found that large employers were much more likely than small employers to have training departments. This finding has been substantiated repeatedly, but almost all these studies suffer from an odd blind spot. They report the presence of a training function or report the presence of a particular type of training and do not identify the proportion of employees receiving training. A company having 50,000 employees may have a training department and programs in a wide variety of different fields while serving a very small proportion of the employees. At the same time, a small company might not have a training department and might offer training programs of only two or three types, yet might be reaching a much larger proportion of its employees. In spite of great gaps in information about training offered by employers, there is general agreement that the larger the company the more likely it is to offer some formal training, and that with most companies, the size of the training program expands and contracts very rapidly in response to short run training needs.

Despite the fact that large employers are much more likely to offer formal training programs than small employers, it is by no means clear that the cost per employee trained through formal and informal methods is higher in large companies than in small. Economies of scale and the presence of internal labor market career ladders clearly seem to suggest that costs per trainee would be lower in large companies. Indeed, the very absence of definitive data on training costs may have been a major factor in securing almost unanimous employer support for passage of the British Industrial Training Act of 1964 and its extension in 1973. This act, which set up industry training boards with authority to levy a training tax on all members of the industry, was hailed by both small and large employers as a means of distributing equitably the costs of training. Clearly, small employers felt that they were bearing an unreasonable proportion of training costs while large employers felt that quite the reverse was true.

One of the major factors leading to short-term goals for much of the training conducted by employers is the fear of competitive disadvantage. If a company invests a substantial amount of money in training an employee only to have the trained worker leave to take employment with a competitor, it has suffered a dual disadvantage. It has lost the money it has spent in training, and it has provided its competitor with a better trained employee than the competitor likely would have been able to recruit otherwise.

The Goal of Training Offered by Employers

Training conducted by employers assumes the presence of workers who are capable of being trained. The section on internal labor markets in chapter 7 points out clearly the importance of *trainability* as an employee selection factor in most industries. Assuming that trainable workers are available, most training programs have one or more of four objectives:

1. increased productivity,
2. increased promotability,
3. increased stability of employment,
4. increased safety.

Almost all employers are extremely cost conscious, and one of the obvious major components of cost is productivity of each worker, from the president of the company down to the lowest level of unskilled worker. Productivity is influenced by skills, knowledges, and attitudes, and hence training programs are used to increase skills, to increase knowledge about the job, the company, the industry, and the economic system, and to change attitudes toward fellow workers and management. A single training program may have all three goals, but more commonly one goal is emphasized.

Programs to enhance promotability are heavily concentrated on supervisory and management personnel. Job rotation training, which familiarizes the supervisor with many different parts of the firm, and many other types of training are used. If a worker must be promoted because of increased seniority, it is obviously advantageous to the employer to have the worker ready for the new position if at all possible. Even more important is the need to have supervisors and managers ready to step into posts of increased responsibility when the need arises.

When a effective employee leaves, a variety of costs are incurred. The employee must be terminated, and a new employee must be recruited, screened, and trained. Each of these steps is expensive. Job satisfaction is one of the major ways of reducing turnover, and training can be one factor which increases job satisfaction.

Poor safety records are expensive in terms of insurance costs and decreased confidence on the part of workers and of the community.

Not everyone in the employing firm has the same training goals. The first-line supervisor and his or her immediate superior are interested in reducing costs in the supervisor's unit through increased productivity. The president of the firm, on the other hand, is most interested in finding managers who have a broad understanding of the firm, the industry, and the marketplace. This leads to differing emphases on selection of workers and on the training of workers once they are employed. The first-line supervisor tells the personnel department to select an experienced worker who can become productive with a minimum of training. The president tells the personnel department to hire people who have a broad liberal education and to tell them that all necessary training will be provided by the company. Complaints about specific individuals who were hired are almost always registered by first-line supervisors rather than by presidents, so the personnel department often attempts to meet the goals of the supervisor, unless the president has recently instructed them to the contrary.

Selection of Employees and Training Needs

The selection of employees invariably is closely related to the need to provide training. If a worker can be lured away from an identical job in an identical industry (that is if he or she can be recruited from a competitor), only a brief orientation need be provided by the employer. When there is a surplus of workers in a particular occupation, this is the method used by most American employers. With a surplus of capable workers, it is likely that a thoroughly trained employee can be found at a salary little above that of a trainee. Since training costs money and since trained employees must be paid more than untrained employees, there is always an economic decision to be made as to whether to spend money on the wages at which a trained worker can be recruited or to spend money on training while paying lower wages. Eventually, of course, the broadly trained worker, whether trained inside or outside the firm, can command premium wages.

Some industries have labor-management agreements which make it almost impossible to bring in trained workers. These agreements give preference in promotions to present employees and virtually insure that each new employee will begin work on an unskilled job. As an opening occurs in a more highly skilled job, the most senior employee has a choice of moving into this job and is allowed to continue on it unless he or she is clearly incompetent. Such a promotion system places a premium on selection of new employees who are untrained but are highly intelligent. If they were well trained, they would not apply since they could get jobs elsewhere which utilized their skills. If they were not intelligent, they could not learn rapidly and thus would not be able to make a large number of major occupational changes successfully. For such a system to work, jobs must be designed so that intelligent workers can learn them rapidly once their seniority entitles them to begin learning.

Vocational education graduates are rarely welcomed in industries that promote entirely from within, unless they are so highly trained that they can be employed as technicians and thus be exempt from the labor-management agreement. If employed as unskilled laborers, they are apt to become dissatisfied as they see less competent but more senior workers receive promotions and to look for employment which can use their skills immediately.

Types of Training

Orientation Training

The most common type of training offered by employers is orientation training. This training is designed to introduce the employee to the employer's business and to show how individual duties are related to the goals of the entire establishment. For ordinary employees, it is seldom more than two days in length and may be conducted in a matter of a few minutes, but for management trainees it may last one to two years. Because of its uniqueness, orientation training must be offered by the individual employer rather than by an outside agency, though public and private vocational education programs should and do offer orientation to an occupational field or to an industry.

Typical content for new hourly paid employees involves delivery of an identification badge or card, a welcoming speech by someone in the personnel department, a description of company regulations, safety and security measures, and a description of the suggestion system (2, p. 41). In unionized firms a copy of the union contract may be handed to the worker. Following a brief question-and-answer period, messengers escort each new worker to the place of work, where the first-line supervisor provides a specific introduction to the job.

A program of orientation for management trainees may involve several days of lectures and discussions about the company organization, history, and goals. After a welcome by a top company official, the trainees may be assigned to different departments or units of the firm, sometimes in different cities or even in different countries with a specific work assignment plus instructions to study and report on what they see. Periodically they may be brought back together for additional instruction and discussion. At the end of the orientation they will be assigned to a specific job, chosen on the basis of their interests and on the needs of the company.

Safety Training

Companies which handle hazardous products or processes probably spend more hours of training on safety than any other type of training program. A weekly safety meeting for all supervisors or even for all employees may be mandatory. A review of recent accidents in the industry, suggestions for improved safety practices, and pep talks with regard to competition in the latest safety contest are featured. The heavy economic penalties of a poor safety record provide the principal incentive for this type of training. Usually the same amount of training is provided to every employee in a particular department, regardless of personal safety record. A few companies, especially in the transportation industry, provide special training in safety to those employees who have poor safety records. Companies which do not have such obvious safety hazards, and small companies regardless of their hazards, rarely devote much time to safety education programs.

Management Training

Clark and Sloan found that in factories, management training was offered more frequently than any type of training except orientation. First-line supervisors were most frequently expected to attend, for the higher a person's status in the company, the less likely he or she was to be required to participate. One of the problems in management training is that the teaching staff consists of company employees who are trainers either on a full or part-time basis, but "status forbids a senior executive from regular participation in a class conducted by a subordinate" (2, p. 16).

Much of management training is not in the formal classroom. Distribution of weekly newsletters, motivational booklets, and company reports is common. Little attempt is made to determine whether or not these materials are read. "Understudy" training is also quite common. Each supervisor is assigned the task of preparing one or more subordinates to be ready as a replacement if the supervisor is promoted. Delegation of authority (but not responsibility), informal coaching, and close observation and evaluation of the trainee's progress is common. Some companies state flatly that they will not promote a supervisor until he or she has prepared a satisfactory understudy.

Job rotation is another commonly used supervisory training practice. It has, perhaps, been developed to the greatest extent in the military, where experience in a variety of different types of jobs is a prerequisite to promotion. The goal of job rotation is not only to acquaint the manager with many different aspects of the firm's operation, but also to observe his or her performance in situations requiring broadly different expertise.

Formal classroom instruction in the plant most frequently uses conference techniques, where questions are proposed and trainees are expected to discuss the questions. Content ranges from how to improve the quality of company products and services to ways of dealing with union officials. Occasionally questions of broad social interest are discussed, but rarely by first-line supervisors. Increasingly, mid-management trainees are being sent to university and trade association sponsored formal training programs where the conference method is supplemented by specific instruction by well-prepared instructors.

When a company is expanding its employment of minority group members, management (and sometimes other employees) is given training on understanding minority group values and problems.

Skill Training

Instruction on how to perform a job efficiently is another common type of training. Its form and extent vary enormously, however, from a simple demonstration by an experienced worker to highly formalized training programs of four or five years in length. Its elaborateness is determined largely by the content of the job. The best measure of the simplicity of a redesigned job is in terms of the length of time required to learn it.

On-the-Job Training (OJT)

On-the-job training usually is a distinctly informal process. A brief job demonstration by a first-line supervisor or by a worker selected by the supervisor, followed by a period of trial-and-error learning, with occasional help from supervisors or from nearby workers characterizes the great majority of such training. If the performance is satisfactory, the on-the-job training may be terminated, and checks on quality and quantity of performance then will be handled as they are for any other worker.

In learning the content of more complex positions, the new employee often serves as a helper to a more skilled person, learning by observation and by trial and error under more direct supervision. The job may be subdivided temporarily, with a particular part being demonstrated, followed successively by practice, additional demonstrations, and additional practice. If the worker is expected to be competent in performing a variety of activities, he or she may acquire these through a planned program of job rotation or may learn new activities only when his or her presence is no longer required on an activity which was learned earlier.

On-the-job training typically occurs during the process of production of goods or services, and it is the quantity and quality of production which indicates whether or not learning has occurred. Both the trainee and trainer occupy dual roles: the trainee serves both as a student and a producer; the instructor serves both as a producer and an instructor.

The inseparability of dual roles and the informality of on-the-job training cause extreme difficulty in measuring its costs. Even where on-the-job training is more formalized, as in the armed forces, the formality often consists only of rotating the trainee through a variety of work experiences to be certain that he or she has been exposed to all of the tasks which will be performed in the future. There have been few serious attempts to measure on-the-job costs even in the military. Although the costs of OJT are not usually identified, they are real. Damage to equipment, low quality and quantity of production (both by the trainee and by the trainer), and wastage of material are common costs in production. Lost sales and dissatisfied customers are their counterparts for on-the-job training in service occupations. Costs of OJT are lowered by utilization of instructors who may be so poor in verbal communication that they could not teach in a classroom. The relevance of instruction is easily apparent, which tends to increase motivation. And instruction is sometimes provided on equipment which otherwise would not be in use or by instructors who otherwise would be resting.

Undoubtedly most blue-collar job skills are learned through training on-the-job (11,p.437; 8, pp. 43–45). For certain blue- and white-collar jobs, there is no alternative to on-the-job training. This is particularly true where workers desire to conceal from management the precise techniques used in production for fear that management will use this knowledge to increase work output. Where the cost of materials is high, where it is impracticable to assemble a group of workers simultaneously needing identical training, and where the cost of equipment is extremely high, on-the-job training is less costly than more formal training programs.

Skills transmitted through on-the-job training are rarely recorded. This leads to direct transmission of skills from worker to successor and to the changing of skills since the process of transmission is incomplete. This, in turn, leads to nonstandard jobs as innovations are introduced without written record. These innovations may or may not be desirable in terms of increasing productivity.

When job skills are specific to a particular firm, present employees tend to have a monopoly on training if OJT is the method of instruction employed. Since on-the-job training is under the control of first-line supervision and other current employees, a worker who is not accepted by these current employees is unlikely to be allowed to learn the job because he or she is subject to sabotage, harassment, and incorrect instruction. On-the-job training requires the approval and close cooperation of experienced employees. Since training is a process by which the supply of skilled labor is increased, it must be apparent to these current employees that an increase in the supply of skilled labor will not be detrimental to their own position. Otherwise they will not cooperate in the training process and will make it almost impossible for a newcomer to learn. Job security and promotions based on seniority help to insure that the newcomer is not an active threat to existing employees (7).

A second method of insuring against too active competition from new workers is the use of labor organizations to restrict worker entry. The craft unions have relied heavily on this method of protection. By controlling entry to the occupation, they have found it much less necessary to rely upon seniority as a control device. Hence, employers are much freer to assign workers from unions having close entry level restrictions than they are workers from industrial type unions which rely much more heavily upon seniority. In either case, proposals for change in the allocation of scarce jobs among the internal labor force through training will almost certainly lead to conflict, and if labor union officials appear to countenance such proposed changes, their positions as leaders are likely to be in jeopardy.

Teaching Speed and Accuracy in Job Performance

On-the-job training is very much concerned with the development of necessary speed and accuracy of performance. The process of acquiring the necessary speed and accuracy can be described for each individual learner as a learning curve which relates output of satisfactory product or service to length of time on the job. The curve showing the amount of satisfactory product eventually levels off. If it levels off at or above the standard required for the job, the worker is said to be trained. If it levels off below the standard required, additional training efforts may be employed or the worker may be transferred or discharged.

One of the hazards of on-the-job training is that it has a potential for permanently lowering work norms. Particularly during periods when there is a tight labor market and employment standards are relaxed, new workers may have difficulty in meeting old job standards. Since these job standards are rarely written but are generally transmitted through the on-the-job training process, they are almost certain to be lowered unless new employees can meet them quickly. Similar problems are involved in the use of on-the-job training to develop behavioral traits such as promptness, regular attendance, and acceptance of criticisms from management. Reductions in behavioral work trait standards during the training period are likely to be incorporated as a permanent feature of the work setting.

Formalized Skill Training

Formal training is emphasized in employment much more frequently during tight labor markets than when adequate numbers of employees are readily available. In part this is a reflection of economies of scale which permit personnel to be assigned temporarily to full-time training duties and to the presence of enough trainees to establish a class. Classroom training in basic mathematical and verbal skills, blueprint reading, and other generalizable, standardizable skills can be organized. When the labor market is loose, these skills can be obtained through a process of selection from the available labor supply and are unlikely to be taught within the plant.

General Education

Clark and Sloan (2) found that general education was the least frequently offered of any type of employer-sponsored training. Even so, the programs classified by employers as being "general education" often sound remarkably specific, e.g., "accounting machine applications," "aircraft flutter and transient loads," "applied electronics," "engineering report writing," "automatic box-loom fixing," plus certain avocational subjects and elementary school and high school subjects which most people would accept as general education. Some employers who reimburse workers for college fees will pay for general courses required for a degree, but others restrict payment to courses approved in advance as being useful on the job.

Decision Making in Employer-Sponsored Training

Two major decisions are necessary once it has been decided that employee performance is not satisfactory. The first decision is whether to recruit or train. Since little is known about the costs of recruitment, and even less is known about the cost of training, this decision is very often made on noneconomic grounds. The presence of skilled, experienced personnel who can be recruited almost always tips the decision in favor of recruitment. If skilled, experienced employees are not available on the labor market, or if management is prohibited from employing them, training will be instituted. The starting of such training often is not as a result of a formal management decision but is done by first-line supervisors forced to institute on-the-job training in order to meet quantity and quality quotas. Formal training programs, on the other hand, almost always require high level management decisions.

Purchasing or Providing Training

If a decision is made that present or prospective employees need training, a second-level decision must be made as to whether to purchase this training outside the company or to provide it internally. Sometimes a combination of these methods is used. The military provides training for officers in service academies and officer candidate schools and purchases training in reserve officer training programs in universities. A large bakery may provide training on-the-job and through formal courses, but it may also purchase training from the American Institute of Baking, which operates a school supported by the industry. General Motors operates its own college, but it also purchases college training for some of its employees. It trains service personnel through a large network of regional service schools, but it also subsidizes vocational programs in schools through gifts of equipment, instructional materials, and low cost teacher training.

Training may be purchased from a variety of sources. Trade associations very frequently have training programs available which may be offered inside or outside the place of employment at a relatively modest cost. Local high schools and community colleges are frequently anxious to provide training programs at even lower costs to the employer.

The availability of vocational education in high schools and colleges and the availability of training services offered by the vendors of equipment often lead employers during tight labor markets to contract for vocational education to be conducted off the job. It is characteristic for such programs to be initiated by the employer rather than by the training agency and be so closely related to the employer that they appear to be extensions of internal training activities. In almost every case, they are designed to provide instruction specific to the needs of the employer rather than to provide basic or general vocational education.

This procedure is in marked contrast to the public statements of most employers that they desire broad general and vocational education programs. Perhaps an explanation lies in the fact that an employer recruiting new employees desires to employ people who have had general and vocational education broad enough to include the specific skill requirements of the firm, but when contracting for the training of current employees does not wish the instruction to be so broad as to include the specific requirements of other employers. Broader training would be more expensive and might lead some employees to seek employment elsewhere. Decisions to provide training rather than to buy it are almost always swayed by such factors as a desire to provide an instructor who "knows our situation," fear of letting outsiders know company secrets, and the desire of workers to have training offered on company time on company premises in order to minimize their personal costs.

Almost invariably, employers prefer to operate their own training program if their size will permit it. With the training directly under their control, no time is spent on instruction they regard as superfluous. Second choice is usually training offered by a trade association, which is at least partially under their contol. Only in the event that these two methods are inadequate do they purchase training from outside educational institutions. Usually, if the training program in a large company must be reduced in size, purchased training is discontinued first. Conversely, purchased training often expands most rapidly when the internal training facilities are fully occupied and additional training is needed.

When training of known high quality is provided at no added cost to the employer, a different set of values is employed. Typists are usually trained in public schools, with all or part of the cost (including foregone earnings) being borne by others. This makes it extremely unlikely that an employer will offer training in typing, unless the number of graduates from outside training agencies is completely inadequate to meet the demand. Even then, a company first is likely to ask the public schools to increase their output.

Some vocational training, however, is so poor in quality that its output is not desirable even if it is free of cost to the employer. If graduates of a program cannot be placed in employment even in times of shortage of employees, the program must be improved or be terminated. If graduates of a program are placed during times of shortage of employees but cannot be placed when the labor market is loose, however, this is not necessarily an indication of poor quality vocational education. Often this is due to employers searching for employees of higher verbal intelligence than the students who are enrolled in that vocational program. High placement rates of school graduates, regardless of the state of the labor market, is a common sign that the vocational program is refusing to serve some of the students who most need its help.

Advantages and Disadvantages of Employer Training

Training offered by employers has numerous advantages. Instruction is almost always relevant and timely in the eyes of the trainee. It is offered in a setting which appears to be relevant to trainee goals. It seldom requires the purchasing of expensive equipment specifically for training. The products and services produced during the process of training are readily sold as regular products of the company. Length of training is not constrained by artifical lengths of class periods, semesters, or school years. Disadvantages are few but important. The business of the employer is to produce products or services other than training, so training is a by-product which inevitably receives less attention than the prime goal of the firm. Not only the training but the trainee is a means to an end. In an educational institution, no one would think of expecting a trainee to continue indefinitely practicing a skill which was already learned. Instead, he or she would be instructed in a new skill. If this process were followed in employer-sponsored training, the company would quickly go bankrupt. The cost of training to an employer can only be recouped by a period of heightened productivity following training. Unless the employee is needed to perform some other process, he or she can expect to continue practicing indefinitely the processes learned most thoroughly.

It is obvious that in some cases human talent is developed more effectively in a production setting than in a school removed from contact with employment realities. On the other hand, it is certain that the development of human talents in an employment setting is often accidental and is almost always subordinate to a production goal.

Training by Organized Labor

Training sponsored by labor organizations has many of the characteristics of employer training. Workers and union officials must be oriented to the goals of the labor organization. Officials must be developed through on-the-job training and through formal educational programs. As with big companies, big unions also are more likely to have sophisticated training programs. Indeed, the AFL-CIO operates a college which in many ways is as sophisticated as those run by General Motors and by International Business Machines.

Apprenticeship training may be sponsored by employers, by labor groups, or may be jointly sponsored. In any case where labor organizations are involved, they regard the apprenticeship program with an almost sacred reverence. Attempts by outsiders to modify the program in any way are regarded with suspicion. In one way, this high regard for apprenticeship training is misplaced. No more than 250,000 people in the United States serve as apprentices at any one time, and, in view of the fact that dropout rates are rather high and programs average four years in length, no more than 50,000 workers can complete apprenticeship programs each year. This amounts to about 2 percent of the yearly additions to the labor force. Even in the construction trades and in certain metal-working crafts, where apprenticeship in the United States is concentrated, apprenticeship rarely provides more than a tenth of the new skilled craftsmen.

On the other hand, the person who completes an apprenticeship program is in a very favored position. He or she is better prepared than any other skilled worker in the field and usually has many positions from which to choose. About a third of the apprentice graduates become supervisors; a third enter technical positions; and a third work directly in the occupations for which they are prepared. This latter third provides a sizable share of the leadership of organized labor. With these facts in mind, it is easy to see why labor guards jealously a program which provides upward mobility for their sons (but still rarely for their daughters) and leadership for their movement.

While the history of apprenticeship is well known, current programs have not been studied intensively. Enough is known, however, to make clear that a far smaller portion of the skilled workers in the United States is provided through apprenticeship than in any other Western industrialized nation. In most other countries, workers in many more occupations, from waiter to technician, are trained through apprenticeship than is the case here. Instead, we tend to rely on OJT which lacks a definite program of job rotation through each of the activities requisite for skilled performance. Moreover, it usually lacks the formal education in the theory and practice of the occupation which accompanies on-the-job training in a well-structured apprenticeship program.

Especially when jobs are scarce, employee groups desire to control educational programs which lead to employment in their industry or occupation. Just as land-owners seek to retain title to their land and to pass it on to their children, so do skilled workers seek to keep their jobs and ensure that their children will have access to these same jobs. This view of jobs as employee property naturally leads to conflict when outsiders seek employment in desirable jobs. If employee groups control access to training programs which lead to such employment, they effectively control who can compete for jobs.

Education in the Armed Forces

Education in the Armed Forces has numerous parallels with education sponsored by any other type of employer. And, since records of armed forces training are much more complete than records of other types of training by employers, we turn to them to note substantial changes in training by employers during America's history. Three general principles seem to have pervaded military training programs:

1. The greater the level of technological advance, the greater the amount of formal schooling provided to cope with these technological changes.
2. Following the introduction of a technological innovation, which requires employees who have new job skills, the first response is to provide a completely inadequate quantity of such training. This is succeeded by a period in which the quantity of trainees is sharply increased and the curriculum is made up of a combination of general education and specific education. This in turn is followed by a sharp curtailment of the curriculum, eliminating many of the general education elements.
3. A shortage of funds is followed almost immediately by sharp curtailment in both formal and informal education programs.

In 1802 the United States Military Academy was established with a curriculum that emphasized engineering. This subject was outside the academic pale of the universities, but it was obviously successful, for not a single fortification designed by West Point graduates was captured by the enemy during the war of 1812. During this same period the Navy depended upon skilled manpower from the Merchant Marine and supplemented their skills by on-the-job training. Its lack of regard for formal instruction was conveyed in an order of 1802 which required the chaplain of each ship to instruct officers ". . . in writing, arithmetic, navigation, and whatsoever may contribute to render them proficients" (quoted in reference 3, p. 16). Very likely the chaplain was the only person on board who could write, though his qualifications for instruction in navigation almost certainly left a great deal to be desired.

In 1814 the first steam powered warship in the United States Navy was constructed by Robert Fulton, but it was not until thirty-one years later that the United States Naval Academy was established, with a curriculum that emphasized steam engineering. The first army airplane was purchased in 1909, but training for aviators lay dormant until 1916. The first army motor truck experiments began in 1904, but when fifty thousand motor vehicles were purchased at the start of World War I, there were no trained technicians for maintenance and repair. The time lag between the introduction of new technology and the preparation of personnel to cope with it continues to decrease. Today the armed forces are usually leaders in an attempt to design educational programs which will produce technicians almost simultaneously with the introduction of new technology.

Formal Schools in the Military

In spite of having the best organized and probably the largest system of on-the-job training of any employer, the United States military still finds a need for more and more formal education. Much of this education is provided through specialized schools operated by the military, but a considerable amount of formal training is acquired through contracts with colleges, universities, private trade schools, and schools operated by vendors of equipment. The level of training ranges from basic literacy education to education at the postdoctorate level. Although they were relatively late in establishing formal schools, the Navy and the Air Force now provide more such training per employee than the Army does, probably because of their higher investment in sophisticated technology. As the rate of technological advance has increased during recent years, the rate of establishment of specialized schools has similarly increased.

Size of the Military Training Effort

Technical training in the military is undoubtedly the largest vocational and technical program maintained by any single establishment anywhere. At any one time between 10 and 15 percent of the personnel of the armed forces in the United States are receiving formal instruction in a school. Over 4,000 resident courses are offered which prepare people for almost 2,500 separate jobs. Since most courses are less than a year in length, it is likely that the number attending formal classes during any one year is considerably higher than 10 to 15 percent and may approximate the number of individuals who enter and leave the armed forces each year (approximately 20 percent). "If all these schools were placed on one contiguous campus, the area covered would probably exceed that occupied by the three cities . . . New York, Los Angeles, and Chicago" (3, p. 1). In addition to those enrolled in formal courses in resident centers, nearly one million students are enrolled in the more than 2,500 correspondence school courses offered by the armed forces.

The Relationship between Military Training and Success in Civilian Life

As is the case with training offered by an employer, all or almost all of military training is designed to enable the trainee to better succeed in military life. Although there have been limited experiments, such as Project Transition, there has been no sustained attempt to design military training which will enable a person better to succeed in civilian life. Inevitably, of course, there is some value in civilian life for many types of military training, and a great deal of civilian value for a very few types of training. Basic training in the military is sometimes accepted by colleges in lieu of health and physical education courses. Language instruction, typewriter repair, medical instruction, certain of the broader electronics training courses, air traffic control, and certain clerical training have very close parallels in civilian occupations. The most striking example of transferability is found in the fact that a very high proportion of commercial airplane pilots received their initial technical instruction and experience in the military. On the other hand, instruction in warfare, cryptography, and the like, has little or no relationship to civilian occupations employing sizable numbers of people.

Even in cases where there is some relationship between skills taught in the military and skills needed in civilian occupations, the number of people trained may bear no relationship to civilian needs (though it certainly will have a close relationship to military needs for personnel).

The Need for Transition Education between Military Technical Training and Civilian Technical Needs

Retirements from the military occur at relatively early ages except for the very few officers who reach the highest levels of command. Many career personnel retire at forty to forty-five years of age. The great majority of non-career personnel leave the armed forces before they are thirty. Most of these people have acquired some skills which would be useful in civilian life. If they go to college, arrangements have been made for them to receive college credit for relevant formal education received in the armed forces. Few such arrangements have been made for credit in apprenticeshp, in vocational and technical education programs, or in occupational licensure.

Planning for Employer Needs

With the exception of the military, very few of even the largest and most sophisticated employers in the United States engage in employment forecasting or planning for any part of their labor force, and those few who do engage in employment forecasting do it almost entirely for their management personnel (6). When the employment office of a company reports that the labor market is tightening, it receives approval to begin advertising for employees, to make contacts with school systems and with public employment services, and to ask current employees to suggest names of friends who might be interested in employment. If the market continues to tighten and insufficient applicants for employment are recruited by these means, the employer then turns to paying bonuses to employees for referrals, pays visiting and moving costs for recruits, activates training and apprenticeship programs, contributes instructors, equipment, and even money to local schools for vocational education, and contacts various organizations to secure referrals of recent arrivals in the community.

Skill shortages also lead to decisions to proceed with job simplification and the substitution of equipment for labor. Davis and Canter (5) pointed out that when new equipment is being designed, it is relatively easy to see what tasks must be performed to operate the equipment. However, the combining of these tasks into jobs depends upon other work being performed nearby, attitudes of union officials, and qualifications of the labor force, and usually must wait until the equipment is in operation. Even minimum job qualifications are almost impossible to foresee, since the new equipment has been operated and maintained by overqualified engineers. During the process of installation of a new technology, as operators assigned to jobs change, the jobs automatically change to take into account the capabilities of the new operators. Enterprises attempt to mold people to jobs, not jobs to people, but in practice people frequently mold jobs.

REFERENCES

1. Belman, Harry S., and Bliek, J.E. "Training Departments in Business, Industry and Government." *Journal of the American Society of Training Directors* 12, no. 9 (September 1968):45–53.

2. Clark, Harold F., and Sloan, Harold S. *Classrooms in the Factories.* New York: New York University Press, 1958.
3. ______. *Classrooms in the Military.* New York: Teachers College, Columbia University, 1964.
4. ______. *Classrooms in the Stores.* Sweetsprings, Mo.: Rocksbury Press, 1962.
5. Davis, Louise, and Canter, Ralph Raymond. "Job Design." *Journal of Industrial Engineering* 6 (January 1955):3.
6. Doeringer, Peter B. et al. "Corporate Manpower Forecasting and Planning." *Conference Board Record* 5, no. 8 (1968):37–45.
7. Evans, Rupert N.; Holter, Arne; and Stern, Marilyn Cheney. "Criteria for Determining Whether Competency Should Be Taught On-the-Job or in a Formal Technical Course." *Journal of Vocational Education Research.* In press.
8. *Formal Occupational Training of Adult Workers.* Manpower/Automation Research Monograph No. 2. Washington, D.C.: U.S. Department of Labor, 1964.
9. Hansen, Gary B. *Britain's Industrial Training Act, Its History Development and Implications for America.* Washington, D.C.: National Manpower Policy Task Force, 1967.
10. Mesics, Emil A. *An Annotated Bibliography on Industrial Training: Training in Organizations, Business, Industrial and Government.* Bibliography Series Number 4. Ithaca, N.Y.: New York State School of Industrial and Labor Relations, Cornell University, 1960.
11. Piore, Michael J. "On-the-Job Training and Adjustment to Technological Change." *Journal of Human Resources* 3, no. 4 (Fall 1968):435–49.
12. Smith, Paul W. of Western Electric Company quoted in Dunlap, J.T., ed. *Work Force Adjustments in Private Industry—Their Implications for Manpower Policy.* Manpower/Automation Research Monograph No. 7. Washington, D.C.: U.S. Department of Labor, 1968.

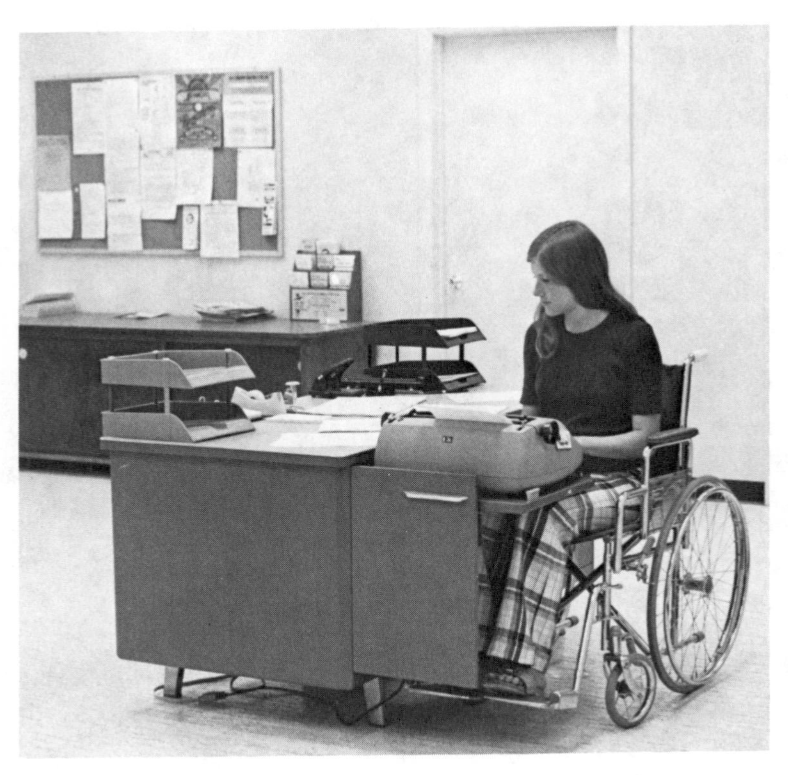

19

Vocational Education Conducted by Other Agencies

When we think of vocational education, we usually think of education conducted in public schools or by employer and employee groups. Undoubtedly the major part of vocational education is provided by these institutions, but a number of other agencies and groups also contribute markedly to vocational education. There is virtually no literature on vocational education of this type.

Organizations Selling Products or Services

A very extensive part of vocational education, but one about which little is known, is that conducted by organizations interested in selling products or services. These educational efforts are particularly intensive when the product or service is so new that formal schools have not yet had an opportunity to incorporate it into their curricula, where the demand for this education is so geographically dispersed that it is impractical for formal schools or even employers to provide instruction, or where vocational educators and employers have failed to provide adequate training (in quantity or quality) for whatever reason.

These training services are expensive, but are justified on the ground that the product or service will not continue to be sold unless its performance is satisfactory. And the only way in which its performance can be guaranteed to be satisfactory is to have capable people who know how to use it or adjust it and repair it. Even where vocational education is not included as a part of the sales or franchise contract, many manufacturers and franchisers are willing to provide training to user organizations, with free or nominal tuition, simply upon request. As a means of expanding the availability of qualified personnel, many such schools allow vocational instructors to enroll with no tuition payment on the assumption that as they acquire the necessary skills, they will pass them on to their students.

Factory Schools

Quite often the manufacturer, franchise owner, or other purveyor of a product or service will organize a school adjacent to the headquarters of the firm. This allows use of their personnel in both production and instruction roles and allows students to see the production of goods or the development of promotional materials firsthand.

Where a relatively expensive product is involved or where large quantities of even inexpensive products are sold, the buyer may receive as a part of the purchase contract an agreement to train a certain number of employees in the factory-operated school. Examples of products which include training as a part of the sales package include computers, digital controlled machine tools, airplanes, and locomotives. Sellers of franchises for hotels, food retailing establishments, and many other service establishments provide a similar type of training in a central school. Often, this training is mandatory, and sometimes retraining at specified intervals (such as once each year) is also mandatory. At least one large manufacturer of automobiles requires personnel from a prospective franchise holder to be trained at a central location before a franchise may be transferred.

Organizations selling petroleum products often require the manager and key personnel of automotive service stations to receive training in a central school. Often this central school may also be a factory-operated service station, which allows personnel to receive not only classroom instruction but also supervised on-the-job training for brief periods of time. In the automotive industry, the critical shortage of skilled repair people has led to the establishment of regional factory schools, each of which provides a site for training conducted by subsidiaries of the parent corporation.

Clinics for Service Personnel

One of the difficulties with factory schools is that it is necessary for the trainee to leave the place of employment for a week or more and travel to some central training area. In order to reach more effectively the people who need training, many organizations have developed mobile training units which travel from town to town, advertise the availability of training, and attract trainees for sessions as short as an hour. Types of organizations which use mobile training include manufacturers of fertilizer, electronic equipment, and automotive equipment. Indeed, almost any manufacturer of a new product which finds it cannot attract students in sufficient quantity to a centralized school is likely to consider seriously the desirability of setting up mobile training units. Often these training units serve not only a training function, but also a sales function, for as people see equipment and services demonstrated, they are often willing to invest in them, particularly if they are assured that additional training will be available as needed.

Technical Information Brochures

A great deal of vocational training is carried on through printed material distributed to users. Ordinarily this method of training works best when the people to be trained have some familiarity with the product or service but need to be introduced to important modifications in it. As in the case of training clinics, technical information brochures serve both a sales and a training function. Indeed, the sales department is often responsible for the preparation and distribution of technical information brochures. In some organizations this leads to conflicts in design of the information to be distributed since sales personnel usually wish to stress advantages of the product or service, while personnel from engineering and training departments wish to call attention to key problems which can be circumvented through adequate training. Advertisements, especially in trade journals, also serve a vocational training function. Usually, however, advertisements are under control of the sales department, and training content is usually incidental to the sales purpose.

University-Affiliated Groups

Cooperative Extension

Although the cooperative extension service was organized in land grant universities to provide educational services to farmers, it has expanded its goals to provide services to city dwellers as well. It has always had a goal of increasing the total well-being of the men and women it serves. Programs range from instruction in art and music to an understanding of better means of marketing home produced goods and services, but a high proportion of the instruction given has been related to increasing occupational competence. A major reason for the success of these programs has been that efforts have been made to determine the needs and interests of the clientele to be served.

University Extension

Most university extension programs began as a way of carrying the standard credit instructional programs of the university off campus. This still continues to be a major goal of people who operate university extension programs, but they have learned many things from cooperative extension. Today the educational programs of cooperative extension and university extension are remarkably similar, and indeed several universities have acted to combine the two. The image of university extension is that its programs serve only professionals and business people. While it is true that these groups ask for and receive a great deal of assistance, a glance at total university extension programs will show that they serve people from almost every walk of life. Programs designed to raise occupational competency, however, tend to be confined to professional and business occupations.

Y.M.C.A.s and Y.W.C.A.s

The Young Men's and Young Women's Christian Associations, while established for religious purposes, have developed a wide range of educational programs to meet the needs of their clientele. As is the case whenever the needs of the students are taken into account, a sizable portion of the educational program is devoted to increasing occupational competence. By meeting the needs of people through inexpensive, well planned occupational education programs, and by being accessible as a result of having large facilities in inner cities, many Y.M.C.A.s and Y.W.C.A.s have built adult education programs which are models of effectiveness.

Opportunities Industrialization Centers

The Opportunities Industrialization Center (OIC) movement began in Philadelphia in the late fifties as a means of increasing the options of blacks. Unlike cooperative or university extension services or Y.M.C.A.s, the OIC program was designed by blacks for blacks. This concept of self-help has appealed to businesses and the federal government, which have provided financial assistance. At the same time, the sense of controlling their own educational and occupational destiny has appealed to blacks. The OIC program has not been entirely occupational, though this has formed its major emphasis. Opportunities Industrialization Centers have spread across the country. While some have failed, largely due to deficiencies in local leadership, others have succeeded very well. As is the case with secondary school vocational education, OIC's programs have attracted more female than male trainees.

Professional and Trade Associations

Most professional associations and associations of employers and employees maintain occupational education programs. These range from correspondence school instruction and short-term seminars to formal instruction in association-operated schools, with the course of instruction lasting a year or more. Traveling lecturers, magazines devoted to education of the members, closed circuit television instruction, and mailed brochures bringing members up to date on recent occupational developments are part of the program of many such groups. The size and scope of these programs have never been tabulated, but it is certain that few people realize their magnitude.

Private Schools

Public schools are supported in large part from taxes, so student fees are relatively low. Private schools, on the other hand, depend largely on student fees to pay their bills, so these fees are often rather high, averaging $500 per course or $1000 per year in 1972 (3, p. 134). How can private schools compete with public schools for students?

A few unethical schools use high pressure sales tactics and fail to deliver quality instruction, but these schools do not stay in business for long because students stop coming and because the remainder of the private school industry refuses to accredit them. The large, stable portion of the industry generally offers services not provided effectively by public schools.

Public schools require general education courses along with occupational education courses. "In contrast, private vocational school programs are specifically designed to *only* contain subjects directly related to the job-oriented course objective," enabling the student "to meet the requirements for job entry in a specific occupation [in] a minimal period of time" (3, p. 30). The cost to the student of enrolling in school includes not only tuition and fees but also foregone earnings (the amount of money the student could have earned if he or she had been working instead of going to school). Since foregone earnings are often much larger than tuition, a short, intensive course with high tuition may cost the student less than a longer course at lower tuition.

Private schools offer vocational instruction through three methods: resident instruction, with services provided to students in a physical facility controlled by the school, home study, with instruction offered by correspondence, and extension, in which instructors travel to meet students in geographic areas away from the school's base facilities. Public schools use these same three methods, but private schools use the latter two much more extensively. Foregone earnings are very low for correspondence and extension instruction, as compared with full-time resident instruction.

Private schools also compete by offering courses as soon as a demand becomes apparent, while public schools often wait until they feel assured that the demand will continue. Private schools are often more effective than public schools in advertising the availability of their services, in acting quickly to replace incompetent instructors, and in operating placement services to secure jobs for their graduates. Private schools have provided vocational eduation for a much longer period of time than public schools, and there is every indication that they will continue to be able to compete successfully.

The first private school which offered vocational instruction in this country taught shorthand. It advertised in 1728 that "any Persons in the Country desirous to Learn this Art, may be having the several Lessons sent Weekly to them to be as perfectly instructed as those that live in Boston" (3, p. 6). By the mid-1800s private business schools operated in every section of the country. Private trade and technical schools also antedated publicly supported instruction in these fields. In fact, it is difficult to find a single vocational subject in which instruction was offered earlier in a public than in a private school.

The early private vocational schools were operated by an individual entrepreneur or by a partnership. This led to their being called *proprietary schools,* but this term is now obsolete since 85 percent of these schools are now controlled by corporations, including some of the largest publicly held conglomerates (3, p. v). Most of these schools seek to make a profit, but there are also a number of nonprofit, private vocational schools which depend on endowments for part of their income.

The number of private schools offering occupational education courses has been estimated at 7000 and the number of students at over 1,500,000 (1, p. 9). This latter figure was probably an underestimate since Illinois alone has over 600,000 students (3, p. 51) but only 393 schools (3, p. 46). Almost all of these schools are at the postsecondary level, though several correspondence schools also offer high school courses. The courses offered cover almost the entire range of entry-level occupations.

Instructors rarely have tenure and are selected on the basis of practical experience, rather than academic degrees. Only a third of them have baccalaureates; 40 percent have no college credits; and few have been taught how to teach (3, p. 122).

Students in trade and technical courses are almost all males, and males predominate in home study instruction. Schools which offer instruction in secretarial and office occupations, art and design, and medical and dental assistant courses have a predominantly female student body. The enrollments by sex are almost identical to those in public schools. The average age of correspondence course students is markedly higher than for students in residence (3, p. 53).

Much more is known about correspondence school students than about students in other private vocational school programs. Students in home study programs tend to come from small cities and rural areas, to earn wages near the poverty level, and to be employed at the lower levels of manufacturing. Students in private vocational schools tend to come from lower or middle socioeconomic levels (3, p. 25, 94). It seems likely that if tuition were subsidized, even more students from low socioeconomic groups would enroll.

Cooperation between public and private schools is making a wider range of vocational education available. Two plans are frequently utilized. More than a thousand high schools allow students to enroll in correspondence courses supervised by the school and accepted for high school graduation (3, p. 159). An unknown proportion of these courses are designed to broaden vocational education offerings of the high school. A second means of broadening the high school's vocational program is to allow students to enroll in a nearby private vocational school for part of the school day or school year. The student's tuition may be paid from state or federal vocational funds if the state approves the program.

Role of the Federal Government

Aside from its support of vocational education activities conducted by secondary and postsecondary schools for in-school youth and adults, the federal government has financed a variety of other training programs for nonprofessional occupations. These other programs have been well described by Levitan and Mangum (4) and by Venn (8).

Vocational Rehabilitation

The oldest of these programs, vocational rehabilitation, began in 1920 to meet the need for retraining people who had been physically disabled as a result of industrial employment. It was gradually expanded to include medical, financial, counseling, and all other types of services needed to return the disabled to employment. At the same time, its clientele was expanded to serve those whose handicaps were the result of birth defects and all types of accidents. Most recently it stated that it can serve anyone who has a physical or mental disability which is a handicap to employment, if rehabilitation services are likely to aid employability.

Like vocational education, vocational rehabilitation requires the participating states to match federal funds and allows the states wide discretion in the ways in which services are provided. A further similarity is that both programs have tended to serve an upper-lower class clientele and to provide inadequate service to lower-lower class people. Two of its strongest points have been the quality of training provided to its counselors and its willingness to purchase quality service for its clients from any agency which can provide the assistance needed (4, pp. 277–331).

Manpower Development and Training Act and Poverty Programs

In 1962 there was fear that technological change would cause unemployment among heads of families. The MDTA was created to ease this dislocation. Within a year, however, it was plain that youth and minority group members had far greater problems, so programs were designed to meet their needs. Many of these took the form of federal grants to neighborhood groups, public and private schools, and employers who provided similar services and competed for students and for employment slots.

Unlike vocational education and vocational rehabilitation, few MDTA and poverty programs operated through state agencies. Most were directed from Washington, and funds were sent to program operators with no intermediaries. Programs were started or stopped on short notice, with little relationship between funding level and quality of program. Costs per trainee were high, ranging up to $10,000 per trainee per year (in the early years of the Job Corps). One reason for high cost was that, unlike vocational education and rehabilitation, MDTA and poverty program trainees were paid to go to school. This was justified on the grounds that it made no sense to pay people more to accept public assistance (welfare) than to receive training which could remove them from welfare rolls. But stipends to trainees were not the only element of high cost. Food, housing, and medical costs were often a far larger proportion of costs than were trainee stipends. Costs of training were high because teachers and administrators had to be paid extra to serve in programs which were temporary. Costs per trainee were inflated markedly by the practice of admitting a specified number of trainees to a program to last, say, forty weeks. As trainees dropped out or were placed in jobs, the instructor might have only two or three trainees by the thirty-fifth week. The teacher's salary and overhead such as rent remained almost constant, sending costs per trainee up sharply.

One reason for funding programs on a short-term basis was refusal to recognize that training programs for unemployed and underemployed adults would be needed for many years. Failure to plan for the institutionalization of such programs increased costs and lowered staff morale. This failure to plan was justified by claims that stopping a project and providing new funds only after a delay of indefinite length allowed local program operators to discharge incompetent instructors. In practice, however, the more competent the instructors, the less likely they were to tolerate a one- to three-month period without pay. In one case, thirty-four of thirty-five instructors took nonteaching jobs within a month.

Skills Centers

A major step toward institutionalization was taken with the establishment of skills centers which were funded on an annual basis. Unlike earlier training programs, skills centers could accept trainees whenever a training slot was open; trainees could change from one occupational goal to another if the first choice proved to be inappropriate; and trainees lived at home (which lowered costs and increased trainee morale).

One group of Washington policy makers felt that private industry could be more effective than nonprofit groups in providing training to the unemployed. In spite of clear evidences of fraud in scattered cases, the private sector has been encouraged to expand its training efforts through a combination of persuasion and payments of approximately $3,000 per trainee per year, through the Job Opportunities in the Business Sector (JOBS) program and similar plans. These programs worked reasonably well so long as unemployment was relatively low, but when unemployment reached 6 percent or above, serious problems arose. Employer training of the unemployed is conducted almost entirely-on-the-job, and the combination of employment during and after training is a major attraction of this means of coping with unemployment. But when former employees are laid off because of lack of work, it is difficult or impossible for employers to take on new workers, even if they might wish to do so because of the government subsidies they would receive. Workers who are on the job are friends of those who are laid off, so they resent and often refuse to train new workers until workers who have been laid off have returned.

Comprehensive Employment and Training Act

After a decade, MDTA was replaced by CETA. The principal effect of this new act was to transfer decision making from Washington to local and state governments. Any local government representing 100,000 people or more could be designated as a *prime sponsor* and could decide which employment and training programs it wished to support. Areas of a state which were not part of a local prime sponsor's territory constituted the *balance of state,* for which the governor served as prime sponsor.

This sudden shift from federal to local planning and decision making found many localities completely unprepared for their new responsibilities. Where local governments were able to hire or train capable staff, CETA worked well, but efforts floundered in other communities.

A major impact of MDTA and CETA programs has been as a force for change in institutionalized training programs. Not only have they demonstrated new methods and demonstrated that a new clientele can be served, but they have also shown a need to shift from matching the *best* person to an existing job to preparing *each* person to fill a suitable job (4, p. 9).

Education of the Disadvantaged and the Handicapped

The federal government has moved more and more strongly, through the Manpower Development and Training Act, the Comprehensive Employment and Training Act, the amendments to the Vocational Education Act, and the rulings of various government agencies, to emphasize its concern for developing the full potential of disadvantaged and handicapped people. Because the unemployment rate is so extraordinarily high for disadvantaged and handicapped youth (higher than for the general population during the depths of the depression), the first efforts were directed toward skill training for immediate employment. It was quickly found that basic educational deficiencies, primarily in reading, needed to be remedied simultaneously.

In its efforts to do something quickly to solve these serious problems some eighteen different federal agencies set up a variety of competing and overlapping programs. Most of these have had little relationship with the formal school structure because (a) there was a general feeling by those in charge that the schools had had their chance and had failed; (b) the formal school structure was not attractive to many of the potential trainees; and (c) most school people were not interested. Soon there were so many programs, with different requirements, different benefits, and starting and stopping at such irregular intervals, that no one could possibly know where to send a person who needed help.

The first attempt to remedy this situation on a nationwide basis was the Cooperative Area Manpower Planning System (CAMPS). This involved state and federal agencies for the first time on a large-scale basis, and brought the various agencies together to tell each other what they were doing. Unfortunately, most agencies chose not to tell what they were planning for fear that some other agency would steal their plans. State-wide plans often consisted of agency plans stapled together into one document. One wag referred to this as "coordination by staple." Schools, in particular, have contributed and received little from CAMPS. They have been represented by state educational officials or in the large cities by central office staff. Most program planning and implementation, however, is done at the local educational agency level. These local people do not want state and central office staff to speak for them.

Due to the inadequacies of CAMPS, decisions on the life and death of federal programs for the disadvantaged continued to be made in Washington, on grounds which appeared to governors, mayors, and community action groups to be capricious. They asked for control, and in the early 1970s they received control of training programs but did not get control of the employment service.

At the same time, public schools were receiving pressure from the courts and from Congress to do more for the disadvantaged and the handicapped. Schools were told that they could no longer neglect these "special needs" students who constituted 5 to 10 percent of youth (6). Twenty-five percent of federal vocational education funds was set aside for this group. Other services were to be funded largely from regular school budgets which already were stretched nearly to the breaking point.

Simultaneously, however, the number of youth of elementary and secondary school age has been declining. This has allowed many communities to retire old, uneconomic buildings and still have space for new programs. CETA prime sponsors are often interested in working with schools to coordinate programs for special needs students of school age with similar programs for those who have left school, and surplus school buildings provide space in which this can be done.

Mechanisms to replace CAMPS as an overall planning agency for service to the disadvantaged and handicapped are being evolved in many states and local communities. These new agencies are aware of the need for coordination of basic education, vocational education, and employment services whether these are provided in or out of school.

If local schools are to become a significant part of this planning, they must be ready to accommodate the needs of the disadvantaged and the handicapped. Governors, mayors, and organized groups representing minorities are apt to be even less tolerant than Washington bureaucrats of the failures of schools to help solve pressing problems of human resource development. Secondary schools which have high dropout rates and community colleges which have little or no remedial work, little or no vocational education, or do not agree to accept students who lack high school diplomas are apt to be particular targets of pressure for change.

REFERENCES

1. Belitsky, A. Harvey. *Private Vocational Schools and Their Students: Limited Objectives, Unlimited Opportunities.* Cambridge, Mass.: Schenkman Publishing Co., 1969.
2. Clark, Harold F., and Sloan, Harold S. *Classrooms on Main Street.* New York: Teachers College Press, 1966.
3. Katz, H.H. *A State of the Art Study of the Independent Private School Industry in the State of Illinois.* Springfield, Ill.: Advisory Council on Vocational Education, 1973.
4. Levitan, Sar A., and Mangum, Garth L. *Federal Training and Work Programs in the Sixties.* Ann Arbor, Mich.: Institute of Industrial and Labor Relations, University of Michigan, 1969.

5. Mangum, Garth, and Snedeker, David. *Manpower Planning for Local Labor Markets.* Salt Lake City: Olympus Pubishing Co., 1974.

6. Phelps, L. Allen; Evans, Rupert N.; Abbas, Elizabeth K.; and Frison, Kent D. *Vocational Education for Special Needs Students.* Urbana, Ill.: Bureau of Educational Research, University of Illinois, 1976.

7. Swanson, Gordon I. et al. *Knowledge and Policy in Manpower.* Washington, D.C.: National Academy of Sciences, 1975.

8. Venn, Grant. *Man, Education, and Manpower.* Washington, D.C.: American Association of School Administrators, 1970.

Teacher Education and Leadership Development

One of the principal reasons for the failure to do more for youth with special needs is the shortage of broad gauge administrators to plan programs and a shortage of teachers and supportive personnel who know what to do. These shortages illustrate a major problem facing vocational education: inadequate emphasis on the preparation and upgrading of educational personnel.

The Labor Market for Vocational Teachers

Any study of supply and demand for vocational teachers must consider the labor market for this field. There is a large overlap in the labor markets for vocational staff and for the staffs of many other human resource development programs. This labor market overlap occurs for teachers, administrators, and other educational personnel employed by

1. Comprehensive Employment and Training Act programs, especially institutional programs such as Skills Centers,
2. Sheltered workshops and other occupational programs for the handicapped,
3. Job Corps,
4. Opportunities Industralization Centers,
5. Vocational education in federal prisons (and in a few state prisons),
6. Private vocational schools, many of which operate training programs under contract to government agencies, as well as programs supported by tuition,
7. Training programs in private business and industry,

8. Armed forces occupational programs,
9. Baccalaureate technical programs.

Educational personnel for the above programs (and this is not an exhaustive list) are interchanged regularly. They come from much the same sources, and shortages or surpluses of personnel in one area quickly affect the others. Who should pay for training these people, and who should forecast demand and supply?

There is still another very large area of labor market overlap. There are about 50,000 industrial arts teachers, 5,000 nonvocational home economics teachers, and 30,000 nonvocational business education teachers, plus an unknown number of former teachers of vocational and practical arts, some of whom are available for vocational teaching under certain conditions. Vocational education planners deny the transferability of many of these teachers, but in practice state departments of vocational education "lower" standards when needed to allow enough of these people into the fold to solve educational personnel shortages temporarily. Indeed, the availability of this pool of people who can be used in an emergency explains in large part how tens of thousands of vocational teachers can be found whenever state or federal vocational education funds are increased sharply. For example, 40,000 teachers were added between 1964 and 1966, and a considerably larger number of teachers were added between 1969 and 1971, though vocational teacher education programs expanded very little during these two periods.

The process works in this way. Nonvocational practical arts teachers usually have a baccalaureate degree but less occupational experience than vocational teachers. They teach courses such as beginning typing, general metals, and general home economics, which are prerequisites to reimbursable vocational courses. Compared to vocational instruction, equipment is less adequate; students are younger (most commonly age thirteen to sixteen); many more classes are taught per day; and class sizes are larger. For these reasons, vocational teaching is often considered to be more desirable.

Public school teachers are employed for approximately nine months per year, so most teachers get summer jobs outside education. Practical arts teachers usually look for employment in occupations related to their school work and, over a period of time, can accumulate considerable occupational experience. When vocational teachers are in plentiful supply, state boards of vocational education discount this summer employment. They seem to feel that full-time commitment to an occupation is better preparation for vocational teaching than short-term employment of people who feel they really are teachers and only temporarily are business or industrial employees. But when there is a shortage of vocational teachers, this objection is waived.

Another sort of interchangeability exists. Particularly in the Midwest, certain teachers spend half of their time teaching vocational courses and half of their time teaching nonvocational courses, usually in the practical arts. The former requires occupational experience, and the latter requires baccalaureate teacher education. Such teachers can and do move to full-time teaching in vocational or in nonvocational fields, depending on supply and demand. Less mobile teachers (from both fields) often regard such dual allegiance with suspicion, feeling that a person should be fully committed to one field or the other.

If shortages in vocational teaching become severe enough that salaries and working conditions are considerably improved, other pools of people become available for full-time vocational teaching. Examples include full-time industrial employees who also teach part-time in vocational programs (they are eagerly sought because their expertise is known), agricultural and home economics extension workers, employees in industrial training departments, and rank and file workers and supervisors. Usually, however, expansion in demand for vocational teachers occurs at the same time or later than expansions in opportunities in private employment.

Still another device to meet shortages of vocational instructors is to employ teachers in a full-time day school program and to pay them extra for teaching evenings and weekends in part-time vocational programs for adults. This not only provides extra hours of teaching service, but it also raises total salaries, making teaching positions more attractive. No one has conducted a thorough study of the effect of long continued overtime on the quality of instruction, but it may be assumed to be deleterious.

Flexibilities of the type described above work reasonably well for teachers. Unfortunately, there seems to be no ready way of similarly enlarging the pool of vocational administrators. Shortages of administrators have occurred each time the vocational program has expanded, but the shortage during the early 1970s was especially severe because administrators, even more than teachers, were in demand for occupational education programs of all types. Fifty percent increases in salaries offered to both teachers and administrators were common as new occupational education programs began by luring experienced staff from public school vocational education.

Administrators are responsible not only for program and facility planning but also for in-service education of teachers. The combination of a shortage of administrators and recruitment of an untrained teaching staff has created a real crisis in in-service teacher education. Realistic planning for development of educational personnel for vocational and technical education must take into account the entire labor market for these personnel. We can no longer afford to assess needs and plan educational development programs based on the public school segment of the market for vocational teachers and administrators.

Supply and Demand for Vocational Staff

In 1973 there were almost 250,000 vocational education faculty members of whom three-fourths were employed full time. Of these full-time staff members, three-fourths were employed in secondary schools (9, p. 27). About 20,000 new secondary school vocational teachers have been being trained each year (2, p. 164).

Several variables affect the supply of teachers:

1. number of new teachers trained (20,000 to 25,000 per year);
2. proportion of new teachers who actually teach(45% to 70%);

3. number (unknown but large) of people returning to teaching or entering teaching from other activities (More than two-thirds came from those sources in one Wisconsin study.);
4. extent to which teachers can shift from one field of vocational teaching to another (unknown, but believed to be small).

A similar range of variables affects the demand for teachers:

1. changes in vocational education enrollment (generally increasing but dependent on birth rates and the relative attractiveness of other curricula);
2. student to staff ratio (approximately one teacher required for each 50 students);
3. proportion of teachers leaving teaching due to death, disability, retirement, and choosing other employment (annual turnover rates are estimated to be between 4 percent and 10 percent).

Data on most of these variables at any given time are quite inadequate. Moreover, all of the variables are affected by changes in the economic situation, and especially by the state of the labor market. Because we know little about the current supply and demand for staff and even less about the future of the economic situation, Somers (2, p. 171) has concluded that no effective national analysis of vocational education staff needs is feasible and that teacher educators and program administrators must rely on analysis of trends in their own institution. Whenever they identify the emergence of local surpluses or shortages of staff, they should take individual corrective action before the situation becomes critical.

Interaction of Supply and Demand and Certification

Another reason for difficulty in the measurement and prediction of supply-demand relationships in teaching is that employment standards are lowered when the supply of teachers is scarce and are raised (gradually on paper and rapidly in actual practice) when the supply is plentiful. Because of working conditions, the supply of a given type of teacher may be plentiful for a wealthy suburb at the same time it is scarce for an inner-city school or a poor rural school. Most states have some type of emergency teacher certification which allows almost anyone to teach in most subject fields, so employment standards effectively are in the hands of the local school district. These standards tend to be high if enough prospective teachers feel working conditions are good in that district and tend to be low if the district cannot recruit better teachers.

In vocational and technical education, however, some states control the number of new teaching certificates, which places power to control quality more in the hands of the state than in the hands of the local district. Many states refuse to certify a vocational or technical teacher until requested to do so by a school wishing to employ that person. This enables the staff of the state board of vocational education to suggest better qualified individuals who might be available. (In practice, this can be a powerful tool for conformity—one gets recommended for a better job only if one is on good terms with one's state supervisor.) In contrast, teachers outside vocational education usually are certified upon completion of a prescribed program of study and experience. The local school district can then select from among the pool of certified applicants.

The practice of limiting vocational certification to teachers who are or are about to be employed has an additional effect. If the state's pool of potential vocational teachers increases in any one subject area, the real requirements for certification will be raised until they may actually reach the requirements specified in the state plan. Refusal to issue certificates until they are required for employment prevents formation of a pool of certified people who might be less qualified than those who could be certified later.

Certification of vocational teachers usually is handled by a state board of vocational education instead of by the certification board operated by the state department of education. Even in states where junior colleges have been declared a part of higher education and hence exempt from teacher certification, a state board of vocational education usually retains authority to approve or reject vocational and technical teachers by approving or withholding reimbursement of salaries. As in the case of the secondary schools, this can be used as a tool for assuring conformity.

All teachers are expected to know their subject matter and how to teach it. Mastery of the art and science of teaching usually is assumed if a certain pattern of courses has been completed. For vocational teachers, depending on state and institutional requirements, this theoretically may require full-time teachers to complete the equivalent of from two to forty semester hours of prescribed courses and require part-time teachers to complete from zero to thirty semester hours of similar courses. In practice, however, some vocational teachers are allowed to teach for twenty years or more with no teacher preparation whatsoever. More commonly, vocational teachers get an initial minimum of training and teach for twenty years or more without updating.

Methods of determining subject matter competency are more varied. For agriculture and home economics teachers (often including agri-business and gainful home economics) the usual requirement is completion of a baccalaureate degree with a prescribed pattern of specialized college courses. No occupational experience is required beyond that which would be acquired by growing up on a farm or in the home, though in the better colleges the trend is toward requirement of occupational experience in gainful employment. In some states, teachers of technicians and office occupations teachers may also be approved as teachers on the basis of collegiate course work, but most states expect them also to have had at least brief occupational experience.

Health occupations teachers are required to have certification as practitioners of the subject taught or certification at the next higher level. Occupational experience for all teachers is regarded as being important, but this experience need not necessarily be in the occupation taught. Dentists teach or supervise the instruction of prospective dental hygienists and dental technicians, but registered nurses teach prospective registered nurses. Registered nurses also teach prospective practical nurses. No one seems to know why these differences exist, though they may be related to the relative lengths of time the occupational fields have existed, and hence to the presumed availability of qualified teachers from the occupation.

Most distributive educators and trade and industrial educators must have had work experience in the occupational field in which they are teaching. This requirement is usually stated as so many years beyond the learner period. In practice, the range of occupational experience required is from approximately eighteen months (in a college cooperative teacher education program) to six years. The length of the learner period is elastic, depending on supply and demand for teachers.

It is generally agreed that the number of years of experience does not correlate well with the criterion of competence, but only a few states have used occupational competency examinations extensively. Even they require a number of years of experience prior to taking the examination. Large school systems often do not depend on state certification but establish their own certification or other approval procedures, occasionally using local advisory committees

Development of Educational Personnel for Vocational Education

In spite of recent improvements, there are still only a dozen or so programs for the development of vocational education personnel in North America. Rather there are programs for the development of agriculture instructors or distributive education instructors or home economics instructors, and so on, with faculty members and students alike rarely talking to their counterparts in the rest of vocational education. The preparation of administrators and teacher educators is in a similar state. If you want to hire a vocational educator, probably the best you can do is to hire the best trade and industrial educator or business educator or similarly specialized person you can find and try to convert this person into a vocational eduator on the job.

This situation arose because the vocational education acts before 1963 had not been vocational acts at all, but rather acts for the support of education in agricultural occupations, home economics, industrial occupations, health occupations, and occupations related to the distribution of goods. As a consequence, teacher education programs for each of these specialties were established as separate departments, often in separate colleges within one university or even in separate parts of each state. In some states certain institutions of higher education wanted no part of these new teacher education programs, and in some states the state board of vocational education thought higher education could not do the job, so certain teacher education programs were operated by the state board or were contracted for outside the state. This fragmentation resulted in variations in recruiting practices, teacher education programs, and teacher certification practices that were tremendous. These variations still exist, not only from state to state, but also from one occupational field to another within each state. Indeed, the latter variations are generally greater than the former.

Where professional education courses are provided, they are almost invariably segregated by occupational field. Thus in the same university it is possible to find several different professional courses duplicated in as many as six different departments. Some states specifically exclude from enrollment in these courses anyone who has not been approved in advance by the state office.

In community colleges, area vocational schools, comprehensive high schools, in the United States Office of Education, and increasingly in state departments of vocational education, there are needs for a variety of educational personnel qualified to study, plan, and administer a broad range of vocational education. With rare exceptions, there are no programs to prepare or upgrade these leadership personnel.

There seems to be no question that better means are needed for coordinating programs of vocational education personnel development. A few universities have established departments of vocational, technical, and practical arts education, usually within a college of education to maximize interaction with other teacher education programs. The Education Professions Development Act fellowship program, which was restricted to "unified" vocational teacher education programs, has helped this move considerably. Other universities have established vocational teacher education coordinating councils which operate across departmental or college lines. A unified department of vocational and technical education tends to

1. eliminate undesirable duplication of courses or units of instruction on topics such as program development, research, philosophy, history, administration, and evaluation of instruction. Using certain of these courses as a common core with individual projects in each student's field of specialization will save staff and money and provide more well rounded instruction.
2. provide better education of planners, researchers, teacher educators, and above all, administrators and other leaders who can see the field more broadly.
3. permit development of programs for general administrators who cannot take several different courses in vocational and technical education, but who need a broad knowledge of the field.
4. facilitate joint development of programs for occupations which cut across two or more content specialties. This need is particularly acute for emerging occupations, which rarely coincide with traditional fields of instruction.
5. allow more efficient allocation of resources. As needs for vocational teachers change, it is easier to shift staff to meet needs. Moreover, specialists (e.g., in international education, career education, and postsecondary education) can be developed to serve all fields.

Advocates of the status quo say that such a program would produce individuals who would have nothing to teach. This is not correct. What we need are people who have something to teach and who know why and how they should teach it. What we need is teacher specialization tied together with a common core of courses and other experiences which also makes them vocational educators and educators. The problem is most difficult in states which have assigned different occupational fields to different institutions. This makes the preparation of broad gauge vocational education personnel very difficult. Indeed, some states have gone so far as to approve vocational home economics teacher education programs in small colleges which have no real home economics program.

Even where teacher education programs for all occupational fields exist in one university, the problem of coordination is not simple. Consider, for example, the frequent situation where 15 to 25 percent of the graduates of a college of agriculture are preparing to be vocational agriculture teachers and where from 50 to 75 percent of the entering freshmen in the college of agriculture are graduates of high school vocational agriculture programs. Such a college may find it difficult to view vocational agriculture as a program designed to prepare students for employment immediately after graduation from high school or junior college. Rather, it is likely to see vocational agriculture as a preparatory program for entrance to colleges of agriculture. And it may not wish to share control of a program involving such a high proportion of its students and its graduates.

Undoubtedly, the coordination of programs for vocational education personnel is being hastened by federal action giving preferential fund allocation to combined or coordinated programs at the graduate level. Since federal action was largely responsible for the development of fragmented programs, this seems to be poetic justice. The amendments of 1968 suggested such preferential treatment, but action has been anemic, especially at the undergraduate level. Indeed, there has been practically no federal support for vocational education teacher or counselor development since the days of the 1917 Smith-Hughes Act. Some federal actions definitely have hampered development of strong programs. Consider these facts:

1. Only in vocational and technical education must college teachers of a subject be approved by the state. (This was instituted to keep colleges from hiring academics who were not interested in vocational education, but almost all states are also unwilling to approve educational specialists or economists, sociologists, and other social scientists who could contribute much to the program.)
2. Vocational education was the only field obviously related to national defense which was excluded from the teacher education sections of the National Defense Education Act.
3. Only vocational education has a sizable program of federal assistance to state and local educational agencies without a parallel program of scholarships, fellowships, and internships to prepare the personnel to enable the program to succeed. (Such a program was envisioned in 1968, but the small amounts allocated have been inadequate and have been used for retraining administrators and teacher educators rather than new teachers.)
4. Vocational education is the only educational field in which the selection of people who are to receive the few fellowships available is in the hands of the state instead of being determined by the employing school or the institution where training would be received.

Why should vocational education be so far behind in the development of education personnel? There seem to be four reasons.

First is the problem of mobility of teachers, combined with state-by-state financing. The state director of vocational education gets from the federal government most of the funds with which to operate programs in that state. Almost all of this money is spent on subsidizing high school and community college vocational programs. Twenty-five percent of it must be used for educating the disadvantaged and the handicapped, but there are few teachers who know how to do this effectively. The state director has urgent demands for all of his or her money. If good teachers can be stolen from another state, money can be saved which otherwise would have been spent on teacher education. But even more important is the fact that if the director pays for collegiate teacher education for a competent individual, he or she knows that this will increase the likelihood of that teacher moving out of state. Often a director decides to spend money on something other than teacher education.

Second, the state director is likely to be a victim of nostalgia. In the "good old days" a vocational educator began as a teacher, moved to the state department, and then to the USOE as a supervisor, then to a local directorship, state directorship, and, eventually, possibly he became director of vocational and technical education in the USOE. Programs were not changing rapidly then, and this job rotation plan was reasonably satisfactory. The group was small and tightly knit. Everyone knew everyone else, and no one outside really mattered. But this system has broken down. Local schools pay more than state offices, so teachers do not want to move to a state job. Local schools reward college credits with pay increases, which brings colleges into the picture and somewhat diminishes the authority of the state director. Moreover, the director may wonder why he or she should pay colleges for teaching courses they ought to be teaching anyway, especially when their staff is better paid.

Third, universities are much more interested in preparing teachers who will send students to higher education than in preparing teachers who will send students directly into employment. College entrance requirements are not geared to the adult worker who wants to learn to teach. Universities tend to resent direction and control by the state board of vocational education unless they are adequately paid to accept it. They cannot understand why the state board, which spends almost all of its money to persuade local schools and community colleges to offer vocational programs, should object to paying the university to conduct vocational teacher education programs. Moreover, they are accustomed to the federal government paying almost all of the direct and indirect costs of nonvocational programs it wants to support, and they see no reason why federal funds channeled through the state should pay only a half or a third of actual costs. For all of these reasons the gap between needs and offerings tends to be greater for vocational teachers than for other teachers.

Fourth, there is an element of self-protection in not training too many education personnel. The need for teachers of elementary education, and indeed for all of general education is closely related to the number of youth in a particular age range. Not so with vocational education, for it expands with amazing rapidity (and would contract as rapidly if it were not for teacher tenure and educational lobbyists who press for continued federal funds). The reason for this is that demand for vocational education has been tied, not to the number of students needing education, but rather to the number of job vacancies for youth and adults. When there is a job market of constant size, vocational education is expected to supply only replacements due to death, resignation, and retirement. When there are shortages of workers, vocational education is expected to supply replacements plus personnel for expansion. When there is a surplus of workers, vocational education is supposed to die temporarily until natural replacements use up the surplus. This is what economists call *acceleration,* and, of course, vocational teacher education is particularly susceptible to this problem. Indeed, it suffers from double acceleration.

In short, many people in vocational education are afraid to train many teachers for fear there will soon be a decrease in demand. After all, most of them can remember the years of 1952 to 1955 when the president was saying federal aid for vocational education should be abolished, and he was joined then by many of the same interest groups who now support vocational education expansion.

It would appear obvious that vocational education, as an integral part of the educational system, should provide education for the good of students and society, not for the good of employers alone. Certainly there is a close relationship between these needs, but the educational philosophy involved is markedly different. One result of gearing vocational enrollments to the number of people who need it would be that we could minimize the effects of acceleration and could prepare teachers on a more regular basis without fear of alternately flooding the market for teachers and suffering from extreme shortages of teachers.

Types of Preservice Programs

There appear to be two basic types of preservice teacher education programs, which differ in the way in which the prospective teacher learns the subject matter he or she will teach. Type 1 assumes that the subject matter will be learned during the course of employment in the occupation to be taught. Type 2, on the other hand, assumes that all or most of the subject matter to be taught will be learned in a school. Both of these types have subtypes. Type 1*a* assumes that what is learned on the job is learned as a by-product of employment. An advocate of type 1*a* believes that the desirable sequence of experience is from worker to teacher, and that a person who plans to be a vocational teacher and secures work experience to that end is missing an identification with the working group essential to successful vocational teaching. An advocate of type 1*b*, however, feels that more efficient learning occurs if prospective teachers approach work experience with plans for learning as much as possible about it because they want to be effective teachers. Prospective teachers who follow plan 2*a* learn their content in a school which is at the same level as the type of school in which they expect to teach. Type 2*b* teachers, on the other hand, learn their content in a school which is at a higher level than that at which they expect to teach. (See table 20–1.)

TABLE 20–1

Types of Preservice Programs	Content Learned in	Primary Identification While Content Is Being Learned
Type 1*a*	Employment	Worker
Type 1*b*	Employment	Prospective Teacher
Type 2*a*	School	Prospective Worker
Type 2*b*	School	Prospective Teacher

Instructors who follow type 1*a* teacher education programs often begin as workers, then teach part-time in evening school, and then become full-time teachers. Teacher education may be provided concurrently with or preceding either of the last two steps. Type 1*b* instructors include practical arts teachers who leave teaching temporarily to gain work experience which will allow them to earn additional money and to become more effective practical arts or vocational teachers. Sometimes this experience is gained through part-time or summer work. Cooperative teacher education programs which provide both college classes and work experience in a baccalaureate program are also of type 1*b*.

Most people who follow pattern 2*a* teach in basic courses in industry, private trade schools, or the military. This type of instructor is so common in the military that a special term, *pipeline instructor,* has been coined by the Air Force. Two or three of the most able students graduating from a technical training course are retained in the pipeline and become instructors after receiving a brief teacher education program. Occasionally, financially embarrassed institutions of higher education retain some of their advanced seniors to teach freshmen, but usually without benefit of teacher education. Some technical education programs in community colleges encourage their best graduates to stay in the pipeline to teach, or encourage them to return to teaching after a brief employment experience.

Most academic teachers receive all of their preparation in programs of type 2*b*. They learn in a college what they are to teach in an elementary, secondary, or postsecondary school. Teachers of teachers and teachers of teachers of teachers usually follow this same pattern of preservice instruction.

The International Vocational Training Information and Research Center studied vocational teacher education in twelve European countries. They identified three patterns of teacher education, but only one pattern was used in a given country. One group of countries recruits teachers who have acquired skill through long experience in employment (type 1*a*). The second group of countries sees teacher training as a continuation of the vocational training system, with able students continuing on and becoming teachers (type 2*a*). A third group of countries sees teacher training for vocational education as being parallel to the training of teachers for general education (type 2*b*). Programs of type 1*b* were not mentioned (8).

Observation of the vastly different types of preservice teacher education used in the United States for the different subject matter fields within vocational education leads one inevitably to the conclusion that we are several countries in one. Until this time, it has been nonsense to talk about *the* philosophy of preparing teachers and administrators of vocational education in this country. We have several contradictory philosophies and must resolve these philosophical problems before we can talk knowledgeably of a single method of preparing staff for vocational and technical education.

In America patterns of preservice education for home economics, agriculture, office occupations, and distributive education are closely parallel to baccalaureate programs for nonvocational teaching (type 2*b*). Portions of the program are allocated to general education, to specialized education in the subject to be taught, and to courses in pedagogy. Students often begin teaching immediately after college graduation. However, as gainful employment occupations in home economics and agri-business occupations in agriculture gain importance, occupational experience outside the home or farm becomes essential and is beginning to be required (type 1*a* or 1*b*).

Office occupations teachers may begin teaching nonvocational business education courses, but shift to teaching vocational courses after they have acquired occupational experience in summer employment or in full-time leaves from school teaching (type 2*b* plus 1*b*). Distributive education teachers have little opportunity for nonvocational teaching, so they often go directly from college to full-time employment in the distribution of goods or services for several years and then begin to teach (type 2*b* plus 1*b*). If they have not acquired teacher education courses as an undergraduate, these may be included in a masters degree program following occupational experience (type 1*a*).

Teachers in health occupations ordinarily follow a sequence of health professions education and occupational experience before beginning to teach and then receive teacher education concurrently with teaching (type 1*a*). Trade and industrial teachers are much less likely than teachers of other vocational and technical subjects to have a baccalaureate degree. The most common sequence is high school graduation, several years of occupational experience, part-time teaching, teacher education, and full-time teaching (type 1*a*). Often the last two steps in this sequence are reversed. An increasing proportion of vocational industrial teachers, however, are coming from the ranks of industrial arts teachers who acquire occupational experience after college graduation (type 2*b* plus 1*b*). The trades and industries teacher who does not have a bachelor's degree usually is allowed to teach only the subject in which he or she has occupational experience. This contributes to inflexibility in the school program once the teacher has acquired tenure.

In all undergraduate vocational and technical programs, increasing use is being made of cooperative work-education to provide occupational experience prior to completion of the baccalaureate degree (type 1*b*). These programs usually require from five to six years for completion. Unless special incentives can be supplied, however, there is little inducement for the student to choose a five-year vocational teacher education curriculum when he or she can complete a practical arts nonvocational curriculum in only four years and find employment after graduation at the same salary.

Canada has developed an excellent pattern for teacher education for trade and industrial and technical teachers which involves payment of a stipend to a skilled worker or technician to induce him or her to attend college for a year. The stipend is nearly equal to a skilled worker's wage and is paid by the federal government, the province (state), and the school in which the student will teach (3).

In this country, much teacher education which should be offered preservice is done in-service or not at all. Preservice programs for vocational administrators are notoriously lacking. Administrators for vocational programs have been developed in sizable numbers at only three periods during the history of the program in the United States: from 1917 to the early twenties, during the early forties, and again since 1963. These were the three periods of rapid program expansion, due almost entirely to sizable infusion of federal funds. In each of these periods the majority of training was by trial and error on-the-job, supplemented by short-term training conferences and summer programs at universities. In recent years, the largest single source of local directors of vocational education has been the industrial arts teacher who acquired enough occupational experience to be certified as a coordinator of a part-time cooperative program. If he succeeded on this latter job, he had learned the needs of the community, had been accepted by its leaders, and in effect had completed an internship and screening process. Both of these processes were unplanned but still were far more effective than other methods of training and selection available. Very few women have become administrators.

A preservice program incorporating a carefully planned internship would be most appropriate for developing administrators and other leadership personnel. The lack of stipends for trainees and the shortage of comprehensive training programs covering all of vocational education have been substantial deterrents to the development of preservice programs for administrators.

Programs of In-Service Development

The United States Office of Education asked the states to indicate the numbers of vocational teachers enrolled in in-service teacher education programs. Replies indicated that about 30 percent of teachers were enrolled in any one year, but almost certainly some people were counted more than once. Unfortunately, no information is available as to the length and quality of such programs. They almost certainly range from one day professional meetings to programs carefully planned and extending over several years.

Responsibility for in-service education programs usually is assumed to be on the shoulders of the local school administration. Unfortunately, however, the greatest need for in-service education comes at a time when programs are expanding and new teachers are being added. This is also a time when local administrators are overburdened with other tasks and when the demand for administrators is so great that new administrators are placed in very demanding positions for which they often are unprepared. This seems to argue for (1) leadership by state offices of vocational education and universities in providing itinerant in-service program leadership, (2) funds to support local proposals for in-service education, and (3) fellowship and institute programs which will allow certain functions of in-service development to be carried out on a statewide or regional basis.

At present, probably the greatest amount of in-service education is accomplished on a purely voluntary and individually planned basis. Teachers decide that they have certain deficiencies which should be corrected. They then map out ways of correcting these deficiencies through such means as

1. reading periodicals and books about teaching or about the subject being taught;
2. securing part-time employment during the week or during the summer in the occupation being taught;
3. attending schools conducted by business or industry;
4. visiting local business and industry;
5. attending technical meetings or meetings of educational personnel.

All of these methods may be effective. Unfortunately very few schools reward participation in them, though an effective administrator will certainly work to facilitate such in-service education by serving as a counselor to the teachers and by serving as a facilitator (e.g., arranging for employment or getting teachers appointed to committees so that their expenses will be paid for attending conventions).

Employers of vocational teachers generally do reward successful completion of college credit courses. Some of these courses are very valuable in improving the quality of teaching, but many are too general or are offered in such remote locations or at such times as to be of little utility. Too often they are chosen on the basis of accessibility. Credit courses offered during the summer force the teacher to choose between spending money on tuition and extra living expense or earning four or five times as much on a job (which may or may not be related to the subject taught). Naturally, summer institutes with stipends for participants are much more attractive to teachers. To date, the scope of summer institutes has been such that no more than 2 percent of vocational teachers could be enrolled. Academic year institutes, which allow more extended study, have been even more rare. The scarcity of institute programs has been such that only the best qualified applicants could be enrolled, and those who need the instruction most are excluded.

One of the more effective in-service education programs conducted by universities is the "first-year teacher" follow-up conducted in agricultural education in a few states. New teachers are visited regularly on the job by university teacher educators. Those who are encountering unusual difficulties are given individual help, and all meet together periodically at a regional center to share ideas and experiences and to get further help from the teacher educator.

Another type of credit course, or institute, is considerably less expensive, yet works well in heavily populated areas. Instruction is offered in a central location in the evening or on Saturday. Participants live at home, but the instructor may travel a considerable distance. Instruction may concentrate on technical or on professional aspects of the teacher's job. Small stipends to compensate teachers for loss of part-time employment occasionally are provided.

One of the most effective in-service educational devices requires year round employment of all professional staff and assignment during the summer to activities which are most needed for the personal development of faculty members and administrators. Staff members may be assigned to curriculum development, attendance at college institutes or other summer programs, or employment in the occupation being taught. Canada uses an extensive sabbatical leave program for these same purposes.

The great majority of institutions, however, find it economically or politically impractical to employ staff on a twelve-month basis or to grant many sabbaticals. The employing institution should have a major voice in determining which of its staff most need fellowship support for study in colleges or for work with business and industry which will allow them to keep up to date. One inexpensive way of doing this is to develop a one- and five-year personal development plan for each staff member and to provide grants for carrying out the plans (3).

Improvement of Staffing in Vocational Education

Six steps for improving the quality of staffing in vocational education seem desirable:

1. Base pay on merit and on supply and demand, rather than on hours of education and seniority.
2. Eliminate certification if it cannot be substantially modified.
3. Limit teacher tenure to ten years, with renewal or notification of nonrenewal near the end of this period.
4. End discrimination by sex in the employment of teachers.
5. Make preservice education in the primary responsibility of the university, with substantial involvement of local and state education agencies.
6. Make in-service teacher education the primary responsibility of the local educational agency, with substantial involvement of universities and state departments of education.

On the average (and of course there are frequent exceptions) teachers who have served approximately five years are at peak effectiveness. Teachers with less experience and teachers with more experience are, on the average, considerably less effective. No one knows for sure whether this is caused by some of the more effective teachers leaving after a few years of teaching, or whether it is a matter of stagnation. Certainly there is no evidence to suggest that in every case, the longer a teacher has taught, the more he or she should be paid. Similarly, we know that there is no relationship between the number of hours of college courses a teacher has had and effectiveness. It is clear that many people who are completely inadequate as teachers return again and again for additional courses in an attempt to have something that allows them to feel superior.

Under present salary structures such insecure individuals are rewarded with additional salary increments. The objection may be raised that merit pay has been thoroughly explored and discarded on the basis that judgments of merit cannot be made accurately. Many colleges do make such decisions and have made them for over a hundred years. No one seems to disagree that the top and the bottom 5 percent or so of teachers can clearly be identified. They should be rewarded in accord with this identification.

Equally important is the matter of pay based on supply and demand. A case occurred in a community college which had an outstanding program in industrial electronics. Graduates of this two-year program regularly started employment at salaries above those earned by the majority of the college faculty. Salaries of the electronics instructors were some two thousand dollars less than they had received in industrial employment but were the highest two salaries on the whole community college teaching payroll. This led to a considerable amount of hostility on the part of some of the academic teachers, but the decision of the college administration seemed exactly correct. To attempt to employ teachers of all types at the same salary schedule will insure that most teachers in fields which are in short supply will be less competent than those teachers who are in plentiful supply. There is no justification whatsoever for providing lower quality education to those students who happen to want to specialize in areas where they are badly needed while at the same time providing superior education for people in fields where they are less in demand.

A local director of vocational education said in a private conversation, "I can employ better teachers for my evening school staff than I can for my day school staff solely because the evening school staff does not have to be certified." This is a sad commentary on the state of certification. College teachers are not certified. Because there are many poor teachers in college, some people have suggested that certification would be in order for them. Why are they poor teachers? Almost invariably it is because they do not know how to teach.

At the secondary school level, where certification is almost universal, we also have many poor teachers. They may be poor because they do not know how to teach, because they do not know what it is that they are supposed to teach, or both. Few college teachers are poor because they do not know their subject matter. Certification, which is supposed to attest both to subject matter and instructional competence, has obviously failed in many cases. Two possible improvements suggest themselves.

1. Have colleges certify teachers upon graduation, have the effectiveness of these teachers reviewed periodically by the state, and take away college authority to certify teachers in a particular field if the graduates of that institution fail to perform satisfactorily.
2. Instead of certification, have the state approve local proposals, program by program, with qualifications of the instructors being part of the package. Have this followed by a post-audit by the state with termination of program approval for poor performance.

Teacher tenure has had many worthwhile effects. Unlimited teacher tenure has had many bad effects as well. A requirement for renewal of tenure at the end of ten years would force a periodic look at faculty competence. At present, we look at faculty competence only at the time of hiring and at the end of a short probationary period. Unfortunately, too many teachers stop professional improvement at the end of their probationary period, though they may go on teaching for several more years. Stated negatively, if vocational education is to survive, it must find some way of getting rid of its deadwood. To put it in a more positive sense, it should be the responsibility of every administrator to build, in cooperation with each staff member, an individualized staff development plan covering five to ten years. If it works, the teacher should be retained. If it does not work, he or she should be released.

One way of insuring that there will be staff development is to use as a key criterion for employment of any administrator, her or his past record of developing staff members. Many industries have a standing rule that no administrator can be promoted unless she or he has developed a possible replacement. This does not mean that a person developed as a replacement would be chosen as the successor, but it does emphasize the role of the administrator as a developer of staff and refuses promotion to those who fail to perform in this role.

In vocational and technical education most often men teach men, and women teach women. Indeed, in the late sixties some went so far as to say that all instruction in "women's occupations" should be provided by women. The occasional female teacher of drafting can testify to the discrimination she faces in professional meetings of drafting teachers. We need to take special steps to recruit teachers (and students) of the minority sex in each of our vocational programs, for exactly the same reason that we need to recruit ethnic minority students and teachers in predominantly white institutions.

Many excellent ideas for an effective preservice education program can be found in B.O. Smith's *Teachers for the Real World* (5). He has a section on "Why Teachers Drop Out." Here he mentions our blind confidence in the value of pooling personal experiences in group discussion in teacher education and suggests that this is valuable only for therapy. He suggests that student teaching should be eliminated and replaced by a carefully structured series of simulated and real experiences, followed by a genuine internship, under supervision, which avoids the make-believe character of much student teaching. Today many universities are engaging in microteaching, pre-student-teaching observations, and competency-based training which embody many of Smith's suggestions and make the internship experience more meaningful. He has a good section on "Bringing the Teacher Trainer Up-to-date," which would be applicable to many of the people in our field. Throughout the book Professor Smith emphasizes close relationships among the university, the local educational agency, and the noneducational community. His section on "Differentiated Teacher Roles" suggests that teacher aides could be recruited from the community. An example of this is the program in Edmonton, Alberta, where an educational specialist works with four craftspeople to provide the best possible instruction for technical students in the printing trades. This is a way of using teacher aides from the community in an excellent pattern of differentiated staffing.

Universities can provide excellent professional training. They can do this job better than institutions designed for other purposes, but they can perform effectively only if they work closely with the groups which use their product.

The most effective pattern of in-service education is one which involves employment of the teacher for twelve months with summers devoted to building strengths and remedying weaknesses. Depending upon the long-term professional development plan which has been prepared for each teacher, summers may be spent in employment, in curriculum development, in further education, or in a variety of other needed activities. Every professional development plan should include the opportunity to visit other schools for brief periods of time. It is amazing how parochial most teachers really are. They have no idea of the strengths and weaknesses of programs in comparable schools in other communities and have little knowledge of employment opportunities outside their own community.

Another highly desirable activity would be a regular exchange program with employers, not only to upgrade the knowledges of the regular teacher but also to acquaint key individuals in business and industry with what is actually going on in the schools.

A third major feature of each professional development package should be attendance at and participation in professional meetings. There is a tendency to have the same people year after year on the same programs. Half of the participants might well be required to be new each year. This would not only improve the competence of the people participating, but it would add a freshness to professional meetings that is badly needed.

The Identification of Leaders

Potential leaders need to be identified as well as to be trained. Too often the identification process has been left to chance. At the local level, vocational education leadership potential is rarely surveyed until an administrative opening has occurred through death, resignation, or expansion of the program. Then the local school officials try to identify an individual who can be immediately promoted and later trained. As was mentioned in the chapter on cooperative programs, a likely candidate will be the cooperative education coordinator because the job of this teacher is most like that of the local director of vocational education. Since no one has been selected and trained by design, the person best trained by accident is often selected. At the state and national level, a wider choice of candidates may be available. A great deal depends on the salaries which can be paid to new supervisory staff and whether or not selection and tenure depend on membership in the political party in power. Low salaries and a requirement of political loyalty obviously decrease the pool of potential candidates.

Regardless of the size of the pool, it is still necessary to identify the best candidates for promotion. Except in the largest cities this is not a great problem for internal promotion at the local level since every insider is likely to be known. Recruitment from outside the system is a different matter. Individuals have made themselves noticeable by appearing on convention programs, by writing, by taking additional college courses, by passing certification examinations, by performing favors for leaders in the profession, and the like. Excellent recent performance in any of these roles helps to bring the individual's name to mind when a current leader is asked to recommend someone for another leadership role.

The federal government has attempted to improve this process by asking for nominations for fellowships and stipends which allow these potential leaders to receive additional training through university courses and internships. This has markedly expanded the pool of potential leadership, for it serves the dual function of identification and training.

Technical Education Teachers

Technicians are aides to professional workers, and technical education is designed to develop technicians. Technicians are needed in every major field of business and industry, and every field of vocational education has a responsibility for conducting technical level education. Technical programs, however, generally require specially prepared teachers.

Most of the earlier comments in this chapter apply to technical education as well as to vocational education. There are, however, certain aspects of the development of technical education personnel which deserve special mention.

The majority of technical education programs are offered in community colleges and other postsecondary institutions, though a few programs begin in the secondary school. About 4 percent of youth reaching age eighteen each year could be accommodated in existing postsecondary technical education programs. Governing boards desire to expand their offerings, but they are understandably reluctant to employ unqualified instructors. Students, too, are reluctant to enroll in technical programs with mediocre instructors. Given a choice between such a program and a college transfer curriculum, they often will choose the latter, for they know that credits from college transfer courses are accepted at face value even if instruction is mediocre, while employers carefully evaluate skills and knowledges possessed by the graduate of the technical curriculum. Both students and employers know that mediocre instructors are not good enough if the technical education graduate is to be acceptable in the occupation.

There are very few teacher education programs designed to prepare staff for technical education. In some cases vocational and technical teachers are taught together for professional courses, e.g., teachers of engineering technicians are grouped with trade teachers. Some of this is desirable; indeed all vocational teachers need some courses in common. But technical education, particularly in the community college, has problems for which teachers need special preparation. Traditional vocational teacher education programs hardly recognize that the community college exists.

Summary

A major reason for the failure of vocational education to do more for youth with special needs is the shortage of broad gauge administrators to plan programs and a shortage of teachers and supportive personnel who know what to do.

There is a distinct shortage of programs and instructional personnel to upgrade adult workers so as to provide room at lower and intermediate levels of employment for youth and for unemployed and underemployed adults.

Data on vocational teachers and teacher educators are conspicuously lacking. The USOE collects information on subjects taught, degrees held, and so on, for teachers reimbursed under the Vocational Education Amendments of 1968, but no plans exist to collect information on preparation for teaching nor will data be collected on teachers in nonreimbursed occupational programs.

The labor market for vocational teachers has never been defined, and predictions of supply and demand neglect the fact that teachers and administrators can and do move from employment in one occupational education program to another and from public to private employment and vice-versa.

Certification for vocational teachers is often restricted to the number of teachers employed. Requirements for certification are raised when there is a surplus of teachers and lowered when there is a shortage.

Teacher education programs and certification practices are even more diverse from one vocational field to another than they are from state to state.

Teacher education programs in separate fields of vocational and technical education badly need careful coordination. There are very few vocational teacher education programs, but rather programs for developing subject matter specialists in isolation from each other. They now exist frequently in separate departments, colleges, and even in separate parts of a state. This fragmentation makes it difficult to prepare teachers who have a full understanding of education for the world of work and has been particularly harmful to the preparation of administrators and other leadership personnel.

Vocational teacher education suffers greatly from acceleration effects since the need for teachers expands very rapidly as the need for skilled workers expands even slightly. Prediction of the need for vocational teachers depends greatly on whether we continue to educate for immediate worker shortages or whether we follow the suggestion of the Vocational Education Amendments of 1968 and serve the needs of students who want and should have vocational education.

Vocational education leaders have paid remarkably little attention to the education of teachers because of shortage of funds, mobility of teachers, and fear of training too many teachers. Universities, likewise, have not done enough, largely because they are interested primarily in college bound students and their teachers.

Certification practices and state approval of teacher educators have tended to exclude educational specialists and social scientists who could aid in the study of vocational programs.

Expansion of vocational and technical education has been slowed by a shortage of qualified teachers, and the development of new programs has been hampered by an extreme shortage of administrators and other leadership personnel.

REFERENCES

1. Arnold, J.P. "Applying Differentiated Staffing to Vocational-Technical Education." *Journal of Industrial Teacher Education* 7, no. 1 (1969):13–20.
2. Evans, Rupert N., and Terry, David R., eds. *Changing the Role of Vocational Teacher Education.* Bloomington, Ill.: McKnight Publishing Co., 1971.
3. Evans, Rupert N. *Vocational Education Staff Development Priorities for the Seventies.* Washington, D.C.: National Advisory Council on Education Professions Development, 1973.
4. Hamilton, Phyllis. *Personnel Development in Vocational Education* Menlo Park, Calif.: Stanford Research Institute, Unpublished Draft, 1974.
5. Smith, B.O. *Teachers for the Real World.* Washington, D.C.: American Association of Colleges for Teacher Education, 1969.
6. Smith, H.T. *Education for the World of Work.* Kalamazoo, Mich.: W.E. Upjohn Institute for Employment Research, 1963.
7. "The Need for Vocational and Technical Educational Personnel." *The Education Professions 1969–70.* Washington, D.C.: U.S. Office of Education, Superintendent of Documents, No. HE 5.258:58032–70.
8. *Training of Vocational Teachers.* Geneva, Switzerland: International Labor Office, 1964.
9. *Vocational and Technical Education.* Selected Statistical Tables. Washington, D.C.: U.S. Department of Health, Education and Welfare, Office of Education, Vocational Education Information No. III, 1974.

part V

The Future of Vocational Education

21

The Future of Vocational Education

Almost every country in the world has more college graduates than can be employed as professionals. This is true in both underdeveloped and developed countries. In many of these countries, the availability of a well-educated but significantly underemployed minority has serious political consequences. In some countries this has created so much of a problem that special efforts are made to recruit these people into government employment. But this does not seem to be a solution which is feasible either economically or in terms of maintaining the self-respect of the embittered college graduate.

There is also a severe surplus of unskilled workers in all except a few nations whose labor supply of certain age groups has been badly disrupted by past wars. This surplus probably exists even in countries which have too few workers of any other type but is concealed by the political necessity of employing every able-bodied person no matter how inept. On the other hand, virtually every nation in the world has had a long continued shortage of skilled workers, clerical workers, sales personnel, and health personnel at every level. Indeed, there are severe shortages of capable workers in almost every occupation which requires more than a year for the average person to master it but which requires less than a baccalaureate degree for entrance. Shortages of workers in occupations which require skills may be masked temporarily by economic recession, but they become apparent again the moment that normal economic activity returns. These are the occupations which produce the goods and services the world needs in the qualities, quantities, and at the prices people can afford to pay. These are the occupations for which vocational education could prepare people. But there has been too little vocational education, and a large proportion of occupations have no public vocational education at all.

As shortages of skilled personnel have increased, and as surpluses of college graduates have increased, normal economic forces are in the process of inverting the pay structures for these two fields. In community after community beginning firefighters, police officers, truck drivers, and people in other occupations for which little or no vocational training has been provided start at higher salaries than school teachers, city planners, architects, and people in many other professional occupations for which four to six years of occupational training has been provided by society. Trends indicate that soon the average salaries will follow the same course that starting salaries have taken. Not only are wages changing, but working conditions are improving as well. Skilled workers who are in short supply can and do demand working conditions equal to those provided to white collar workers in every respect.

These changes seem to signify a new era of status for the well qualified nonprofessional, and consequently a new status for the vocational education instructor who can meet society's needs. On the other hand, it seems likely that vocational instructors who turn out unqualified graduates will be subject to closer scrutiny that has ever been true in the past and will have to increase their efficiency or lose their justification for continued employment.

A Major Change in Emphasis

Until 1963 federal legislation directed vocational education to meet the needs of the labor market. Students were to be admitted only if they could profit from the instruction then being offered. Local advisory committees dominated by labor and management were strongly recommended. Prior to 1946 instruction could be offered only for occupations which required a long time to learn (and were in short supply). The 1963 act changed this philosophy to one of meeting the needs of individual students, but most vocational education continued business as usual.

In 1968 Congress made it clear that it was not making an idle suggestion in 1963. Twenty-five percent of appropriations were set aside for vocational education for the disadvantaged and the handicapped effective with the 1969–70 school year. Earlier expenditures from vocational education funds for these two groups certainly did not exceed 5 percent. This new requirement raised the proportion of vocational students with below average academic ability since the mentally handicapped and many of the disadvantaged were well below average in verbal skills. It did not decrease the number of above average students since total appropriations were increasing markedly.

The primary effect on postsecondary schools has come from additional encouragement of vocational students to attend college. While very few vocational teachers have ever discouraged students from attending college, state and federal officials have discouraged publicity on the numbers of students attending college. It is a general public impression, as a result, that it is impossible for graduates of the secondary school vocational curriculum to attend college. The best way to counteract this false impression is for counselors to point out that virtually every college will admit vocational graduates and that they are preferred in many technical curricula.

Coordinated Planning for Vocational Education and Other Occupational Education

The chapter on training offered by other groups has a section on the need for coordinated planning. Some vocational educators feel that their field should not be included in a statewide or metropolitan area-wide coordinated plan. There is an attempt to justify such exclusion on the ground that vocational education has objectives in addition to meeting the worker needs of the nation. This is true, but Comprehensive Employment and Training Act programs also have additional objectives, such as alleviating poverty and providing basic general education, so the differences are more apparent than real. General education, vocational education, and CETA are all part of the same education continuum which ranges from the very general to the very specific. These three types of education are not points on the continuum. They are ranges, and the ranges overlap considerably. If vocational education is excluded from comprehensive planning and coordination of training and employment, the effect is almost certain to be the development of two separate, parallel school systems—one of college preparation and the other for occupational preparation. Such separation is undesirable because it promotes socioeconomic segregation and thus hampers the education of the poor. From a selfish point of view, separation leaves vocational education with no home. It would be completely unwelcome in the college preparatory school and largely unwelcome in the occupational education schools operated by the Department of Labor, as can be seen in the many countries which operate such dual systems. Thus, on educational grounds and on the ground of self-preservation, vocational education has every reason to support comprehensive high schools and community colleges. Vocational educators must insist that these schools include Comprehensive Employment and Training type activities for youth and adults and insist that in-school vocational education be coordinated with occupational education activities in the private sector.

Local, State, and National Advisory Committee Development

The earliest proponents of vocational education in the schools recognized that if school administrators and teachers attempted to set up vocational education programs without advice from employers and employees, two major problems would probably occur:

1. Programs might be established which did not meet local worker needs.
2. Employers and employees, not having been involved, would regard vocational education as "their program" rather than as "our program."

The establishment of local advisory committees worked very well for both purposes in the early days of vocational education. Local surveys of employment needs were undertaken, and programs were established to meet local needs. Having been involved from the inception, both employers and employees tended to be satisfied with the results.

Two types of committees usually were established: a general advisory committee concerned with the entire vocational education program and a series of occupational advisory committees, one for each occupational program. These committees generally worked well so long as worker shortages existed in the local community. But in city after city, when economic recession or changing employment patterns appeared, conflicts arose in local advisory committee meetings. Some representatives of employees could see no need for the school to continue to turn out vocational graduates when experienced adult workers were unemployed. Some employers could see no need to spend tax money on keeping the program up to date, or even on the relatively high cost of maintaining the program as it was. Some school officials were reluctant to accept advice if it was contrary to the desires of the professional staff, or to close classes, re-assign, retrain, or dismiss teachers on tenure. These conflicts came to the surface most frequently in advisory committee meetings so the majority of vocational educators simply stopped calling advisory committee meetings, tightened their belts, and waited for the next shortage of trained workers to bring them added support.

There was a resurgence of interest in advisory councils in the late sixties (1). In part, this was due to recurring worker shortages, but it was also due to the studies of S.M. Burt (3) which helped to convince Congress that advisory committees should be mandated at the local, state, and national level.

State and national advisory committees add an important dimension to vocational education. Shortages and surpluses of workers can be assessed more accurately by people removed from local pressures. One reason is that a shortage of people in one occupation in one community is often cancelled by a surplus in another community. Educational needs for occupations employing only a few people in any one community can best be assessed at state and national levels. But an even more important reason is that administrative and legislative decisions affecting vocational education are made more and more by state and federal governments. These decision makers need advice as much as do decision makers at the local level.

The developing social consciousness of employers and employee groups is likely to lead them to accept all of the goals of vocational education insted of concentrating only on the goal of meeting needs for employees. This argues well for continued usefulness of advisory committees.

Cyclical Changes in Demand for Vocational Education

The cyclical changes in demand for vocational education have had an important effect upon the development of effective programs for the education of vocational education staff members. When vocational education was seen as having a single objective of meeting the worker needs of the nation, it was inevitable that as the needs of the nation increased on a short-term basis, the demand for vocational education increased sharply, and as the level of economic activity decreased, vocational education was expected to lie dormant for an extended period of time. This made the development of in-service programs for staff members almost impossible and made programs for teacher education almost as difficult.

Now there seems to be general agreement that vocational education should assume the additional objectives of increasing the options of the individuals it serves and of lending intelligibility to general education. Moreover, there is understanding, in at least some quarters, that we should serve long-term needs of society for workers rather than the short-term fluctuations from month to month. All of these changes suggest increased stability for vocational education which will allow long-term planning and the development of competent personnel to meet the needs of students, both youth and adults.

The next major cyclical change apt to affect vocational education will be the shortage of young workers during the 1980s. This shortage will occur because of a low number of births during the 1960s. The experience of Germany and Japan (which have had similar shortages but for different reasons) suggests that youth will be more highly valued, both by society and by themselves. This leads to fewer school dropouts, more vocational education, less unemployment, and higher wages for youth. If national policy decides to fill the shortage of youth with nonresidents, vocational education can expect to need staff who have expertise in Spanish and Portugese and who are comfortable in working with students from other cultures.

The Targets of American Education

Perhaps the most persistent criticism of American education is that, as presently structured, it best meets the needs of the minority of people who will someday become college graduates. The National Advisory Council on Vocational Education (22), in their first annual report to Congress, contended that academic education aimed at preparing students for four year colleges and universities has predominated in our public education system and that high schools have emphasized preparation for college at the expense of preparation for employment. The Council tied this educational emphasis to social unrest, violence, the unemployment of youth, and irrelevance in education.

The statistics typically cited to support the above concerns include some variation of the fact that less than 20 percent of the secondary school population receive a program of specific occupational education while 80 percent of our youth do not graduate from college. A similar perspective on this matter is the projection that of those students in high school only three out of ten will go on to four year college level academic pursuits. Of these, one-third will drop out before completing the baccalaureate degree.

Looking at the matter from another vantage point, some observers cite Department of Labor estimates that only 7 percent of the work force now hold jobs dependent upon college and university education and projections that by 1980 four out of every five jobs still will not require a four year degree for job entry. Taken quite literally, such projections can be used as a devastating indictment of misplaced perspective in the target groups to which the bulk of American education is addressed. However, as Ottina points out:

> What often gets lost is the other half of this projection—that most of these jobs will require training beyond high school. In other words, the new technologies and service industries have created a new middle ground of job opportunities that call for one or two years of training beyond high school, but do not require a four-year college degree. Blue-collar jobs as we have known them in the past are fast disappearing. (25, p. 84)

Koschler and Parker (17, p. 12) have argued that Ottina's middle ground is technical education. It is their projection that given the current characteristics of the occupational structure (which has been described as a knowledge economy requiring rising cognitive levels in work) 35 percent to 55 percent of the work force should be composed of technicians and comparable specialists. These workers would require training beyond the secondary school but not in the form typically provided by baccalaureate degree programs. They further observe that of the 9,204,000 students enrolled in higher education in 1972 only 2,107,000 were in occupational programs recognized as technical education by the U.S. Office of Education. The number of people actually being trained at the technical education level is still far short of the number necessary to maintain or advance the American economy.

Other observers address the question of the target group to which American education is directed somewhat differently, though the conclusions tend to be the same. Ralph Tyler, in testifying in 1970 before the Sub-Committee on Education of the House of Representatives, stated:

> The schools are steeped in the academic traditions which emphasize scholarship, not effectiveness in performing one's roles. . . . Although presumably dedicated to the education of all children and youth, the instructional programs are related specifically to the needs of the academically able students and little deviation is provided for the needs of nonacademic students. (26, p. 794)

Kohlberg and Gilligan (16) stated that American education has created a two-track educational system dividing adolescents into two groups, an elite capable of abstract thought and hence of profiting from a liberal education and the masses who are not. Essentially, this system has assumed that one either has the capacity for abstract thought or one does not—that it cannot be stimulated or developed. Wall (35, p. 51) observed that the Morrill Land Grant Act in 1862 was directed at the same conditions in higher education which now plague elementary and secondary education. He has argued that public education is geared to the needs and desires of a minority, the third who enter college rather than the masses needing vocational and technical education.

The statistics and observations cited suffice to give credibility to the argument that American education is out of balance with the needs of its consumers and the occupational structure. The alternative, however, is not simply diminishing the numbers entering higher education or the general education components of public education.

Educational priorities must be redefined and assumptions about the capabilities of learners must be reassessed. Rigid tracking of students must be diminished. The development, rather than simply the reinforcement, of existing capabilities must assume greater importance in educational philosophy and action. Education must deal with life rather than the intellect in isolation from life. All students, regardless of the setting to which they aspire, need to be assisted to find a vocational identity and the means to implement that identity. The proportion of emphasis given to vocational-technical education in higher education must be increased.

The challenges just cited are enormous. They do not simply give vocational educators a ticket to do significantly more of what they are now doing. The economic and philosophical realities of the moment argue that vocational educators like general educators must be more creative than that.

Vocational educators need to design curricula for occupational preparation not now being provided. They must consider the findings of Reubens (26) and others that general training in vocational skills is to be preferred to specific training, that clusters of job skills are to be preferred to simple job skills. Vocational educators must avoid creating their own elite by setting the standards for admission to vocational education programs so high that few students can qualify; the results being that the masses of students still remained unserved by the schools. Ways must be found to exploit the vocational education potential of community sites to provide training in areas beyond the capability of the public school sector in a particular locale. The expansion of cooperative education in secondary and higher education needs attention. The conversion or reorientation of selected aspects of general education in colleges and universities to technical education must be systematically explored.

Finally, vocational educators must consider their assumptions about students. Are they willing to provide programs for students at all intellectual levels or for only the most intellectually capable? Are they allowing the boundaries defined by specific occupational tasks—e.g., bookkeeping, nursing, carpentry—to inhibit preparation in cluster skills or the provision of short-term experiences in vocational education for some students? Are all students seen as capable of learning some set of occupational tasks or are many seen as incapable of developing such skills? In the final analysis, how such questions are answered will determine whether American education will simply substitute one form of elitism for another or whether its priorities and programs will come into balance with student needs and occupational realities.

Education of Disadvantaged or Minority Individuals

Since the passing of the Vocational Education Act of 1963, the sensitivity of vocational educators to the needs of disadvantaged or minority individuals has been heightened. So it has been throughout education.

While not very precise, the terms *minority* and *disadvantaged* frequently merge to include black, American Indian (Native American), Spanish, Mexican, and Puerto Rican populations as well as the poor Appalachian rural dweller. The essential point of the concept of *disadvantagement* is that there are social, cultural, and economic circumstances which act systematically to discourage or prevent children in certain geographical places and with certain environmentally imposed constraints from obtaining adequate education, income, and dignity.

It has become reasonably clear that where one's family fits into the nation's social structure has a great deal to do with the types of information about opportunity, encouragement, or education one is likely to obtain. The disadvantaged are seen as getting inadequate information, sparse encouragement, and inadequate training to move out of poverty. Thus popular critics as well as researchers have observed that in most instances neither general education or vocational education has effectively responded to the special needs of the disadvantaged/minority student populations of the nation.

Some indication of the magnitude of the problem of the minority/disadvantaged person in this country is indicated by the fact that in 1973 blacks accounted for about 20 percent of the unemployed, 22 percent of those with inadequate employment and earnings, and about 16 percent of labor force participants with less than high school education (13). Their joblessness rate continues to be roughly double that of whites in the same age range.

It has been cited frequently that Appalachian youth manifest a higher dropout rate that whites in other parts of the nation and that in too many cases the educational and vocational opportunities available to these young people are very limited. Bass and Burger (2) have pointed out that the Native American (Indian) population is the most disadvantaged rural group. In comparison to the general population, their income was only two-ninths as much, their unemployment rate almost ten times greater, their life expectancy seven years less, half again as many of their infants died, their school dropout rate almost double that of the general population, and they had less than half the years of schooling.

A theme which runs through much of the literature concerning the disadvantaged is that schools are not only failing to educate disadvantaged students effectively, but also they may not know how to do so. Davis (8), in exploring the failures of compensatory education in America, contends that such programs are concerned "only with bringing the student up to a predetermined norm. In the process they ignore the possibility that a whole new range of norms may be more appropriate."

Speaking more specifically to vocational education Feldman (11) has argued, "Vocational education has a serious and important message to deliver in the education of the poor for reasons that are even more important than the fact that it does provide economic mobility. . . . The processes of vocational education require the student's active participation and greatly enhance his motivation to learn. They help relate his educational experience to any number of adult roles as well, which are particularly applicable to the poor."

Fundamentally, vocational educators are being challenged to recognize that while the disadvantaged are likely to have the same ambitions and wishes as other people, their personal history has frequently not provided them the adult models, the understandings of alternative work styles or opportunities, or the basic academic skills required to compete with their advantaged contemporaries. Thus vocational educators, rather than expecting these behaviors in such students, are going to have to work to develop them. Sometimes this will involve extensive collaboration and prevocational involvement with general education colleagues. At another level, it is likely to involve helping such students identify a set of goals to which they might aspire and specific detail about how to acquire the skills necessary to achieve them. In addition, vocational educators in the future will likely need more involvement of adult representatives of minority and disadvantaged populations in planning educational experiences which take into account the attitudes, needs, and goals of disadvantaged students.

As vocational education moves into the immediate future, pluralism among student characteristics—racial, ethnic, economic—will become a growing issue. Assumptions and generalities about such students will be inadequate. Flexible, diverse, and developmental vocational education experiences attuned to both the strengths and deficits of disadvantaged students will have to become the rule rather than the exception.

Education of the Handicapped

Although Congress gave the same "marching orders" to vocational education regarding the handicapped as it did with regard to the disadvantaged, the handicapped have received far less attention. Two related reasons for this neglect seem to be paramount: other agencies such as special education and vocational rehabilitation have expertise in working with the handicapped, so it has been easy to let them continue to assume responsibility; and vocational educators have not been taught how to deal with their population. A third reason applies particularly to the mentally handicapped: some vocational educators do not want mentally handicapped students because they fear it will lower the image of their program and hence the employability of their graduates.

In recent years the term *special needs students* has been applied to the entire population of the disadvantaged and handicapped. This term has some utility because similar methods of diagnosing and remedying problems can be applied to some parts of these two groups. It may have the disadvantages, however, of allowing some types of students to be forgotten and of minimizing the real differences in the causes of difficulties in learning and performing. The mentally and the phsyically handicapped have quite different needs, and both are different in many ways from the disadvantaged. There are many types and severities of handicaps, and these differences cannot be overlooked in planning sound educational programs.

Estimates of the number of handicapped people in this country range as high as twenty-five million. Special education has been particularly concerned with the portion of this population of elementary school age or younger. Vocational rehabilitation has paid most attention to adults of working age. Problems of the adolescent or aged handicapped have been ignored, relatively speaking.

Since 1977 federal legislation has mandated that schools provide a wide range of services to the handicapped. One of the major needs of handicapped youth is vocational education. Vocational educators know much more than special educators about what should be taught to these students, but special educators are far more knowledgeable about how to teach them. There is an obvious need for both groups to work together, not only in providing direct service to the handicapped but also in designing teacher education programs which will prepare and retrain the staff needed to serve this large group of citizens whose needs have been virtually ignored.

Education of Women

Until comparatively recently, secondary school occupational education for women has been confined almost exclusively to homemaking and clerical occupations. Today these two programs have two-thirds of the total enrollment in reimbursed secondary school vocational education, and perhaps 90 percent of the female enrollment. This has been somewhat reasonable since many women become homemakers and since 70 percent of the women high school graduates who do not go to college are employed as clerical workers (21, p. 243). It has, however, provided very few opportunities for women to break out of these two rigid molds. In community colleges, nursing and business education provide most of the opportunities for vocational education for women. For some reason, after an initial surge, the rate of increase in health occupations has been relatively low, but enrollments in business education are large and expanding.

The most rapidly expanding occupational programs for women have been in home economics wage-earning occupations. This classification covers a variety of fields, including child care, foods, and textiles and includes both production and service occupations.

More and more women are enrolling at the secondary school level in occupational education courses which were at one time the exclusive province of men. Men are beginning to be welcomed into "women's" occupational courses. Beyond question the amount of secondary school occupational education for women now exceeds that for men, but its breadth is increasing far too slowly. The goal should be to eliminate sex as a criterion for admission to any educational program.

Who Should Receive Vocational Education

As blue-collar jobs become more attractive, and as the status of vocational education rises, it seems likely that the proportion of students seeking vocational education will increase dramatically. In the past, when vocational educators have been faced with more applicants than they could educate, they have responded in almost every case by accepting those applicants who least need vocational education services: those with highest verbal intelligence, highest grades in school, and influential parents. This type of selection makes the teacher's task easier, but it is questionable whether it has served the best interests of the total student body.

The supply of vocational education services should be increased to the point where all students who want vocational education can be admitted. Data from several studies indicate that half of high school freshmen want vocational education, but only one-fourth of them can be accommodated. The proportion of students who want vocational education is almost certain to increase more rapidly than the supply of available instruction. With substantial increases in state and federal support, this long-term imbalance between supply and demand can gradually be overcome. But where there are temporary unavoidable discrepancies between demand and supply of vocational education, we need a measure of "value added by vocational education" which will enable us to determine which students will receive the greatest benefit from vocational education as compared with other educational or noneducational programs. Those students who will benefit most from vocational education are the ones who should be admitted.

Development of Parallel School Systems

Most other nations have separate, parallel systems of secondary education for vocational and for college preparatory students. Educational reform in these countries concentrates on developments similar to our comprehensive high schools. But at various times and places, separate systems have existed in this country as well; the National Youth Administration (NYA) schools which ended in the early forties and the Wisconsin system which existed for half a century are two examples of such programs which have been totally or partially abandoned. Most of our large cities built separate vocational high schools, but these are gradually being phased out, largely because they became racially segregated.

This does not mean that the concept of separate parallel schools is dead. Rosen expressed the prevailing point of view of the Department of Labor when he said, "The time has come for us to recognize that the good vocational schools are capable of making an important contribution in developing the supply of our skilled workers. However, the only way they can really carry out this function is to separate out those students who need special treatment by developing a new institutional arrangement so that they can be taught in separate schools" (27, p. 10). Job Corps centers and, more recently, Skill Centers have been set up to provide this special treatment which has not been available in most public schools.

The most rapidly growing organizational structure in vocational education has been the area vocational school. It serves principally small city and rural areas which will not or cannot consolidate secondary schools to achieve the two thousand to four thousand student enrollment which seems necessary for a fully comprehensive high school. The area vocational school has a potential for encouraging school consolidation by making people aware for the first time of the services which can be provided by a full scale vocational program. But it can also postpone consolidation by providing certain of these services without requiring the trauma of closing small high schools.

Both of the above solutions, one sponsored by the Department of Labor and the other by the United States Office of Education, have numerous advantages. These advantages seem completely outweighed, however, by one tremendous disadvantage; they segregate students by socioeconomic level. Data are not available on the effect of these patterns of school organization on the rate of attendance in postsecondary education. It is likely, however, that both types of segregated occupational education will decrease the college-going rate.

Another type of parallel school system, the private vocational school, has considerable potential for competition with community colleges. Schaefer and Kaufman report that a survey of twenty-five hundred private vocational schools indicates that only 7 percent of them (primarily barber and beautician colleges) will accept people who do not have a high school diploma (28, pp. 92, 100). In view of the small proportion of private vocational schools accepting high school dropouts, this source of training is not likely to be an important factor at the secondary school level.

One argument in favor of specialized educational institutions for college transfer programs and for vocational and technical education is that only in this way will administrators be selected who will allow and encourage full development of this specialized program. All other arguments seem spurious. Sufficient size to operate programs effectively can be obtained in either specialized or comprehensive institutions. Moreover, as the size of the secondary school population base declines, fewer high schools can afford to release their students to attend area schools.

It seems likely that the administrator is indeed the key to the success of technical institutes, area vocational schools, and other specialized segregated vocational school organizations. But the administrator is important in a different way than is generally assumed. Study after study shows that general education administrators in comprehensive institutions place a higher value on vocational education than do vocational educators in these same institutions. If the vocational educator were being held back by the general educator, such a difference in values could hardly be found to exist.

There is no question but that there is a grossly inadequate supply of adequately prepared administrators for vocational education. Thus it seems likely that the more capable vocational administrators are being attracted to positions where pay and working conditions are most attractive to them. The administrative head of a separate vocational school is almost invariably paid more than the head of a vocational program in a comprehensive school organization, even though the qualifications and duties are not too dissimilar. Moreover, the head of such a specialized school has a freedom of action not accorded to the high school vocational director who must report to a high school principal or perhaps to an assistant superintendent for secondary school education. Similarly, the head of a technical institute has greater freedom of action than a dean of occupational education who must report to an official two or three steps down the administrative hierarchy in a comprehensive community college. This suggests that the more able vocational administrators are more likely to be attracted to separate vocational institutions, while comprehensive institutions are able to attract people willing to accept poorer working conditions and in the main less competent. Twin remedies for this situation would seem to be (1) greatly expanded programs of development of vocational education administrators so that the supply of competent personnel is somewhere near the demand, and (2) improved working conditions for capable people in vocational education in comprehensive institutions so that these positions will be considerably more attractive than they have been in the past.

The fatal defect of most school organizations which separate vocational and general education is the fact that such an organization results in segregation of student bodies by social class. Middle and upper class students will attend the college transfer school, while lower class students will attend the vocational school. This pits class against class, limits social mobility, and, in accord with findings of the Coleman Report, results in decreased rates of learning in the lower class institution.

It seems likely that as the supply of well prepared vocational education administrators is increased and as the findings of the Coleman Report become part of the conventional wisdom, separate institutions for vocational and for college transfer programs will decrease sharply in both number and proportion, and comprehensive institutions at every level will become the norm.

In contrast, imagine the effect of widespread application of the system reported in the *Wall Street Journal:*

> The local school board has proposed a conversion to an "integrated two-track" system, with the present white high school providing college preparatory work and the present black high school offering vocational training. Students would be selected for one or the other on the basis of achievement tests. White school officials are hoping such a system would deposit most whites in the college prep school and funnel most blacks to the vocational school. (14, p. 1)

Public versus Private Vocational Education

Public awareness of the importance of vocational education is almost sure to be accompanied by public willingness to spend public funds on vocational education. The availability of substantial finances, however, almost certainly will increase the competition for those finances. Some private industry which was not at all interested in training personnel except for a small proportion of their own needs leaped at an opportunity to train workers on the production line when federal payments for training disadvantaged workers reached three thousand dollars per trainee per year (though other employers were not interested even at this price). The expansion in private-for-profit vocational schools was phenomenal following the passage of the GI Bill for veterans and the Manpower Development and Training Act for disadvantaged workers. Where there is a job to be done, and money to be made, the private competitive industrial system of the United States usually responds rapidly.

The chief deterrent to efficient vocational education in the private sector has been the fact that business and industrial corporations have had production as their primary goal, while education played a distinctly secondary role. In the private vocational school, however, education is a primary goal. A few proprietors have sought for quick profits and have given a bad name to some of the remaining schools which lacked the advantage of a long established reputation. But the principal problem of the private vocational school has been the high cost of recruiting students. Cost of advertising, sales commissions, and the cost of collecting unpaid tuition have in a number of cases amounted to more than the cost of providing instruction and job placement.

Many private vocational schools have been bought and established by large organizations which can recruit students more efficiently. Not only can advertising dollars be spent more effectively on a chain of business education schools stretching from coast to coast than on a school operating in a single locality, but unsuccessful applicants for jobs in the parent corporation can be referred to the school with promise of further consideration after they have completed training successfully. Not only will the parent corporation be able to earn a profit on tuition charged, but it will have first pick of the better quality graduates.

It is difficult to predict the outcome of such competition between public and private vocational schools, but the beneficiary of such competition should be the student, provided that society insures that the competition is conducted in a way which protects the consumer of vocational education.

Cooperative Work-Education

The future should see cooperative work-education greatly expanded in size, with major expansions coming in community colleges. Work-study programs should rapidly be converted into cooperative education so that educational and employment goals are coordinated. Truck driving, heavy equipment operation, and similar occupations which require large capital and operating costs are quite suitable for cooperative education. Addition of courses in such fields would broaden markedly the typical school offerings. In small schools which cannot afford specialized coordinators for each of several occupational fields, the trend is likely to be toward approval of a coordinator who can serve vocational education needs in all fields.

Level of Vocational Education

Youth and adults who need and want vocational education have suffered because of controversies as to the level at which vocational education ought to be offered. General educators who desire more time for their own instructional program have been almost unanimous in demanding that vocational education be postponed until after high school. They have been joined by certain technical educators in the community colleges who feel that education for occupations below the level of technician is worthless and should be eliminated both from high schools and from community colleges.

So long as emphasis was placed on meeting the needs of the labor market, it was logical to postpone vocational education until just prior to the time when the student would enter the labor market. This was particularly true for programs which emphasized the development of specific skills, because such skills become obsolete more quickly than do general principles. In spite of the changes suggested in chapters 3 and 4, vocational education necessarily has a considerable tie to the labor market, if for no other reason than that to date it has been evaluated only on the basis of the success of its graduates in employment. If the thirteenth and fourteenth years of education become nearly universally accepted, almost all vocational educators will do all they can to get specific skill training moved to that level.

It is generally true, however, that middle class people, including vocational educators, want a different type of education for their children than they prescribe for the disadvantaged. The most likely solution should seem to be expanded enrollments in vocational education for all types of students (both high school graduates and dropouts) in community colleges, where almost everyone (regardless of class) is pursuing an occupational or professional goal.

If we assume that the more specific types of vocational education should be provided close to the time when the graduate will use them in employment, there is no question that as the average age of leaving school increases, the average age of the vocational education student who is receiving specific instruction will also increase. At the same time, if we assume that all students who need and want vocational education should have it available to them, it is crystal clear that we must continue to offer vocational programs in the high school for the foreseeable future. Moreover, for those students who are likely to drop out at the age of compulsory attendance, we must insure that vocational education programs are provided to at least some students prior to age sixteen.

The high schools of the nation have access to almost every youth, and they are accessible to almost every adult. Postsecondary education institutions, however, are attended by considerably less than half of our youth and, because of their geographic dispersal, are practically inaccessible to a high proportion of adults. To argue that vocational education programs for either youth or adults should be conducted only in postsecondary education institutions is completely unrealistic. Vocational education programs suitable to the needs of the student are needed and will be needed for the foreseeable future, at every level of education and for every age of student from early childhood to retirement from the labor force.

Basic Academic Skills in a Changing Society

Many who write about education and its problems advocate a greater emphasis on basic academic skills. Typically these educational critics interpret basic academic skills as reading writing, and computation. However, another group of observers contend that while basic academic skills are gaining renewed importance in a society where technological advances and rising cognitive requirements in occupations seem to be the rule, basic academic skills are not confined to reading, writing, and arithmetic. For example, the basic academic skills related to work success include communication skills, computational skills, manual dexterity or motor skills, and group organization and human relations skills.

Coleman (5) argues that there are several basic skills which the educational system should provide to all students before they become eighteen years of age. In addition to intellectual skills (reading, writing, arithmetic), he would include skills of some occupation that may be filled by a secondary school graduate, decision-making skills acquired in complex situations where consequences follow, skills that allow the young person to deal with physical and mechanical problems which one finds outside work, in the home, and elsewhere. Coleman also believes that students should acquire skills that help them deal with a bureaucratic organization, an employee, a customer, a client, a worker, or an entrepreneur.

Neither of these perspectives downgrade the importance of reading, writing, and arithmetic. Indeed, most thoughtful critics appear to accept the observation of Drucker (9) that America has become a knowledge society in which traditional cognitive skills have become highly important in most work activity. One indication of how important such skills have become is that there is clearly a reduction in the number of unskilled jobs available to absorb dropouts or people unequipped with appropriate academic skills however they are defined. Venn (34, p. 13) has illustrated this point by observing that only 5 percent of the jobs available today require no education and no specific job skills as compared with 25 percent of the jobs twenty years ago.

What do these observations about basic academic skills mean for the future of vocational education? While it is not possible to predict with certainty, several likely trends seem probable. First, American education is currently undergoing a subtle but significant reassessment of its goals and priorities in relation to social and economic change. As part of this reassessment, an increasing number of observers are viewing the outcomes of high school level vocational education, entry level occupational skills, as basic academic skills important to all students, not simply to those intending to enter the labor market on a full-time basis directly from high school.

To the degree that vocational education is *mainstreamed,* becomes a part of the educational experience of all students, it will be challenged in ways not true in the past. A variety of questions will need to be answered. Can vocational educators deliver entry level skills in shorter periods of time and in modules which allow students to keep their other educational options open and flexible? What groups of entry level skills are most appropriate for mainstreaming? If vocational education facilities are not now as available in some parts of the country as the current demand would justify, how can the use of existing facilities be maximized and made more efficient? How can vocational educators help other educators teach basic academic skills in less abstract ways than now seems to be the norm?

A second trend of concern to vocational education is the growing interest in including among basic academic skills, understanding and coping behaviors related to organizational and bureaucratic forms as well as interpersonal human relations skills. These trends also stimulate a number of important questions. How should understanding of work settings, the ingredients of work adjustment, and the differences in organizations for work best be included in vocational education curricula? Should vocational educators and general educators collaborate to teach such understandings and skills to all students? How can students be introduced most effectively to supervisory-employee relations or employee-employee relations?

A third trend is the growing concern for developing decision-making skills as part of basic academic skills. At one level, this means providing within vocational education curricula opportunities and experiences which help students to explore different vocational education specialties and to match these to their future life-style and career pattern goals. At a second level, this means providing information and orientation to students considering vocational education as an educational option but who have little understanding of the specialties available or outcomes likely or how to relate these to their personal decision making. At a third level, there is the matter of helping students make decisions in regard to the application of the occupational tasks they are learning to different work problems they are confronted with and to live with the consequences of these decisions.

A reappraisal of basic academic skills in American education will clearly cause increased scrutiny of the importance of such skills within vocational education. It will be found that most forms of vocational education are increasingly dependent upon and, indeed, give life to reading, writing, arithmetic, interpersonal skills, and understandings of bureaucratic organizations. What remains a priority concern in American education is how vocational educators and general educators can learn to understand, respect, and use the contributions each can make to the instructional goals of the other.

Meaning in Education

A large number of observers have critized American high schools and colleges for offering meaningless education to many students. This charge includes several aspects. Some believe that current educational structure is discipline oriented and fragmented with little or no attempt to relate the information taught to the lives of children. Such people believe that much information is taught because it exists, not because it is related to the personal questions about life and work that students are trying to answer.

Some observers contend that the boredom and confusion which many students experience is related to the school's inattention to certain questions: Why are we studying this? Why is it importnat? To what does it relate? Still other observers argue that feelings of educational meaninglessness experienced by some students is a function of the school's lack of response to individual differences in rate of learning or to a range of human talents which go beyond the traditional areas of abstract verbal and numerical reasoning.

As a result of such conditions, many students leave the high school goal-less, unable to function effectively as wage earners or in related life roles as citizens, homemakers, or parents. Shoemaker (29, p. 18) argues that "there can be no relevance in a curriculum unless it is related to student goals, and I submit that the success of vocational education is due to the fact that it is goal-centered education based upon the student's choice of a goal." This may well be true, but as indicated in the section on basic academic skills, many students do not have the decision-making skills or the information about vocational education to commit themselves to it in a meaningful fashion. As Gordon has indicated:

> It seems evident that youth do not persist in job skill programs unless the programs are relevant to the self-perceived needs of youth, nor do they continue in programs if their successful completion of the program does not result in a job that is worth the effort required for completing the program. (13, p. 2)

Specific data really do not exist about the number of people who find or do not find meaning in what they learn in school and what happens after they leave school. However, there are related data which bear on the matter. For example, Johnson and Johnson (15) have reported on a three-year follow-up study of almost 900 high school graduates. They found that over one-half of the employed graduates had jobs related to their course of study in high school and that there was a direct relationship between job satisfaction, satisfaction with high school preparation, and whether or not an individual's occupation was related to her or his course of study in high school.

Eggeman, Campbell, and Garbin (10) queried a national sample of 763 Youth Opportunity Center Counselors about the major problems faced by youth in the transition from school to work. Eighty-six percent of the counselors in the sample reported that the major problem was job preparation. This included inadequate training, inadequate job skills, lack of information about work and training opportunities, lack of knowledge of real demands of work-employer expectations, lack of education requirements, and lack of prior work experiences. Slightly more than 71 percent of the sample counselors indicated a third ranked category of worker adjustment was vocational behavior. Included were poor work habits (absenteeism, tardiness, etc.), inability to fill out forms and handle interviews, inability to accept supervision, inability to get along with fellow workers or to cope with real demands of work, and poor attitudes toward work.

Other studies and conjecture could be cited which relate to what happens to students in school or after they leave the school. Collectively, these observations represent a significant amount of data that schools do not have meaning for a lot of young people. The voids in meaning are seen as results of not tying content or instructional modes to student needs and the personal questions with which they are coping or giving students reasons for the learning they are exposed to. These are pragmatic perspectives on how to make education more meaningful. As such, they treat the rationale for education in terms of how it prepares people for their subsequent life experiences.

As was suggested in the section on basic academic skills, increasing meaning in education will likely require collaborative efforts between vocational educators and general educators. In such a relationship, vocational educators need to provide a resource to help students understand more clearly the relationships between different kinds of school learning and the opportunities for their application in occupational and educational roles likely to be available in the future. In addition, vocational education in the future will need to serve as a stimulus to the larger educational community to provide educational opportunities geared to a larger spectrum of human talents and learning styles than has been traditional so that students can select from a wider range of options and plan with more comprehensive purpose. In order to contribute to increased meaning in education, however, vocational educators cannot allow themselves to be smugly complacent about their capability to respond to student needs but must consider organizational and content implications for broadening and making more flexible access to vocational education of different kinds.

Self-Understanding and Decision-Making Skills

A perspective which has grown in acceptance since the sixties is that technical skills alone are insufficient for work adjustment and satisfaction. Employability also includes the attitudes and values which the worker brings to the job. In the study by Eggeman, Campbell, and Garbin (10) previously cited, 78.2 percent of the Youth Opportunity Counselors surveyed reported that personality problems hamper youth's adjustment to the world of work. More specifically, 72 percent mentioned job-seeking and/or on-the-job behavior as a major problem. Garbin, Campbell, Jackson, and Feldman (12) found that the maladjustment of secondary students in the work place may be more highly related to poor interpersonal skills than to inadequate technical skills; the major problem is not finding a job, but keeping one.

Implicit in these observations is that vocational skills or employability include opportunities for people to come to terms with a variety of personal questions and with clarifying their self-concepts. From the vantage point of higher education, Livingston has observed:

> One reason university graduates have had so much difficulty making the transition from academic life to the world of work is that they have failed to develop in school the self-identities needed to enable them to make firm career commitments. Their formal education has not nurtured the traits of individuality, self-assurance, and responsibility or developed the attributes that would permit them to become active agents in their own career success. (20, p. 35)

These self-understandings and decision-making skills are not only important in the university setting; they are also important ingredients of success in the public school and in relation to work. For example, Sievert (23) has reported that achievement in industrial education is related to the degree of congruency between the self-concept and the occupational concept of the subject matter; there is a positive relationship between the self-occupational congruence and achievement in the school shop. He suggests, as several other researchers would, that a partial reason for a student's aggressive acting out in shop or in other school dimensions is because the particular setting is not congruent with her or his self-concept.

O'Hara (24) has demonstrated that the self-concept relates not only to occupational choice but to high school achievement as well and that these relationships increase from ninth to twelfth grades. The implication of this correlation seems to be that students who persist in school are those who can find meaning in what they are learning in relation to the ways they view themselves and their goals; those who do not find such a condition in school act out or drop out. Oakland (23), too, has reported relationships between levels of high school achievement and a variety of personal traits including self-awareness, responsibility, and planning.

The longitudinal portions of Super's Career Pattern Study (31) have found that the educational and occupational levels attained by age twenty-five are significantly related to information about training and education, occupational information, planning and interest maturity in the ninth and in the twelfth grades.

Virtually all career development research currently available indicates that students need self-knowledge and career decision-making skills. Specifically, they need to be able to differentiate personal values and interests as they are related to personal strengths and weaknesses in abilities—verbal, quantitative, psychomotor. They also need to be able to relate this self-information to the vocational, educational, and social choices available to them. Other elements of importance to students are being helped to link what they are doing educationally at particular points in time to future options they will have both in education and work. They need to be able to determine what personal factors are relevant to success in different curricula and how the various curricula are linked to different field and level responsibilities in the occupational world.

While many other studies could be cited, the point should be made that self-understanding and decision-making skills are important to employability and vocational adjustment. However, there are also a number of studies like that of Tierney and Herman (32) which indicate that many students do not have the skill to make realistic self-estimates and that such a skill is apparently not being developed by schools. It seems obvious that the rise of affective education, psychological education, and, to some extent, career education during the early seventies are testimonies to these deficits in American education.

These trends have placed upon the school a requirement to acquaint the young with personal and vocational alternatives which in an earlier day were the responsibility of the family or the church. This need to serve as a surrogate for parents and other social institutions is now confronting schools with providing education for choice as a central priority of education.

Vocational educators particularly are challenged by the awareness that employability or placeability are perhaps as much affective as they are technical.

Thus, vocational skill development must include ways of developing self-knowledge, career planning, and constructive attitudes about oneself as a worker. This means that vocational educators, and other educators, must incorporate in their programs the realization that the overarching goal of education is not simply helping youth acquire the technical skills to be competent in academic or occuaptional tasks. Rather, the task is to help them attain personal competence—a goal which couples technical skill acquisition with the acquisition of values, understandings, and attitudes which permit students to use such skills wisely and effectively.

Elimination of the General Curriculum

The general curriculum in the secondary school has so little to commend it that it is sure to disappear. Both the vocational and the college preparatory curricula are expanding slowly, and this expansion comes at the expense of the general curriculum. Elimination of the general curriculum will result in higher rates of college attendance since it has by far the highest dropout rate of the present three high school curricula and has by far the lowest rate of college attendance by its graduates.

In the long run, the vocational and college preparatory curricula should merge and form a single basic curriculum for the secondary school based on general education (not the general curriculum). This requires deleting as well as adding courses for it is clear that many high schools now require certain mathematics, physical science, and foreign language instruction that is not needed by all citizens.

A few very interesting programs which could lead to a single secondary school curriculum are underway. Most prominent among these is career education, which has a goal the integration of knowledge about the world of work, occupational preparation, and the rest of general education and seeks to prepare all students for life outside the school as well as for postsecondary specialization. It is too early to predict the direction of the single curriculum which may result, but it is apparent that many people are working hard to bring it to reality.

Work: The Major Untaught Subject

Work is an essential ingredient in the survival of any society and in the development of every individual's talents and personality. Consequently the study of work is a basic academic skill, but work is almost never studied systematically in school. As a result, students learn about work piecemeal, by chance, and inaccurately.

One reason why work is not studied is that our educational system has been based on Greek philosophy, which assumed that work would be done by slaves. The modern verson of this philosophy believes that work is hated by the worker but will soon disappear as mechanical or electronic slaves take over all work.

Therefore, it is assumed that work should not be studied because it will soon vanish. However there is no evidence that work will become less important to society, and there is much evidence that work has and will continue to have enormous effect on individuals (18).

Several aspects of work deserve study. Among these are

1. praxiology (the science of efficient action),
2. work values and work ethics (individual and societal),
3. job satisfaction and work design,
4. effects of education on opportunities for work,
5. effects of governmental fiscal planning on work.

Career education offers promise of encouraging the study of work as a part of basic academic skills and of facilitating close working relationships between vocational and academic educators. But regardless of whether they are part of a career education program, vocational educators have a prime responsibility for teaching their students about work as a whole, as well as about work in the teacher's special field.

Specific versus General Vocational Education

The issue of whether or not vocational education is too specific has been raised constantly since its inception. Too often the argument has generated more heat than illumination because those who say vocational education is too specific tend to rely on assumptions rather than facts. Vocational education has almost never been so specific as to warrant the frequently made charge that it prepares individuals for a single occupation. On the other hand, in response to demands from general educators, it occasionally has become so general as to have practically no occupational relevance.

Relevance to the needs of youth and of society is a far more important test than is a measure of generality or specificity. Almost certainly, irrelevance is caused most frequently by instructors who are out of touch with the world of work. Equipment, texts, materials, and instructional organization can all contribute to a lack of relevance, but most of these deficiencies can be overcome by a competent instructor. It is to be hoped that a combination of improved evaluation techniques and greatly increased emphasis on teacher education programs for vocational instructors will lead to the elimination of the teacher as a major cause of irrelevance.

A charge of too great specificity is usually accompanied by a statement that occupations rapidly become obsolete; hence, it is charged that vocational education will be of no value a few years after it is completed. A variation of this theme admits that vocational education may be of value but claims that since no one knows which occupations will survive, each student should be prepared for all occupations. Undeniably, if a form of vocational education could be devised which prepared all students for all occupations, it would be a great boon to society. But it has not been devised, and it is unlikely that it will be devised. The difficulties involved in preparing a person for all skilled occupations are roughly comparable to the difficulties of devising a single graduate school program which would prepare students for all professions.

Barring some miracle which would produce a universal vocational education program, the best assurance of continued usefulness of vocational education is the provision of well-prepared teachers. It is a well known fact that within any occupation, obsolete practices exist for years alongside the most modern practice. A capable instructor will be several years ahead of the generality of practice in the occupation he or she teaches, and simply by being ahead of general practice can provide students with competencies which will insure that their skills and knowledges will be obsolete much less quickly than is true for the occupational field as a whole.

There is, however, one side of the question of generality of instruction on which most vocational educators have a blind spot. Because they have suffered for many years from inadequate resources to accomplish the tremendous task which faces them, they tend to be jealous of the resources that they have and to be wary about sharing these resources with other parts of the school system. Vocational education, and indeed all of education, is hampered greatly by the fact that education about the world of work begins so late in the student's educational career. It does no good to complain that general educators should recognize that education for the world of work is a basic part of the education needed by everyone. They have not seen this in the past, and they are unlikely to deal with it effectively in the near future unless they have help. The only plausible remedy is to use public funds to prepare curriculum materials and to train classroom teachers in their use so that an understanding of the world of work can be a part of the educational program from early childhood education onward. This will make the task of vocational education easier when students arrive at the point that they are ready for more specific occupational instruction. But equally important, the general citizenry will in the long run become aware of the importance of vocations to the national welfare and will insist that increasing educational resources be devoted to their development.

Curriculum Development

In some ways, vocational education has had an embarrassment of riches in text material. Specialized trade magazines, extremely specialized books on industrial processes, highly specific catalogues and sales brochures, motion pictures designed to sell products or services, and a wealth of other materials have been available. Moreover, in many cases they have been available at low cost, and vocational educators have been urged in no uncertain terms to accept them. On the other hand, until comparatively recently, there have been very few texts designed specifically for vocational education instruction. Unlike the English teacher or the foreign language teacher, the vocational educator rarely has, even today, a choice of more than one or two suitable texts, and in many occupational fields there are none.

Even worse is the fact that there have been no large scale curriculum development projects designed to prepare a course of study, select or develop instructional aids, prepare examinations, and train teachers to use these revised curricula in any field of vocational education. The closest we have come has been the federally supported work in industrial arts curriculum development in two university centers. In contrast, the physics course, which enrolls no more than 5 percent of high school students, has had over ten million dollars of foundation and federal money spent on the development of curriculum materials. A similar expenditure on the development of curriculum materials for orientation to the world of work in the elementary school, which would reach every student, could produce far greater results. Not only do we know more about developing curriculum materials than we did twenty years ago when the new physics course was begun, but the new physics course replaced a series of old physics courses which were reasonably satisfactory; the development of curriculum materials for orientation to the world of work would meet a pressing need which is now not met at all satisfactorily.

The development of sound curricula to meet the needs of the occupational fields covered by vocational education will be an extremely time-consuming and expensive task. It is unlikely that a competent job can be done for less than five million dollars per occupational cluster. Yet it can and must be done if vocational education is to be maximally effective. The present system of curriculum development, where a few states operate independent curriculum laboratories, investing ten to twenty-five thousand dollars per curriculum, duplicating each other's services, and in many cases being unable to distribute their products beyond the borders of the state, is grossly inefficient. The regional curriculum development effort has helped somewhat but has had far too few resources to do the job. They must be strengthened or replaced by federally supported curriculum development projects, adequately funded, and with only enough duplication of effort to give the teacher a choice of two or three excellent curriculum packages which can be modified to meet regional needs. The Committee on Vocational Education Research and Development of the National Academy of Sciences found that in spite of all its problems, curriculum development had more measurable impact than any other type of vocational education research and development (6).

Vocational Education in Developing Countries

Vocational educators from the United States have provided instruction in a number of developing countries around the world. In addition to teaching in the classroom, they have worked to develop appropriate curricula and establish vocational education institutions. A few vocational educators have even become proficient at securing funds for such endeavors. In the course of this employment, vocational educators from the United States have learned a great deal, much of it through trial and error. One of the things they have learned is that similar teams of vocational educators from such countries as England, Japan,

Germany, and Russia are on similar missions. In some countries, teams from five or more nations have been in active competition.

Valuable as this type of vocational education foreign assistance has been for the development of the vocational educators involved, it is not a realistic long-term approach to the development of vocational education abroad. In the long-term, vocational education must be provided by individuals who share the culture of the students being educated. This is true for two reasons. One is national pride, which demands that key educational positions be staffed by nationals of the country for whom the training is given. The second reason is goals and methods in different cultures are so diverse and even contradictory that an outsider not only has difficulty in communicating, but may indeed be suggesting solutions which are entirely inappropriate or even offensive to the culture in which he or she is teaching.

The only serious attempt to solve this problem has been the assignment of "counterparts" from the country being served. In addition to carrying on the assigned role as a teacher or administrator of vocational education,the American (foreign) expert has been expected simultaneously to train one or more counterparts who can carry on after the foreigner leaves. In practice, this counterpart system has not worked well. Sometimes this has been because the wrong people were assigned as counterparts, but equally often it has been because the American vocational educator was more interested in doing the work alone than in training a replacement.

These considerations sugest a few remedies:

1. Most Americans have little appreciation of cultures which exist outside their continent, and indeed have little understanding and appreciation of values held outside the American middle class from their own particular section of the country. As vocational educators are forced to work with lower class leaders who demand respect, these attitudes may gradually change. Another step toward the understanding of other cultures would be full-scale American participation in international conferences on vocational education. At present, these are regarded as unimportant, and only token American representation is sent, if any is sent at all. Generally, those people who are selected to attend are bureaucrats who are felt to deserve a vacation from the conflicts within the federal office of education. Substantial representation by those who regard international conferences as a professional opportunity instead of as a vacation would teach us much and might teach foreign vocational educators some things as well.
2. Most of our foreign assistance in vocational education should be transformed into teacher and administrator training activities conducted on a part-time cooperative basis here and abroad. A staff of educators in this country who had had meaningful foreign experience could conduct an educational program for foreign nationals who would spend half of their time working on a college campus and half of their time in observation and participation in vocational education institutions in this country. After perhaps a year of such instruction, the locale of training could be shifted

abroad, with foreign educators being developed through formal instruction which supplemented actual work as a teacher or administrator in schools or in training programs conducted by business and industry.

The Future

The years ahead call for more and better vocational education. This book has tried to describe some of the dimensions of *better.* If even a small proportion of the events predicted here come to pass, there will be more work for vocational educators than we can accomplish. As we recruit others to the task, we need to remind them and ourselves that our goals are to serve students, youth and adult, by helping to meet the needs of the nation (and of the world) for effective workers, increasing individual options of students, and lending intelligibility to all of education.

REFERENCES

1. American Vocational Association. *The Advisory Committee and Vocational Education.* Washington, D.C.: American Vocational Association, 1969.
2. Bass, W.P., and Burger, H.G. *American Indians and Educational Laboratories.* Albuquerque, N.M.: Southwestern Cooperative Educational Laboratory, 1967. ERIC: ED 014 369.
3. Burt, Samuel M. *Industry and Vocational-Technical Education.* New York: McGraw-Hill Book Company, 1967.
4. Cochran, Leslie H.; Phelps, L. Allen; and Skupin, Joseph F., Jr., of Advisory Committees. Lansing, Mich.: Michigan Department of Education, Vocational Education Services, 1974.
5. Coleman, James A. "How Do the Young Become Adults?" *Review of Educational Research* 42 (Fall 1972).
6. Committee on Vocational Education Research and Development. *Assessing Vocational Education Research and Development.* Washington, D.C.: National Academy of Sciences, Assembly of Behavioral and Social Sciences, National Research Council, 1976.
7. Darcy, Robert L. "Manpower in a Changing Curriculum." *American Vocational Journal* 44, no. 3 (March 1969):57–60.
8. Davis R.H. "The Failure of Compensatory Education." *Education and Urban Society.* 4 (February 1972):234–47.
9. Drucker, Peter F. *The Age of Discontinuity: Guidelines to Our Changing Society.* New York: Harper and Row, 1969.
10. Eggeman, D.F.; Campbell, R.E.; and Garbin, A.P. *Problems in the Transition from School to Work as Perceived by Youth Opportunity Center Counselors.* Columbus, Ohio: The Center for Vocational and Technical Education, The Ohio State University, December 1969.
11. Feldman, M.J. Vocational Education for the Disadvantaged: Lessons from Ford Foundation-funded Programs. Paper presented at the National Workshop on Vocational Education for the Disadvantaged, Atlantic City, New Jersey, March 1969.
12. Garbin, A.P.; Campbell, R.E.; Jackson, Dorothy P.; and Feldman, R. *Problems in the Transition from High School to Work as Perceived by Vocational Educators.* Columbus, Ohio: The Center for Vocational and Technical Education, The Ohio State University, 1967.

13. Gordon, J.E. *Testing, Counseling, and Supportive Services for Disadvantaged Youth.* Washington, D.C.: Manpower Administration, U.S. Department of Labor, Undated.

14. "Integrating Teachers," *Wall Street Journal* 30 (January, 1970), p. 1.

15. Johnson, Larry, and Johnson, Ralph H. "High School Preparation, Occupation and Job Satisfaction." *Vocational Guidance Quarterly* 204 (June 1972):287–90.

16. Kohlberg, Lawrence, and Gilligan, Carol. The Adolescent as a Philosopher: The Discovery of the Self in a Post-Conventional World. *Daedalus* 100, no. 4 (Fall 1971):1051–86.

17. Koschler, Theodore A., and Parker, Allen L. How Broad Is Technical Education? *Technical Education Reporter* 1, no. 1 (May-June 1974):11–19.

18. Levitan, Sar, and Johnston, William. *Work Is Here To Stay, Alas.* Salt Lake City: Olympus Publishing Co., 1973.

19. Levitan, Sar; Johnson, William; and Taggart, Robert. "Manpower Programs in Black Progress." *Manpower* 6, no. 6 (June 1974):2–10.

20. Livingstown, J.S. "The Troubled Transition: Why College and University Graduates Have Difficulty Developing Careers in Business." *Journal of College Placement* 30 (1970):34–41.

21. Mangum, Garth. "Second Chance in the Transition from School to Work." *Transition from School to Work.* Princeton, N.J.: Industrial Relations Section, Princeton University, 1968.

22. National Advisory Council on Vocational Education. *6th Report—Counseling and Guidance: A Call for Change.* Washington, D.C.: The Council, June 1972.

23. Oakland, J.A. "Measurement of Personality Correlates of Academic Achievement in High School Students. *Journal of Counseling Psychology* 16 (1969):452–57.

24. O'Hara, R.P. "Vocational Self-Concepts and High School Achievement." *Vocational Guidance Quarterly* 15 (1966):106–112.

25. Ottina, John R. "Career Education Is Alive and Well." *The Journal of Teacher Education* 24, no. 2 (Summer 1973):84–86.

26. Reubens, Beatrice G. "Vocational Education: Performance and Potential." *Manpower* 6, no. 7 (1974):23–30.

27. Rosen, Howard. *Job Training of Blue Collar Workers: Implications for Vocational Guidance.* Unpublished speech. Washington, D.C.: Office of Manpower Research, Manpower Administration, U.S. Department of Labor, undated.

28. Schaefer, Carl J., and Kaufman, J.J. *Occupational Education in Massachusetts.* Boston: Massachusetts Advisory Council on Education, 1968.

29. Shoemaker, Byrl R. "People, Jobs and Society: Toward Relevance in Education." In *Contemporary Concepts in Vocational Education,* edited by Gordon F. Law. First Yearbook of the American Vocational Association, Washington, D.C.: The American Vocational Association, Inc., 1971, pp. 17–21.

30. Sievert, Norman W. "The Role of the Self-Concept in Determining an Adolescent's Occupational Choice." *Journal of Industrial Teacher Education* 9, no. 3 (Spring 1972):47–53.

31. Super, D.E. "Vocational Development Theory: Persons, Positions and Processes." *The Counseling Psychologist* 1 (1969):2–9.

32. Tierney, Roger J., and Herman, Al. "Self-Estimate Ability in Adolescence. *Journal of Counseling Psychology* 20, no. 4 (1973):298–302.

33. Tyler, Ralph. "Schools Needed for the Seventies." In the General Sub-Committee on Education of the Committee on Education and Labor of the House of Representatives, *Needs of Elementary and Secondary Education for the Seventies.* Washington, D.C.: U.S. Government Printing Office, 1970, pp. 794–95.

34. Venn, Grant. "Career Education in Perspective—Yesterday, Today and Tomorrow." *N.A.S.S.P. Bulletin* 57, no. 371 (March 1973):12–14.

35. Wall, Carlton D. "Career Education: A Better Way." *Education* 93, no. 1 (October 1972): 51–53.

Index